Rhetorical Traditions and Contemporary Law

Edited by

BRIAN N. LARSON

Texas A&M University

ELIZABETH C. BRITT

Northeastern University

CAMBRIDGE
UNIVERSITY PRESS

CAMBRIDGE UNIVERSITY PRESS

Shaftesbury Road, Cambridge CB2 8EA, United Kingdom

One Liberty Plaza, 20th Floor, New York, NY 10006, USA

477 Williamstown Road, Port Melbourne, VIC 3207, Australia

314–321, 3rd Floor, Plot 3, Splendor Forum, Jasola District Centre, New Delhi – 110025, India

103 Penang Road, #05-06/07, Visioncrest Commercial, Singapore 238467

Cambridge University Press is part of Cambridge University Press & Assessment, a department of the University of Cambridge.

We share the University's mission to contribute to society through the pursuit of education, learning and research at the highest international levels of excellence.

www.cambridge.org
Information on this title: www.cambridge.org/9781009524094

DOI: 10.1017/9781009524087

First published 2025

Cover image: Figure of Justice by Diana K. Moore

A catalogue record for this publication is available from the British Library

Library of Congress Cataloging-in-Publication Data
NAMES: Larson, Brian N. (Brian Nicholas), 1966- editor. | Britt, Elizabeth C. (Elizabeth Carol), 1964- editor.
TITLE: Rhetorical traditions and contemporary law / edited by Brian N. Larson, Texas A & M University; Elizabeth C. Britt, Northeastern University, Boston.
DESCRIPTION: Cambridge, United Kingdom ; New York, NY : Cambridge University Press, 2025. | Includes bibliographical references and index.
IDENTIFIERS: LCCN 2024052723 (print) | LCCN 2024052724 (ebook) | ISBN 9781009524094 (hardback) | ISBN 9781009524049 (paperback) | ISBN 9781009524087 (epub)
SUBJECTS: LCSH: Law–Language. | Law–Methodology. | Rhetoric. | Rhetoric, Ancient. | English language–Rhetoric.
CLASSIFICATION: LCC K487.L36 R49 2025 (print) | LCC K487.L36 (ebook) | DDC 340/.14–dc23/eng/20241107
LC record available at https://lccn.loc.gov/2024052723
LC ebook record available at https://lccn.loc.gov/2024052724

ISBN 978-1-009-52409-4 Hardback
ISBN 978-1-009-52404-9 Paperback

RHETORICAL TRADITIONS AND CONTEMPORARY LAW

Rhetorical Traditions and Contemporary Law is a collection of twelve case studies that explore the often-overlooked intersections of law and rhetoric. Drawing from rhetorical traditions of the past and present, the multidisciplinary roster of contributors analyzes contemporary legal theory and practice, from judicial opinions to legal scholarship, using significant texts or concepts in a rhetorical tradition. The essays demonstrate how legal texts function and to what end, while also considering how they might have worked differently. The volume sheds light on the usefulness of rhetoric in addressing some of today's most pressing legal and social challenges. This title is also available as Open Access on Cambridge Core.

Brian N. Larson is Research Fellow and Arts and Humanities Fellow and was formerly Associate Professor of Law at Texas A&M University School of Law. He co-edited *Classical Rhetoric & Contemporary Law* (2024) and has published numerous book chapters and articles on legal theory, law and rhetoric, and data use and information privacy.

Elizabeth C. Britt is Professor of English at Northeastern University. She is the author of *Reimagining Advocacy: Rhetorical Education in the Legal Clinic* (2018) and *Conceiving Normalcy: Rhetoric, Law, and the Double Binds of Infertility* (2001), as well as numerous articles and book chapters.

To Bob, for whom no more words are necessary, and to my many mentors, including Professor Brad Clary, Dr Mary Lay Schuster, Dr Lee-Ann Kastman Breuch, Professor Jay Mootz, Dr Kirsten Davis, and others too numerous to name here.

BNL

For Jeff, who keeps me grounded.

ECB

Contents

List of Contributors — *page* ix
Acknowledgments — xi

PART I INTRODUCTION

1 **Rhetoric and Law: A Mosaic** — 3
Elizabeth C. Britt and Brian N. Larson

PART II KEY RHETORICAL CONCEPTS ANIMATING CONTEMPORARY AMERICAN LAW

2 **The Ethos of Originalism** — 17
Mark A. Hannah and Francis J. Mootz III

3 **The Role of Tradition in Classical and Contemporary Argument** — 42
Vasileios Adamidis and Laura A. Webb

4 **Practical Reason in Peril: From Cicero to *Texas Health Presbyterian*** — 70
Brian N. Larson

PART III FAÇADE OF NEUTRALITY

5 **Deciphering *Dobbs*: Syllogism and Enthymeme in Contemporary Legal Discourse** — 97
Susan Tanner

6 **Eradicating Ethos: Language, Circumstances, and Locke's Empirical Language Ideology in the Anglo-American Hearsay Principle** 119
Jennifer Andrus

PART IV PERMEABLE BOUNDARIES

7 **Searching for Legal *Topoi* in the Shadow Docket** 141
M. Kelly Carr

8 ***Sensus Communis*, Voter-Inflicted Harms, and *Schuette v. BAMN*** 158
Laura J. Collins

9 **(Vernacular) Rhetorics for Women's Rights** 181
Rasha Diab

10 **<Police Power> to Stop-and-Frisk: A Pattern for Persuasion** 205
Lindsay Head

PART V LAW'S POWER TO EXCLUDE VOICES

11 **Framing the War on Drugs: Judith Butler and Legal Rhetorical Analysis** 229
Erin Leigh Frymire

12 **Ensnared by Custom: Mary Astell and the American Bar Association on Female Autonomy** 248
Judy M. Cornett

13 ***Dissoi Logoi*, Rhetorical Listening, and Legal Education** 273
Elizabeth C. Britt

PART VI LOOKING OUTWARD AND FORWARD

14 **An Unconventional Call for Proposals** 295
Brian N. Larson and Elizabeth C. Britt

Index 301

Contributors

Vasileios Adamidis is an Associate Professor of Law at Nottingham Trent University, UK. He has written in the field of legal history and rhetoric, especially in the context of Athenian democracy, identifying intersections between ancient and modern concepts and practices.

Jennifer Andrus is Professor of Writing and Rhetoric Studies at the University of Utah. Her work has primarily consisted of analyses of discourses circulating in the intersections between domestic violence, law, and law enforcement.

Elizabeth C. Britt is Professor of English at Northeastern University. She is a feminist rhetorical theorist and critic whose research focuses on legal rhetoric. She has written most recently about domestic violence advocacy and legal education as rhetorical education.

M. Kelly Carr is Associate Professor of Communication at the University of West Florida. Her research explores the nexus of law and public discourse, primarily as implicated through Supreme Court opinion writing. She is the author of *The Rhetorical Invention of Diversity: Supreme Court Opinions, Public Argument, and Affirmative Action* (2018).

Laura J. Collins is Assistant Professor of English at the University of Colorado, Colorado Springs. Her research focuses on legal rhetorics and their relationship to political advocacy. She has written about the Second Amendment and antidiscrimination law.

Judy M. Cornett is the College of Law Distinguished Professor at the University of Tennessee College of Law, where she teaches Law and Literature. Her published work includes rhetorical analyses of eighteenth-century British novels, Harper Lee's *To Kill a Mockingbird*, and opinions of the Tennessee Supreme Court.

Rasha Diab is Associate Professor of Rhetoric and Writing at the University of Texas at Austin. Her work centers on the rhetorics of peacemaking, Arab(ic)-Islamic rhetorics, feminist rhetorics, and revisionist historiography. She is the author of *Shades of Ṣulḥ* (2016), which explores the cultural, legal, and political dimensions of Arab(ic)-Islamic rhetorics of reconciliation.

Erin Leigh Frymire is Senior Lecturer in Rhetoric and Writing and Co-director of the Global Health Humanities Gateway program at Trinity College in Hartford, CT. Her work focuses on rhetorics of law and the body, as well as developing pedagogical strategies for cultivating empathy and for teaching rhetoric in nontraditional spaces.

Mark A. Hannah is Associate Professor of English at Arizona State University. He has written broadly about the relationship between law and rhetoric, applications of rhetoric in the professions, and rhetorics of multidisciplinary communication. He is a co-author of *Law and Rhetoric: A Primer* (2024).

Lindsay Head is Assistant Professor of Law at Jacksonville University College of Law. She centers her research on the intersections of rhetoric, culture, and law. Her recent work examines cultural influences on Fourth Amendment jurisprudence and interrogates notions of authorship in legal discourse.

Brian N. Larson is Research Fellow, Arts and Humanities Fellow, and formerly Associate Professor of Law at Texas A&M University School of Law. His scholarship focuses on legal argumentation and its rhetorical, logical, and cognitive dimensions.

Francis J. Mootz III is Professor of Law at McGeorge School of Law at the University of the Pacific. He has written extensively about the relevance of hermeneutics and rhetoric to legal theory. He is author of *Rhetorical Knowledge in Legal Practice and Critical Legal Theory* (2006).

Susan Tanner is Associate Professor of Law at Brandeis School of Law at the University of Louisville. Her scholarship is focused on law and language, with particular focus on privacy and technology law, using methods that range from computational linguistics to traditional rhetorical and legal analyses.

Laura A. Webb is Professor of Law, Legal Practice at the University of Richmond School of Law. She has written about legal education as well as the intersection of classical rhetoric and contemporary law.

Acknowledgments

We are grateful to Northeastern University and the Dee J. Kelly Law Library and the Arts & Humanities Fellowship at Texas A&M University, among others, for their pledges of financial support to permit this volume to be published open access. We are grateful, too, to Robert Gaines, who helped us get this project started, and to the contributors to the volume, who played along with our "contributors' symposium," resulting we hope in a stronger collection from all of us. Finally, thanks to the anonymous reviewers, who provided helpful insight into some issues that we would not otherwise have treated fully.

PART I

Introduction

1

Rhetoric and Law

A Mosaic

Elizabeth C. Britt and Brian N. Larson

1.1 INTRODUCTION

With this book, we offer the beginnings of an answer to this question: "How can we understand and intervene in contemporary legal practice using texts from the rhetorical tradition?" We envisioned this volume as a mosaic of rhetorical theories and texts from various historical traditions juxtaposed with contemporary legal texts. Our goal was for the contributions to show a picture of the continued vitality and potential utility of rhetorical traditions – construed broadly – for understanding, interrogating, and criticizing contemporary legal texts. As to the latter, we hoped to depict the utility of rhetorical traditions as applied to a greater variety of contemporary legal texts than those that are often the focus of rhetorical criticism: the opinions of American courts, often the US Supreme Court. We are confident that the contributions to this volume succeed in these tasks. We see this effort as contributing tesserae – the small pebbles, tiles, and sometimes pieces of glass that lie in the matrix of mosaics – to a broader picture.

In the Western tradition, rhetoric has always been about particulars. In his translation of Aristotle's *On Rhetoric*, George Kennedy interposed the word into Aristotle's definition of the topic of study: "the ability, in each [particular] case, to see the available means of persuasion" (Aristotle, 2007, p. 27). Nevertheless, the oldest surviving treatises on the topic in the West, including Aristotle's, often treat it as a whole. These treatments create big, theoretical pictures, but if we think of those big pictures as mosaics, we can imagine the application of those theories to particular cases or situations as tesserae.

The ancient Western theoretical treatments also tended to deal with law, as the two disciplines (at least as they were practiced in the West) were born together in the Eastern Mediterranean during a brief experiment in democracy by Greek city states in the fifth and fourth centuries BCE (Larson & Tiscione, 2024). Though they grew together through most of the ensuing two millennia, they have become estranged: Rhetoric has broadened its attention to include many other forms of symbolic action (such as workplace, medical, and social media communication, and even some non-human objects of study), while law has turned its back on rhetoric. Contemporary legal theory continues to ignore, and even deny, the rhetorical nature of law, but some legal scholars over the last two to four decades have brought rhetorical theory to bear on the law.

Two recent volumes have brought attention to the interplay of rhetorical traditions and contemporary (American) law. Together, they sketch or outline some of the mosaic, representing pictures of the intersection of these disciplines. In *Critical and Comparative Rhetoric: Unmasking Privilege and Power in Law and Legal Advocacy to Achieve Truth, Justice, and Equity*, Elizabeth Berenguer, Lucy Jewel, and Teri A. McMurtry-Chubb (2023) outline a sweeping segment of the picture that attempts to correct the overreliance of the American legal system – and approaches to rhetorical criticism of it – on classical Western thinking. They argue first that Western rhetorical traditions and their contemporary manifestations in law are grounded in hegemonic impulses of white European men. They then argue that some of the responsibility for contemporary socio-legal problems lies with deduction and the syllogism, which they see as inherent to the ancient Western models. Finally, they argue that the introduction of rhetorical traditions from other places and times – that is, texts from the "Indigenous, African Diasporic, Asian Diasporic, and Latine" traditions (Berenguer et al., 2023, p. 18) – can help to remedy the resulting problems. Their volume approaches the mosaic from a bird's-eye view, outlining the contours of the rhetorical tradition they critique and the traditions they offer as alternatives.

Meanwhile, Francis J. Mootz III, Kirsten K. Davis, Brian N. Larson, and Kristen K. Tiscione have edited a collection titled *Classical Rhetoric and Contemporary Law: A Critical Reader* (2024) that takes a close-up look at the mosaic. The central thesis of their volume contradicts a main premise of *Critical and Comparative Rhetoric*, that the ancient Western rhetorical tradition is bound up with deduction and the syllogism. Instead, the volume asserts that this tradition is concerned with judgment "grounded in practical wisdom addressing probabilities rather than in formal, deductive certainties" (Davis & Mootz, 2024, p. 3). In addition, the volume treats the Western rhetorical tradition as heterogeneous, identifying the locales where various tesserae might be found, from the pre-Socratic sophists to Augustine of Hippo. It includes lengthy excerpts from these texts, providing critical questions and inviting readers to apply them to contemporary American legal texts.[1]

Our volume complements these books by offering detailed and careful analyses of both rhetorical traditions and contemporary legal texts.

We take analysis of the primary texts of rhetorical traditions to be an important part of their use in contemporary law. We think we know what contemporary legal

[1] This is a category in which the editors included court opinions – of course – but also lawyers' appellate briefs, amicus curiae briefs, and jury instructions.

texts are supposed to do, because we inhabit their context.[2] But traditional rhetorical texts are often unmoored from their contexts. Careful reading of traditional texts – as done by the contributors to this volume – coupled with careful reading of more contemporary readings of those traditional texts (see, e.g., Hannah & Mootz, Chapter 2 in this volume) is essential to understanding their ideas and adapting them to contemporary practices. As scholars, we have a duty to understand and acknowledge what we owe to those who came before us, but we must also ensure that what we have inherited merits our attention and use. Indeed, the volume by Mootz and colleagues concludes with a set of questions that we should ask about any traditional text, whether ancient Western or not, if we wish it to "tell ... us something insightful and informative about contemporary law" (Larson, 2024, p. 246):

- Is [the] text widely known, either among scholars or among some broader human community?
- Is it, or was it, influential in its historical or cultural context?
- Does it relate sufficiently to contemporary legal discourse to say something about that discourse?
- Does it offer insights into how legal language and argument operate?
- Does it help scholars see something about the law that is more difficult to reveal without its help?
- What voices are or were absent from it? Are there characteristics of its author or their milieu that may limit its perspectives?
- Can it offer something emancipatory, helpful, insightful, or revelatory even if the text or its author(s) exhibited biases and limitations ... that were inherent in their cultural contexts and norms?

The contributions in this volume address these questions, guiding scholars from both fields – law and rhetoric – to use each other's work. Through analyzing each legal text's rhetorical moves, each chapter shows not only how the text works and to what ends but also how it might have worked otherwise. In other words, the analyses point to the possibility for change. By focusing on contemporary legal texts, the volume demonstrates the usefulness of rhetoric for considering today's most pressing problems.

In the rest of this introduction, we offer our sense of why rhetoric is integral to the law and then provide an overview of the chapters. Given that all but one of the chapters in this volume contribute tesserae to the mosaic from Western rhetorical traditions and contemporary American legal texts, this introduction provides an imperfect and incomplete description of the scholarly matrix in which this volume intervenes.

2 Of course, careful analysis can sometimes expose misunderstandings of contemporary contexts. Our senses of our lived experiences are not *knowledge* until they are examined thoughtfully.

1.2 RHETORIC IS INTEGRAL TO THE LAW

Although the contributors to this volume draw on different definitions of rhetoric, we broadly define it here as the use of symbols to influence thought, belief, and action. The symbols through which rhetoric does its work permeate law, from the more obvious (think closing arguments, judicial opinions, legislation) to the less so (think rules, client communications, law textbooks).[3] These symbols influence not just the lawyers, judges, and jurors in courtroom settings, but also publics beyond the courtroom's narrow confines. The symbols of law matter profoundly. They tell us who we can marry, whether we are entitled to health care, and how we will choose our leaders.

Like all rhetoric, law's symbols are choices and therefore assert a point of view. These choices are made on a number of fronts. In the opening statement of a trial, for example, an attorney would choose how to tell a compelling story favorable to their client, including choices about narrative structure and character development. But even everyday legal texts like the forms used to obtain a restraining order involve choices that inevitably assert a point of view (for example, whether to call the act at issue "abuse," "violence," or something else). The point of view asserted is not necessarily that of the speaker or writer. Instead, it is one that the audience is invited (successfully or unsuccessfully) to adopt. These invitations are not always intentional or conscious. From a rhetorical perspective, the intent of the speaker or writer is less significant than how their choices potentially influence an audience and how, over time, these choices accumulate to construct the law as a social system.

In the Western world, law and rhetoric were born together nearly 2,500 years ago in the Mediterranean. In the newly emerging democracies of Athens and other city-states, citizens spoke for themselves in the law courts, defending themselves or bringing charges against others. Because knowing how to persuade others took on such importance (and could be a matter of life and death), learning rhetoric for legal purposes became a fundamental part of citizenship. As a result, teachers and scholars of rhetoric in ancient Greece and Rome, including the sophists, Isocrates, Plato, Aristotle, Cicero, and Quintilian, developed theories and pedagogies that would become the foundation of the Western rhetorical and legal traditions.

Larson and Tiscione (2024, p. 12) recount rhetoric and law's intertwined history from that time until the end of the nineteenth century, at which time they describe a "rupture between training in rhetoric and law ... that has only gradually begun to heal." Law's rhetorical roots have largely been forgotten. In the late nineteenth-century American context, legal practice and education moved away from the apprenticeship model by which most attorneys had been trained. At the forefront of this movement was Harvard University, which instituted broad reforms aiming to intellectualize the professions, including law. Reformers there saw law as a science,

[3] Many, but not all, of these genres are represented in this volume.

with rules that could be derived from legal opinions and then neutrally applied to other scenarios. As explained by James Boyd White, the legal scholar widely credited with founding the law and literature movement, this conception treats law as a bureaucratic "machine acting on the rest of the world," with legal decisions abstracted from their lived contexts and evaluated through a cost–benefit logic (Boyd White, 1985, p. 686). This view of law now predominates in the American context, manifesting primarily as legal formalism, or the application of quasi-formal logic to determine the outcome of cases.[4]

Ironically, one of the central features of the rhetoric of legal formalism is, as put by legal scholar Gerald Wetlaufer (1990, p. 1555), "the systematic *denial* that it is rhetoric." To admit the rhetorical nature of law would be to admit its partiality, or the point of view inevitably inscribed with every textual choice. Denying law's rhetorical nature is a way of constructing an impartial façade, thereby shoring up law's legitimacy and authority.

Because law denies its rhetorical nature, calling attention to legal rhetoric is sometimes seen as trivial or, worse, as distracting from justice, law's ultimate aim. Such criticisms are as old as the connection between rhetoric and law: Plato himself condemned the popular teachers of legal rhetoric of his time, saying that they taught speakers to say what audiences wanted to hear without regard for truth or justice. We instead see attention to law's rhetoric as essential to justice. Legal scholar Patricia J. Williams embraces this view, focusing on the tendency of law to favor abstractions rather than the complexities of lived experience. As she writes: "That life is complicated is a fact of great analytic importance. Law too often seeks to avoid this truth by making up its own breed of narrower, simpler, but hypnotically powerful rhetorical truths. Acknowledging, challenging, playing with these *as* rhetorical gestures is … necessary for any conception of justice" (Williams, 1991, p. 10).

Heeding Williams' call, this volume challenges law's truths by engaging in rhetorical criticism. If rhetoric is about subjectivity, contingency, and specificity, law purports instead to be about objectivity, certainty, and universality. By denying its rhetorical nature, law maintains its authority and therefore its power. Calling attention to law's rhetoric – through rhetorical criticism – is therefore an important check on its power.

The contributions in this volume are by no means alone in this work, as many others have added tesserae to this mosaic. For example, many scholars of rhetoric, cultural studies, and law and society have added facets to the picture, including authors in this volume, along with Alden (2020), Amsden (2016), Campbell (2012), Camper (2018), Chávez (2016), Coulson (2012, 2023), Craig and Rahko (2016), Gibson (2018), Hasian (1997), Hasian et al. (1996), Johnson and Smith (2024), Langford (2018), Pham (2015), Rountree (2007), Schuster and Propen (2011),

[4] Many chapters in this volume discuss this view (e.g., Hannah & Mootz, Chapter 2; Larson, Chapter 4; Tanner, Chapter 5).

Sciullo (2019), Somerville (2005), West (2008, 2019), and some of the contributors to Brooks and Gewirtz (1996), Mootz and Frank (2023), Sarat and Kearns (1996), and Slocum and Mootz (2019). Similarly, many from the legal academy have worked on problems there using rhetorical lenses, including Berger (2010, 2013), Inniss (2009), Provenzano (2022), Venter (2021), White (1985, 1990), Williams and Spedding (2024), and other contributors to the edited volumes mentioned previously. Other scholars, harder to classify, work regularly at the intersection of rhetoric and law, including Constable (2004, 2014b, 2014a) and Vats (2016, 2019, 2021).

Some other recent scholarly interventions deserve special attention. A symposium issue of the *Nevada Law Journal* brought together scholars from law and rhetoric to bridge "classical" or ancient Western rhetoric and contemporary legal practice (Cedrone, 2020; Dauphinais, 2020; Davis, 2020; Hannah & Salmon, 2020; Johnson & Koenig, 2020; Mootz, 2020; Provenzano & Larson, 2020; Rountree, 2020; Webb, 2020; Weresh, 2020). The *Feminist Judgments* series, beginning in America with Stanchi and colleagues (2016), but owing its genesis to earlier developments in the United Kingdom and Canada, is not rhetorical criticism, but rather a set of rhetorical performances and analyses of them using feminist theory, designed to highlight differences between the actual opinions and those they could have been. Finally, some scholars from the field of legal writing make use of rhetorical theory when offering their own contemporary rhetorical handbooks (e.g., Tiscione, 2016), not uncommonly looking for a synthesis of rhetorical theory with cognitive science (e.g., Berger & Stanchi, 2018).

1.3 THIS VOLUME'S CONTRIBUTIONS

This volume brings together an interdisciplinary group of scholars with the goal of showing how contemporary legal texts are constructed rhetorically. Each chapter connects a significant text or concept from or constituting a rhetorical tradition and a contemporary legal text or body of scholarship.

We have organized the volume in a way that we hope will most effectively demonstrate what rhetorical criticism can explain about how law works. Part II lays the foundation for the rest of the volume by focusing on the rhetorical construction and function of three key concepts central to US law: originalism, traditionalism, and determinism. The chapters in Part III then examine the legal syllogism and enthymeme and Enlightenment ideology about language, two means by which law presents itself as rational and neutral. Part IV demonstrates that law is not a system separate from culture and ideology but integrated with them. Finally, the chapters in Part V provide examples of the mechanisms by which law operates in exclusionary ways. Other groupings would have highlighted different connections across the chapters, connections we encourage readers to make on their own.

In the first chapter in Part II, "The Ethos of Originalism," Mark Hannah and Jay Mootz explore today's dominant judicial interpretive tenet of "originalism," that the meaning of a legal text is the ordinary meaning that the text had at the time of its enactment for the average competent speaker of the language, which purportedly provides an objective basis for judging with integrity. They embrace Martin Heidegger's ontological reinterpretation of Aristotle's concept of ethos to show that the proponents of originalism do not prevail by persuading others through logic or dialectical reasoning (logos) nor by promoting their audience's disposition to hear their argument (pathos). Instead, originalists bring force to their claims by establishing and projecting an ethos, but not solely the ethos of originalism's proponents.

In "The Role of Tradition in Classical and Contemporary Argument," Vasileios Adamidis and Laura Webb analyze the use of tradition in the legal arguments of the Attic orators, including Demosthenes, Lycurgus, and Aeschines, and in contemporary US Supreme Court cases, including the controversial gun rights case, *District of Columbia v. Heller*. They give particular attention to the Commonwealth of Virginia's amicus curiae brief in *Obergefell v. Hodges*, where the Supreme Court upheld same-sex marriage as a fundamental right. There, the Commonwealth of Virginia sought to abandon its prior approach of framing fundamental rights with a narrow focus on tradition, which had put it on the "wrong" side of cases such as *Loving v. Virginia* (interracial marriage) and *Brown v. Board of Education* (school desegregation) and instead endorsed a broader framing consistent with the "full measure of freedom" protected by the Fourteenth Amendment.

In "Practical Reason in Peril: From Cicero to *Texas Health Presbyterian*," Brian Larson contrasts the interpretive methods that Cicero put forward in his early work, *De Inventione*, dating to the early first century BCE, with those presented by a greatly influential 2012 book coauthored by Justice Antonin Scalia, *Reading Law*. Larson contends that *Reading Law* departs from a millennia-old tradition of practical reason and instead embraces a *determinist imaginary* about contemporary judging. Larson illustrates the contrast in the two approaches by discussing a Texas Court of Appeals opinion – which exhibits Ciceronian practical reason – and the Texas Supreme Court's opinion in the same case – which exhibits Scalian determinism.

Part III illuminates two rhetorical means by which law maintains its façade of neutrality: the legal syllogism and Enlightenment ideology about language. In "Deciphering *Dobbs*: Syllogism and Enthymeme in Contemporary Legal Discourse," Susan Tanner shows that the conception of the "legal syllogism" popular among lawyers, judges, and law scholars is not the iron-clad deductive case that they make it out to be. Rather, she shows that the enthymematic structure of legal reasoning has profound effects on the logic and rhetoric of US court decisions that cannot be fully understood through the traditional paradigm of the legal syllogism. She applies her resulting model to *Dobbs v. Jackson Women's Health Org*, the 2022 US Supreme Court opinion that overturned the 1973 case *Roe v. Wade* and unsettled American reproductive rights law in ways whose ramifications are only slowly becoming understood.

In "Eradicating Ethos: Language, Circumstances, and Locke's Empirical Language Ideology in the Anglo-American Hearsay Principle," Jennifer Andrus explores Locke's theory of language in the *Essay Concerning Human Understanding* and its history of influence on judicial thinking about hearsay evidence. Hearsay is distrusted, she suggests, because it is language all the way down – testimony based on second-hand narrative – rather than language grounded in the empirical world. She analyzes three contemporary US Supreme Court opinions using her framework: *Ohio v. Roberts* (1980), *Crawford v. Washington* (2004), and *Davis v. Washington/Hammon v. Indiana* (2006).

Part IV examines the permeable boundary between law's rhetoric and public discourses. In "Searching for Legal *Topoi* in the Shadow Docket," Kelly Carr explores the US Supreme Court's "shadow docket," the growing number of emergency orders and summary decisions that lack the transparency and consistency of cases granted and decided on their merits. Carr examines the Court's practices in the shadow docket through the lens of the modern classic, Perelman and Olbrechts-Tyteca's *The New Rhetoric*, which itself adapted and adopted many concepts from the ancient Western rhetorical tradition. She applies this lens particularly to *Roman Catholic Diocese of Brooklyn v. Cuomo*, a 2020 shadow-docket case relating to state restrictions on religious gatherings during COVID.

In "*Sensus Communis*, Voter-Inflicted Harms, and *Schuette v. BAMN*," Laura Collins argues that Giambattista Vico's *sensus communis* helps explain why a court's earlier decisions can fail to anticipate decisions in new cases and how courts end up discerning stark breaks between their precedents and cases at bar. Vico defines *sensus communis* as "judgment without reflection," shared by an entire community, which evolves but endures. Importantly, *sensus communis* is "sedimented in language itself" such that a community's values and judgments are confined and animated by its language. She applies this lens to the US Supreme Court's decision in *Schuette v. BAMN*, a 2014 case adjudicating the application of Michigan's statutory ban on affirmative action.

Rasha Diab's chapter, "(Vernacular) Rhetorics for Women's Rights," broadens our focus beyond US law. Tracing early Arab-Islamic iterations of women's rights, Diab revisits Prophet Muḥammad's "Farewell Speech" (*khuṭbat al-wadāʿ*), which is often in/directly invoked in vernacular discourses to structure arguments for women's rights. Diab sheds light on early Arab-Islamic discourses on women's rights and uses the concept of vernacular rhetoric of human rights to draw attention to more recent iterations of women's rights. Diab fast-forwards to a speech on women's rights by Malak Ḥifnī Nāsif (1886–1918), Egyptian writer, intellectual, and reformer, who proposed ten articles to promote women's rights, including marital and epistemic rights. Finally, Diab moves to 2019 and the highly publicized Arab Charter on Women's Rights issued by the Federal National Council of the United Arab Emirates in conjunction with the Arab Parliament. She uses these three iterations of women's rights to underline key topoi of (women's) rights discourse.

In "<Police Power> to Stop-and-Frisk: A Pattern for Persuasion," Lindsay Head draws on Michael Calvin McGee's characterization of the ideograph as a link between rhetoric and ideology to explore the development of the ideograph <police power> in the time leading up to, and the court's opinion in, the landmark case *Floyd v. City of New York* (2013). In this case, a bright spot in New York's sullied history of stop-and-frisk, twelve Black and Hispanic individuals succeeded in a class action lawsuit against the city, alleging that the NYPD's use of stop-and-frisk policy violated their Fourth Amendment right to be free from unreasonable searches and seizures and their right to equal protection of the laws under the Fourteenth Amendment. Head shows that ideographic inquiry offers more than a useful tool for education and analysis or a method for predicting societal beliefs and behaviors: It is a force for persuasion.

Part V focuses on law's power to exclude voices. In "Framing the War on Drugs: Judith Butler and Legal Rhetorical Analysis," Erin Leigh Frymire uses Butler's concepts of *frames of war* and *precarious life* to analyze the 1986 Anti-Drug Abuse Act (ADAA), which infamously mandated the same minimum sentence for the possession of 100 times as much powder cocaine as crack cocaine. The two forms of the drug are pharmacologically equivalent and yet the sentences arise from causes not chemical but social and rhetorical, as the two forms are associated with distinct socioeconomic and racial groups. Frymire uses Butler's frames of war and precarious life to highlight not only the rhetorical strategies used in the ADAA and the political discourse surrounding it but also to illuminate how the ADAA is itself a rhetorical strategy for maintaining a racist status quo.

In "Ensnared by Custom: Mary Astell and the American Bar Association on Female Autonomy," Judy Cornett compares two very different authors separated by almost four centuries on the problem of women's social position. Mary Astell, one of the earliest English feminists, examined these questions in 1694 in *A Serious Proposal to the Ladies*. She believed that women were not living up to their intellectual potential and were relegated to the realm of trivia and frivolity by the social norms of the period. In 2019, the American Bar Association published a report entitled *Walking Out the Door: The Facts, Figures, and Future of Experienced Women Lawyers in Private Practice*. Focusing on America's 350 largest law firms, the report found that women with more than fifteen years of experience are leaving law firms in droves. Like Astell, the report attributed this failure to thrive to male-created cultural norms. Although the two authors agree that women should be able to thrive in a man's world but aren't doing so, they rhetorically engage the problem very differently.

In "*Dissoi Logoi*, Rhetorical Listening, and Legal Education," Elizabeth Britt examines the anonymous *Dissoi Logoi*, attributed to a sophistic author in Greece in the late fifth century BCE. She uses the ancient text, and the practices of listening that it implies, to imagine how law students might be taught to listen rhetorically to the materials they encounter in their training. To focus the discussion, she analyzes how a contemporary law school casebook teaches *State v. Norman*, a case about a woman convicted of voluntary manslaughter in the death of her abusive husband. The case is included in a number of criminal law casebooks to teach theories of self-defense; it is also widely cited and discussed by scholars of intimate partner violence law and advocacy. Britt argues that casebooks have the potential to encourage students to listen to arguments on either side of a question but that this potential can be thwarted by editorial decisions. She suggests ways that readers can listen rhetorically to law school materials to hear not only the multiple voices present (and missing) from cases but also the voices framing the cases.

In Part VI, the afterword, we offer an unconventional call for proposals to carry on the work to which this volume contributes.

REFERENCES

Alden, A. A. (2020). *Disorder in the court: Morality, myth, and the insanity defense*. University of Alabama Press.

Amsden, B. (2016). Rhetorical interventions in the law: Interpreting "I ♥ Boobies!" *First Amendment Studies*, 50(1), 1–13. https://doi.org/10.1080/21689725.2016.1152907

Aristotle. (2007). *On rhetoric: A theory of civic discourse* (G. A. Kennedy Trans.; 2nd ed.). Oxford University Press.

Berenguer, E., Jewel, L., & McMurtry-Chubb, T. A. (2023). *Critical and comparative rhetoric: Unmasking privilege and power in law and legal advocacy to achieve truth, justice, and equity*. Policy Press.

Berger, L. L. (2010). Studying and teaching "law as rhetoric": A place to stand. *Legal Writing: The Journal of the Legal Writing Institute*, 16, 3–64.

(2013). Metaphor and analogy: The sun and moon of legal persuasion. *Journal of Law and Policy*, 22(1), 147–196.

Berger, L. L., & Stanchi, K. M. (2018). *Legal persuasion: A rhetorical approach to the science*. Routledge.

Brooks, P., & Gewirtz, P. (Eds.). (1996). *Law's stories: Narrative and rhetoric in the law*. Yale University Press.

Campbell, P. O. (2012). The procedural queer: Substantive due process, *Lawrence v. Texas*, and queer rhetorical futures. *Quarterly Journal of Speech*, 98(2), 203–229. https://doi.org/10.1080/00335630.2012.663923

Camper, M. (2018). *Arguing over texts: The rhetoric of interpretation*. Oxford University Press.

Cedrone, M. J. (2020). Cicero and Barack Obama: How to unite the republic without losing your head. *Nevada Law Journal*, 20(3), 1177–1208.

Chávez, K. R. (2016). Protecting LGBT migrants: The rhetoric of identity and the expansion of the prison-industrial complex. In E. J. Hartelius (Ed.), *The rhetorics of US immigration: Identity, community, otherness* (pp. 70–90). Penn State University Press.

Constable, M. (2004). On not leaving law to the lawyers. In A. Sarat (Ed.), *Law in the liberal arts* (pp. 69–83). Cornell University Press.

(2014a). Law as language. *Critical Analysis of Law*, 1(1), 63–74.

(2014b). *Our word is our bond: How legal speech acts*. Stanford University Press.

Coulson, D. M. (2012). Persecutory agency in the racial prerequisite cases: Islam, Christianity, and martyrdom in *United States v. Cartozian*. *University of Miami Race and Social Justice Law Review*, 2, 117–188.

(2023). *Judicial rhapsodies: Rhetoric and fundamental rights in the Supreme Court*. Amherst College Press. https://doi.org/10.3998/mpub.12752816

Craig, B. B., & Rahko, S. E. (2016). Visual profiling as biopolitics: Or, notes on policing in post-racial #AmeriKKKa. *Cultural Studies ↔ Critical Methodologies*, *16*(3), 287–295. https://doi.org/10.1177/1532708616634775

Dauphinais, K. A. (2020). Quintilian's curriculum. *Nevada Law Journal*, *20*(3), 917–934.

Davis, K. K. (2020). [Classical] lawyers as [Digital] public speakers: Classical rhetoric and lawyer digital public commentary. *Nevada Law Journal*, *20*(3), 1137–1176.

Davis, K. K., & Mootz, F. J., III. (2024). Contemporary law through the classical lens. In F. J. Mootz, III, K. A. Davis, B. N. Larson, & K. Tiscione (Eds.), *Classical rhetoric & contemporary law: A critical reader* (pp. 3–10). University of Alabama Press.

Gibson, K. L. (2018). *Ruth Bader Ginsburg's legacy of dissent: Feminist rhetoric and the law*. University of Alabama Press.

Hannah, M. A., & Salmon, S. (2020). Against the grain: The secret role of dissents in integrating rhetoric across the curriculum. *Nevada Law Journal*, *20*(3), 935–966.

Hasian, M. (1997). Judicial rhetoric in a fragmentary world: "Character" and storytelling in the Leo Frank case. *Communication Monographs*, *64*(3), 250–269. https://doi.org/10.1080/03637759709376419

Hasian, M., Condit, C. M., & Lucaites, J. L. (1996). The rhetorical boundaries of "the law": A consideration of the rhetorical culture of legal practice and the case of the "separate but equal" doctrine. *Quarterly Journal of Speech*, *82*(4), 323–342. https://doi.org/10.1080/00335639609384161

Inniss, L. B. (2009). A critical legal rhetoric approach to *In Re African-American Slave Descendants* litigation. *St. John's Journal of Legal Commentary*, *24*(4), 649–696.

Johnson, K. A., & Smith, C. R. (2024). *Fear and the First Amendment: Controversial cases of the Roberts court*. University of Alabama Press.

Johnson, L. D., & Koenig, M. L. (2020). Walk the line: Aristotle and the ethics of narrative. *Nevada Law Journal*, *20*(3), 1037–1078.

Langford, C. L. (2018). *Scalia v. Scalia: Opportunistic textualism in constitutional interpretation*. University of Alabama Press.

Larson, B. N. (2024). Afterword. In F. J. Mootz, III, K. A. Davis, B. N. Larson, & K. Tiscione (Eds.), *Classical rhetoric & contemporary law: A critical reader* (pp. 243–246). University of Alabama Press.

Larson, B. N., & Tiscione, K. K. (2024). Classical rhetoric: Then and now. In F. J. Mootz, III, K. A. Davis, B. N. Larson, & K. Tiscione (Eds.), *Classical rhetoric & contemporary law: A critical reader* (pp. 11–25). University of Alabama Press.

Mootz, F. J., III (2020). Corpus linguistics and Vico's lament: Against vivisectional jurisprudence. *Nevada Law Journal*, *20*(3), 845–854.

Mootz, F. J., III, & Frank, D. A. (Eds.). (2023). *The rhetoric of judging well: The conflicted legacy of Justice Anthony M. Kennedy*. Penn State University Press.

Mootz, F. J., III, Davis, K. A., Larson, B. N., & Tiscione, K. (Eds.). (2024). *Classical rhetoric & contemporary law: A critical reader*. University of Alabama Press.

Pham, V. N. (2015). Our foreign president Barack Obama: The racial logics of birther discourses. *Journal of International and Intercultural Communication*, *8*(2), 86–107. https://doi.org/10.1080/17513057.2015.1025327

Provenzano, S. E. (2022). How rhetoric reveals judicial motives in employment discrimination cases. *Tennessee Law Review*, *90*(1), 149–221.

Provenzano, S. E., & Larson, B. N. (2020). Civil procedure as a critical discussion. *Nevada Law Journal*, *20*(3), 967–1035.

Rountree, C. (2007). *Judging the Supreme Court: Constructions of motive in Bush v. Gore*. Michigan State University Press.

(2020). Kairos and American legal praxis. *Nevada Law Journal*, *20*(3), 855–876.

Sarat, A., & Kearns, T. R. (Eds.). (1996). *The rhetoric of law*. University of Michigan Press.

Schuster, M. L., & Propen, A. D. (2011). *Victim advocacy in the courtroom: Persuasive practices in domestic violence and child protection cases*. Northeastern University Press.

Sciullo, N. J. (2019). Queer phenomenology in law: A critical theory of orientation. *Pace Law Review*, *39*, 667–709.

Slocum, B. G., & Mootz, F. J., III (Eds.). (2019). *Justice Scalia: Rhetoric and the rule of law*. University of Chicago Press.

Somerville, S. B. (2005). Queer loving. *GLQ: A Journal of Lesbian and Gay Studies*, *11*(3), 335–370.

Stanchi, K. M., Berger, L. L., & Crawford, B. J. (2016). *Feminist judgments: Rewritten opinions of the United States Supreme Court*. Cambridge University Press. https://books.google.com/books?id=aVCeDAAAQBAJ [https://perma.cc/XY79-Y7RH]

Tiscione, K. K. (2016). *Rhetoric for legal writers: The theory and practice of analysis and persuasion* (2nd ed.). West Academic.

Vats, A. (2016). (Dis)owning Bikram: Decolonizing vernacular and dewesternizing restructuring in the yoga wars. *Communication and Critical/Cultural Studies*, *13*(4), 325–345. https://doi.org/10.1080/14791420.2016.1151536

(2019). Prince of intellectual property: On creatorship, ownership, and Black capitalism in purple afterworlds (Prince in/as Blackness). *Howard Journal of Communications*, *30*(2), 114–128. https://doi.org/10.1080/10646175.2018.1523760

(2021). Temporality in a time of *Tam*, or towards a racial chronopolitics of intellectual property law. *IDEA: The IP Law Review*, *61*(3), 673–734.

Venter, C. M. (2021). Dissenting from the bench: The rhetorical and performative oral jurisprudence of Ruth Bader Ginsburg and Antonin Scalia. *Wake Forest Law Review*, *56*(2), 321–385.

Webb, L. A. (2020). Speaking the truth: Supporting authentic advocacy with professional identity formation. *Nevada Law Journal*, *20*(3), 1079–1136.

Weresh, M. H. (2020). Ethos at the intersection: Classical insights for contemporary application. *Nevada Law Journal*, *20*(3), 877–916.

West, I. (2008). Debbie Mayne's trans/scripts: Performative repertoires in law and everyday life. *Communication & Critical/Cultural Studies*, *5*(3), 245–263. https://doi.org/10.1080/14791420802206841

(2019). Wedding cakes, equality, and rhetorics of religious freedom. *First Amendment Studies*, *53*(1–2), 1–21. https://doi.org/10.1080/21689725.2019.1604246

Wetlaufer, G. B. (1990). Rhetoric and its denial in legal discourse. *Virginia Law Review*, *76*(8), 1545–1597.

White, J. B. (1985). Law as rhetoric, rhetoric as law: The arts of cultural and communal life. *University of Chicago Law Review*, *52*(3), 684–702.

(1990). *Justice as translation: An essay in cultural and legal criticism*. University of Chicago Press.

Williams, L., & Spedding, M. (2024). The First Amendment and constitutive rhetoric: A policy proposal. *NYU Law Review*, *99*(4), 1338–1397.

Williams, P. J. (1991). *The alchemy of race and rights*. Harvard University Press.

PART II

Key Rhetorical Concepts Animating Contemporary American Law

2

The Ethos of Originalism

Mark A. Hannah and Francis J. Mootz III

We are all originalists

Solicitor General Elena Kagan (2010)

2.1 INTRODUCTION

Originalism has positioned itself as the *au courant* doctrine of legal interpretation in the United States. Proponents argue that originalism is a core element of our democratic identity and should be adopted by every judge. The originalist tenet[1] – that the meaning of a legal text is the ordinary meaning the text had when it was enacted – purportedly provides an objective basis for judging with integrity. Despite originalists' grandiose claims, critics have lodged many well-reasoned objections that problematize originalists' goals and methods (Chemerinsky, 2022; Mootz, 2017; Segall, 2018). Why, then, has originalism gained such widespread prominence? In this chapter, we offer a rhetorical analysis that explains its ascendence and strange persistence.

Our thesis is that originalists do not prevail primarily by persuading others through logic or dialectical reasoning (*logos*) or by promoting their audience's disposition to hear their argument (*pathos*). Instead, originalists bring force to their claims by establishing and projecting an *ethos*. They draw on ethos when claiming to be principled legal advocates who are persons of good character and wisdom. However, "ethos" has a broader scope than the speaker's reputation or character exhibited in an effort to persuade. Embracing "ethos" in its broadest sense reveals that *originalism* itself – distinct from its individual supporters – has an ethos in the form of a communal indwelling. Only by acknowledging this dimension of ethos can we explain how originalists have dominated recent jurisprudential debates.

[1] Originalism seemingly has morphed into as many iterations as there are theorists. Subtle differences among the various theorists are not relevant to our analysis of the ethos of originalism writ large.

The ethos of originalism is a dynamic social reality that has evolved over time. In Section 2.2, we reconceptualize "ethos" and recover its full meaning as developed by Martin Heidegger in his 1924 lectures on Aristotle. In Section 2.3, we describe the emergence of modern originalism in the work of Professor Raoul Berger and analyze his promotion of an ethos of originalism through proper acts of deference. In Section 2.4, we trace how Justice Antonin Scalia initially advanced the cause of originalism by narrowing its ethos of deference to a judicial model of rule-following. He later veered from originalism's cause when his writings eschewed deference in favor of performative, individually motivated reasoning, but his reliance on the ethos of indwelling remained. In Section 2.5, we contrast Scalia's efforts with those of Professor Lawrence Solum, the most prominent contemporary academic proponent of originalism. We demonstrate that, although more sophisticated and restrained than Scalia, Solum also relies on the ethos of indwelling to overcome originalism's deficiencies.

Berger, Scalia, and Solum did not secure a place of pride for originalism solely through the ethos of personal character and effective reasoning. Rather, we demonstrate that they succeeded by connecting their work to a deep-seated shared sense of communal identity. This demonstration is a critical starting point for developing effective critical interventions in future jurisprudential debates about the merits of originalism as a theory of legal meaning.

2.2 THE CONCEPT OF "ETHOS"

In the absence of compelling logical demonstration, Aristotle locates the power of persuasion primarily in the trust that the audience places in the speaker. Aristotle contends that the speaker can be deemed trustworthy in three ways (Aristotle, 2007, p. 112). First, the speaker may display personal excellence in the virtues (*arete*), such as courage, temperance, and fairness. Second, they might demonstrate practical wisdom in their argument (*phronesis*), such as by choosing apt metaphors and cogent analysis. Third, they may exhibit goodwill toward the audience (and the entire community) (*eunoia*), which is an ethical relationship of shared regard. The combination of these three elements constitutes the speaker's ethos. Logos and pathos are also forms of persuasion (*pisteis*) (Aristotle, 2007, p. 38), but Aristotle regards ethos as the most important because it looks beyond technique to the persuasion effected by the speaker as a person. As Gene Garver concludes, Aristotle ultimately regards rhetoric as "an art of character" (Garver, 1995). Ethos carries a weight that shapes future reasoning, which Garver explains with the concept of an "ethical surplus" (Garver, 2004, pp. 73–76). In practical reasoning, one is always committed to more than the logical entailments of one's position. For example, in *Brown v. Board of Education* (1954), the Court committed the nation to racial desegregation beyond the specific question of educational equity presented in the case (Garver, 2004, pp. 83–85). We explain this powerful amplification of ethos by drawing on Heidegger's reading of Aristotle.

2.2.1 *The Speaker's Display of Ethos:* Arete *and* Phronesis

"Ethos" often is loosely translated as the speaker's "character," with attention to how it affects the speaker's ability to persuade an audience. It is uncontroversial to suggest that an audience is more likely to trust the arguments of a person of high character. However, this limited sense of "ethos" as the speaker's pre-established *arete* fails to capture how that ethos operates in and beyond the rhetorical situation. One of Aristotle's advances was recognizing that ethos is evinced in the rhetorical act itself and not solely an antecedent fact about the speaker. This understanding that the speaker's manifestation of ethos is dual in nature is summarized by Quintilian's dictum that the ideal rhetor is a "good man speaking well." One's ethos as a trustworthy person is certainly augmented by one's ability to generate appropriate arguments in a case (Garver, 1995, p. 15). Ultimately, Aristotle contends that the speaker's ethos is revealed more by skill in practical reasoning than by virtue (Smith, 2004, p. 5).

2.2.2 *The Speaker's Participation in Communal Ethos:* Eunoia

This reading of Aristotle's definition of "ethos" is incomplete. There is a component of ethos that goes beyond the individual speaker and a particular argumentative challenge. In his 1924 lectures, Heidegger recuperated Aristotle's "hermeneutics of everydayness" as an exploration of the meaning-laden background resources that gird ethical thought and action (Hyde, 2004, pp. xvii–xx; McNeill, 2006, pp. 77–94). Heidegger characterizes "ethos" as an exhibition of virtue activated by deliberative activity that draws on shared fore-understandings in the moment, a thoroughly futural comportment toward action rather than a stable and preexisting capacity (McNeill, 2006, p. 95). This is the critical difference that Heidegger draws between *arete* as virtuous activity and *techne* as merely adapting one's established craft to particular circumstances.

Heidegger's key insight is that our pre-thinking existence with others generates the call of conscience that spurs deliberations about shared conceptions of the good (Hyde, 2004, p. xx). This dimension of ethos is a way of being in which we dwell rhetorically, drawing from a community's rhetorical resources to generate meaning but also being shaped by the community's fore-understandings before consciously developing arguments for a particular position. The goodwill described by *eunoia* is rooted in the ethical indwelling shared by the speaker and audience.[2]

[2] The principal text is Heidegger's famous lectures from the 1924 summer course on Aristotle (Heidegger, 2009). Heidegger reads the *Nicomachean Ethics* and the *Rhetoric* as phenomenological accounts of how we exist together prior to reflection, our dwelling together in speech. Heidegger emphasizes that living, "for the human being, means speaking" (Heidegger, 2009, p. 14) and there is an equiprimordiality of being with (*mitsein*) and speaking (p. 45). This deep shared dimension is the wellspring of rhetorical engagement, in that "Rhetoric is nothing other

We can render Heidegger's dense theorizing more accessible through several of his commentators. Walter Jost (2004, p. 75) connects this broad notion of "*ethos* as dwelling" to the "rhetorical places or topoi, more or less undefined terms, categories, cases, and the like useful for exploring ... indeterminate practice problem[s]." Put differently, in Heidegger's "way of seeing things, [ethos] is not something that a rhetor uses, it is something that uses him" (Kenny, 2004, p. 36). Calvin Schrag (2004, p. vii) characterizes this broader conception of ethos as "a region of knowing and working together in advance of strategies to achieve consensus in the public forum." Viewed this way, ethos is "the dwelling or abode from which our communicative practices of entwined discourse and action take their rise and to which they return for their validations of sense and reference" (Schrag, 2004, p. vii). The ethos subtending a community is dynamic. Each rhetorical engagement not only draws on ethos, it also contributes to its evolution by creating a surplus for other community members to engage. A speaker has a personal ethos in the sense of demonstrated "character," but the speaker's character arises out of a shared ethos with the audience that provides the very possibility of having an individualized ethos. This is particularly true when a speaker seeks to motivate the audience to modify their practical reasoning and values. Accomplishing this is possible only by drawing from and embodying the discursive practices that constitute the communal ethos and then revealing to the audience a better "character" that exhibits the community's values in deliberation (Smith, 2004, p. 13).[3]

We use the concept of "ethos" in the full sense developed above. Originalists use ethos – construed as exhibiting good character and practical reasoning through deferring to the Framers' original intentions – to persuade others of the correctness of originalist methods. The speaker's character is general in that their audience already knows them as trustworthy, but their character is also developed and revealed in how they persuade. But ethos does not arise out of thin air, or simply by the speaker's force of will. Rather, the speaker's ethos is evinced through embodying the community's fore-understanding, namely its rhetorical commitments as represented in the values, topics, genres, and modes of argumentation that define the community and provide the resources for the exercise of practical wisdom. One cannot understand the power of ethos in persuasion without illuminating the constitutive effects of this indwelling.

than the interpretation of concrete being there, the hermeneutic of being-there itself" (p. 75). He concludes: "We are better off since we possess the Aristotelian *Rhetoric* rather than a philosophy of language. In the *Rhetoric* we have something before us that deals with speaking as a basic mode of the being-with-another of human beings themselves ... [T]he *Rhetoric* gives access to this original phenomenon" (Heidegger, 2009, p. 80; see Canzonieri, 2017). Heidegger's *Being and Time* takes a more understated approach to *mitsein* as the primordial experience of understanding (Heidegger, 1996, pp. 116–126), but his *Letter on Humanism* continued this theme (Heidegger, 1977).

3 Feminist scholars have also reassessed ethos as an abiding yet dynamic abode subtending the attribution of character according to a society's biases (Ryan et al., 2016a).

2.2.3 *An Example of Ethos as Communal Indwelling*

We illustrate these different senses of "ethos" by describing Martin Medhurst's (2004) argument that the country was not as rigidly divided during the 2000 presidential campaign as many assumed. He contends that the electorate shared Judeo-Christian values and sought a return to public spiritual values in the wake of the Clinton presidency. Medhurst traces the operation of ethos in the political debates at all three levels. First, Al Gore and George W. Bush both presented themselves as moral and upstanding men. Gore and his wife, Tipper, were widely admired as a loving couple. Bush had overcome alcoholism and other wayward behavior and offered himself as a committed Christian. Gore's running mate, Joe Lieberman, advertised he would be working for the American people "24/6," humorously using his devotion to the Sabbath to underscore his character. Moreover, the candidates demonstrated moral leadership by pitching their political arguments in respectful tones.

The ethos of the campaign was not limited to the candidates' characters or how they exercised practical reasoning. Both candidates also drew upon American citizens' deep belief in, and reverence for, the ideas embodied in American exceptionalism, that is, the principles of freedom, democracy, and the rule of law established at the nation's founding. Americans longed for virtuous leadership and spiritual renewal, and these desires were actualized through the candidates' dwelling within these principles. The candidates both tapped into and aligned their characters with this dimension (*eunoia*) of ethos, demonstrating a shared civic connection that was obscured by the campaigns' hurly-burly politicking. Medhurst argues that the campaign revealed "an ethos to our democracy – a dwelling place – that is shared across parties, across religions, across geography, across races, and even, to some extent, across ideologies" (Medhurst, 2004, p. 115). Medhurst illustrates how a complex ethos that begins in shared preunderstandings ultimately was reflected in the candidates' rhetorical practices, providing a model of our critical inquiry in this chapter. We apply this same heuristic to two of the "original" originalist thinkers, Professor Raoul Berger and Justice Antonin Scalia,[4] and one of its contemporary defenders, Professor Lawrence Solum.

2.3 RAOUL BERGER: ESTABLISHING DEFERENCE AS THE ETHOS OF ORIGINALISM

Professor Raoul Berger is widely credited with being originalism's first proponent. Berger worked in private and government practice and also as a law professor writing extensively on topics such as impeachment, executive privilege, and the death

[4] Robert Bork is generally regarded as a third "original" originalist, or perhaps the proto-originalist (see Bork, 1971, p. 7), and our analysis applies equally to him.

penalty. He is most well-known for his 1977 book *Government by Judiciary: The Transformation of the Fourteenth Amendment* (Berger, 1997), in which he argues that constitutional interpretation must be constrained by the original intentions of the Framers who authored the US Constitution (Berger, 1997, p. 18). Berger wrote *Government by Judiciary* because he was deeply concerned by judicial revision of the Fourteenth Amendment (Berger, 1985–1986, p. 297). As an originalism manifesto (Segall, 2017, p. 47), *Government by Judiciary* clarified the basic contours of originalism (O'Neill, 2005, p. 131) through passionately calling for judges to restrain their work by deferring to text and original meaning rather than implementing evolving contemporary values (Segall, 2017, p. 47). The arc of Berger's theory lives on today through academic scholarship and judicial dicta commenting on its merits and limits. Some go so far as to argue that "almost everything being written, explicitly or implicitly, [about originalism] is a response to *Government by Judiciary*" (O'Neill, 2005, p. 131).

2.3.1 *Berger's Theory of Original Meaning*

Berger's originalism is traceable to his frustration with the activist decisions in the New Deal era that fundamentally altered the relationship between the state and the federal government (Presser, 2018). Berger did not want courts to be engines of progressive change, and he argued the Fourteenth Amendment's purpose was "merely to provide a Constitutional basis for the 1866 Civil Rights Act … which was designed to guarantee that the newly freed Blacks would have the same rights to enforce contracts, to possess property, and to enjoy the security of life and limb as did whites" (para. 6). By exceeding this purpose, Berger argued that judges undermined traditional democratic and rule-of-law values.

Berger's conception of originalist argument is animated by the conviction that judges cannot revise the Constitution (Berger, 1997, p. 21) because it is the covenant that operates at the heart of American civil religion (p. 394) and is the bulwark of people's liberties (p. 321). Fealty to the Constitution runs deep in America, and Berger deeply respected the consent-based majoritarian nature of democratic systems (O'Neill, 2005, p. 112). Notably, he understood the Constitution as fundamental law that derived its obligatory force from the sovereignty of the people who ratified the Constitution. Berger believed the intentions of the sovereign people demanded obedience (Berger, 1997, p. 407) as people have the right to control their own destiny (p. 18). Encroaching on the Framers' intentions, which were an expression of the people's value choices (p. 301), thwarted this liberty.

Berger's advocacy for an interpretive method grounded in original meaning also displayed his commitment to the rule of law (Berger, 1997, p. 6). He insisted that we are bound to the Constitution and strict rules and precedents (p. 329) and asserted that "preestablished rules serve the requirements of certainty and predictability so that people may conduct themselves accordingly" (p. 467). Perhaps the greatest rule to follow was the formal processes for amending the Constitution (p. 19). Berger characterized judicial discretion as an act of informal amendment that subordinated the law to judge's predilections and ultimately displaced the Framers' choices that expressed the people's will (p. 461). In undermining this will, jurists created conditions for rule by elites and experts rather than democratic self-governance.

To uphold democratic and rule-of-law values, Berger centered deference as foundational to originalist practice. Though Berger did not explicitly conceptualize his theory of originalism as deference, his advocacy clearly intimated the need for a yielding influence in judicial decision-making. For example, Berger believed deference hobbles the exercise of judicial power and thus short-circuits activists' opportunities to take advantage of the natural susceptibility of language (Berger, 1987–1988, p. 351). Importantly, such disabling ensures that judges merely expound and interpret the law and not make it (p. 351). Through its disabling work, deference establishes an objective critical practice that is immune to subjective disagreements about the merits of jurists' interpretive work. When done properly, deference legitimates originalist interpretation as credible, trustworthy, and loyal to the Framer's vision.

2.3.2 *Berger's Ethos as a Display of Character and Practical Reasoning*

Though Berger does not expressly claim to be a good man speaking well, he was widely regarded as a principled theorist, known for his temperance (in the sense of appropriate restraint), truthfulness, and keen sense of justice (in the sense of sustaining American democratic and rule-of-law principles) (see O'Neill, 2005). His work criticizing President Nixon's invocation of "executive privilege" during the Watergate crisis is representative of what it means for a legal advocate to work in a non-partisan manner, eschewing predilections for policy positions and standards of morality (Presser, 2018) in their decision-making. At times, Berger admittedly was irreverent (for example, his coining of phrases such as "judicial squatter sovereignty" (Berger, 1986–1987, p. 15) or "a cloud of post-Warren court euphoria" (Berger, 1997, p. 4), but at the heart of his projected character was an unmistakable quality of deference that turned on a profound well of respect for the Framers' articulation of constitutional rights.

Berger's virtue was put into question by his criticism of *Brown v. Board of Education* (1954). His display of character when criticizing the decision purported to be a principled approach to constitutional decision-making, such that he argued "intellectual honesty demands that the 'original understanding' be honored across the board" (Berger, 1997, p. 460) and that intellectual honesty in *Brown* requires that judges recognize that "the historical warrant for desegregation in the due process clause" is controversial (p. 7). In the face of overwhelming criticism, Berger reinforced his integrity by acknowledging he also held the political views of the judicial activists seeing to advance racial justice.[5] Nevertheless, the rule of law demanded he cabin these personal views in deference to the law. Making this choice was difficult, as are all constitutional decisions involving core American values, and Berger evinced courage in making the "right" argument, something unprincipled Justices avoid when facing an unpalatable situation.

This tack was essential to Berger's appeal. As a historical matter, it is clear that originalism arose as a political theory for reversing the Warren Court advances rather than as a legal theory of argumentation (Greene, 2009a; TerBeek, 2021). Many who developed the political dimensions of originalism, such as Attorney General Edwin Meese, offered weak and partisan arguments to support their position. Berger's broader historical and political account sought to neutralize the racist underpinnings dedicated to undermining *Brown* by insisting that the rule of law had some regrettable effects that must be corrected legislatively.

Berger's display of character included a well-developed communal sensibility illustrated through his centering of the locus of power in a community's rhetorical commitments. Berger (1997, p. 52) recognized the "[Framers]' concern with the rights of the community rather than the individual." Honoring the Framers' communal concerns thus requires acts of self-abnegation, the sacrifice of one's predilections and morals that preserves the authority of the "we" and its values that were instantiated through ratification. Berger (1986, p. 14) understood the people have a fundamental right to rule themselves, and more importantly, that only they can revoke such authority. Not centering authority in the community creates the conditions that enable judges to upend and revoke that authority against the Framers' constitutional designs.

Like Aristotle, Berger understood that the ability to persuade an audience turns on more than a speaker's character and involves how the speaker makes their case. For originalism, this "how" dimension of ethos is cultivated by the speaker looking only to the meaning of the authoritative text when it was enacted, eschewing crude appeals to the audience's emotions or hubristic efforts to define the "just" rather than the "legal" result. Berger (1986–1987, p. 10) framed the "how" dimension of ethos as a problem of evidence and "always insisted on the test of empirical evidence in the written record as the only legitimate source of constitutional law" (O'Neill, 2005, p. 112). In *Government by Judiciary*, for example, he argued it "is necessary to pile proof on proof" (Berger, 1997, p. 9) to demonstrate the overwhelming nature of an appeal to original meaning. Berger criticized activists for ignoring these evidentiary demands, and, as a corrective, suggests three features of originalist arguments – temporality, textual integrity, and authorial reputation – that judges and legal advocates ought to advance.

[5] Though a lifelong liberal (Berger, 1987–1988, p. 352), Berger refused to pursue political goals out of concern it would corrupt his writings (Gangi, 1988, p. 802).

Berger's emphasis on original meaning demands that originalist argument be temporally attentive (Berger, 1985–1986, p. 321). In originalist thought, skillful argument relies on evidence close to the founding – "contemporaneous construction" – because it more accurately reflects the Framers' intentions (Berger, 1942, p. 625). It is not simply a matter of judges accepting a quantifiable expression of time, that is, texts written a certain number of years ago. Rather, judges use the time of a text's creation to identify the contours of the rhetorical context that confine their considerations of rhetorical factors like audiences, events, and constraints[6] in their arguments (Berger, 1997, p. 9).

Regarding textual integrity, Berger inhabited a procedural disposition shaped by well-defined guidelines for identifying and using appropriate texts. For example, Berger encouraged judges to use texts that had a stenographic quality (Berger, 1997, p. 7). Namely, he encouraged judges to draw from verbatim accounts developed during the time of an event's occurring, as statements made in those accounts counted as facts rather than opinion (p. 7). As facts, such evidence is free from the distortions of recollection and thus more reliable (p. 7). Berger also was highly critical of unprincipled citation practices. In particular, he argued judges should not have a free and easy way with texts and criticized any incompatibility between sources and their application (Berger, 1985–1986, p. 331). Implicated in Berger's concern with incompatibility is an understanding that there are appropriate genres for anchoring constitutional arguments. As an example, Berger describes the preservation of journals from the Convention that could be used to rebut false claims about the Framers' intentions (Berger, 1985–1986, p. 313). Ultimately, skillful textual practices establish a relationality that induces deference to dampen judges' speculative instincts to consider extralegal factors, like politics, which are at odds with the Framer's original intentions. Significantly, Berger makes room for judges to consider policy texts when historical texts run out (Berger, 1942, p. 637), and in acknowledging such potential, Berger bolstered his character as a credible advocate who recognized originalism's limits.

Concomitant with Berger's concern with textual integrity is the character of the authorial voice that establishes the original meaning of the Constitution's words, namely the voice of historical contemporaries and not modern theorists (Berger, 1997, p. 9). Berger deferred to trustworthy voices like Alexander Hamilton, James Madison, and other Framers (p. 427) whose words set the originalist community's boundaries. Relatedly, Berger deferred to the voices of Senators who signed the Fourteenth Amendment and recertified the democratic will of the citizenry to alter the Constitution (Berger, 1985–1986, p. 297). He was suspicious of scholarship animated by personal bias and how it undermined the pull of deference to the community voice instantiated through the Constitution's ratification (p. 323). To offset bias concerns, Berger insisted that the voice of competing arguments,

6 For a discussion of the "rhetorical situation" in law, see Hannah and Salmon (2020).

represented by discrepant evidence and opposing inferences, be part of the evidentiary record for claims regarding the Framers' original understanding (Berger, 1997, p. 10).

2.3.3 *Berger's Resonance with Communal Ethos as Indwelling*

We interpret Berger's theory of original meaning coupled with his display of character and practical reasoning as emerging from a region of knowing (Schrag, 2004, pp. 4–5) shaped by the democratic and rule-of-law principles that defined the American legal community. In particular, his advocacy of deference was shaped by the ethos of indwelling that was behind and always already supporting his display of character and practical reasoning. The ethos of originalism's indwelling is a pre-thinking existence that operates in advance of argumentative strategies and exegetical claims. Berger's demonstration of communal sensibility along with his attention to issues of temporality, textual integrity, and authorial reputation embodied a persistent mode of deference that took its rise from the region of knowing and then came back for its validation through subsequent enactments of deference to original meaning.

Returning to Berger's willingness to jettison *Brown*, we can see that it was not fatal because it hewed closely to rule-of-law principles from which the conservative white majority wanted to draw to undo the civil rights ethos. By expressly putting his character into question, Berger's originalist argument regarding *Brown* evinced a principled argumentative approach that was – on its own terms, as a matter of logic – unassailable. He enacted a contextual sensibility by constraining his assessment to the parameters of *Brown* and not speculating about the decision's moral rightness. His approach was ensconced in the rule of law and aimed to preserve the ideal of democratic self-governance that subtended originalism's communal ethos. Berger's assessment of *Brown* establishes that originalism is inherently conservative and state centered. As we show next, Justice Scalia embodied and amplified this very nature through his originalist practice that drew from and was validated through originalism's indwelling ethos.

2.4 JUSTICE ANTONIN SCALIA: REVISING THE DEFERENTIAL ETHOS OF ORIGINALISM BY FOCUSING ON RULES THAT GENERATE CERTAINTY IN RESULTS

Berger successfully promoted originalist theory by projecting an ethos of deference to democratic rule. As an academic commentator, he succeeded in placing the topic at the center of jurisprudential debates. Ultimately, however, his ethos suffered when he declared that *Brown* was illegitimate. This abrasive disturbance of shared social values cast a dark shadow on his methodology. Deference to a fault with respect to *Brown* was unappealing to the vast majority of scholars, judges, and lawyers, even those with originalist convictions. And yet, originalism still got off the ground, most famously through the jurisprudence of Justice Antonin Scalia. To avoid negative ethos, Justice Scalia paid scant scholarly attention to Berger's work and, like most originalists, contended that the result in *Brown* was consistent with his originalist methodology (Scalia & Garner, 2012, p. 88; see Calabresi & Perl, 2014). Nevertheless, Justice Scalia faced his own difficulties in maintaining ethos as a judge.

2.4.1 *Justice Scalia's Theory of Original Meaning*

Justice Scalia promoted originalism as the least problematic – but by no means perfect – method for promoting certainty and consistency in adjudication.[7] Early in his tenure on the Supreme Court he, like Berger, championed a practical theory of judicial self-restraint capable of constraining judges to defer to democratic rule. Unlike the case-by-case weighing of equities by common law judges, Justice Scalia argued that modern judges confronting binding legal texts must follow the rules established by democratically responsive government branches. His measured articulation of this approach is reasoned and pragmatic and therefore able to promote adherence through a strong ethos.

Similar to Berger's interest in strong empirical foundations, Justice Scalia argued that his commitment to following a statute's ordinary textual meaning provides an invariant, empirical foundation upon which binding rules may be established (Scalia, 1989a, pp. 1184–1185). Certainly, judges will exercise discretion to choose among several plausible rules, but this activity should be minimal if the judge is committed to defer to the statute's original meaning (pp. 1186–1187). Justice Scalia readily admits that originalism is imperfect, but he insists that the question

> is not whether originalism is perfect. . . . The question is whether it is better than anything else. . . . And that is not difficult. . . . The reality is that originalism is the only game in town – the only real, verifiable criterion that can prevent judges from making the Constitution say whatever they think it should say. . . . The living constitutionalist is a happy fella, because it turns out that the Constitution always means precisely what he thinks it ought to mean. (Scalia, 2017, pp. 210–212)

Originalism, then, is the "lesser evil" when compared to other jurisprudential approaches (Scalia, 1989b).

2.4.2 *Justice Scalia's Ethos as a Display of Character and Practical Reasoning*

Justice Scalia presents a measured and reasonable defense of adhering to the value of certainty to the extent possible, even while acknowledging the epistemic and

7 This section draws heavily from Mootz (2019).

volitional obstacles to achieving complete adherence. He puts his faith in a jurisprudence of rules, grounded in the fixed, original understanding of the governing text, but he is astute enough to recognize we will fall short in our good-faith effort to follow this rigorous path. His point is a practical one. Non-originalists invite a wholesale failure of the judicial function, but realistic (faith-hearted and imperfect) originalists suffer only occasional concessions to human frailty while generally holding firm to rule-of-law values.

Justice Scalia's definition of originalism trumpets the virtue of judges who ignore the lure of power and defer to clear rules. Like Berger, he projects the image of a stalwart adherent to the rule of law who bravely overcomes his own all-too-human desire to effectuate justice on a case-by-case basis. He presents himself as a fallen angel trying to defer to legislative rules but acknowledging that he too, for his sins, will almost certainly write some opinions that rest on undisciplined weighing of incommensurable equities (Scalia, 1989a, pp. 1186–1187). A quick gloss of Scalia's words suggests he is a virtuous jurist aware of his limitations, yet the coy reference to himself as a fallen angel also intimates a desire to draw attention to himself. Through self-references like these, Scalia unwittingly laid the grounds for the undoing of his judicial character. Over time this undoing became a reality, as he became known for a communicative style characterized by florid prose and rhetorical excess (Shanske, 2019) which cuts at the heart of his presumably restrained and forthright judicial character.

Unlike Berger, Justice Scalia does not regard originalism as a truly attainable goal as much as an aspiration. Rather than hewing to a rigid philosophy, his ethos is one of practical attunement to the realities of judging, a sensibility Berger explicitly rejects. For example, Scalia readily accepted (undoubtedly with cases like *Brown* in mind) the virtue of *stare decisis* with his customary flourish: "The way I like to put it is: I am a textualist, I am an originalist. I am not a nut. You cannot go back and redo everything" (Scalia, 2015, p. 588). Though some argue that Scalia's originalist defense of *Brown* is so unpersuasive that it actually weakens his ethos (Turner, 2014), Scalia managed to project a strong ethos through humor, humility, and a sense of duty. He protects the rule of law not by wildly speculating about what the law ought to be but instead by constraining his work to what the law is.

Over time, though, Justice Scalia's ethos eroded as he became a visible proponent of a conservative political movement rather than a judge writing about, and employing, a distinctive interpretation theory (Segall, 2018, pp. 10–11). The tenor of his dissenting opinions and public speeches evidenced anger and intolerance that far exceeded Berger's occasional irreverence. In the string of gay rights cases authored by Justice Kennedy, Justice Scalia's intemperance spiraled out of control. He declared *Romer* "an act, not of judicial judgment but of political will" (*Romer v. Evans*, 1996, p. 653), *Lawrence* a "product of a Court . . . that has largely signed on to the so-called homosexual agenda" (*Lawrence v. Texas*, 2003, p. 2496), and *Obergefell* so bad that if he were to join the majority he would have to hide his "head in a bag," given that it was written in the "mystical aphorisms of the fortune cookie" to veil a "Judicial Putsch" (*Obergefell v. Hodges*, 2015, pp. 718–719).

Beyond these cases, Scalia continued leveling searing critiques against the motives and honesty of other Justices (Mootz, 2019, p. 97 n. 2), thus making him seem more like a partisan political figure (Berman, 2017; Newman, 2006–2007, p. 909). Through his behavior, it was increasingly clear he no longer made difficult choices constrained by law's rhetorical commitments but instead expedient ones that merely served conservative goals. This perceived alignment between his legal positions and the conservative political movement cast a long shadow over his case for originalism and thereby pitted his jurisprudential ambitions at odds with the American vision of liberty, democracy, and rule of law that girded Berger's theorizing of originalism. Ultimately, rather than building consensus around his view of proper judicial deference, Justice Scalia's lack of virtue and character defects undoubtedly put off many scholars, originalist and non-originalist alike.

Notwithstanding his irascible personality, Justice Scalia garnered widespread attention for his jurisprudential methodology. Adhering to meaning that is fixed at the time of a text's enactment promises to convert legal questions into empirical historical inquiries that have a correct and determinable answer. Justice Scalia unremittingly takes up this task, seeking to persuade his readers that legal meaning stands apart from political calculation and policy implementation.

The primary appeal of originalism is that it can serve as a constraining method whose results can be reviewed objectively. Perhaps the best demonstration of the ethos of Justice Scalia's practical argumentation is found in his majority opinion in *District of Columbia v. Heller* (2008). In it, Justice Scalia looks to the stable, unchanging bedrock of historical fact as an anchor against profound changes in society since the founding. Disregarding the contentious debates among professional legal historians about the nature of historical knowledge given the inevitable hermeneutical character of understanding, he assumes that constitutional provisions have an unchanging meaning that is grounded in the historical understanding of the text when it was enacted. Consequently, he spends more than fifty pages crafting a thick citational web of sources to analyze the "meaning of the Second Amendment" before turning "finally to the law at issue here" (*District of Columbia v. Heller*, 2008, p. 628). His dense narrative confirming that the Amendment grants gun owners protection for self-defense purposes appears unassailable; by working with texts from the time of the Amendment's enactment, Scalia ostensibly was imbuing his analysis with a sense of temporal and textual integrity anchored in a strong empirical record. However, as Justice Stevens' dissent regarding the deeply disputed history of the Amendment makes clear, histories like the one developed in *Heller* are highly contested as a matter of both political theory and historical truth. As such, those histories can open the door to smuggling in the values that originalism sought to eliminate.

Scalia's originalist method accrues ethos by centering deference to minimize doubt and indeterminacy, yet his *actual performance* in *Heller* falls short. First, his practical reasoning suffers from *hubris* in that he rarely recognizes the possibility that others may have insights into textual meaning that is not the product of originalist method. Furthermore, his "rhetoric of constitutional absolutism" rings hollow in the ears of those in the legal community who strive to balance incommensurable values and weakens the force of his argument (Berger, 2015). His aggressive method of judging in *Heller* (Segall, 2018, pp. 123–124, 140) also was rejected by many professional historians (pp. 143–144), and a failure to provide a convincing, empirically sound historical account is a failure at the core of originalist practice. Just as Justice Scalia's judicial character was highly suspect, so too his activity of practical reasoning was highly questionable.

2.4.3 *Scalia's Resonance with Communal Ethos as Indwelling*

Justice Scalia's originalism is part of a broader commitment to a norm of rule-following and institutional deference, as expressed by Berger, which compels judges to abstain from imposing their policy views and to adhere to democratically enacted laws. These commitments are deeply seated in democratic sentiments and corresponding principles of the separation of powers. Our assessment of the ethos of originalism as indwelling is buttressed by Eric Segall's (2018) characterization that originalism is more a matter of faith than a matter of reasoned deliberation about the best means for legal decision-making.

> Why was Scalia so effective advocating for a theory of constitutional interpretation he did not [in practice] adopt? The answer may be that originalism is not a theory of constitutional interpretation judges can effectively use to decide cases but a symbol, an article of faith, that links judicial review and the rule of law. (Segall, 2018, p. 183)

What binds the proponents of originalism is just "the faith that some combination of text, originalist-era evidence, and history can constrain Supreme Court decision-making (Segall, 2018, p. 193).[8] Our point is that this "faith" subtends the reasoned arguments about our practices as an affective feature of the indwelling that operates as an always already rhetorical force in constitutional interpretation.

John Manning explains Scalia's success promoting originalism in terms that fit our model. Manning argues that Scalia gained traction not through his personal ethos but because "his emphasis on standardless judicial discretion tapped into a preexisting, and deeply rooted, strain of American legal culture that aspires to

[8] Segall's metaphor is apt. In the Christian faith, "indwelling" is the presence of the Holy Spirit in the believer, a presence that empowers the person to be hermeneutically astute and discerning. Extending Segall's analysis of originalism as a matter of "faith," Benjamin Priester analogizes originalism to the kind of "fandom" that arises around iconic cultural events such as the Star Wars movies. Despite divisiveness and infighting about the "true" way to understand the franchise, the faithful are collectively committed to the claim that it expresses a universal and unchanging truth (Priester, 2021, pp. 37, 40).

judicial objectivity and constraint" (Manning, 2017, p. 771). His "anti-discretion principle reflects a persistent strain of thought in the American legal tradition" (p. 776), with "the aspiration to identify external legal constraints upon judging [continuing] to have a pull" (p. 778). Ironically, Manning notes, Scalia's deconstructive critique of judicial rhetoric was his great contribution to the cause, demonstrating that judges everywhere were arrogating discretion to themselves in their interpretive practices (pp. 779–781). In all of this, we recognize Scalia's opposition to judicial discretion, though in a markedly different tone, as furthering Berger's original lament. His tone led to the undoing of his personal character, but it reverberated with the American legal community's shared fore-understanding of values and modes of argumentation that gave shape to Berger's rhetoric of deference.

2.5 LAWRENCE SOLUM: GENERATING CERTAINTY IN JUDGING THROUGH THE FIXED MEANING OF LANGUAGE

Professor Berger's argument for a principled approach to constitutional decision-making that constrained judges set the stage for Justice Scalia to develop the judicial disposition of originalism, albeit with only a crude epistemological backing. Professor Lawrence Solum has been the most ardent and cogent defender of originalism as a correct hermeneutical theory of legal meaning, revisiting Berger's theory and Scalia's judicial practice in a sophisticated theoretical account that fully displays the ethos of originalism.

2.5.1 *Solum's Theory of Original Public Meaning*

There are many varieties of originalist theory, but most "contemporary originalists aim to recover the public meaning of the constitutional text at the time each provision was framed and ratified" (Solum, 2019, p. 1251). This definition seeks to avoid the problems raised by Berger's efforts to "discover" the intentions of the drafters.

> "Originalism" is a family of contemporary theories of constitutional interpretation and construction that share two core ideas. First, the communicative content of the constitutional text is fixed at the time each provision is framed and ratified – The Fixation Thesis. Second, constitutional practice should be constrained by that communicative content of the text, which we can call the "original public meaning" – The Constraint Principle. (Solum, 2017, p. 269; see also Solum, 2019, pp. 1270–1271)

Solum concedes there are different kinds of meaning, and he emphasizes he is interested only in the communicative (public) meaning of legal texts, as opposed to the drafters' intent or the purpose of the enactment (Solum, 2015, pp. 20–21; see also 2013a, p. 479). By focusing on fixed communicative meaning, Solum narrows the interpretive field and achieves certainty despite the "linguistic drift" of meaning over time (Solum, 2015, pp. 62–63). For example, a constitutional reference to "domestic violence" has a fixed meaning from the time of the founding that differs from the meaning the phrase might have today (US Constitution, art. IV, sec. 4).

Why is original public meaning the necessary touchstone for legal interpretation? Solum asserts that, from "the very beginning, American constitutional jurisprudence has recognized that the meaning of the constitutional text does not change" (Solum, 2018, p. 237). The normative obligation of judges to defer to the text's fixed meaning rather than enforce their own preferences is assumed rather than argued. Having identified a source of fixed meaning, it follows that the constraint principle will restrain judges from contradicting or exceeding that meaning. Critics object that historians do not take such a simplistic view of the past, but Solum emphasizes that uncovering the fixed communicative meaning of a text does not entail the same difficulties that professional historians encounter, inasmuch as they have competing objectives beyond recuperating communicative meaning.[9] In short, if "originalists are right about the Constraint Principle, then the truth of the Fixation Thesis should have important implications for constitutional practice" because it is the only plausible source for that constraint (Solum, 2015, p. 78).

Solum does not adequately account for the epistemological and motivational difficulties of judging. The Fixation Thesis does not ensure that the fixed meaning is pellucid, nor is the conversational meaning self-executing in a manner that definitively resolves interpretative problems. Judges begin with the original meaning of the text and then "construct" a result in the case at hand in line with a variety of judicial norms. Applying a text to a specific controversy requires judgment and the construction of a legal rule (Solum, 2010, 2013b). Even if the fixed linguistic meaning is clear, the judge must often engage in contemporary assessment of the legal rule for a case, working within what Solum calls the "construction zone." The construction zone is both "ubiquitous" and "ineliminable" in judicial practice (Solum, 2013b, p. 516).

To Solum's credit, he doesn't dodge the instability inherent in the trilogy of fixed meaning, the normative justification of constraint, and the practical necessity for construction. Because he fails to resolve these tensions, he roots his theoretical construct with a diverse ethos that strives to compensate for the weakness of his logos.

2.5.2 *Solum's Ethos as a Display of Character and Practical Reasoning*

Solum writes in a neutral scholarly voice that defends his position based wholly on the cogency of his arguments. Although he does not expressly invoke his character,

9 Solum notes that many historians have other concerns, including inquiries into the motives and purposes of constitutional actors, the construction of constitutional narratives that illuminate the causal processes that explain constitutionally salient events, and tracing the development of constitutional ideas over time. These inquiries intersect with originalist inquiry, but they are sometimes orthogonal to the central aim of originalism – the recovery of the original public meaning of the constitutional text (Solum, 2017, p. 292).

Solum does make an implicit appeal along these lines. First, he carefully circumscribes the scope of inquiry by admitting that defining originalism is an ongoing task he doesn't claim to have fully achieved. Solum often notes that applications of his theoretical claims must "wait another day," because they would require "deep and comprehensive research" (Solum, 2015, pp. 29, 70, 75). More important, he never claims to provide a complete analysis of a single legal dispute using originalist methodology (Solum, 2018, p. 237). With abundant humility, like early Justice Scalia, he claims only to be clarifying the conceptual terrain so as to provide a *lingua franca* for continuing jurisprudential debates (Solum, 2013a, pp. 518–519, 2013b, p. 536, 2019, p. 1296).

Solum's restrained claims are most apparent in his review of Jack Balkin's effort to link originalism with progressive politics and judicial practices. In various works, Balkin has argued that we can reconcile the original understanding of legal texts with efforts to apply them so as to overcome the Framers' limited vision (Balkin, 2011a, 2011b). Balkin suggests that the meaning of the text provides some measure of constraint on the elaboration of constitutional principles in a progressive manner. Balkin thereby combines fidelity to a fixed meaning with faith in redemptive judicial practices. This appears to put the theory at war with itself, precisely the kind of uncertainty that originalism is supposed to preclude (Solum, 2012, p. 162).

In response, Solum argues that courts are not bound by original meaning when they are operating in the "construction zone" to elaborate on vague or ambiguous terms. Thus, it is possible to assimilate the living constitutional method of construction with the fixation thesis of meaning, without engaging in a logical error. But this expansion must be duly circumscribed if it is not to undermine originalism. Solum indicts Balkin for embracing Philip Bobbit's (CITE) modes of argumentation without scrupulously distinguishing the modes for finding the text's fixed meaning from those that can be used only in the "construction zone" in the absence of a controlling fixed meaning.

> There may be special cases of irreducible ambiguity – where resort to context is insufficient to yield clear communicative content. In those special cases, we are in the construction zone, and originalists might concede that [Bobbitt's approaches of] precedent, ethos, and consequences are relevant. (This will depend on one's theory of constitutional construction – a topic outside the scope of this essay.) (Solum, 2012, p. 171)

Living constitutionalism may well be an appropriate strategy for legal construction, but one must steadfastly resolve not to collapse the initial inquiry into fixed meaning into an unguided "construction" of opaque provisions to address the case at hand. Solum concludes that Balkin ultimately must "face squarely the central dilemma of contemporary constitutional theory. If faith in constitutional redemption cannot be reconciled with fidelity to constitutional text, then which shall yield?" (Solum, 2012, p. 173). Solum encourages scholars to reject the appeal of progressive construction that threatens to eviscerate the constraining effect of fixed meaning. As a practical matter, Solum understood there is no way to avoid this slippage, other than fidelity to original meaning whenever it can be discerned and applied. Solum rejects the lure of becoming a philosopher king who heroically pronounces the appropriate constitutional doctrine, claiming for himself a small role in preserving democratic and rule-of-law values.

The nature of Solum's argumentation also evinces ethos. Like Berger, he is non-partisan and does not argue in favor of any particular conception of constitutional law. Rather, he is committed to uncovering original meaning to serve as an independent constraint on judging that produces both liberal and conservative results (Solum, 2018). Thus, a self-effacing judge or scholar truly constrained by the original meaning should sometimes be surprised by the applicable rule provided by the fixed meaning.

Moreover, Solum consistently defers analysis of particular disputes. Unlike Justice Scalia, operating under the time constraints of appellate litigation in deciding *Heller*, Solum can sketch a method that appears objective in nature but is never fully put to the test of resolving an actual legal dispute. This clever approach makes it difficult to challenge originalism as practiced rather than as conceived. Interestingly, though, Solum feels the need to make the case that *Brown* might be justified by originalist method, recognizing that a "large question is raised" if the canonical *Brown* can't be accommodated by one's theory (Solum, 2018, pp. 259–260). Solum argues that an originalist understanding of the Privileges and Immunities Clause might provide justification for *Brown* that is difficult to sustain under the original meaning of the Equal Protection Clause. Resisting the need to speculate about the drafters' expectations of how the text would be interpreted, Solum favors the original meaning of the Privileges and Immunities Clause as being more protective (Solum, 2018, pp. 265–266). Of course, Solum does not put himself at risk by making the full argument regarding *Brown*'s legitimacy.

Finally, Solum's practical reasoning is expressly pragmatic. Because some believe that justice would be improved by moving beyond original textual meanings, Solum appeals to the idea of originalism as a compromise rather than vacillating between "liberal" and "conservative" courts by endorsing originalism and the sometimes surprising results it produces (Solum, 2018, pp. 270–272). People across the political spectrum sometimes will see their political positions adopted by the Court if decision-making is driven by fixed meaning with varying applications rather than substantive political positions. "An originalist jurisprudence would lead to a mix of outcomes – conservative, liberal, progressive, and libertarian – if the original meaning of the constitution were fully implemented" (Solum, 2018, p. 277). This pragmatism resonates with Berger's insistence that practical legal reasoning should not be filtered through a single political perspective.

2.5.3 *Solum's Resonance with Communal Ethos as Indwelling*

There is a sense in which originalism is so foundational to preserving the ideals of American democracy and its rule-of-law commitments that it is immune from critique. Thus, Justice Kagan "surrenders" to the reality, and perhaps even the perceived necessity, that today we are all originalists. As Eric Segall (2018) summarizes, drawing from Solum's testimony in connection with Judge Neil Gorsuch's nomination to the Supreme Court, the defense of originalism appeals to universal values that deeply inform our understanding even before we begin to make specific arguments.

> Professor Solum ended his testimony with the following statement: "The whole idea of the originalist project is to take politics and ideology out of law. Democrats and Republicans, progressives and conservatives, liberals and libertarians – we should all agree that the Supreme Court Justices should be selected for their dedication to the rule of law." This idea, that only originalism can make judging and judicial review consistent with the rule of law, and that only originalism can "take politics and ideology" out of the Supreme Court are constant refrains of many originalists. (Segall, 2018, p. 176)

Although these grand claims are not realized in judicial practice, "originalism as a brand is selling better today than ever before" precisely because it resonates with these deep values that are a matter of our constitutive civic "faith" rather than the product of reason (Segall, 2018, p. 185).

Our characterization of the ethos of originalism as indwelling best explains the "faith" that supports originalism's continuing influence.[10] Interestingly, Solum directly addresses the indwelling ethos when arguing against Bobbit's "ethical" mode of constitutional argumentation that looks beyond the Constitution's text.

> Nonconstitutional texts might serve as evidence of what Philip Bobbitt calls "ethos," the shared values of the American people. Some constitutional theorists may believe that such values trump the communicative content of the constitutional text, but the constraint principle commits originalists to the view that ethos can play only a supplementary role. Deploying the terminology of the interpretation–construction distinction, ethos (as evidenced by canonical nonconstitutional texts)

[10] Jamal Greene offers a similar explanation of originalism's success, developing an account of the "*ethos* of originalism" in terms of the modalities of constitutional argument described by Philip Bobbit (Greene, 2009a). He concludes that the "success of originalism results not from its penetrable logic but from its consistency with a political morality defended most ardently by originalism's opponents … In short, many non-originalist theoretical models need not only to acknowledge, but also to accommodate the success of originalism as a political practice" (Greene, 2009b, pp. 695, 701). We write in the spirit of Greene's critique, although we develop ethos as indwelling in expressly rhetorical terms. The ethos of originalism is more than a canny use of political manipulation, which is why it is not so easily identified and overcome.

> could guide constitutional actors in the construction zone – but would have no direct relevance to constitutional interpretation. (Solum, 2013c, pp. 1974–1975)

Solum regards ethos as a concession to the necessity for construction and does not understand how much his theory is underwritten by implicit appeals to a pre-argumentative ethos of deference. More specifically, he concerns himself only with those contemporary values operating in the construction zone while simultaneously ignoring the shared values animating the will of the people instantiated through ratification.

2.6 CONCLUSION

The success of originalist theory and its apparent staying power is explained by its ethos. Not the individual ethos projected by Justice Scalia and Professors Berger and Solum through a demonstration of their character and reasoning, but rather the communal ethos that they were able to invoke and draw from as a rhetorical well of prejudgments and commitments. We offer this conclusion not only as an explanation of how originalism could succeed against the odds with such weak logos and personal ethos but also as a first step in explaining how critics of originalism must respond if they hope to be effective in jurisprudential debates. Put simply, critics can overcome an argument deeply rooted in an ethos of indwelling only by offering a counterargument that is rooted in an alternative indwelling.

Unfortunately, we have an all too vivid example of the challenges facing those who seek to argue against originalism. Donald Trump was popular enough to win the US presidency despite what should clearly have been disqualifying traits. The ethos exhibited in his character and argumentation was wholly negative by any reasonable account. And yet, he won the presidency with fervent followers who found his appeal compelling. Tapping into dimensions of our dwelling together in meaning – American exceptionalism, national security, racial protectionism, and anti-elitism, to name a few features – Trump tapped into a strong ethos of indwelling to overcome his substantial personal deficits. His critics continually failed to understand that pointing out his personal flaws or his warped reasoning was utterly beside the point. The real battleground was the marshalling of the communal ethos to point to a particular political expression of our deepest values (or, more accurately in this case, an expression of our deepest fears).

A rhetorical analysis of the success of originalism by three of its most notable proponents reveals that ethos has secured the apparent temporary victory. To effectively respond, originalist critics must also draw from our communal indwelling without pretending to render it fully present as a logically compelling argument. Indwelling supports and sustains our thinking; it is not a subject we can take up at arm's length and use like a tool. Without engaging in rhetoric at this deep level, critics cannot hope to counter originalism's force.

We now return to the testimony of then-Solicitor-General Kagan that "we are all originalists." She felt compelled to make this concession because it was unthinkable to reject the constraints provided by originalist theory through its insistence on deference to democratic and rule-of-law values. But, her testimony was not a capitulation to Justice Scalia's opportunistic use of originalism to secure conservative results. Instead, she found in "original understanding" a confirmation of the dynamic character of the Constitution and its commitments to sustaining the Framers' choices that expressed the people's will. Consider her testimony in its broader context:

> [T]he Framers were incredibly wise men, and if we always remember that, we will do pretty well, because part of their wisdom was that they wrote a Constitution for the ages. And this was very much in their mind. This was part of their consciousness. ... They were looking generations and generations and generations ahead and knowing that they were writing a Constitution for all that period of time, and that circumstances and that the world would change, just as it had changed in their own lives very dramatically. So, they knew all about change. ... And I think that they laid down – sometimes they laid down very specific rules. Sometimes they laid down broad principles. Either way we apply what they say, what they meant to do. So, in that sense, we are all originalists. (Kagan, 2010, pp. 61–62)

Originalism is neither the question nor the answer. What originalism means, what values it calls forth in support of our polity, is the issue at hand.

We now briefly outline strategies for confronting ethos as indwelling to prop up originalist arguments. Indwelling is precognitive; it is best understood as operating at the level of the symbolic realm, rather than as a discursive elaboration of a cognitive capacity (Arnold, 1962). Gene Garver's concept of "ethical surplus" explains the rhetorical logic at work in the reference to ethos as indwelling and provides insight into how we can generate persuasive critiques of originalism.[11]

The foundational symbols that structure our shared indwelling are polysemic and non-discursive. Moreover, these symbols are in tension with each other. Exploiting the ambiguities in the symbolic realm is the only realistic manner to challenge the originalist ethos. Originalists have particularly focused on our shared commitment to certainty, objectivity, and univocity in the exposition of law, anchoring arguments to support originalism that otherwise would be susceptible to criticisms. Critics should begin by linking their arguments to these same principles.

Perhaps the single most important strategy is to connect certainty and objectivity with a need for judicial transparency. Arguing against the fantasy of semantic univocity, critics should adopt Karl Llewellyn's theory that the law becomes more certain when it is less technical and participates in the shared values of the

[11] For a more expansive analysis of how "ethical surplus" provides a critical purchase on the rhetoric of the "war on immigration," see Mootz and Saucedo (2012).

community.[12] The availability of a plurality of approaches for resolving a particular interpretive question is not problematic if the decision-maker engages in practical reasoning honestly and in good faith. Critics can thus unite the three elements of ethos. Justice Kennedy's approach in the "gay rights" cases evinces the kind of reasonable development over time that demonstrates the operation of ethical surplus and is not merely a matter of the Justice's subjective will. Indeed, in *Lawrence*, Justice Scalia expressed his concern that the "ethical surplus" of Justice Kennedy's reasoning in *Lawrence* would almost certainly unfold and result in *Obergefell*.[13] Ironically, by this prediction, Justice Scalia proves the case that non-originalist legal reasoning generates some degree of "certainty."

Our brief outline of how ethos as indwelling should power the critique of originalism is not unprecedented. A number of scholars have pursued some of these strategies, and we have discussed several examples in this chapter. The essential point is that the criticisms don't take hold to the extent that they focus on the ethos of the speaker's characteristics, rather than focusing on the ethos of indwelling. Using ancient Greek understandings of persuasion through ethos, we are better positioned to develop more specific strategies that rebut the ethos of originalism when the interpretive theory is advanced in an unprincipled manner.

REFERENCES

Aristotle. (2007). *On rhetoric: A theory of civic discourse* (G. A. Kennedy, Trans.). Oxford University Press. (Original work published fourth century BCE.)

Arnold, T. W. (1962). *The symbols of government* (Harbinger ed.). Harcourt, Brace and World. (Original work published 1935.)

Balkin, J. M. (2011a). *Constitutional redemption: Political faith in an unjust world*. Harvard University Press.

(2011b). *Living originalism*. Harvard University Press.

Berger, E. (2015). The rhetoric of constitutional absolutism. *William & Mary Law Review*, 56(33), 667–757.

Berger, R. (1942). Constructive contempt: A post-mortem. *University of Chicago Law Review*, 9(4), 602–642.

12 For example, in his famous article on the "dueling canons" of statutory interpretation Llewellyn (1950) argued that the availability of multiple arguments about meaning does not impair the consistent development of the law through reasoned elaboration. Legal practice is consistent and predictable because the "construction contended for must be sold, essentially, by means other than the use of the canon: The good sense of the situation and a *simple* construction of the available language to achieve that sense, *by tenable means, out of the statutory language*" (Llewellyn, 1950, p. 401).

13 In response to Justice Kennedy's assurances that the decriminalization of gay sex in *Lawrence* did not undermine all manner of "morals legislation," Justice Scalia responded with scorn (*Lawrence*, 2003, p. 586). He concluded his dissent by arguing that this "case 'does not involve' the issue of homosexual marriage only if one entertains the belief that principle and logic have nothing to do with the decisions of this Court" (*Lawrence*, 2003, p. 605).

(1985–1986). Original intention in historical perspective. *George Washington Law Review*, 54(2–3), 296–337.
(1986). New theories of interpretation: The activist flight from the constitution. *Ohio State Law Journal*, 47(1), 1–46.
(1986–1987). Some reflections on interpretivism. *George Washington Law Review*, 55(1), 1–15.
(1987–1988). Originalist theories of constitutional interpretation. *Cornell Law Review*, 73(2), 350–358.
(1997). *Government by judiciary: The transforming of the Fourteenth Amendment* (2nd ed.). Liberty Fund. (Original work published 1977.)
Berman, M. N. (2017). The tragedy of Justice Scalia. *Michigan Law Review*, 115(6), 783–808.
Bobbitt, P. C. (1989). Methods of constitutional argument. *University of British Columbia Law Review*, 23, 449–458.
Bork, R. H. (1971). Neutral principles and some First Amendment problems. *Indiana Law Journal*, 47(1), 1–35.
Brown v. Board of Education of Topeka, 347 U.S. 483 (1954).
Calabresi, S. G., & Perl, M. W. (2014). Originalism and *Brown v.* Board of Education. *Michigan State Law Review*, 2014(3), 429–552.
Canzonieri, A. (2017). Heidegger on rhetorical language: The 1924 lecture course on the "Basic Concepts of Aristotelian Philosophy." *Logoi.ph – Journal of Philosophy* – N, 3(9), 236–246.
Chemerinsky, E. (2022). *Worse than nothing: The dangerous fallacy of originalism*. Yale University Press.
District of Columbia v. Heller, 554 U.S. 570 (2008).
Gangi, W. (1988). On Raoul Berger's federalism. *Law & Social Inquiry*, 13(4), 801–823.
Garver, E. (1995). *Aristotle's Rhetoric: An art of character*. University of Chicago Press.
(2004). *For the sake of argument: Practical reasoning, character and the ethics of belief*. University of Chicago Press.
Greene, J. (2009a). On the origins of originalism. *Texas Law Review*, 88(1), 3–89.
(2009b). Selling originalism. *Georgetown Law Review*, 97(3), 657–721.
Hannah, M. A., & Salmon, S. (2020). Against the grain: The secret role of dissents in integrating rhetoric across the curriculum. *Nevada Law Journal*, 20(3), 935–966.
Heidegger, M. (1977). Letter on humanism. In D. F. Krell (Ed.), *Basic writings* (pp. 190–242). Harper and Row.
(1996). *Being and time* (J. Stambaugh, Trans.). State University of New York Press.
(2009). *Basic concepts of Aristotelian philosophy* (R. D. Metcalf & M. B. Tanzer, Trans.). Indiana University Press.
Hyde, M. J. (2004). Introduction: Rhetorically, we dwell. In M. J. Hyde (Ed.), *The ethos of rhetoric* (pp. xiii–xxviii). University of South Carolina Press.
Jost, W. (2004). Sweating the little things in Sidney Lumet's 12 Angry Men. In M. J. Hyde (Ed.), *The ethos of rhetoric* (pp. 75–88). University of South Carolina Press.
Kagan, E. (2010, June 29). The nomination of Elena Kagan to be an associate justice of the Supreme Court of the United States. *Senate Hearing 111-1044: Hearing before the Committee on the Judiciary, United States Senate, One Hundredth Eleventh Congress.* 2nd Session.
Kenny, R. W. (2004). Truth as metaphor: Imaginary vision and the *ethos* of rhetoric. In M. J. Hyde (Ed.), *The ethos of rhetoric* (pp. 34–55). University of South Carolina Press.
Lawrence v. Texas, 539 U.S. 558 (2003).
Llewellyn, K. N. (1950). Remarks on the theory of appellate decision and the rules or canons about how statutes are to be construed. *Vanderbilt Law Review*, 3(3), 395–405.

Manning, J. F. (2017). Justice Scalia and the idea of judicial restraint. *Michigan Law Review*, *115*(6), 747–782.
McNeill, W. (2006). *The time of life: Heidegger and ethos*. State University of New York Press.
Medhurst, M. J. (2004). Religious rhetoric and the *ethos* of democracy: A case study of the 2000 presidential campaign. In M. J. Hyde (Ed.), *The ethos of rhetoric* (pp. 114–135). University of South Carolina Press.
Mootz, F. J., III. (2017). Getting over the originalist fixation. In B. G. Slocum (Ed.), *The nature of legal interpretation: What jurists can learn about legal interpretation from linguistics and philosophy* (pp. 156–190). University of Chicago Press.
(2019). Party like it's 1989: Justice Scalia's rhetoric of certainty. In B. G. Slocum & F. J. Mootz III (Eds.), *Justice Scalia: Rhetoric and the rule of law* (pp. 97–110). University of Chicago Press.
Mootz, F. J., III & Saucedo, L. M. (2012). The "ethical" surplus of the war on illegal immigration. *Journal of Gender, Race & Justice*, 15(2), 257–279.
Newman, S. A. (2006–2007). Political advocacy on the Supreme Court: The damaging rhetoric of Antonin Scalia. *New York Law School Law Review*, 51(4), 908–926.
Obergefell v. Hodges, 516 U.S. 644 (2015).
O'Neill, J. (2005). *Originalism in American law and politics: A constitutional history*. Johns Hopkins University Press.
Presser, S. (2018, May 15). The coming resurrection of Raoul Berger? A remembrance of *Government by Judiciary*. Last modified May 15, 2018. https://perma.cc/4N3H-Q8HG
Priester, B. J. (2021). Is originalism a fandom? http://dx.doi.org/10.2139/ssrn.3775043.
Romer v. Evans, 517 U.S. 620 (1996).
Ryan, K. J., Myers, N., & Jones, R. (Eds.). (2016a). *Rethinking ethos: A feminist ecological approach to rhetoric*. Southern Illinois University Press.
Scalia, A. (1989a). The rule of law as a law of rules. *University of Chicago Law Review*, 56(4), 1175–1188.
(1989b). Originalism: The lesser evil. *University of Cincinnati Law Review*, 57(3), 849–865.
(2015). A look back: 1994 William O. Douglas lecture series transcript. *Gonzaga Law Review*, 51(3), 583–600.
(2017). *Scalia speaks: Reflections on law, faith, and life well lived* (C. J. Scalia & E. Whelan, Eds.). Crown Forum.
Scalia, A., & Garner, B. A. (2012). *Reading law: The interpretation of legal texts*.Thomson/West Publishing.
Schrag, C. O. (2004). Foreword. In M. J. Hyde (Ed.), *The ethos of rhetoric* (pp. vii–viii). University of South Carolina Press.
Segall, E. J. (2017). Judicial engagement, new originalism, and the fortieth anniversary of *Government by Judiciary*. *Fordham Law Review Online*, 86, 47–58.
(2018). *Originalism as faith*. Cambridge University Press.
Shanske, D. (2019). Rhetoric, jurisprudence, and the case of Justice Scalia: Or, why did Justice Scalia of all judges write like that? In B. G. Slocum & F. J. Mootz III (Eds.), *Justice Scalia: Rhetoric and the rule of law* (pp. 123–135). University of Chicago Press.
Smith, C. R. (2004). *Ethos* dwells pervasively: A hermeneutic reading of Aristotle on credibility. In M. J. Hyde (Ed.), *The ethos of rhetoric* (pp. 1–19). University of South Carolina Press.
Solum, L. B. (2010). The interpretation–construction distinction. *Constitutional Commentary*, 27(1), 95–118.
(2012). Faith and fidelity: Originalism and the possibility of constitutional redemption. *Texas Law Review*, 91(147), 147–173.

(2013a). Communicative content and legal content. *Notre Dame Law Review*, 89(2), 479–519.
(2013b). Originalism and constitutional construction. *Fordham Law Review*, 82(2), 453–537.
(2013c). Originalism and the unwritten constitution. *Illinois Law Review*, 2013(5), 1935–1984.
(2015). The fixation thesis: The role of historical fact in original meaning. *Notre Dame Law Review*, 91(1), 1–78.
(2017). Originalist methodology. *University of Chicago Law Review*, 84(1), 269–295.
(2018). Surprising originalism: The Regula lecture. *ConlawNOW*, 9, 235–277.
(2019). Originalism versus living constitutionalism: The conceptual structure of the great debate. *Northwestern University Law Review*, 113(6), 1243–1296.

TerBeek, C. (2021). "Clocks must always be turned back," *Brown v. Board of Education* and the racial origins of constitutional originalism. *American Political Science Review*, 115(3), 821–834.

Turner, R. (2014). A critique of Justice Antonin Scalia's originalist defense of *Brown v. Board of Education*. *UCLA Law Review Discourse*, 62, 170–184.

3

The Role of Tradition in Classical and Contemporary Argument

Vasileios Adamidis and Laura A. Webb

3.1 INTRODUCTION

For centuries, advocates have used arguments grounded in tradition to persuade legal decision-makers. The appeal of tradition – whether "tradition" refers to long-standing cultural practices, the alleged intentions and beliefs of revered historical figures, or a narrative about the historical path of a people – is well-established. What is less well-established is how classical rhetorical structures and concepts of tradition can be used to reflect on and even challenge contemporary social injustices or inequalities. In this chapter, we discuss how advocates on both sides of an issue – even the side challenging the status quo – might effectively use tradition to advance their cause. We explore the role of tradition in forensic Athenian rhetoric and identify similarities in contemporary American legal argument. We then identify specific rhetorical strategies used by advocates in both systems in an effort to shed light on how such tools may be used by advocates, even ones for whom tradition may seem to be an unlikely ally.

We start our journey with the forensic rhetoric of classical Athens. Traditionalism, as a central feature of classical Athenian ideology, was evident in the literary works and political agendas of the period (Dover, 1994, p. 7; Hansen, 1991, pp. 296–297). References to the *patrios politeia* (ancestral constitution) and the achievements of the ancestors were common in the popular and political discourse of classical Athens. Respect for tradition was manifest in the legal system too; the expediency of old laws was unquestionable,[1] as was the authority of lawgivers of the past such as Solon and Draco (Gagarin, 2020a, p. 26). This popular appeal of tradition allowed

[1] The homicide laws of Draco, dated around 632 BCE, were attributed a divine origin (Dem. 23.70; Antiph. 5.48) and, due to their ancestry, they were valued above all other laws at least until the late fourth century (Antiph. 5.14, 87–89; 6.2–4; Dem. 23.70–79.). Note: For readers seeking the original text and the translations of the Attic Orators cited in this chapter, please refer to the index of Abbreviations and Translations provided at the end of this chapter. The numbers in the citations of the works of the Attic Orators refer to the orator's speech and

orators to claim that "the public conduct of a state, like the private conduct of a man, should always be guided by its most honorable traditions" (Dem. 18.95; Aeschin. 1.185; 3.178–183). Making the most of this ideological inclination, litigants frequently evoked tradition to indicate the right course of action; in deciding a case, Athenian dicasts[2] were encouraged to imitate the methodology and practices of their ancestors (Adamidis, 2024). In that respect, speakers referred to Athenian tradition both to argue for the "correct" interpretation of the law and to project a certain *ethos* that allowed them to identify with the audience and alienate the adversary.

Classical rhetoricians understood that systematically identifying types of possible arguments for a particular matter was a critical part of the process of creating persuasive arguments. Aristotle, in his *Rhetoric*, listed a number of *topoi*: lines of argument that could help the advocate invent appropriate arguments and then effectively articulate those arguments to an audience (Aristotle, 2007).[3] For example, a deliberative orator speaking publicly about legislative matters would be well-advised to consider lines of argument focused on "finances, war and peace, national defense, imports and exports, and the framing of laws" (Aristotle, 2007, 1.4.7, 1359b). Contemporary American advocates and jurists have followed Aristotle's lead by identifying common types of argument or common sources from which legal arguments can be formed, and checking to see which type or types may be most helpful in a specific client matter. For example, Wilson Huhn has identified "five types of legal argument," including tradition as well as text, intent, precedent, and policy (Huhn, 2014). Huhn argues that law students and lawyers should recognize these types and assess their strengths and weaknesses for a particular situation, so that advocates can effectively use a combination of types to create persuasive arguments. Tradition is thus a type of argument relied upon by both classical rhetors and contemporary lawyers; for the latter, arguments grounded in tradition and history can be particularly effective, perhaps most notably in the context of constitutional arguments (Balkin, 2013, 2018; Huhn, 2014).

This chapter identifies intersections between forensic Athenian rhetoric and contemporary American legal rhetoric on the use of tradition-based legal arguments and explores the use of tradition on the rhetorical battleground. We argue that advocates, both past and present, have found tradition so compelling that both sides

the section of the speech respectively. For example, reference to Dem. 18.95 refers to Demosthenes' speech 18, *On the Crown*, section 95.

2 The term dicast (judge/juror) refers to the male Athenian citizen over the age of thirty who was selected by lot as a member of a panel empowered to decide legal cases in the popular courts. In a system without professional judges to regulate what the jury can hear, the vote of dicasts was based upon all questions of fact and law, thus combining the functions of modern judges and jurors.

3 Aristotle identified both "special topics" or "lines of argument that were especially suited to one type of rhetorical setting" (Herrick, 2009, p. 90), as well as "common topics," rhetorical strategies useful in any setting encompassing "a wide range of arguments and strategies that might be employed in all sorts of debates" (p. 91).

on an issue may use arguments with foundations in tradition, and advocates will use "tradition" both to support long-standing practices *and* to argue that those practices should be overturned. "Tradition" may be broadly construed by the speaker to be long-standing custom or repeated practices, views attributed to historical figures, or even an evolving social identity, depending on what formulation best suits the speaker's argument. In this way, even the Western-centric structure and approach of classical rhetoric may be utilized by modern advocates to challenge – and combat – contemporary social injustices such as discrimination based on sexual orientation. Creative advocates may use tradition to justify outcomes that are, in some sense, truly non-traditional. And jurists wishing to provide rationales for such outcomes are likely to use tradition – in one way or another – to explain why that outcome is consistent with the past even as it achieves societal change.

Intuitively, we might expect that only advocates who support the superficially "traditional" position would rely on long-standing cultural practices, the intentions of respected figures from the past, or historical references, while advocates on the side of progressive causes might be expected to argue that "tradition" should be rejected in favor of policy reasons supporting a change. Certainly, advocates supporting the status quo use tradition-type arguments, and advocates opposing it often rely on policy rationales that compel change. However, rhetors are not necessarily as limited in their approaches as one might initially suspect. In many instances, advocates challenging ingrained social norms have effectively argued that tradition – as they define and explain it – supports their cause. And aligning their position *with* tradition, and not *against* it, can make these arguments stronger in a system that values (perhaps even valorizes) the past. While it is by no means certain that integrating tradition into a progressive argument will guarantee success, the prevalence and desirability of aligning tradition (even if creatively defined) with contemporary legal positions is notable.

Below, we first provide background about the appeal of tradition-type arguments in both systems and identify, in each system, specific examples of how tradition arguments have been used to interpret law and identify rights. With this background and foundation in mind, we then explore how specific rhetorical strategies may be used in connection with tradition-type arguments and identify specific examples of how advocates in each society used those strategies.

3.2 TRADITION AND LEGAL ARGUMENT: ATHENS AND THE UNITED STATES OF AMERICA

It is easy to understand the appeal of tradition in legal argument. A legal system that values tradition supports "predictability and reliability interests" (Mazrui, 2011, p. 293), encourages social stability, and reinforces social and cultural identity. These values and interests were important to classical Athenians and remain important to modern Americans, despite the potential downside of an overreliance on tradition, which may perpetuate and reinforce a problematic status quo, thus inhibiting progress and change. Similar considerations apply for arguments based on previous decisions of the court. The foundation of a common law system is *stare decisis*, or "letting the decision stand." Stare decisis requires courts to rely on precedential decisions to guide current rulings. The foundational respect for precedent represents a reliance on tradition and a reverence for the past. "Letting the decision stand" accepts the idea that we should be governed by the past and act today as we have acted before. Precedential decisions can be seen as a major cognitive contribution to thinking about current problems, as they act as "storehouses of possibly relevant analogies to our present problems, ways of thinking about such problems, and successful and unsuccessful attempts to solve them" (Krygier, 1986, p. 257).

3.2.1 *The Role of Tradition in Each Society*

The Athenians saw a benefit in interpreting the law in line with earlier decisions and with the intent of the lawgiver, as this served the aim of consistency and predictability of decision-making. Despite the absence of a single formal reasoning for the verdicts (which would be impossible with the several dicasts voting secretly), and the underdevelopment of detailed law reports and systematic records, the importance of public memory, and the audience's knowledge and expertise, should not be underestimated. Precedent was still invoked by Attic forensic speakers (Harris, 2013, pp. 246–273; Lanni, 2004). Dicasts were encouraged to remain consistent with earlier decisions and practices, and litigants expected that the court decisions would set the standards for subsequent behavior.[4] The orators would often rely on their own or logographer's (expert speechwriter's) knowledge and interpretation of previous rulings, but they were careful to refer to famous or recent cases that the experienced audience would be expected to know (Harris, 2013, p. 271).[5]

The tremendous importance and persuasive appeal of tradition means that advocates – then and now – on either side of an issue benefit by claiming that tradition is on their side. Indeed, the draw of tradition is so strong that claiming a practice as a "new tradition" (surely a contradiction in terms) gives weight to the practice (Mazrui, 2011, p. 292). Thus, advocates in both systems – and on both sides

4 On dicasts, see for example Lys. 26.15; Lys. 30.25. On the precedent as the benchmark of subsequent decisions see, for example, Lys 14.4; cf. Lys. 22.20; 27.7–8; 28.10; 30.23, 35; Aeschin. 1.192; Lyc. 1.9–10, 15, 27, 52–54, 110, 120–122.

5 The use of precedent included both previous verdicts of the court, when there was uncertainty about the meaning of the law (e.g., Lys. 3.43 on the meaning of "premeditation"), and earlier cases whose facts appear to resemble the factual dispute at hand (e.g., Lys. 16.8; Lys. 22.18; Aeschin. 3.252). In some cases, the use of precedent was to highlight a particular practice of the court that the speaker wants the current panel to implement (e.g., Lys. 3.42–43 on "proportionality"; Lyc. 1.12–13 on "relevance"; Hyp. 4.2 on "impeachment"; Hyp. 4.36 on "just decision-making"; Dem. 19.297 on the "rule of law").

of a given issue – have been motivated to identify traditions that would support their positions. We can observe this phenomenon in classical Athenian speeches. Since tradition was a reference point for the rhetoric of litigants, different versions of it, or even conflicting traditions, were presented by the speakers. For example, in *Against Leocrates*, Lycurgus anticipated that his opponent, Leocrates, would argue that his departure to Rhodes in a time of emergency could not amount to treason because their ancestors had also evacuated Athens in the face of Persian danger before the naval battle of Salamis. Alleging that Leocrates was misrepresenting tradition, Lycurgus replied that the ancestors "did not desert the city but only moved from one place to another as part of their brilliant plan" (Lyc. 1.68–71).

American legal rhetoric developed in reliance on classical rhetoric, and it should come as no surprise that modern American advocates take a similar approach in using tradition to support their legal arguments. "Anyone who studies the classical treatises soon discovers that, with some adaptations for modern taste and modern legal practice, the classical rhetorical principles are as applicable today as they were 2500 years ago" (Frost, 2005, p. vii). Indeed, legal writing scholars are encouraged to familiarize themselves with classic rhetoric in part because modern "[c]ourt rules and common practice for appellate briefs specify the same organizational requirements as those first formulated by Corax of Syracuse" in the fifth century BC (Berger, 2010, p. 50, internal citations omitted). More controversially, recent scholars have asserted that this reliance taints contemporary American legal rhetoric because it "sits on a foundation that is White-supremacist, patriarchal, and elitist" (Berenguer et al., 2020, p. 207).[6] That critique raises challenges for progressive advocates, who (if they accept this critique) may wonder how can they use rhetoric that is ostensibly grounded in injustice and inequality as they work to achieve social justice and equality? How can they integrate tradition into their arguments to change society?

When contemporary American advocates discuss tradition, they carefully identify and frame a tradition that supports their position and desired outcome. For example, when considering relevant "traditions" governing the use of firearms in an effort to interpret the scope of the Second Amendment in a 2008 Supreme Court case, both sides claimed that tradition supported their competing positions. In *District of Columbia v. Heller*, one side pointed to the individual right to self-defense as a traditional aspect of American society, noting that the "natural right" of individuals "to keep arms for their own defence [sic]" was a customary part of colonial society (*District of Columbia v. Heller*, Resp. Brief, 2008, p. 35). The other side drew the reader's attention to a different tradition, asserting that "[t]he Nation's capital has

[6] Berenguer et al. (2020, p. 207) argue that "[t]raditional legal rhetoric derives from Aristotle and Plato, both of whom accepted human hierarchy and inequality in a society that encompassed male domination, slavery, and elitist governance norms." Similarly, scholars such as McMurtry-Chubb (2019, p. 259) assert that contemporary American legal writing is rooted in "Eurocentric ways of knowing and being." Readers interested in a robust discussion of this critique will wish to review Berenguer et al. (2023).

regulated guns for two centuries" (*District of Columbia v. Heller*, Pet'r Brief, 2008, p. 3) and summarizing the Congressional tradition of gun regulation.

The fact that both sides could plausibly claim a relevant tradition to support their positions is not all that odd. After all, there must have been contrasting definitions and conflicting traditions even at the time of enactment. Audiences might well wonder:

> Whose tradition? English, American, African-American, Native-American, city, country, South, North? Tradition as expressed over what duration of time? Since the thirteenth century? Since the sixteenth? The eighteenth? Does the historical evidence relevant to a tradition end in 1791, in 1868, in 1930, or 2016? At what level of abstraction is the tradition to be drawn? And what of conflicting traditions . . .? (Miller, 2016, p. 225)

The value of the rhetorical strategy lies not in its accurate identification of a relevant tradition but in its ethotic appeal to the audience. If the audience is willing to accept the reference to traditional values or beliefs, it can succeed regardless of competing or missing historical evidence to support the claim of a single tradition. For that reason, tradition arguments can be successfully used to support a wide variety of positions. One study of five terms of the Roberts Court concluded that "traditionalism has been used regularly, in many different contexts, and by many different Justices with different jurisprudential viewpoints" (Virelli, 2011, p. 63). The Court's reliance on tradition in the 2021–2022 and 2022–2023 terms underscores its importance.

3.2.2 *Using Tradition to Interpret Laws and Identify Legal Principles: Examples from Athens and the United States*

Tradition, whether combined with precedent or not, has held high value in both systems as a stand-alone basis for persuasive argument. In both systems, arguments grounded in traditional values have been used both to (1) interpret the meaning of legal terms and (2) identify rights and legal principles not specifically articulated in the law.

3.2.2.1 Legal Interpretation

The "open texture" of Athenian law, meaning that quite often the law is intentionally indeterminate and vague (Hart, 1994, pp. 121–127), triggered questions of correct interpretation, a fact that allowed Attic orators to frequently resort to arguments from tradition to persuade the audience for their view as to the meaning and the scope of the law.[7] In cases involving a dispute about the interpretation of a statute, framing an

7 For application of Hart's concept of "open texture" to Athenian law see Harris (2013, chapters 5–6).

argument in a way which ostensibly aligned with Athenian tradition gave the speaker an advantage based on the belief that a practice continued over time by our ancestors is presumed to have value.

One example is the speech of Lycurgus, *Against Leocrates*. There, the objective facts were more or less undisputed, but whether the defendant's acts satisfied the legal definition of "treason" was unclear. The background behind the speech is this: Shortly after the defeat at Chaeronea in 338 BCE, there was panic in Athens, with the city implementing emergency measures to prepare for what was believed to be an imminent invasion of Attica by Philip of Macedon. At this time, Leocrates sailed to Rhodes, ostensibly for trade. After leaving Rhodes, he settled at Megara, where he resided as a metic (resident alien) for six years before returning to Athens in 331. Upon his return, Lycurgus charged Leocrates and claimed that his desertion amounted to treason.

Lycurgus based his arguments on a creative interpretation of the term "treason," using tradition as the canvas of legal interpretation. He explained that Leocrates' specific acts were not included in the statute simply because the lawgiver could not anticipate such an outrageous scenario, which was far worse than any of the activities he listed in the law (Lyc. 1.9). This fact alone rendered Leocrates liable for the offense. To prove this wide scope of the statute, Lycurgus attempted to discern the Athenian traditional values intentionally betrayed by Leocrates that amounted to treason (Lyc. 1.1–2). These values of "Athenian-ness" were evident in the list of offenses provided in the law and the previous decisions of the court (e.g., Lyc. 1.52), but also in the Athenian tradition: the conduct of the ancestors (Lyc. 1.14, 127), the oaths (Lyc. 1.76, 80), and the literature (e.g., Lyc. 1.100–109). By reference to multiple examples from Athenian history, Lycurgus asked the dicasts to "consider your [their] traditions and opinions on this matter" (Lyc.1.75).[8] He contrasted Leocrates' behavior with their ancestors' in similar circumstances and wondered: "Would any of these men of old have perhaps tolerated such a crime? Wouldn't they have stoned to death the man who brought shame on their own courage?" concluding that: "It would be the most terrible thing of all if your ancestors had the courage to die for your city's reputation, but you do not punish those who cover it in shame" (Lyc. 1. 82). Pointing to the harshness with which previous panels punished these crimes (Lyc. 1. 111), he urged the dicasts not to fall below the standards set by the ancestors (Lyc. 1.116), reminded them that it is not in their "nature or traditions to cast a vote that is unworthy" of them, and urged that it was their "traditional duty" to put Leocrates to death (Lyc. 1. 123).

Lycurgus lost the case by a single vote. However, his innovative interpretation of treason, framed by reference to Athenian tradition, had substantial impact and shows how Athenian orators used tradition and traditional values to interpret a general term and identify specific acts encompassed within that term.

[8] On the use of examples from the past, see Maltagliati (2020).

American advocates have used similar approaches in American constitutional argument. For example, as mentioned above, advocates relied on traditional customs to define the scope of the Second Amendment right to bear arms in *Heller*. The facts in *Heller* revolved around a DC law that prohibited individuals from possessing handguns in the home (*District of Columbia v. Heller*, 2008). A special police officer, who was authorized to carry a handgun while on duty, sought to force the city to allow him to lawfully keep his firearm at his home. The police officer argued that the Second Amendment's right to "bear arms" provided an individual right for a single person to keep and use arms for lawful purposes such as individual self-defense (*District of Columbia v. Heller*, Resp. Brief, 2008); in contrast, opponents argued that the Amendment's language referring to the right to bear arms in the context of "a well-regulated militia" meant that the right should be constrained to connection with service in a militia (*District of Columbia v. Heller*, Pet'r Brief, 2008). If the former were true, then the DC law banning handgun possession in the home had to be evaluated with the level of scrutiny appropriate for a law impinging on Constitutional rights (*District of Columbia v. Heller*, 2008, p. 628). If, instead, the officer's individual Constitutional rights were not impacted, a lesser degree of scrutiny would be appropriate in assessing the law. Both advocates relied on tradition to persuade, although each focused on different aspects and sources within their arguments; those aspects and sources were carefully chosen to show that a decision in their favor would be consistent with tradition as they framed it.

The advocate for the police officer, who ultimately prevailed in this argument, drew the Court's attention to traditional customs. The brief explicitly focused on the idea that an individual right to self-defense was a traditional aspect of American society, noting that the natural right of individuals to keep arms for their own defense was a customary part of colonial society (*District of Columbia v. Heller*, Resp. Brief, 2008). Referring to the Supreme Court's 1997 articulation in *Washington v. Glucksberg* that the fundamental rights protected by the Constitution are those "rooted in the traditions and conscience of our people," the police officer's attorneys argued that interpreting the Second Amendment as an individual right was appropriate because this Amendment, properly interpreted, protects "the most fundamental rights of all – enabling the preservation of one's life and guaranteeing our liberty" (*District of Columbia v. Heller*, Resp. Brief, 2008, p. 57, internal citations omitted).

And these arguments worked, even though (as detailed in the following section) the opposing party *also* argued that tradition supported its position. The Court's opinion, written by Justice Scalia, explicitly accepted not only the officer's position but also the basis for that position as grounded in tradition. The Court agreed that the right of the people to bear arms was protected in the Second Amendment in part because it protected a preexisting traditional right, one that had become "fundamental" by the time of the country's founding (*District of Columbia v. Heller*, 2008, p. 594). The Court referred to both tradition and text, noting that "[t]here seems to us no doubt, on the basis of both text and history, that the Second Amendment conferred an individual right to keep and bear arms" (p. 595). The Court also relied on specific historical traditions and customs to support the position about the meaning of the words and to provide specific substance to the term "bear arms."[9]

The *Heller* case illustrates how tradition-type arguments can be utilized by each side in the briefs and by the Court in its opinion deciding the case. But it is by no means the only illustration of this point. Advocates asserted similar arguments in the more recent case of *New York State Rifle & Pistol Association v. Bruen* (2022), which was argued before the Supreme Court in November 2021. *Bruen* focused on whether New York's requirement – that those who wished to carry concealed firearms must obtain a special license – improperly burdened Second Amendment rights. There, advocates on both sides similarly argued that tradition and history supported their respective positions.[10] Unsurprisingly, in its decision, the Supreme Court also relied on tradition and history as part of its rule and rationale, even elevating their role beyond what was articulated in *Heller*.[11] The Court in *Bruen* found that the state's regulation did not pass Constitutional muster. But even if it had found in favor of New York, one imagines that the Court's focus would have been on history and tradition, using those forces to explain why relevant traditions of firearm regulation justified the restriction.

3.2.2.2 Identification of a Particular Right or Legal Principle

In addition to using tradition to interpret the meaning of a particular law, speakers in Athenian courts also used tradition to argue that a particular right or privilege existed within the law. For example, Athenian legal tradition provided that no person could be put to death without a trial (Carawan, 1984). Although certain criminal procedures, such as *apagoge* (summary arrest) and *endeixis* (denunciation), appear to have permitted the immediate execution of a criminal caught *in flagrante delicto* and confessing his guilt (Hansen, 1976), by the latter half of the fourth century BCE

[9] Justice Scalia, writing the majority opinion, also discussed the meaning of the Court's prior 1939 decision in *United States v. Miller* and decided that the Second Amendment does not protect weapons "not typically possessed by law-abiding citizens for lawful purposes" because of the "historical tradition prohibiting the carrying of 'dangerous and unusual weapons'" (*District of Columbia v. Heller*, 2008, p. 627).

[10] In *Bruen*, one side asserted the right to carry arms outside the home was a custom of early America that was also enshrined in legislation and judicial decisions (*New York State Rifle & Pistol Association v. Bruen*, Pet'r Brief, 2021, pp. 29–34), while the other argued that restrictions on individuals carrying concealed firearms "have continuously been a part of the AngloAmerican legal tradition" (*New York State Rifle & Pistol Association v. Bruen*, Resp. Brief, pp. 21–31).

[11] In *Bruen*, the Court rejected a two-step framework that "combine[d] history with means–end scrutiny" in favor of a test that when regulating conduct covered by the Second Amendment "the government must demonstrate that the regulation is consistent with this Nation's historical tradition of firearm regulation" (*New York State Rifle & Pistol Association v. Bruen*, 2022, p. 17).

magistrates would have been very reluctant to condemn the accused to death without trial (Carawan, 1984, p. 121), thus acknowledging the sovereign jurisdiction of the courts applying this norm. This right to trial was linked with the democratic tradition and was often contrasted to the oligarchic practice of execution without a hearing.[12]

In *Against Aristocrates* (Dem. 23), the prosecutor, Euthycles, accused the defendant of proposing an illegal decree granting special protection for the general Charidemus. The main ground for the decree's illegality, according to the questionable interpretation offered by the speaker, was that it deprived any person who might kill Charidemus for any reason, even accidentally or lawfully, of the right to a trial, and subjected that person to seizure and immediate retribution by anyone (Dem. 23.22–81). Arguing for the need to provide anyone accused with a fair trial due to the Athenian commitment to the presumption of innocence (Dem. 23.25–26, 29, 36), the speaker analyzed relevant statutes which were directly violated by the decree and, taken together, revealed the underlying principles of Athenian law against which this proposal should be evaluated. Firstly, since homicide was an offense that incurred pollution, namely a traditional religious belief in the impurity of the killer which could bring disaster to his relatives or the community, the lawgiver was "concerned about protecting the city's respect for religion" (Dem. 23.25) and thus granted the right to trial to ensure that the person convicted and put to death is indeed the perpetrator. Secondly, the Athenian commitment to the rule of law precluded the option of taking the law into one's own hands and dictated the surrender of the suspect to the relevant officers; as the speaker suggests, "it certainly makes the greatest difference whether the law or a personal enemy has the power to punish" (Dem. 23.32). Thirdly, the decree attempted to abolish the powers of the most respected Athenian courts with jurisdiction over cases of homicide (Dem. 23.65–81), which had its roots in old stories handed down by oral tradition involving gods and mythical heroes (Dem. 23.66–67, 81). Therefore, ostensibly, by allowing execution without trial, the decree violated not only existing statutes but also the underlying traditional principles of Athenian law. The speaker thus used tradition to identify a substantive right within the law that had not been specifically identified by the law itself.

We can identify a similar use of tradition in the modern American legal system, when advocates and jurists explicitly refer to American traditions to find (or fail to find) a fundamental right, such as a due process right within the Fourteenth Amendment. In many instances, lawyers have relied upon long-standing customs in American society to support an assertion that a fundamental Constitutional right

[12] For example, Lysias, the famous speechwriter whose brother Polemarchus was executed without trial by the Thirty Tyrants (Lys. 12.17), frequently referred to this as an outrageous oligarchic practice deserving the severest penalty (Lys. 12.36). Cf. Lys. 12.81–82; 26.13; Isoc. 7.67; 20.11; Dem. 40.46.

exists. For example, in the 1997 *Washington v. Glucksberg* case, the Court used a "backdrop of history, tradition, and practice" to decide whether there was a fundamental right to assisted suicide (*Washington v. Glucksberg*, 1997, p. 719). Chief Justice Rehnquist noted that that "we have regularly observed that the Due Process Clause specially protects those fundamental rights and liberties which are, objectively, deeply rooted in this Nation's history and tradition" (*Washington v. Glucksberg*, 1997, pp. 720–721). In *Glucksberg*, the Court refused to find a right to assisted suicide because it found no American custom supporting a tradition of assisting death, even for terminally ill patients. Instead, the Court noted the country's "constant and almost universal tradition that has long rejected the asserted right" (p. 723) and followed that tradition by rejecting the proposed right as well. In contrast, in the 1977 case of *Moore v. City of East Cleveland*, the Court relied upon a "venerable" social custom "of uncles, aunts, cousins, and especially grandparents sharing the household along with parents and children" (*Moore v. City of East Cleveland*, 1977, p. 504) when it found that a city could not constitutionally criminalize multiple generations of a family for living together in a dwelling limited to a "single family." And in the highly controversial 2022 *Dobbs v. Jackson Women's Health Organization* decision, the Court took the unusual step of overturning its prior decisions on abortion, stating its "inescapable conclusion ... that a right to abortion is not deeply rooted in the Nation's history and tradition" (*Dobbs v. Jackson Women's Health Organization*, 2022, p. 250).

The intersections between American and Athenian uses of tradition are not limited to using a specific historical custom to interpret the law. Both systems also have asserted original intent of revered historical figures as a persuasive argument, even when that intent may be difficult or even impossible to ascertain and thus may be available to both sides in an argument. In classical Athens, the evocation of the authority of the lawgivers, such as Solon and Draco, sought to reveal the timelessness and merit of Athenian laws, making each verdict an act of historical importance and a continuation of a respected tradition.[13] Lawgivers of the past personified the Athenian traditional norms of behavior and served as the benchmark for the proper conduct of subsequent legislators.[14] A commonplace in Athenian forensic rhetoric provided that the correct meaning of the law in accordance with Athenian traditional values could be discerned by reference to the ostensible intent of the lawgiver

[13] On the historical importance of decisions, see: Aes. 3.6–7, 3.14, 3.108, 3.112, 3.175, 3.178; Dem. 20.12,20. 89–93, 20.135, 20.142, 20.154; 22.35,22. 94–99; 24.38.

[14] For example, Aeschines, in *Against Timarchus*, contrasted the unrestrained behavior of Timarchus to the respectable Solon to prove the former's unworthiness to be a public speaker (Aeschin. 1.25–26). Similarly, Demosthenes devoted a large part of his speech in *Against Timocrates* to comparing the legislative practice of his opponent with Solon's, claiming that Timocrates fell well below the standards set by the Athenian legislative tradition (Dem. 24. 103–115; cf. Aeschin. 3.257–258).

(Adamidis, 2017a, pp. 186–187; Gagarin, 2020b, p. 37).[15] Although discerning the real intent of these historical figures was almost impossible, litigants quite often referred to it as if they knew it (and presented it, persuasively, in a way that supposed that the audience knew the original intent too).[16]

Similarly, to persuade the audience as to the validity of their interpretation of the law, Athenian advocates relied upon the general underlying Athenian values encapsulated in the laws and connected those explicitly to the alleged beliefs of quasi-mythical figures. In the speech *Against Athenogenes*, the speaker Epicrates, in an effort to nullify a contract, contended that the law required that for agreements to be valid they must also be just (Hyp. 3.13). To prove the existence of such an underlying principle, Epicrates offered a series of (remotely relevant) laws.[17] Claiming that this principle is endorsed by the lawgiver, Epicrates concluded that "Solon believed that even a decree that was legally proposed should not override the law; but you [Athenogenes] expect even unjust contracts to override all the laws" (Hyp. 3.22).

In the American system, advocates and jurists similarly refer to the intent of respected historical figures to support their interpretation of constitutional words and phrases. The briefs and opinion in *Heller* provide us with an example of this approach. As noted above, the advocates there on both sides of this case referenced historical customs to bolster their arguments. Both sides also referenced historical figures. The winning brief relied extensively on lawgiver intent, spending considerable time parsing through historical documents to show that "the Framers" supported this interpretation of the Amendment (*District of Columbia v. Heller*, Resp. Brief, 2008, pp. 19–40). And that argument appealed to the Justices in the majority. The Court's majority opinion reviewed a variety of historical sources to identify the meaning of the Second Amendment's words to the public at the time of ratification and through the nineteenth century (*District of Columbia v. Heller*, 2008, pp. 581–619). It also referenced well-known and respected Founding Fathers, including Thomas Jefferson and James Madison. In doing so, the argument invoked the ethical authority of honored heroes of our cultural past.

Advocates' confident assertion of historical intent allows them to persuasively suggest that the audience shares a knowledge of the revered lawgivers' intentions, based upon the traditions of the past. The views of honored historical figures, like identification of longstanding customs, can often be used to support either side of an

[15] On Greek lawgivers, see Szegedy-Maszak (1978). On Solon, see Harris (2010) and Adamidis (2017b).

[16] For example, see Lys. 3.42; Aeschin. 1.183; 3.2, 26, 175; Dem. 21.45–50; Dem. 22.25–32; Dem. 23.30, 51, 79.

[17] Inter alia, the laws presented by Epicrates provided that (i) the seller was forbidden from making false statements in the agora about his products (Hyp. 3.14); (ii) in the case of the sale of a slave, the owner was required by law to inform the buyer of any physical defects the slave might have; otherwise, the buyer could return the slave and demand his money back (3.15); (iii) lawful betrothals are valid and unlawful ones are invalid as "the simple act of betrothal ... did not satisfy the lawgiver" (3.16), similarly to wills (3.17).

argument. In *Heller*, the losing side similarly relied on writings of historical figures to demonstrate that the Framers intended that the amendment comprise a right of keeping arms only as related to militia service, not as an individual right (*District of Columbia v. Heller*, Pet'r Brief, 2008, pp. 17–35).

Moreover, assertions about the intentions or values of respected historical figures can be made even without specific evidence relating to specific figures.[18] Just as Athenian advocates could probably not have known the true intentions of Solon or Draco, American advocates face a similar situation and employ a similar approach when they make general assertions about what "the Founders" or "the Framers" intended. Rather than attempting to identify a specific intention of a particular historical person, these arguments seek to appeal to the cultural and traditional memory of revered historical figures. Jack Balkin offers, as an example of an argument invoking "cultural memory" (Balkin, 2013, p. 676), the concurring opinion of Justice Louis Brandeis in the 1927 Supreme Court case *Whitney v. California*. There, Justice Brandeis referred to "those who won our independence" (*Whitney v. California*, 1927, p. 375) to support his argument that only speech that presented a "clear and present danger" should be punishable. In referencing "those who won our independence" rather than specific individuals who wrote the Constitution, Brandeis appealed to cultural memory.[19] As Balkin notes, arguments that conflate different groups or "appeal to the Founders and Framers as an undifferentiated whole" (Balkin, 2013, p. 677) are arguments grounded in tradition and American cultural memory rather than actual assertions about specific intent of particular lawgivers. For the purpose of the argument, it does not matter whether "the Founding generation disagreed about protecting politically unpopular speech, whether some of the Founders were selective in their support of free expression, or whether some members of the Founding generation actually wanted to suppress particular dissenters" (Balkin, 2013, p. 678). What matters is the ethos-based appeal to an understanding of cultural memory of the group, a narrative about the origins of the country and the values of the people who founded it, and a sense of tradition of "who we are" as Americans. Advocates' confident assertion of historical intent allows them to persuasively suggest that the audience shares a knowledge of the revered lawgivers' intentions, based upon the traditions of the past.

3.3 TRADITION AND RHETORICAL STRATEGIES

In our work thus far, we have sought to provide foundational information about the relevance and use of tradition-type arguments in classical Athenian and

[18] For ways that this shared knowledge might be used without expressly invoking it, see Tanner's discussion of enthymemes (Chapter 5 in this volume).

[19] Balkin (2013, pp. 676–677) observes that the Framers of the Constitution and the revolutionaries "who won our independence" are "not identical; however, in American cultural memory, the two groups tend to merge into one."

contemporary American systems. In this section, we turn to rhetorical strategies accessible to advocates in classical times and today. In both systems, advocates have used specific rhetorical strategies to effectively develop tradition-based arguments. These strategies include a deliberate focus on shared identity and the development of an attractive narrative integrating the historical arc of the audience's culture. Using these tools creatively and wisely has enabled lawyers and jurists to argue that tradition actually supports apparently non-traditional causes such as same-sex sexual activity, coeducational military education, and even same-sex marriage.

3.3.1 *Rhetorical Strategies: Shared Identity and Narrative*

By highlighting shared identity between the orator and the audience based on shared values and traditions, an advocate can simultaneously forge connections with the audience and, by placing opponents outside that shared identity, marginalize those opponents (Adamidis, 2024).[20] Interestingly, the varying "traditions" that can be identified and exploited result in a rhetorical situation where both sides may claim the "tradition-based" position, even as they argue for different positions. This provides an opportunity for creative modern advocates to use tradition to promote outcomes that might not immediately be identified as tradition, in the sense of long-standing custom. Although the American legal framework, as it evolved and adapted from classical times to the present, has been criticized as inherently Western-centric, patriarchal, and biased,[21] contemporary advocates can find creative ways to use rhetorical techniques for social justice and equality.

The American legal system's foundational reliance on *stare decisis* provides a default preference for tradition, in the sense that precedential decisions govern our current decisions. No court – or lawyer – is starting from scratch in a current case; all must contend with prior rulings on similar questions and build upon them. Advocates know that arguing to *overturn* precedent is much more difficult than arguing that their case is *consistent* with a different view of that precedent, either

[20] The artful creation of shared identity with the audience through rhetoric can be analyzed by reference to the psychological theory of social identity, developed in the 1970s by Tajfel and Turner (1979). Readers who are interested in learning more about the theory of identification would be well advised to consult Kenneth Burke's work in A *Rhetoric of Motives* (1950), because Burke's theory of identification was a significant contribution to modern rhetoric. The work of stressing commonality between a rhetor and an audience requires rhetoricians to be "skilled psychologists or soul-knowers" (Herrick, 2009, pp. 70–71) so that they can effectively assess their audience and determine how to align the audience's interests with those of their client.

[21] Berenguer et al. (2020, p. 211) argue that because American founders held the ideas of the Enlightenment and classical Greco-Roman thinkers in such high esteem, the ideas, which included justification of "violent race-based enslavement" on the Aristotelian belief that "out-group individuals must be ruled and subjugated because they do not have the capacity for deliberative reason" became embedded in the foundation of American law. For a more thorough discussion of this critique, see Berenguer et al. (2023).

because the cases are distinguishable or because the rule of the prior case can be framed in such a way as to allow for a favorable decision in the current matter. Even the Supreme Court, which has the ability to overturn its own decisions as well as those of lower courts, is never eager to do so. While *stare decisis* is not an inexorable command, it is a critical cornerstone of our system. One need only examine the reaction to *Dobbs v. Jackson Women's Health Organization* (2022), in which the Supreme Court overturned two prior rulings on abortion, to understand how unusual such a step was. And one need only review the *Dobbs* opinion to see how painstakingly the Court tried to explain why such action was appropriate.

Just as clever advocates find ways to frame precedential decisions so that they appear consistent with a favorable ruling in the current situation, advocates can also frame "tradition" so that it supports their position. It may be more difficult for advocates promoting change and challenging the status quo to incorporate tradition into their arguments, but it is arguably even more important for them to do so to combat the default preference for the status quo that results from our legal system's structure.

One useful rhetorical strategy for these advocates is what Kenneth Burke (1950) called identification, a tool by which rhetors find "commonality between a rhetor and an audience" (Herrick, 2009, p. 10). Effective advocates assess their audience and determine how to align the audience's interests and values with those of their client; this rhetorical strategy dates back to Plato's recommendations in the *Phaedrus* that a speaker must identify "the kind of discourse suitable for each kind of soul" and "order ... and embellish ... his discourse accordingly" (Plato, 1921, p. 277). Using tradition allows advocates to create a sense of shared identity between their audiences, honored and respected authorities or practices, and the current client. Of course, if the audience does not "identify with the country's traditions, arguments from ethos and tradition will have little purchase" (Balkin, 2013, p. 673). Thus, the advocate must choose the tradition carefully. For example, an advocate on one side might rely upon a specific cultural custom, while the opposing side favors a broader political concept as the relevant tradition. Each advocate can identify and use a tradition argument, depending on which one supports the client's position and with which one the audience is likely to identify.

In addition to creating shared identity, effective advocates in both systems have constructed narratives that place the past tradition and the current position in a historical story that their audience will be willing to accept (Gagarin, 2003, p. 207). An argument grounded in tradition is, by definition, grounded in history: the story of our past. As such, these arguments are particularly amenable to use of narrative techniques to increase their persuasive appeal (Balkin, 2013, p. 680). A variety of stories can give meaning to a single reality.[22] An effective advocate can construct a

[22] L. H. LaRue points out that the law itself can be viewed as "fiction" because "judicial opinions are filled with 'stories' that purpose to be 'factual' but that are 'fictional'" (LaRue, 1995, p. 8).

narrative that will trigger the audience's recollection of "master stories or myths" and serve as "a template, or path, for a wide variety of other similar stories to follow" (Sheppard, 2009, p. 261).[23] The narrative framework thus infuses meaning into the current situation, as the audience experiences not only the specific story of the case at bar, but also perhaps subconsciously remembers other, similar stories, and experiences the emotional connection from these other stories in a way that can both draw upon and "reinforce traditional, cultural, and societal values" (Sheppard, 2009, p. 262). By identifying people or traditions in the past that the audience will respect, advocates identify the "right side of history, as judged by the present" (Balkin, 2013, p. 684) and suggest that siding with their client today will align the current decision-maker with that right side. And just as identification can connect the audience *to* or *away from* specific cultural practices and connection with a conceptual political tradition, these narratives can be used to show the audience how either *following* or *abandoning* a specific practice may be desirable. For either approach, the advocate can selectively choose honored authorities for further positive identification (Balkin, 2013). Rhetorical choices matter, for both advocates and jurists. For example, progressive Constitutional scholar Kate Shaw, in the podcast *Strict Scrutiny*, noted Justice Ketanji Brown Jackson's rhetorical choice to use the term "'framers,' "without modification" to describe the authors of the reconstruction amendments, reminding us that they should occupy the same place in our kind of constitutional constellation as the people who drafted the original Constitution" (Litman et al., 2023).

Athenian orators used both techniques successfully in classical arguments, and American advocates have followed their lead. Both sets of advocates employed *ethos* as they created shared identity and *pathos* as they employed narrative to argue either that they were acting consistently with historical tradition *or*, more inventively, to identify a narrative in which a broader tradition was evolving and the advocate's position was on the right side of history. The latter approach allows innovative advocates to ostensibly use tradition as they validate outcomes that are inconsistent with – or even contradictory to – long-established social customs.

3.3.2 *Using Tradition as a Rhetorical Tool: Examples from Athens and the United States*

Athenian and American advocates have often evoked tradition to argue that their position is on the right side of the historical narrative with which the audience

Just as legal arguments are not purely logical, as Tanner (Chapter 5 in this volume) illustrates, they may also not be purely "factual" in LaRue's sense of the word. Readers who are intrigued by the role of narrative in legal argument may enjoy LaRue's discussion of stories of limits, growth, and equality in constitutional law, and the literature of legal writing is replete with discussions of narrative in persuasive argument.

[23] Amsterdam and Bruner (2000, pp. 77–109) have thoughtfully analyzed Justice Scalia's opinion in *Michael H. v. Gerald D.* as a narrative of adultery as combat myth.

should align. In the adversarial setting of Athenian courts, tradition arguments were often embedded in the narrative as the focal point of the litigants' speeches, in an effort to create shared identity with the audience and to marginalize the opponent through the projection of a certain ethos.[24] Dicasts expected that the speakers would strictly adhere to widely accepted traditional norms of behavior, and a person who understood himself as an integral part of the community perceived these norms as the benchmark of ethical conduct.[25] Therefore, the speaker whose actions or arguments were artfully presented as consistent with tradition had more chances to persuade the audience of their expediency.

The debate about awarding a crown to Demosthenes offers insight into this use of tradition, namely how the rhetorical presentation of different versions of it provides the benchmark for the evaluation of current practice. In the spring of 336 BCE, an Athenian citizen named Ctesiphon proposed a decree for a golden crown to be conferred by the Athenian people to Demosthenes claiming that he "continually advises and acts in the best interests of the people" (Dem. 18.57).[26] In the ensuing debate about whether Demosthenes should receive such a crown, both Demosthenes and the plaintiff, Aeschines, used different interpretations of tradition to suggest that their position was the correct course of action based on how the historical narrative should flow.

First, Aeschines attacked Ctesiphon's proposed decree. Aeschines focused both on the illegality of the motion and on an assessment of Demosthenes' political career (Aeschin. 3.9–48, 54–167).[27] After a detailed grim review of Demosthenes' disastrous policies which eventually led Athens to its defeat by Macedon, Aeschines contrasted his opponent with the true public benefactors of the past who made Athens great and whose deeds indicate what is the "right side" that the dicasts must take. In light of this, he asked them to be associated with the ancestors, instead of Demosthenes' cowardice, and to imagine that the heroes of the past stand before them on the platform asking for justice against Demosthenes' plotting and treason (Aeschin. 3.247, 257–259).

Demosthenes, in reply, claimed that the right side of history, as indicated by Athenian tradition, was to resist tyranny even against the odds, not to erase the noble and just achievements of the ancestors (Dem. 18.63) by submitting voluntarily to Philip (18.68). Athens always fought for the first prize in honor and glory (18.66) so "the only remaining course of action was to oppose on the side of right everything

[24] According to Aristotle (2007), argumentation from ethos belongs to the *entechnoi* (artful, i.e., invented by the orator) *pisteis* (means of persuasion) (see *Rhet.* 1355b35; cf. *Rhet.* 1356a 10–14).

[25] For example, Aeschines, ostensibly defending the laws of the city and the traditional norms of decency and restraint, advised the dicasts to stand with him, condemn Timarchus and not put at risk the whole moral and education system of Athens (Aeschin. 1.1–2, 34, 192; cf. Aeschin. 2.146–152; Lyc. 1.82–83; 111–123, 127).

[26] Also, see Aeschin. 3.49, 101, 237.

[27] On the legal arguments of both sides, see Harris (2013, pp. 225–233). On Demosthenes' speech, see Yunis (2001).

that he [Philip] did to wrong you [Athenian dicasts]" (18.69). Regardless of the outcome, "both individual citizens and the city as a whole must ever strive to act in accord with the noblest standards of our tradition" (18.95; cf. 96–99, 101, 200). Surrendering "was not part of the Athenian heritage" and "since the beginning of time, no one has ever been able to persuade the city to side with the powerful but unjust and to find safety in servitude" (18.203, 204). Demosthenes' policies resembled "those made by the eminent citizens of the past and have the same goals as did theirs" (18.317). Right from the beginning, the path he chose was "straight and honest: to foster, to enhance, to remain true to the country's honor, power and prestige" (18.322). According to this approach, awarding Demosthenes the crown would be consistent with the desired historical narrative and the continued story of who Athenians were, consistent with the past.

Athenian advocates acknowledged the value of tradition as the benchmark for the evaluation of current practice, and often evoked it as a strong argument for resisting or advocating change (or, more accurately, a return to a more commendable approach taken in the past). In lawsuits against purportedly unlawful legislation, prosecutors argued that they were defending the city's existing laws against fresh statutes which, if endorsed, would undermine the integrity of the legal system and the Athenian traditional values.[28] In fact, contrasting the reverent lawgivers of the past and their well-tried, old-established laws against a current lawgiver introducing a fresh, inexpedient statute was a rhetorical commonplace which reveals the Athenian belief in and the rhetorical force of tradition.[29] In a prosecution against an inexpedient law, Demosthenes contended that the law proposed by Leptines violated the spirit of Solon's old laws (Dem. 20.89–104). Observing that the law is "far removed from the city's character," Demosthenes argued that "it is more advantageous both to you (Athenians) and to Leptines for the city to persuade him to adopt its ways than for it to be persuaded by this man to adopt his ways" (Dem. 20.14; cf. 20.111).

On the other hand, speakers criticized the purported deviation of current practice from tradition and recommended a return to a previous, more expedient, approach. In Aeschines' speech *Against Ctesiphon* and in Demosthenes' speech *Against Aristocrates*, the speakers questioned the current readiness of the Athenians to distribute honors to ostensibly unworthy individuals. Aeschines claimed that the whole practice was discredited by "giving crowns out of habit, not on purpose" as opposed to "those days when distinctions were scarce in our city and the name of virtue was an honor" (Aeschin. 3.178; cf. 3.181–189, 231).[30] Similarly, Demosthenes argued that "[m]en in the past used to grant awards to citizens in a way both noble and in their interest, but we do it in the wrong way" (Dem. 23.199). In the speech

28 See, for example, Dem. 20.10, 14; 22.76; 23.201, 208–210; 24.142–143, 182–186.

29 E.g. Dem. 24.137, 139, 142, 153; cf. Dem. 20.8–9, 18.

30 To this, Demosthenes replies that he should not be compared to the ancestors but with his contemporaries (Dem. 18.314–319).

On the Dishonest Embassy (Dem. 19), Demosthenes encouraged the dicasts to live up to the standards of their ancestors who considered matters of corruption a capital crime (19.269–270). Offering a series of examples showing how "repugnant and harmful" corruption was considered by them, Demosthenes criticized the current lenient approach of the courts (19.275; cf. 23.204–206). By helping the dicasts identify with revered Athenian traditions, these speakers used the rhetorical strategy of creating a shared identity with the audience to further their persuasive arguments.

In addition to being used as a rhetorical tool to highlight the shared identity between the orator and the audience, arguments from tradition could be employed to marginalize the adversary and cast him as an outsider.[31] If a speaker could show that his opponent was breaching Athenian traditional norms, this would be probative of his propensity to break Athenian law. For example, in Aeschines' charge (*dokimasia rhetoron*) against Timarchus, challenging his fitness to address the Athenian Assembly due to having prostituted himself, the speaker framed his arguments within a wider context by reference to the longstanding Athenian values of decency, restraint, shame, and honor. He contrasted Timarchus to the great legislators of the past, Solon and Draco, who showed a "great concern for decency" (Aeschin. 1.6), and alleged that Timarchus' way of life was contrary to all their laws (1.8–32, 37) and Athenian patterns of behavior (1.25–26, 182–184). Consequently, Aeschines told the court that considering "the view of your fathers on the issues of shame and honor" (1.185), it would be unthinkable to "acquit Timarchus, a man guilty of the most shameful practices" (1.185) and, thus, "overturn the whole educational system" (1.187).[32]

Americans have also relied upon shared identity in their tradition-based arguments. In the section above, we noted that American advocates used tradition in arguments that relied upon long-standing customs in American society, or assertions about the historical and traditional meaning of words or the intentions of revered historical figures. Advocates supporting the status quo find natural alignment with tradition-type arguments, and it is not surprising to find tradition-type arguments in the work of those advocates. What may be surprising, however, is to find the

[31] This was a central (and, judging by the result, quite successful) strategy in Demosthenes' masterpiece *On the Crown*, where the orator presented himself as the exponent of the ancestral values to which the present audience was also committed (Dem. 18.72, 101, 206–208, 281, 293), whereas his adversary, Aeschines, was presented as an ethical and political outsider (Dem. 18.200, 280, 282). The marginalization and alienation of the opponent through invective, following the interpellation of the audience by reference to an idealistic view of it, and the creation of a shared identity with the speaker who ostensibly is the protector of venerated traditional values, is a technique commonly employed in populist rhetoric. For further discussion, see Adamidis (2021, 2022).

[32] For examples of similar argumentation, see Aeschin. 3.77–78; Andoc. 1.124–131; Lys. 6.51–54; Lys. 12.17–18; Lys. 30.26–28; Lys. 31.21–23, 31). In Dem. 21, Meidias' impiety and disrespect for Athenian customs and behavioral standards could be used as evidence that he should be held liable for the offense of hubris for assaulting Demosthenes for the purpose of humiliating him during a public religious festival (Dem. 21.51, 55, 61, 66, 69, 79, 98).

instances where advocates use tradition-type arguments to creatively support positions that are not, at least on an obvious level, "traditional" at all. For example, American advocates have effectively employed the concept of tradition in argument grounded in political traditions and a narrative about the historical arc of the country. When focusing on a more concrete, specific, longstanding custom would suggest an undesirable outcome, lawyers and jurists have chosen a more general, overarching principle that could support the desired outcome and yet still be classified as tradition within an evolving historical narrative.[33] Using narrative reinforces the positive identity created: The narratives "explain who Americans are by explaining where they have come from and where they are going" (Balkin, 2013, p. 680). In this way, clever advocates have used the rhetorical tactic of marginalizing the outsider to create arguments that end up bringing "out-groups" into the protection of American anti-discrimination law.

This type of tradition argument, which is less intuitively obvious than the cultural tradition argument, invokes a particular, often evolving, tradition within the political life of the country. The evolving tradition is often more conceptual and broad than a cultural custom (e.g., nondiscrimination or privacy), usually relates to important cultural aspects of American society as reflected in the law, and asks the audience to identify a tradition of who we are as a people moving through history: a more general principle to which Americans are committed, rather than a specific act or practice that has been customary.[34] These tradition arguments "often call for us to remember what 'we' – here a transgenerational subject – fought for, what we stand for, what we promised we would do, and what we promised we would never let happen again" (Balkin, 2013, p. 684). This type of argument encourages the audience to view the past and determine which position ended up on the right side of history and follow the approach and principles of that position. Advocates making such an argument might invoke the views of particular Founding Fathers, if interpreting words of the Constitution (while ignoring the views of others), or might identify with social movements that, even though unpopular at the time, have come to be seen as correct in the present.

This type of narrative tradition-based argument can actually be used to advocate for turning *away* from tradition in the sense of a customary practice. For example, consider the progression of arguments in two Supreme Court cases focused on same-sex activity. In the 1986 *Bowers v. Hardwick* decision, the Court relied on tradition in the form of a long-standing custom to reject a gay rights challenge to state laws criminalizing sodomy. In that case, the Court considered a Georgia statute that criminalized "any sexual act involving the sex organs of one person and the

33 Cf. Turner (2016), who argues that this approach, as seen in *Obergefell*, is properly viewed as a "generational" interpretation of the due process clause and a rejection of tradition rather than a reframing of it.

34 Readers who are interested in the question of whether such appeals to an audience actually constitute and create particular identities may wish to review Charland (1987).

mouth or anus of another" (*Bowers v. Hardwick*, 1986, p. 188 n. 1). Michael Hardwick was charged with violating the law. Hardwick's attorneys argued that the statute was unconstitutional because it violated Hardwick's fundamental right to consensual intimate activity; they noted that America's "constitutional traditions have always placed the highest value upon the sanctity of the home against government intrusion or control," particularly with respect to "individuals' most intimate affairs" (*Bowers v. Hardwick*, Resp. Brief, 1986, p. 4). The Court found that the statute was constitutional. In doing so, the Court framed the legal issue as "whether the Federal Constitution confers a fundamental right upon homosexuals to engage in sodomy and hence invalidates the laws of the many States that still make such conduct illegal and have done so for a very long time" (*Bowers v. Hardwick*, 1986, p. 190). The Court explicitly noted that "to claim that a right to engage in such conduct is 'deeply rooted in this Nation's history and tradition' or 'implicit in the concept of ordered liberty' is, at best, facetious" (p. 194). Because the court found that the traditional custom was to ban such conduct, it rejected the assertion that individuals had a "a fundamental right to engage in homosexual sodomy" (p. 191).

But less than twenty years later, in the 2003 case *Lawrence v. Texas*, the Court overturned the *Bowers* case – which relied on tradition as a primary rationale for its decision – while still citing tradition as a rationale. The Court considered – and found unconstitutional – a Texas statute criminalizing "deviate sexual intercourse with another individual of the same sex" and defining such "deviate" intercourse as including "any contact between any part of the genitals of one person and the mouth or anus of another person" (*Lawrence v. Texas*, 2003, p. 563). *Lawrence* mirrored *Bowers* in that a man who had been convicted under the law for engaging in consensual same-sex activity in his own home challenged its constitutionality. But the Court now found that this behavior was protected by the Constitution.

How could the Court justify overturning *Bowers*, which relied on long-standing custom to reject a right of same-sex intimate activity in a situation where two consenting adults engaged in such in the privacy of their own homes, in a decision that claimed to be justified by tradition? It could do so in part because its framing of the type of relevant tradition in *Lawrence* was, in important ways, different from the longstanding custom upon which the Court initially relied in *Bowers*. Writing for the Court in *Lawrence*, Justice Kennedy asserted that the *Bowers* Court had "misapprehended the claim of liberty presented to it" (*Lawrence v. Texas*, 2003, p. 567). Although Kennedy did argue that the prior decision may not have been entirely correct in finding a long-standing custom disfavoring same-sex activity,[35] the

[35] Justice Kennedy argued that *Bowers* had been wrong to suggest that there was a longstanding custom against same-sex sodomy "as a distinct matter," instead suggesting that prior laws criminalizing sodomy had been focused on prohibiting "nonprocreative sexual activity more generally" (*Lawrence v. Texas*, 2003, p. 568). Kennedy concluded that "the historical grounds relied upon in *Bowers* are more complex than the majority opinion and the concurring opinion by Chief Justice Burger indicate" (p. 571).

Lawrence decision did not simply assert that the prior decision got the tradition wrong. Instead, it suggested that a different and broader tradition was more relevant. Justice Kennedy declined to focus on a particular custom disfavoring same-sex sodomy, but instead noted that "in our tradition the State is not omnipresent in the home" (*Lawrence v. Texas*, 2003, p. 562) and identified as a more general tradition of principle and policy: the traditional right of citizens to be free from government interference in private matters in their homes. Kennedy also identified an *evolving* tradition or "emerging recognition" about intimate relationships generally, noting that the "laws and traditions in the past half century are of most relevance here" (pp. 571–572). Because those more recent traditions "show an emerging awareness that liberty gives substantial protection to adult persons in deciding how to conduct their private lives in matters pertaining to sex" (pp. 571–572), Kennedy concluded that the traditions upon which the Court relied in 1986 were not dispositive.

One might argue, as Justice Scalia did in his *Lawrence* dissent, that an "emerging awareness" is not a tradition at all, at least by the definition of a long-standing custom (*Lawrence v. Texas*, 2003, pp. 597–598). Justice Kennedy's opinion appeared at some points to concede this point by noting that "[h]istory and tradition are the starting point but not in all cases the ending point of the substantive due process inquiry" (p. 572, internal citations omitted). But by framing the issue as an "emerging *recognition*" regarding intimate relationships rather than simply a "new practice," Kennedy was able to draw support from history and tradition despite the apparent tension (or even contradiction) inherent in the concept of what might otherwise be framed as a "new tradition."

The contrasting opinions of Justice Ginsburg (writing for the Court majority) and Justice Scalia (dissenting from the Court's decision) in the 1996 case *United States v. Virginia* offer an even clearer example of one type of tradition argument – long-standing custom – pitted against another – narrative historical arc and evolving political identity – with evolving political identity carrying the day for social justice. There, the Court found that Virginia Military Institute's (VMI) practice of excluding females and maintaining single-sex education exclusively for male students violated the Constitution. To reach this decision, Ginsburg's opinion (for the Court majority) had to overcome a tradition argument of the first type: longstanding custom. Justice Scalia, in his dissenting opinion, focused on the "long tradition, enduring down to the present, of men's military colleges supported by both States and the Federal government" (*United States v. Virginia*, 1996, p. 566). Justice Ginsburg, writing for the majority, effectively countered the longstanding cultural tradition of single-sex education by identifying a new and evolving tradition that represented the country's political movement toward equality. First, she identified a negative tradition aligned with the single-sex education endorsed by VMI, noting that "our Nation has had a long and unfortunate history of sex discrimination" (p. 531, internal citations omitted). Then she reviewed the history of other American colleges and universities (including within Virginia) who had shifted from single-sex to coeducational (pp. 536–538). Towards the end of her argument, she identified the new political tradition, dating from "a generation ago," of equal treatment for men and women as a counter to the longstanding custom of all-male military education (p. 556). "A prime part of the history of our Constitution," Ginsburg concluded, "is the story of the extension of constitutional rights and protections to people once ignored or excluded" (p. 557, internal citations omitted). Justice Ginsburg's identification of the political tradition of non-discrimination thus trumped the cultural tradition argument offered by Justice Scalia.[36] In this view, non-discrimination on the basis of sex represents who Americans are and who they are becoming.

Why, and when, might progressive advocates choose to rely on tradition as a basis for support even as they argue for social change? Reliance on tradition alone might be ineffective or even appear disingenuous in an argument to change laws related to problematic social norms. In some cases (such as certain constitutional inquiries), references to tradition and history are unavoidable because of the legal rules already in place. In others, even if not absolutely necessary, such references may be strategically desirable. Creative advocates understand that weaving multiple types of argument together create a stronger argument overall. Including backward-looking tradition-type arguments alongside forward-looking policy arguments can lessen opposition to action that might otherwise be perceived as unbridled judicial activism or overturning (as opposed to reframing) settled precedent.

Clever advocates in the past have integrated the narrative approach to their advantage while also relying on shared identity. The Commonwealth of Virginia's amicus brief in the 2015 case *Obergefell v. Hodges* demonstrates both these techniques. In advocating on behalf of the petitioners who wished the Supreme Court to find a fundamental right to same-sex marriage, Virginia had to overcome a specific cultural tradition identified by the opposing side: the longstanding custom of marriage as composed of a man and a woman rather than two members of the same sex. To do so, Virginia explicitly identified (and invited the Court to identify) with "the right side of this issue" despite its own prior positions on the "wrong side" of cases such as *Brown* (on school desegregation) and *Loving* (on interracial marriage) (*Obergefell v. Hodges*, Brief of Commonwealth of Virginia, 2015, p. 6). By referencing cases in which a long-standing custom had been cited as sufficient rationale for racial discrimination, Virginia reminded the Court that one type of tradition argument might place the Court in a position that would later be overturned.

[36] Justice Ginsberg's opinion, of course, included much more than these points; the summary here is intended to focus readers' attention on the competing concepts of tradition and not to fully encapsulate all reasoning within the majority opinion. Readers interested in the contrasting views of Justices Scalia and Ginsburg on the appropriate role of tradition in legal interpretation in another Supreme Court case may wish to read Keenan (2023).

> Virginia submits this amicus brief in support of reversal because its experience on the wrong side of *Brown* and *Loving*, and on the right side of this issue, has taught us the truth of what the Court recognized in *Lawrence v. Texas*: "those who drew and ratified … the Fourteenth Amendment" chose not to specify the full measure of freedom that it protected because they "knew [that] times can blind us to certain truths and later generations can see that laws once thought necessary and proper in fact serve only to oppress." (*Obergefell*, Brief of Commonwealth of Virginia, 2015, p. 6)

With that single sentence, the brief told a story of regret and redemption: Virginia had been wrong, had seen the error of its ways, and now sees – and shares – the true path that is aligned with a correct political tradition of non-discrimination. This narrative plays upon a stock story of redemption. If the Court sides with Virginia, it positions itself on the right side of history. Virginia also reminded the Court of past instances where the Court had initially made a decision that it later reversed, by referencing *Lawrence*'s reversal of *Bowers*. And it offered an alternative tradition to the one proposed by the opposing party (the traditional view of marriage as one man and one woman), by framing the traditional right as the right of an individual to marry (*Obergefell v. Hodges*, Brief of Commonwealth of Virginia, 2015, p. 17).[37]

Was it successful? The Court's opinion in *Obergefell* suggests that line of argument was influential. Writing for the Court, Justice Kennedy noted that "[t]he right to marry is fundamental as a matter of history and tradition" (*Obergefell v. Hodges*, 2015, p. 671).[38] His focus on the general right of an individual to marry stood in stark contrast to the tradition invoked by the opponents to same-sex marriage: the tradition of marriage involving a man and a woman rather than two members of the same sex. Once more, a "traditional" argument had prevailed for an outcome that may have seemed, by some definitions, decidedly untraditional.

3.4 CONCLUSION

Incorporating tradition has been and continues to be persuasive as a strategy to enhance an argument's legitimacy and appeal. We can identify intersections between Athenian forensic rhetoric of the fourth century BCE and American rhetoric of the twentieth and twenty-first century in the use of and reliance upon tradition. Both sets of advocates find tradition so compelling that even when they argue against a tradition (in the sense of a longstanding custom), they frame the argument as advancing a tradition (in the sense of a political tradition or principle or

[37] Virginia reminded the Court that "[n]o case before *Loving* involved interracial marriage; no case before *Zablocki* involved betrotheds behind in their child-support obligation; and no case before *Turner* involved marriage to a prisoner. But the Court nonetheless described each case as involving the right to marry, a right 'of fundamental importance for *all* individuals'" (*Obergefell v. Hodges*, Brief of Commonwealth of Virginia, 2015, p. 17).

[38] Note, however, that the Court simultaneously opined that "[h]istory and tradition guide and discipline this inquiry but do not set its outer boundaries" (*Obergefell v. Hodges*, 2015, p. 664).

historical narrative). Both sets of advocates have employed ethos (in establishing shared identity) and pathos (with narrative techniques) as they try to persuade their audiences that tradition supports their position. In both systems, advocates rely upon tradition as a central tenet of persuasive argument and use it as a rhetorical battleground. And for proponents of equality, social justice, and nondiscrimination, tradition can be used as a force to propel society into the future rather than allow it to remain moored in the past. For example, an advocate might strategically choose to establish a specific view of shared communal identity to support a broader view of tradition – one that would encompass progressive views regarding equality and consideration of historically marginalized groups.

The structure inherited from classical rhetoric may not appear to lend itself to these uses. Classical rhetors might have been surprised at the outcomes. But even within a Western-centric structure that has been critiqued as hostile to contemporary notions of equality, the tools of the past can be used to create a new and more egalitarian future. And given the structure in which we operate, an advocate who chooses to neglect these tools does so at their peril; integrating them will not guarantee success, but ignoring them will increase the likelihood of failure. The power and allure of tradition has held fast for centuries and shows no sign of diminishing. Unless and until we see dramatic change in our legal system's operation, we must embrace tradition and find strategies to incorporate it into even "non-traditional" arguments.

REFERENCES

Adamidis, V. (2017a). *Character evidence in the courts of classical Athens: Rhetoric, relevance and the rule of law*. Routledge.

(2017b). Solon the lawgiver: Inequality of resources and equality before the law. In D. A. Frenkel (Ed.), *Role of law, human rights and social justice, justice systems, commerce, and law curriculum: Selected issues* (pp. 121–138). ATINER Publications.

(2021). Populist rhetorical strategies in the courts of classical Athens. *Athens Journal of History*, 7(1), 21–40.

(2022). Populism in power? A reconsideration of the Athenian democracy of the late 5th century BC. *Journal of Ancient Civilizations*, 37(1), 33–64.

(2024). Mind the audience: Forensic rhetoric, persuasion, and identification by reference to the social identity of Athenian dikastai, *Rhetorica*, 42(1), 1–30.

Amsterdam, A. G., & Bruner, J. (2000). *Minding the law*. Harvard University Press.

Aristotle. (2007). *On rhetoric: A theory of civic discourse* (G. A. Kennedy, Trans.) (2nd ed.). Oxford University Press. (Original work published ca. 360 BCE.)

Balkin, J. M. (2013). The new originalism and the uses of history. *Fordham Law Review*, 82(2), 641–720.

(2018). Arguing about the Constitution: The topics in constitutional interpretation. *Constitutional Commentary*, 33(2), 145–260.

Berenguer, E., Jewel, L., & McMurtry-Chubb, T. A. (2020). Gut renovations: Using critical and comparative rhetoric to remodel how the law addresses privilege and power. *Harvard Latinx Law Review*, 23(2), 205–232.

(2023). *Critical and comparative rhetoric: Unmasking privilege and power in law and legal advocacy to achieve truth, justice, and equity*. Bristol University Press.
Berger, L. L. (2010). Studying and teaching law as rhetoric: A place to stand. *Legal Writing: Journal of the Legal Writing Institute*, *16*(1), 3–64.
Bowers v. Hardwick, 478 U.S. 186 (1986).
Bowers v. Hardwick (No. 85-140), Brief for Respondents, 478 U.S. 186 (1986), 1986 WL 720442.
Burke, K. (1950). *A rhetoric of motives*. Prentice-Hall Inc.
Carawan, E. M. (1984). *Akriton Apokteinai:* Execution without trial in fourth-century Athens. *Greek, Roman, and Byzantine Studies*, *25*(2), 111–121.
Charland, M. (1987). Constitutive rhetoric: The case of the *peuple Quebecois*. *Quarterly Journal of Speech*, *73*(2), 133–150.
District of Columbia v. Heller, 554 U.S. 570 (2008).
District of Columbia v. Heller (No. 07-290), Respondent's Brief, 554 U.S. 570 (2008), 2008 WL 336304.
District of Columbia v. Heller (No. 07-290), Brief for Petitioners, 554 U.S. 570 (2008), 2008 WL 102223.
Dobbs v. Jackson Women's Health Organization, 597 U.S. 215 (2022).
Dover, K. J. (1994). *Greek popular morality in the time of Plato and Aristotle*. Hackett Publishing. (Original work published 1974.)
Frost, M. H. (2005). *Introduction to classical legal rhetoric: A lost heritage*. Ashgate.
Gagarin, M. (2003). Telling stories in Athenian law. *Transactions of the American Philological Association*, *133*(2), 197–207.
(2020a). *Democratic law in classical Athens*. University of Texas Press.
(2020b). Storytelling about the lawgiver in the Athenian orators. *Cahiers des études anciennes*, *57*, 33–44. http://journals.openedition.org/etudesanciennes/1434 [https://perma.cc/6A4A-SS8X]
Hansen, M. H. (1976). *Apagoge, endeixis and ephegesis against kakourgoi, atimoi and pheugontes*. Odense University Press.
(1991). *The Athenian democracy in the age of Demosthenes: Structure, principles, and ideology*. Blackwell.
Harris, E. M. (2010). Solon and the spirit of the law in archaic and classical Greece. In E. M. Harris, *Democracy and the rule of law in classical Athens* (pp. 3–28). Cambridge University Press.
(2013). *The rule of law in action in democratic Athens*. Oxford University Press.
Hart, H. L. A. (1994). *The concept of law*. Clarendon Press.
Herrick, J. A. (2009). *The history and theory of rhetoric: An introduction* (4th ed.). Pearson Education.
Huhn, W. (2014). *The five types of legal argument* (3rd ed.). Carolina Academic Press.
Keenan, R. T. (2023). Functional federal equity. *Alabama Law Review*, *74*(4), 879–916.
Krygier, M. (1986). Law as tradition. *Law and Philosophy*, *5*(2), 237–262.
Lanni, A. (2004). Arguing from "precedent": Modern perspectives on Athenian practice. In E. M. Harris and L. Rubinstein (Eds.), *The law and the courts in ancient Greece* (pp. 159–171). Duckworth.
LaRue, L. H. (1995). *Constitutional law as fiction: Narrative in the rhetoric of authority*. Pennsylvania State University Press.
Lawrence v. Texas, 539 U.S. 558 (2003).
Litman, L., Shaw, K., & Murray, M. (Hosts) (2023, July 3). *What else can the Supreme Court get away with?* [Audio podcast episode]. In *Strict Scrutiny*. Crooked Media. https://crooked.com/podcast/what-else-can-the-supreme-court-get-away-with/ [https://perma.cc/6E99-ED42].

Maltagliati, G. (2020). Persuasion through proximity (and distance) in the Attic orators' historical examples. *Greek, Roman, and Byzantine Studies*, 60, 68–97.
Mazrui, K. F. (2011). Tradition as justification: The case of opposite-sex marriage. *University of Chicago Law Review*, 78(1), 281–344.
McMurtry-Chubb, T. A. (2019). Still writing at the master's table: Decolonizing rhetoric in legal writing for a "woke" legal academy. *Scholar: St. Mary's Law Review on Race and Social Justice*, 21(2), 255–292.
Miller, D. A. H. (2016). Second Amendment traditionalism and desuetude. *Georgetown Journal of Law & Public Policy*, 14(1), 223–232.
Moore v. City of East Cleveland, 431 U.S. 494 (1977).
New York State Rifle & Pistol Association, Inc. v. Bruen, 597 U.S. 1 (2022).
New York State Rifle & Pistol Association, Inc. v. Bruen (No. 20-843), Brief for Petitioners, 597 U.S. 1 (2022), 2021 WL 3017303.
New York State Rifle & Pistol Association, Inc. v. Bruen (No. 20-843), Brief for Respondents, 597 U.S. 1 (2022), 2021 WL 4245013.
Obergefell v. Hodges, 576 U.S. 644 (2015).
Obergefell v. Hodges (Nos. 14-556, 14-562, 14-571, 14-574), Brief of Commonwealth of Virginia as Amicus Curiae in Support of Petitioners, 576 U.S. 644 (2015), 2015 WL 1022690.
Plato. (1921). *Phaedrus* (Wright, J., Trans.). MacMillan & Co. (Original work published early fourth century BCE.)
Sheppard, J. (2009). Once upon a time, happily ever after, and in a galaxy far, far away: Using narrative to fill the cognitive gap left by overreliance on pure logic in appellate briefs and motion memoranda. *Willamette Law Review*, 46(2), 255–296.
Szegedy-Maszak, A. (1978). Legends of the Greek lawgivers. *Greek, Roman, and Byzantine Studies*, 19, 199–209.
Tajfel, H., & Turner, J. (1979). An integrative theory of intergroup conflict. In W. Austin & S. Worchel (Eds.), *The social psychology of intergroup relations* (pp. 33–47). Brooks/Cole Publishing Co.
Turner, R. (2016). Marriage equality and Obergefell's generational (not Glucksberg's traditional) due process clause. *Duke Journal of Gender Law & Policy*, 23(2), 145–162.
United States v. Miller, 307 U.S. 174 (1939).
United States v. Virginia, 518 U.S. 515 (1996).
Virelli, L. J., III. (2011). Constitutional traditionalism in the Roberts court. *University of Pittsburgh Law Review*, 73(1), 1–64.
Washington v. Glucksberg, 521 U.S. 701 (1997).
Whitney v. California, 274 U.S. 357 (1927).
Yunis, H. (2001). *Demosthenes: On the Crown*. Cambridge University Press.

TRANSLATIONS

Aeschines:

Text in *Orationes, Bibliotheca Scriptorum Graecorum Et Romanorum Teubneriana*, ed. Mervin R. Dilts (Leipzig, DE: De Gruyter, 1997), trans. Chris Carey, *Against Timarchus*, in *Aeschines*, trans. Chris Carey, The Oratory of Classical Greece 3, ed. Michael Gagarin (Austin, TX: University of Texas Press, 2000).

Demosthenes:

Text in Demosthenis Orationes Vol. II, Part i (Orationes XX–XXVI.), Oxford Classical Texts, ed. Mervin R. Dilts (Oxford: Oxford University Press, 2005), trans. Edward M. Harris, Against Aristocrates, in Demosthenes, Speeches 23–26, trans. Edward M. Harris, The Oratory of Classical Greece 15, ed. Michael Gagarin (Austin, TX: University of Texas Press, 2018).

Text in *Demosthenes: On the Crown. Cambridge Greek and Latin classics*, ed. Harvey Yunis (Cambridge: Cambridge University Press, 2001), trans. Harvey Yunis, *On the Crown*, in *Demosthenes, Speeches 18 and 19*, trans. Harvey Yunis, The Oratory of Classical Greece 5, ed. Michael Gagarin (Austin, TX: University of Texas Press, 2005). Also, see Aeschin. 3.49, 101, 237.

Hyperides:

Text in M. Marzi, P. Leone, & E. Malcovati (Eds.) (1977). *Oratori attici minori, 1: Iperide, Eschine, Licurgo*. Unione Tipografico – Editrice Torinese. Trans. Craig Cooper, *Against Athenogenes*, in *Dinarchus, Hyperides, & Lycurgus*, trans. Ian Worthington, Craig Cooper, and Edward M. Harris, The Oratory of Classical Greece 5, ed. Michael Gagarin (Austin, TX: University of Texas Press, 2001).

Lycurgus:

Text in Licurgo. *Orazione contro Leocrate e frammenti*, ed. Enrica Malcovati (Rome, IT: Tumminelli, 1966), trans. Edward M. Harris, *Against Leocrates*, in *Dinarchus, Hyperides, & Lycurgus*, trans. Ian Worthington, Craig Cooper, & Edward M. Harris, The Oratory of Classical Greece 5, ed. Michael Gagarin (Austin, TX: University of Texas Press, 2001).

4

Practical Reason in Peril

From Cicero to Texas Health Presbyterian

Brian N. Larson[*]

4.1 INTRODUCTION

Judging requires practical reason, in each case a decision about what to do rather than one about scientific truth (Bix, 2022, p. 14; see also Aristotle, 1934; Burton, 1989; Larson, 2019). Writing sixty years apart, legal theorists Lon L. Fuller (1946) described an "antinomy" between reason and fiat, what Francis J. Mootz III (2018) called an "in-betweenness" in judging: The conclusion that judges necessarily exercise some discretion, because their decision cannot be the results of geometric proofs and deduction. In the face of this necessity, Mootz called for judges to exercise "rhetorical knowledge," "a practical accomplishment that achieves neither apodictic certitude nor collapses into a relativistic irrationalism" (Mootz III, 2018, p. 16).

In short, Fuller's whole theory of law and Mootz's in-betweenness acknowledge *underdeterminacy*, a state where more than one outcome is reasonably and rationally possible in many (or even all) cases. It lies between the extremes of *determinacy*, where there is only one possible answer and one possible way to reach it, and radical *indeterminacy*, where any outcome is acceptable simply as an exercise of the court's power. Judges should thus not pretend to engage in a deductive enterprise or pure fiat, but they should instead *show their work* in their practical judgments by writing opinions that exhibit a reasonable route to their conclusions. The admonition is important because the argumentation in judicial opinions is often the only evidence we have of the reasoning of the judges behind them, and it is of central concern to

[*] Research for this paper was supported by the Texas A&M University Arts & Humanities Fellowship and by summer research grants from the Texas A&M University School of Law. I am grateful for the exceptional research assistance of Claire Fecteau and Joseph Glover. Thanks are also due to the other contributors to this volume, Professors Susan E. Provenzano and Elizabeth S. Miller, and participants at the 2023 Texas Junior Scholars Faculty Workshop for their comments on earlier versions of this essay.

democracy and judicial legitimacy that the arguments judges present are cogent enough to secure (at least grudging) assent of those bound by them (Bencze & Ng, 2018; Larson, 2019). This use of rhetorical invention in the law has ancient roots in the West and a family tree that leads to the founding of the United States.

Nevertheless, express appeals to rhetorical invention in law have become unfashionable since the mid-twentieth century, while the focus of much rhetoric *about* the functioning of law and the reasoning of judges has shifted to what I call the contemporary *determinist imaginary*. An imaginary is what philosopher Charles Taylor labels "the ways people imagine their social existence, … how things go on between them and their fellows, the expectations that are normally met, and the deeper normative notions and images that underlie these expectations" (Taylor, 2004, p. 23). The imaginary is "carried in images, stories, and legends," and it "makes possible … a widely shared sense of legitimacy."

Like most of the present, the determinist imaginary is an outgrowth of the past. During the centuries before the framing of the US Constitution, most English (and thus American colonial) law was *common law*, or judge-made law. On the one hand, those judges told the story that they were merely uncovering law that was already there, often on natural-law bases. On the other, it was clear that their decisions could have "discovered" quite different laws that were equally rational (if they were rational at all). Around the time of the framing of the US Constitution, Supreme Court Justice Joseph Story – whose legal treatises were widely read in the nineteenth century – seized on the view that judicial opinions could be demonstrations, much like geometrical proofs, and that legal principles could be *deduced* – either from natural law or from other principles (Eisgruber, 1988). A similar view reached its apex in the teaching methods of Harvard Law School dean C. C. Langdell, who purported late in the nineteenth century to derive the principles of law scientifically by induction from reading court opinions. Already at the time of Langdell, however, there were theorists pushing in a different direction. For example, Oliver Wendell Holmes Jr. argued that law was a prediction about what courts would do.[1] So the imaginary swung away from determinism during the first two-thirds of the twentieth century, with more talk of Holmes' probabilities than of mathematical or scientific deduction and Langdell's induction.

But the advent of modern textualism and originalism (see Hannah & Mootz, Chapter 2 in this volume) in the latter decades of the twentieth century corresponded with the new determinist imaginary. The contemporary determinist imaginary is like older claims of determinism, in that it portrays a world where there is one right answer to each legal question and, indeed, one right way to arrive at that answer.

[1] Note, however, that some contemporary theorists of law have accused Holmes himself of being a determinist, but based on social or scientific perspectives external to the law (Burton, 1989).

The determinist imaginary's stories and legends blossomed as "a series of reactions and countermobilizations from different segments of society" to the New Deal, the civil rights movement, and the Warren Court's arguably liberal decisions (Balkin, 2009, p. 69). In that sense, the contemporary determinist imaginary is an outgrowth of conservative backlash to arguably activist, arguably liberal judging during that earlier era. But the result has been an arguably activist conservative judiciary cloaking sweeping decisions in questionable claims of certainty. In this way, determinism destabilizes the public's understanding of judging and brings into question the legitimacy of the judiciary.

This chapter cannot describe all the antecedents, all the pernicious consequences, or even all the current manifestations of the determinist imaginary (though there are many). Rather, it presents a case study comprising two treatises and the conversation into which they can be set, along with two recent opinions in the Texas Court of Appeals and Texas Supreme Court. The case study shows how the determinist imaginary obscures underdeterminacy in the interpretation of authoritative legal texts.

The first treatise is *De Inventione* (Cicero, 1949), an early work of Marcus Tullius Cicero, probably the most famous orator of the ancient West. *De Inventione* provides a checklist for practical reasoning for the invention of arguments in legal reasoning about texts, is candid about the tensions between competing interpretations, and does not dress them in the rhetoric of determinacy. I illustrate this approach in the first part of a case study, an opinion of the Court of Appeals of Texas in *D.A. v. Texas Health Presbyterian* (2017; "*THP I*"). I then discuss *Reading Law: The Interpretation of Legal Texts*, the work of Supreme Court Justice Antonin Scalia and lexicographer Bryan Garner (2012). Scalia was a self-proclaimed textualist and is one of the revered figures of the new determinist imaginary. Their book employs sweeping rhetoric to portray legal reasoning as determinist. But for their work to be practically useful to advocates and judges – as it has unquestionably been – it must subtly acknowledge the underdeterminism of all its precepts. Thus, Scalia and Garner's rhetoric *about* legal reasoning is part of the new determinist imaginary, but their description of rhetorical invention *as* legal reasoning lays bare law's underdeterminacy.

I illustrate the consequences of Scalia's determinist rhetoric with the second half of the case study: The Texas Supreme Court in *Texas Health Presbyterian v. D.A.* (2018; "*THP II*") purports to resolve the same case based on an entirely questionable assessment of grammar and punctuation. Its rhetoric about legal reasoning flees from the underdeterminacy that even *Reading Law* must acknowledge (if only in the fine print) and imagines instead judges calling "balls and strikes" (Roberts, 2005), exhibiting the perfect reason of law, and limiting judicial discretion. I wrap up with a summary of the broader strokes of Scalia and Garner's portrayal of the determinist imaginary and oppose it by urging a return to the tradition of practical reason that we can inherit from Cicero.

4.2 PRACTICAL REASON'S PEDIGREE

[N]othing at all could be done either with laws or with any instrument in writing … if everyone wished to consider only the literal meaning of the words and not to follow the intentions of the speaker.

Cicero, *De Inventione* ([1st century BCE]1949, 2:140)

The sort of practical reasoning available to contemporary US courts traces its origins to the ancient Mediterranean. Aristotle (2007) offered one model, perhaps in hopes of settling a debate between those who valued rhetoric and those who considered it unethical. Building on Hellenistic thinkers who were the heirs of Aristotle's thought, Cicero's *De Inventione* (1949) provided a method for interpreting texts whose meaning is uncertain, a method well familiar to many jurists of eighteenth-century England, to the framers of the US Constitution, and to American lawyers through the nineteenth century.

4.2.1 *Starting a Debate in Greece*

On the one side were the Greek sophists of the late fifth century BCE, teachers of rhetoric or philosophy or both, depending on who you asked. The fragments of Gorgias and the *Dissoi Logoi* (see Britt, Chapter 13 in this volume) illustrate the argumentative techniques of these teachers, producing arguments on both sides of any issue and arguments in the alternative (*The Greek Sophists*, 2003). The practical value of this type of training, and the practical reasoning of which it was evidence, could not be denied in litigious Athens during its brief experiment in democracy. On the other side was the idealism of Plato (2004, 463b) and others who decried rhetoric's focus on winning and its failure to focus on truth. For Plato, rhetoric was a pale imitation of reason – it was "cookery" or merely a "knack."

Mediating between the sophists and his own teacher Plato in the *Ethics*, Aristotle (1934, p. 337) distinguished the kind of reasoning used in geometry and the sciences, "about things that cannot vary," from the deliberation necessary for action. Because action in the public sphere requires persuasion, Aristotle's *On Rhetoric* (2007, p. 27) embraced the need for the "ability, in each [particular] case, to see the available means of persuasion"[2] and provided the first extant theoretical account of rhetoric in the West.

4.2.2 *Cicero and* De Inventione

Marcus Tullius Cicero was certainly the most famous ancient Roman orator and wrote several texts on rhetoric, including *Topica, De Oratore* and *Brutus*. This

[2] The emendation appears in the 2007 translation by Kennedy.

chapter deals with his early work *De Inventione* (Cicero, 1949). It addresses the first of the five canons of rhetoric, invention – the discovery of arguments available to the orator appearing before a tribunal – and introduces us to arguments about text, "when some doubt arises from the nature of writing" (Cicero, 1949, II.116). Though such doubts arise from several sources, I will restrict my treatment here to ambiguity and letter and intent, as they are the most salient for the discussion that follows.

For Cicero (1949, II.116), ambiguity appeared when "the written statement has two or more meanings." He gave the example of a will where the testator required that "my heir give to my wife a hundred pounds of silver plate as desired."[3] Both heir and wife desired to select which silver plate the widow would receive. The author could have cleared matters up by saying "as desired *by my heir/my wife*." Cicero offered a variety of bases for arguing on each side of the case: trying to show there is no ambiguity; the immediate linguistic context; looking at the author's "other writings, acts, words, disposition and in fact his whole life" (Cicero, 1949, II.117); the "convenience" for the state of implementing one interpretation over the other (II.118); whether one interpretation gives a result that is "more expedient, more honourable or more necessary" (II.119); whether another law determines the outcome (II.119–120); and how the author would have worded the text were the other side's interpretation correct (II.120).

Cicero (1949, II.121) discussed a second type of dispute about text that involves whether "the letter" – "the exact words that were written" – conflicts with the author's intent. We can extend the previous example, assuming that the testator required that "my heir select a hundred pounds of silver plate to give to my wife." Perhaps numerous witnesses, friends both of the testator and his wife, witnessed the testator saying – after writing his will – that he intended his wife to receive particularly a set of very valuable silver goblets, weighing some twenty pounds, that she cherished. Would this expression constrain the complete freedom that the will's text appeared to grant the heir?

On the one hand, the advocate for the author's intent would look outside the text of the writing itself to consider whether the author had some specific end in mind or to equitable considerations, where enforcing the language as written would have unexpected and undesirable consequences (Cicero, 1949, II.122–124). The advocate would urge against the letter on grounds that injustice would result from enforcing the letter in this instance and "that there is no law which requires the performance of any inexpedient or unjust act" (II.138); that the law requires that judges should exercise discretion; or that following the law as the other side urges would require it to be ignoble or "base" (II.140). The advocate for the author's intent may argue "that

3 Though the example in Cicero and here is of a will, a document unlike a law in that it does not bind other citizens to its pronouncements, Cicero proposed the same interpretive techniques for laws as for private documents. Scalia and Garner (2012) also asserts that *Reading Law* is generally applicable to interpreting contracts, statutes, and constitutions.

we value the laws not because of the words, which are but faint and feeble indications of intention, but because of the advantage of the principles which they embody, and the wisdom and care of the law-makers" (II.141). Such an advocate could conclude that "the true nature of law . . . consist[s] of meanings, not of words, and that the judge who follows the meaning may seem to comply with law more than one who follows the letter" (II.141).

On the other hand, the advocate for enforcing the letter of the text could first argue that it is *always* best to follow the letter, considering the following lines of argument: Where the text is clear, it is the best evidence for the intention of the author (Cicero, 1949, II.127–128); authors know well how to draft exceptions, so they should not be inferred (II.130–131); if exceptions are allowed it is "nothing more than repealing the law" (II.131); departing from the letter of the law makes the law unpredictable (II.134). Finally, if the judge alters the law by exception, they deny the legislators or the people an opportunity to approve this version of the law.

The advocate may also seek to show that, *regarding this text*, it is better to follow the letter, including the following lines of argument: that this law is "of the highest importance" or "sanctity" (Cicero, 1949, II.135); or that this law "was so carefully framed, that such provision was made for every situation and proper exception" (II.135). Finally, the letter's advocate can argue that *in this case* it is better to follow the letter by arguing, for example, that allowing for an exception here would create an inequitable result.

From this brief treatment, we can see that Cicero by no means saw reference to intent to be applicable only when a text was ambiguous. He acknowledged both the strength of the letter and that the strongest attack on the letter occurs when the equities favor intent. His willingness to look to extrinsic evidence in any case demonstrated his open embrace of the antinomy and underdeterminacy that letter and intent represent in this type of argument.

4.2.3 *The Through-Line from Cicero to the Framers of the US Constitution*

Cicero's *De Inventione* was available almost continuously in the Western Middle Ages and Renaissance. The guidance in this work heavily influenced the medieval *ars dictaminis* and the *ars notaria*, the proto-legal-writing practices of Western Europe (Larson & Tiscione, 2024, p. 18). Martin Camper (2018) has noted the pervasive effect of *De Inventione* in arguments about texts – including functioning as the seed for hermeneutics of the Bible – in the West from that time through the sixteenth century. Nevertheless, Cicero's ideas began to play a less prominent role after the beginning of the seventeenth century, as "influential thinkers of the day insisted that empirical evidence, mathematics, and strictly logical premises and proofs were the only suitable means by which to discover new knowledge" (Camper, 2018, p. 5). So, for example, Hobbes and Locke derided the abuses of rhetoric (Andrus, Chapter 6 in this volume; Larson & Tiscione, 2024, p. 20). The apotheosis of the movement to make even practical reasoning "logical" is possibly Emmanuel Kant's *Critique of Practical Reason* (1909), appearing in 1788, around the time that the United States was adopting its Constitution.

Nevertheless, leaders in the legal profession in the early United States were familiar with Cicero. President and lawyer John Quincy Adams was an ardent Ciceronian and first Boylston Professor of Rhetoric at Harvard. As late as the 1890s, a professor at Yale Law School, William C. Robinson, published *Forensic Oratory: A Manual for Advocates* (1893), a legal textbook that relied heavily on Cicero.

Cicero lived in a culture with its own imaginaries – imperfectly accessible to us, of course, as two millennia separate us – and those imaginaries evolved with the times through church and monarchy to parliamentary and congressional forms of government. But the focus of this chapter is on what I have called the contemporary *determinist imaginary*. To illustrate some of its practices, this chapter presents a case study in two parts, the first engaging practical reason of the sort that Cicero would have recognized, and the second embracing the rhetoric about legal reasoning that Scalia and Garner espouse.

4.3 CASE STUDY: PART 1

The words of a governing text are of paramount concern, and what they convey, in their context, is what the text means.

Antonin Scalia and Bryan A. Garner (2012, p. 56)

This section introduces "statutory construction" and the litigation in the *Texas Health Presbyterian* opinions that provide the case study for this chapter. It then measures the opinion of the Texas Court of Appeals in *THP I* against the approach that Cicero proposed.

In the United States, statutes are the enactments of the federal Congress and state legislatures, and courts must frequently interpret or construe[4] these statutes to apply them to particular circumstances. It is helpful to think of the tools of statutory interpretation as consisting of different levels of text and context. Just as we saw in Cicero, in the contemporary United States there is wide consensus that one must begin with the text of the enacted provision that is subject to interpretation. The "text" could be something as short as a word, a prepositional phrase, a sentence, or a section of a statute. Within that text are words and punctuation, and there are generally recognized guidelines in the law – known as *canons* – for interpreting certain combinations of them. It is also generally accepted, even by staunch

4 Note that many distinguish "interpreting" and "construing" (e.g., Scalia & Garner, 2012, pp. 13–15; Solum, 2010), but I'm not taking up that issue.

advocates of textualism, that none of these canons is, by itself, dispositive of what the meaning of a text is, that the different canons can cut in different directions and with different weights (e.g., Scalia & Garner, 2012, p. 59; see also Llewellyn, 1950).

Outside the statutory text under consideration, there is a statutory context: other provisions of the same statute and other statutes adopted in the same jurisdiction. Though we could call this *textual context*, I'll refer to it as *intrinsic context*. This terminology will help to distinguish it from context outside the body of statutes enacted in the jurisdiction, what various commentators refer to as extrinsic aids to statutory construction. The latter might include legislative history – reports of the debates and committees in the legislature that led to adoption of the statute – events in the jurisdiction at the time of enactment or interpretation, evidence of the likely consequences of a particular interpretation, and so on.[5] Self-described textualists usually eschew any use of extrinsic context in interpretation of statutes (e.g., Scalia & Garner, 2012). For them, the meaning of a statutory provision, for purposes of applying it as law, can be found *only* in the provision and in its intrinsic context. Unlike Cicero, these jurists permit recourse to extrinsic aids only when the text of the statute is ambiguous, and some of them would prohibit it even then.

As we shall now see, however, while looking at the opinion in *THP I*, even textualist judges are wise to engage in the type of weighing and balancing that Cicero advised.

4.3.1 *The* Texas Health Presbyterian *Litigation and Its Statutory Context*

In the course of the *Texas Health Presbyterian* case, the Texas Court of Appeals in *THP I* (*D.A. v. Texas Health Presbyterian*, 2017) reversed a trial court determination, and the Texas Supreme Court in *THP II* (*Texas Health Presbyterian v. D.A.*, 2018) reversed the appellate court. The factual context of the *THP* case study is a procedure that Dr. Marc Wilson performed in an obstetrics unit during the birth of baby "A.A." An emergency condition during the birth prompted Dr. Wilson's procedure, but he allegedly performed it negligently, injuring A.A. and resulting in long-term effects. The plaintiffs "D.A." and "M.A." were the child's parents, suing on his behalf. For the sake of simplicity, this discussion refers to D.A., M.A., and A.A. as "the plaintiff" and to "Dr. Wilson" and "the defendant" interchangeably, though Texas Health Presbyterian Hospital of Denton and a limited liability company that provided nursing services were also named defendants. At issue was whether the defendant had acted not just negligently, but with "willful and wanton

[5] *Black's Law Dictionary* (Garner, 2019) defines "extrinsic material" as "[i]nformation that is not included in a statute ... subject to interpretation but that may be helpful to understanding its meaning." For a balanced, thorough, and digestible summary of these materials and the other canons commonly in use in contemporary US federal courts, see Brannon (2023).

negligence" (*D.A. v. Texas Health Presbyterian*, 2017, p. 129), causing the injuries to A.A.

"Willful and wanton negligence" is a higher burden of proof for the plaintiff and would protect Dr. Wilson. The Texas Medical Liability Act (Section 74.153) spelled out that the higher standard applied:[6] "[i]n a suit . . . arising out of the provision of emergency medical care in a hospital emergency department or obstetrical unit or in a surgical suite immediately following the evaluation or treatment of a patient in a hospital emergency department." Wilson asserted that because he was rendering "emergency care" during the procedure, and he did so in an obstetrical unit and not a surgical suite, the plaintiff had to meet the willful-and-wanton standard. The plaintiff argued instead that the clause "immediately following the evaluation . . . of a patient in a hospital emergency department" applied to the whole phrase beginning "arising out of . . ."[7] If the plaintiff was correct, the willful-and-wanton standard would not apply to their case. In other words, because A.A. and his mother had never been in the emergency department, they would need to prove only ordinary negligence.

Like many states, Texas has statutes that direct courts how to interpret its statutes, and Texas courts commonly refer to them when interpreting or construing statutory language.[8] The Texas Government Code also permits Texas courts to consider several other "construction aids" – regardless of "whether . . . the statute is considered ambiguous on its face" – including, among others, the "object sought to be attained," "circumstances under which the statute was enacted," "legislative history," and "consequences of a particular construction" (Tex. Gov't Code § 311.023).

4.3.2 *Opinion of Texas Court of Appeals*

In *THP I*, the Appeals Court of Texas reversed the trial court, which had accepted Dr. Wilson's interpretation. The appellate court nodded to the requirement that "the source for legislative intent is found, whenever possible, in the plain language of the statute itself" (*D.A. v. Texas Health Presbyterian*, 2017, p. 433). To assess the plain language of the statute, the court began with the grammar and punctuation of the sentence. It illustrated the potential ambiguity with a diagram, a relatively rare sight in a court opinion (p. 437):

6 The provision appears here as it was when the courts decided *THP I* and *THP II*. The Texas legislature amended the statute in 2019, changing the applicable language. 2019 Tex. Sess. Law Serv. Ch. 1364 (H.B. 2362) (Vernon's).

7 Section 74.001 of the act defined "emergency medical care" as "bona fide emergency services provided after the sudden onset of a medical or traumatic condition manifesting itself by acute symptoms of sufficient severity . . . such that the absence of immediate medical attention could reasonably be expected to result in placing the patient's health in serious jeopardy, serious impairment to bodily functions, or serious dysfunction of any bodily organ or part."

8 See, e.g., *Wal-Mart Stores, Inc. v. Forte* (Tex. 2016); *Atmos Energy Corp. v. Cities of Allen* (Tex. 2011).

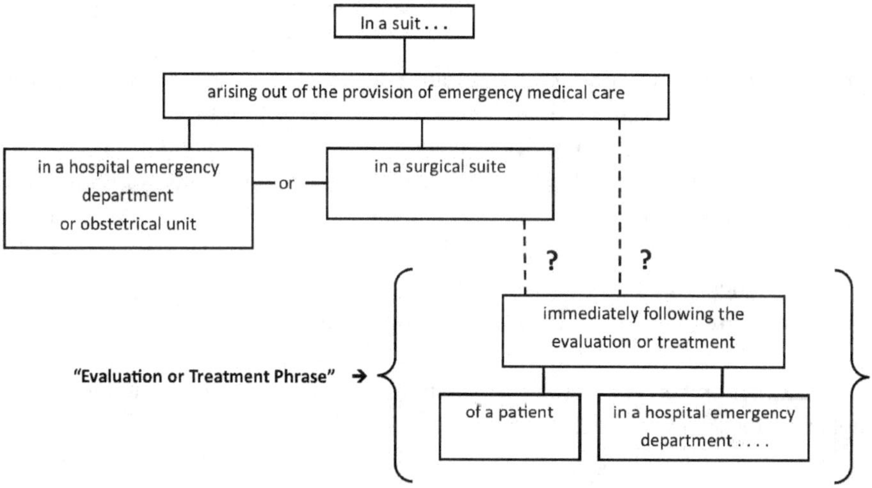

The question marks show the possible points of attachment for the limiting clause, which the court called the "Evaluation or Treatment Phrase": (1) to the participle phrase beginning with "arising" and thus governing all the locations, a reading that would favor the plaintiffs or (2) to the prepositional phrase "in a surgical suite" and governing only it, a reading that would favor Dr. Wilson. The Court of Appeals grappled with the question whether the sentence would have surplus words or absurd consequences if the Evaluation or Treatment Phrase applied to all three locations, with one reading being "arising out of the provision of emergency medical care in a hospital emergency department . . . immediately following . . . treatment of a patient in a hospital emergency department." Wasn't the second "emergency department" redundant or absurd and therefore surplusage under this reading?[9] The Court of Appeals rightly concluded that the two instances were not redundant, as one might receive "emergency medical *care* in a hospital emergency department" only after receiving "*evaluation* . . . in a hospital emergency department." The disjunctive "or" in the Evaluation *or* Treatment Phrase saved the clause from being redundant or absurd under either party's reading of the statute. The court thus concluded that grammar permitted either reading.

To select the correct attachment point, the appeals court then considered four canons of construction: the last-antecedent, series-qualifier, nearest-reasonable-referent, and related-statutes canons, finding the first two did not apply, the third favored Dr. Wilson, and the fourth favored the plaintiff.[10] The last-antecedent canon provides that a "pronoun, relative pronoun, or demonstrative adjective

[9] On the reluctance of courts to regard statutory words as surplus, see the discussion of the surplusage canon below.

[10] The court of appeals erroneously referred to these as "extrinsic aids," but as I noted previously, and also within Scalia and Garner's textualist model discussed below, they are part of the statutory, and therefore *intrinsic*, context.

generally refers to the nearest reasonable antecedent" (Scalia & Garner, 2012, p. 144 [emphasis added]). Because the Evaluation or Treatment Phrase in *THP* was not a pronoun, relative pronoun, or demonstrative adjective, the Texas Court of Appeals concluded that this canon did not apply.

The series-qualifier canon provides that when "there is a straightforward, parallel construction that involves all nouns or verbs in a series, a prepositive or postpositive modifier *normally* applies to the entire series" (Scalia & Garner, 2012, p. 147 [emphasis added]); the nearest-reasonable-referent rule holds that when "the syntax involves something other than a parallel series of nouns or verbs, a prepositive or postpositive modifier *normally* applies only to the nearest reasonable referent" (Scalia & Garner, 2012, p. 152 [emphasis added]). The Court of Appeals noted that the construction here did not involve "all nouns and verbs in a series" and it thus did not apply the series qualifier. Nevertheless, it concluded that the nearest reasonable referent applied, working in favor of Dr. Wilson by limiting the Evaluation or Treatment Phrase only to surgical suites, its nearest reasonable referent.

Finally, the related-statutes canon provides that "affiliated statutes" – the body of law enacted "for the same purpose" – "are to be interpreted together, as though they were one law" (Scalia & Garner, 2012, pp. 252–253). The Texas Court of Appeals carefully examined adjacent portions of the Texas Medical Liability Act, identifying other circumstances that referred to the higher standard of "wanton and willful negligence." In each, the court found that the higher standard of proof against a healthcare provider applied where "the situation presented an emergency requiring medical care by a provider who had no prior knowledge, or realistic opportunity to acquire knowledge, about the patient's history" – that is, the typical emergency room visit (*D.A. v. Texas Health Presbyterian*, 2017, p. 442). Because Dr. Wilson had a prior relationship with the plaintiff, this canon favored the plaintiff.

Taking these facts about the text into account, the court concluded that both potential attachment points for the limiting clause were reasonable (*D.A. v. Texas Health Presbyterian*, 2017, p. 439). In the presence of this ambiguity, the court looked to extrinsic aids in its construction of the statute, as the Texas Government Code had invited it to do (even absent any ambiguity). It relied on an exchange between two state senators while they debated the bill, which "the Senate voted unanimously to publish in the Senate Journal … 'to establish legislative intent regarding'" the statute (*D.A. v. Texas Health Presbyterian*, 2017, p. 442):

SEN. HINOJOSA: [This version of] the bill adds in the words "obstetrical unit" and "surgical suite" to the new section on the standard of proof now required for emergency care. Does this mean that now the higher standard applies to emergency care in these areas of the hospital, not just the emergency room?

SEN. RATLIFF: Only if the same emergency that brought the patient into the ER still exists when the patient gets to the OR or Labor and Delivery area.[11]

The Texas House also published excerpts, including Representative Nixon's unopposed claim that "it is the intent of this legislation that emergency situations [sic] where you do not have a prior relationship with the patient is [sic] the one given the protection" (*D.A. v. Texas Health Presbyterian*, 2017, p. 443).[12] In light of these discussions "about the application of this statute to a fact scenario nearly identical to the one" the appeals court considered, it could not "ignore what plain grammar also [shows] is a reasonable reading of this ambiguous statute." The court concluded that the limiting phrase applied to all three treatment locations, in favor of the plaintiff, and reversed the trial court.

* * *

The appeals court here engaged in practical reason of a kind that Cicero would have recognized. It carefully examined the text and its intrinsic context. The court could have weighed the canon favoring one party more than the one favoring the other and gone either way. But given the uncertainty that remained under those analyses, the court widened the circle of context – as recommended by the Texas Government Code – and found important evidence in the legislative history to support the plaintiff's conclusion. The court showed its work. Throughout this process, the court cited Scalia and Garner's *Reading Law* for their methodology and interpretive method – the self-same methods that textualists urge for legal reasoning – but as we shall see, the Texas Supreme Court later fell prey to Scalia and Garner's *rhetoric about* their methods.

4.4 SCALIA AND GARNER ON INTERPRETING STATUTES

Scalia and Garner published *Reading Law: The Interpretation of Legal Texts* in 2012. The text is influential: As of November 2023, nearly 3,200 court opinions had cited it, often as authority for a court's selection and application of a general principle or canon for statutory interpretation.[13] In *Reading Law*, Scalia and Garner grudgingly acknowledged in descriptions of their methods that often canons must be balanced against each other and weighed with the discretion of the judge. The results are

[11] *Quoting* S.J. of Tex., 78th Leg., R.S. 5003 (2003), www.journals.senate.state.tx.us/sjrnl/78r/pdf/sj06-01-f.pdf.

[12] *Quoting* H.J. of Tex., 78th Leg., R.S. 6041 (2003), www.lrl.state.tx.us/scanned/HouseJournals/78/day84final.pdf.

[13] By comparison, the fifty-year-old landmark reproductive rights case *Roe v. Wade* (U.S. 1973) had been cited in barely 4,500 opinions as of the same date.

necessarily underdeterminate. But when describing those methods, their rhetoric soared in support of deterministic goals. Note here that I'm not attacking textualists for not following their own methods; others have done so, arguing that self-described textualists sneak consequentialist and other non-textualist arguments into their interpretation quite regularly.[14] Instead, I propose to show that textualists using methods on their own terms illustrate Fuller's antinomy: The rhetorical weighing and balancing of the intrinsic tools of textualist statutory interpretation requires some fiat, but textualists' rhetoric about the tools emphasizes claims that their methods result in determinism (Fuller, 1946).

In the introduction of *Reading Law* and its section on fundamental principles, the rhetoric about its methods emphasizes the determinist perspective – that legal questions have right answers and right ways of reaching them. This approach also dominates in the balance of the text, which explores eighteen "semantic" canons, seven "syntactic," and fourteen "contextual" (but always relating to intrinsic context); and twenty-one canons "applicable specifically to" statutes and other enacted law. It continues the trend in its treatment of ambiguity and legislative intent, particularly in the latter part of the book, which "exposes" thirteen "falsities."

As this section shows, *Reading Law*'s rhetoric about its methods is determinist, root and branch. It denies the complexity of the interpretive task using rhetorically effective but rationally questionable arguments. Nevertheless, in statements of principle and in the explanatory notes for almost every one of the canons, *Reading Law* acknowledges that the judge must balance them against each other, addressing those that are applicable and ignoring those that are not. We can account for these acknowledgements, and to an extent the popularity of the book with judges, by noting that Scalia and Garner meant the text to be a handbook for those actually engaged in statutory construction.[15] Tellingly, *Reading Law* describes the canons only in isolation and provides no advice to the reader about how to balance them. As the case study in this chapter shows, the result is that judges must often choose between results that would be equally plausible but for the judge's decision to weigh one canon more than another – or not – much as the Texas Court of Appeals did in *THP I*. The denial of this reality results in opinions like that of the Texas Supreme Court in *THP II*, which I take up in Part 2 of the case study.

4.4.1 *Fundamental Principles*

From the very beginning, *Reading Law* emphasizes the determinist perspective. It provides a long block quotation from a law professor writing nearly 100 years earlier and asserting that "the demand for *certainty* and predictability requires an *objective basis* for interpretation" (Scalia & Garner, 2012, p. 34 [emphasis added]).

[14] For a recent example, see Krishnakumar (2024).

[15] Note that book also covers contractual language, but that is not the focus here.

Immediately after that quote, Scalia and Garner (2012, p. 34 [emphasis added]) emphasized those words: Professor "De Sloovere . . . was right to insist on *certainty, predictability, objectivity*, reasonableness, rationality, and regularity." They claimed that "most interpretive questions have a right answer" and that "[v]ariability in interpretation is a distemper" (p. 6). And they used the language of determinism when, for example, they claimed that "we will *demonstrate* . . . [that] the textualist routinely takes purpose into account, but in its concrete manifestations as *deduced* from close reading of the text" (p. 20 [emphasis added]).

Nevertheless, the book struggles to maintain the determinist imaginary in the face of practical constraints: It asserts that its methods provide determinist answers, but it must in many cases acknowledge the underdeterminacy of those self-same answers and that its methods might justify more than one outcome. Scalia and Garner's solution was, on the one hand, to use a strongly deterministic rhetoric when describing their approach, and even particular canons. On the other hand, their blackletter[16] characterizations of the canons and occasional acknowledgments quietly (and fairly) allow for the contingency that is inherent in natural language – in other words, for underdeterminacy.

For example, they began their exposition of their method with a series of "fundamental principles" that represent the foundation of their approach. *Reading Law* (Scalia & Garner, 2012) sets each off in its own short section. Two of the first three begin with blackletter maxims or headings that seem quite underdeterministic:

1. Interpretation Principle: Every application of a text to particular circumstances entails interpretation. (p. 53)
2. Supremacy-of-Text Principle: The words of a governing text are of paramount concern, and what they convey, *in their context*, is what the text means. (p. 56 [emphasis added])
3. Principle of Interrelating Canons: *No canon of interpretation is absolute* [emphasis added]. Each may be overcome by the strength of differing principles. (p. 59)

We expect the content of each section to develop the subject in the heading, but the book does so in a complicated way.

The whole description of the principle in section 1 and at least the clauses in sections 2 and 3 that I have italicized here seem to acknowledge that there will be underdeterministic practical reasoning going on. The text that follows these headings in sections 1 and 3, however, works hard to undermine the underdeterminacy implied by the headings. Section 1 quotes nineteenth-century legal theorist

16 Blackletter statements are common in legal treatises such as Scalia and Garner's, where the principle of law appears at a section's beginning in bold type. The rest of the plain-type text explains or justifies the main principle. This approach also appeals to the reader's sense that blackletter principles are settled and not subject to dispute.

Frederick Pollock (1896): "Given a rule of law that [those] conditions generically described as A produce a certain legal liability or other consequence X, does the specific fact or group of facts *n* fall within the genus A?" (Scalia & Garner, 2012, p. 54). Scalia and Garner gave that passage this gloss: "You read an authoritative legal text to discover A (a major premise). You find facts to discover *n* (the minor premise). Then you draw your conclusion" (p. 54). In other words, Scalia and Garner reconfigured the *interpretation* referred to in the section heading as a *deduction*.

Section 2, which has the blackletter maxim that seems most determinist, asserts that extrinsic context (such as legislative history) is an unacceptable aid. The text of this section is among Scalia and Garner's most determinist, asserting that "the purpose must be defined *precisely*" and as "*concretely* as possible, *not abstractly*," and that "purpose ... *cannot be used to contradict text or to supplement it*" (Scalia & Garner, 2012, pp. 56–57 [emphases added]).

Though the blackletter statement that begins section 3 seems highly underdeterministic, most of its text argues against the view that the canons have no value and for the view that they restrain prejudice and provide near-certainty. Scalia and Garner's conclusion, quoting Bishop (1882), is that "[t]he sound view is that 'statutory interpretation is *covered as absolutely by rules* as anything else in the law'" (Scalia & Garner, 2012, p. 61 [emphasis added]). *Reading Law* argues that the canons are stable, and it claims – without any argument or support – that "[t]hey *should* be stable ... despite the efforts of many moderns to destabilize them" (p. 62).

Importantly, these fundamental-principle sections offer brief nods to reality: "Yes, [the canons] can be abused, but every useful tool can be abused," and "This is not to say that it is always clear what results the principles *produce*" (Scalia & Garner, 2012, p. 61). But *Reading Law* provides absolutely no guidance how the judge should mediate or weigh the interaction of the canons pointing in different directions, probably because acknowledging the necessity of that process would emphasize the underdeterminacy of the result.

4.4.2 *Complexity and Its Denial*

Reading Law continues these practices of emphasizing determinism while scantly acknowledging markers of underdeterminism, including in its presentation of the canons and its treatment of ambiguity and legislative history. Throughout its discussion of the canons of interpretation, the book exhibits the tension between determinist rhetoric and underdeterminist reality. But because *THP* implicates particular canons, I will discuss several of them briefly: the grammar, last-antecedent, series-qualifier, nearest-reasonable-referent, punctuation, surplusage, interpretive-direction, and related-statutes canons. I add some notes about Scalia and Garner's stance on the use of legislative history.

The blackletter of *Reading Law*'s grammar canon provides: "Words are to be given the meaning that proper grammar and usage would assign them" (Scalia &

Garner, 2012, p. 140). As to punctuation, it "is a permissible indicator of meaning" (p. 161). The text of the grammar section begins: "Judges rightly presume ... that legislators understand [grammar]. No matter how often the accuracy, indeed the plausibility, of this presumption is cast in doubt by legislators' oral pronouncements, when it comes to what legislators enact, the presumption is *unshakable*" (p. 140 [emphasis added]). But a paragraph later, it acknowledges that "[t]he presumption of legislative literacy is a *rebuttable* one; like all the other canons, this one can be overcome by other textual indications of meaning" (p. 140 [emphasis added]). The presumption is both unshakable and rebuttable? *Reading Law* also notes that "some grammatical principles are weaker than others" (p. 142). Meanwhile, the section on the punctuation canon makes an extended argument for the permissibility of the use of punctuation in interpretation, again apparently relying on the literacy of legislators. Nowhere does it suggest the punctuation is a *conclusive* aid to interpretation. Nowhere in these sections is there guidance about which grammatical principles and punctuation rules are stronger and how one should weigh them against each other or against other canons.

The last-antecedent canon has been criticized by linguists and legal theorists (e.g., Kimble, 2017). *Reading Law* states the blackletter principle simply: "A pronoun, relative pronoun, or demonstrative adjective *generally* refers to the nearest reasonable antecedent" (Scalia & Garner, 2012, p. 144 [emphasis added]). As the "generally" in the blackletter statement would suggest, the last paragraph of the section contains a "caveat," that this "canon may be superseded by another grammatical convention" (p. 146). We receive an example but may be left wondering, are there others? I presented the series-qualifier and the nearest-reasonable-referent canons in part 1 of the case study (Section 4.3). Again, after many easy cases given as examples discussing those canons, *Reading Law* admits: "Perhaps more than most of the other canons, [these two are] highly sensitive to context" and "subject to defeasance by other canons" (p. 150). By which canons, and under which circumstances, it does not say.

Under the surplusage canon, "*[i]f possible*, every word and every provision is to be given effect ... None should *needlessly* be given an interpretation that causes it to duplicate another provision or to have no consequence" (Scalia & Garner, 2012, p. 174 [emphasis added]). Again, I highlight the words "if possible" and "needlessly" here to emphasize the contingency of this canon, and one would expect a court disregarding a word as surplus should explain the need. In fact, *Reading Law* provides an example: In *Moskal v. United States* (1990), a majority of the Supreme Court concluded that "falsely made" meant something other than "forged, altered, or counterfeited" on grounds that if "falsely made" meant the same as "forged" in this list, it would be surplus. In dissent, Scalia maintained "falsely made" *did* mean "forged" and blistered that the "entire phrase is *self-evidently* not a listing of differing and precisely calibrated terms, but a collection of near synonyms" (Scalia & Garner, 2012, p. 178 [emphasis added]). By "self-evidently," Scalia meant that he didn't think his view needed explanation. But departing from this canon seems to demand it.

The related-statutes canon provides that "affiliated statutes" – the body of law enacted "for the same purpose" – "are to be interpreted together, as though they were one law" (Scalia & Garner, 2012, pp. 252–253). It is important to note that for Scalia and Garner, related statutes are not an extrinsic aid to interpretation. They are part of the same body of statutes in the same jurisdiction. Again, the authors acknowledged that "[t]he critical questions are these: Just how affiliated must 'affiliated' [statutes] be, and what purposes are the same? The cases provide – properly in our view – a good deal of leeway" (Scalia & Garner, 2012, p. 253). And again, there are no guidelines here.

The interpretive-direction canon acknowledges that legislatures sometimes provide some interpretive machinery of their own, defining terms they use in statutes and even providing interpretive guidance. These provisions are enacted law just as much as the statutes they are to help interpret. "Definition sections and interpretation clauses are to be carefully followed" (Scalia & Garner, 2012, p. 225) according to the blackletter, but the section that follows includes Scalia and Garner's lengthy ruminations on the limits of the ability of legislatures to adopt statutes that dictate how they want their own statutes to be interpreted. *Reading Law* asserts there are many such limits, but often without supporting arguments and often with the only authority supporting them being a few citations to law-review articles. Again, the reader receives mixed signals, as if the authors are saying: "Carefully follow interpretation clauses, but we'll let you know when they go too far."

In addition to canons that *Reading Law* endorses, it abjures some interpretive tools, including legislative history. It is a common perception among attorneys that one either should not consider legislative history – an extrinsic aid to interpretation – at all or that one should consider it only if the statutory text is ambiguous. *Reading Law* does not adopt the view that "[w]hen the words of a statute are unambiguous, [the] first canon is also the last: 'judicial inquiry is complete'" (*Connecticut National Bank v. Germain*, 1992, p. 254). In fact, the treatise suggests that the question of ambiguity is not a central one and can usually be resolved by selecting the proper word sense.[17] It argues instead that problems consistently arise from "vagueness."[18] It urges that "[m]ost interpretive canons apply to both ambiguity . . . and vagueness" (Scalia & Garner, 2012, p. 33), though it does not say which ones do not apply or when.

[17] E.g., "*[T]able* could refer either to a piece of furniture or to a numerical chart" (Scalia & Garner, 2012, p. 31).

[18] "A word or phrase is ambiguous when the question is which of two or more meanings applies; it is vague when its unquestionable meaning has uncertain application to various factual situations" (Scalia & Garner, 2012, p. 32).

One controversial view that *Reading Law* firmly espouses is that legislative history, an extrinsic aid to interpretation, should never be used.[19] Well, almost never: The treatise acknowledges the utility of history as evidence "establishing linguistic usage" at the time of the enactment or for showing that an interpretation by the court is not absurd if even one legislator maintained that view in the legislative history (Scalia & Garner, 2012, p. 388). But a section making up nearly 5 percent of the book's pages appeals to judges to avoid it in all other cases.

* * *

Scalia and Garner peppered their exposition of the canons with assertions of determinism and self-evidence, especially in the excerpts of Scalia's own opinions. But as I have shown, their treatise acknowledges – indeed, must acknowledge – several things: First, canons compete, and their weighting when they do is uncertain. Second, canons' presumptions are rebuttable, though it is unclear when. Third, canons require conduct only generally or abjure it only when it is needless. Fourth, canons are sensitive to context, though how sensitive and to how great a context is uncertain. And finally, the statutes' own internal rules for interpretation work only to an extent, but to what extent, it is hard so say.

If we take at face value the canons as *Reading Law* explains them, they are at best a checklist of lenses through which courts should view an interpretation problem, rules of thumb to solve a problem that will require the give and take of practical reason, the result of which is often – if not always – underdeterminate. They are a complex toolset for judges, requiring subtle judgments so difficult to balance that *Reading Law* does not even try. But its rhetoric *about* the canons is consistently determinist.

Cicero, the Texas Court of Appeals, and the explanations of *Reading Law* seem to be in complete agreement (with the exception of legislative history): Interpreting statues is a complicated act of practical reasoning, rarely resolved by any zinger of a rule. Though the Texas Court of Appeals seemed to understand the underdeterminate reality in *THP I* and showed its work, the Texas Supreme Court instead embraced the determinist rhetoric of *Reading Law* when it decided *THP II*.

4.5 CASE STUDY: PART 2

The Texas Supreme Court reversed the appeals court's decision in *THP II* (*Texas Health Presbyterian v. D.A.*, 2018, p. 137). The Supreme Court stepped through the facts of the case and the procedural history at the trial court and Court of Appeals. The Supreme Court disposed of Dr. Wilson's arguments based on the punctuation

[19] For the contrary view, see the concurrence of Justice Stevens in *Connecticut Nat. Bank* (1990, p. 255), arguing that "[w]henever there is some uncertainty about the meaning of a statute, it is prudent to examine its legislative history."

and nearest-reasonable-referent canons, concluding that it was "left with an unpunctuated phrase containing a modifier that – in light of its location within the phrase – could modify the entire series or only the last item in the series" (p. 132). It nevertheless concluded there are "two features that make the family's construction unreasonable" (p. 133). The first is the location of the clause "in a" in the text, which the court illustrated by parsing the text in the way that Dr. Wilson would:

[1] ***in a*** hospital
  [a] emergency department or
  [b] obstetrical unit or
[2] ***in a*** surgical suite immediately following the evaluation or treatment of a patient in a hospital emergency department.

And in the way that the plaintiff would:

[1] ***in a***
  [a] hospital emergency department or
  [b] obstetrical unit or
  [c] ***in a*** surgical suite
[2] immediately following the evaluation or treatment of a patient in a hospital emergency department.[20]

The court concluded that the plaintiff's reading required it to ignore the second "in a," violating the surplusage canon and, with reference to Scalia and Garner, the nearest-reasonable-referent canon. The court accepted Dr. Wilson's reading of the clause, claiming "[i]t simply permits no other reasonable reading."

The court nevertheless considered a second reason, grounded solely in the clause they interpreted. The reason was that the plaintiff's reading required the court to accept a gloss of the statute it deemed nonsensical: "treatment in a hospital emergency department . . . immediately following . . . treatment of a patient in a hospital emergency department" (*Texas Health Presbyterian v. D.A.*, 2018, p. 134). It failed to note the Court of Appeals' conclusion that the "or" between "evaluation" and "treatment" permitted this gloss: "treatment in a hospital emergency department . . . immediately following the evaluation . . . of a patient in a hospital emergency department." Given that treatment, even in the ER, always follows some kind of evaluation or assessment of the patient's condition, this gloss seems quite reasonable. Nevertheless, the Supreme Court concluded that the plaintiff's reading "would create a redundancy that deprives the phrase of any linguistic sense" (p. 135).

The Supreme Court entirely ignored the appeals court's use of the related-statutes canon, failing to account for evidence in other sections of the same statute that it is meant to protect doctors providing emergency care who have no familiarity with their patients. It did, however, expressly discount the appeals court's and the family's

[20] The emphasis in these two excerpts reproduces the Texas Supreme Court's in the original.

use of legislative history: "[T]he family relies heavily on statements individual legislators made during floor debates" (*Texas Health Presbyterian v. D.A.*, 2018, p. 136). The court responded that "statements explaining *an individual legislator's* intent cannot reliably describe the *legislature's intent.*" Here, though, the court relegated to a footnote the fact – pointed out in the appeals court decision – that the exchange between Senators Hinojosa and Ratliff appeared in the Senate report only after *unanimous consent* of the Senate, a threshold higher than the majority required to pass the statute in the first place.

4.6 RESTRAINT AND TRADITION

Reading Law argues throughout its length for an approach to judicial decision-making on grounds that it promotes judicial restraint and supports democratic values and that it enacts traditional jurisprudence. Judicial restraint is part of a story in the determinist imaginary that in the mid-twentieth century judges moved away from the principles Scalia and Garner espoused, and the result "has weakened our democratic processes, and has distorted our system of government checks and balances" (Scalia & Garner, 2012, p. xxvii). They claimed that "nontextual means of interpretation ... erode society's confidence in a rule of law that evidently has no agreed-upon meaning" (p. xxviii). Of course, by telling that story, they simultaneously responded to and helped to perpetuate populist beliefs that judges should not exercise discretion in applying the law, that they should do only what the text of the law demands.

But Scalia and Garner (2012) also had to acknowledge that textualist judges can abuse their discretion as can non-textualist judges. They claimed that "in a textualist culture, the distortion of the willful judge is much more transparent, and the dutiful judge is never *invited* to pursue the purposes and consequences he [sic] prefers" (Scalia & Garner, 2012, p. 17). The transparency they asserted seems to require that if a court draws a practical conclusion, it should provide considerable explanation for the public, other judges, and lawyers to understand how it reached that conclusion (Larson, 2022). The Texas Court of Appeals and Texas Supreme Court in *THP* were both textualist-minded courts, given that both liberally cited Scalia and Garner. But the Texas Court of Appeals showed its practical reasoning, balancing the arguments of the parties and its own inventive efforts, while the Texas Supreme Court ignored or misconstrued arguments in its effort to give a conclusive answer based on questionable grammatical analysis.

The Texas Supreme Court embraced the determinist imaginary, just as Scalia had in his own opinion-writing, where he often claimed his answers were self-evident. Unfortunately, his example and the impulse to make conclusions sound determinist have worked to obscure courts' reasons, as *THP II* showed. Rather than showing their work as they evaluated and balanced the canons, they often claimed abruptly that one is determinative. The Supreme Court's opinion in *THP II* represents what even Scalia and Garner might call a "crabbed" reading that hangs on deterministic conclusions about the meaning of the text based on contestable grammatical claims. Citing *Reading Law*, the court did not employ the balancing that the treatise's explanations counseled, and it failed to consider the intrinsic context of the related-statutes canon or the wider extrinsic context of the legislative history, which the legislature had invited it to do. It is difficult to describe *THP II* as more restrained than *THP I*.

Scalia and Garner further propped up the determinist imaginary with frequent appeals to a tradition before the twentieth century, where they said judges behaved according to their standards. But some of their appeals to tradition seem to cut both ways, and in other cases they proposed *abandoning* the old ways. *Reading Law* relies on frequent claims about the historicity of its approach, claiming that today "judicial invention replaces what used to be an all-but-universal means of understanding enacted texts [resulting in] the distortion of our system of democratic government" (Scalia & Garner, 2012, p. xxviii). It asserts that its "approach is consistent with what the best legal thinkers have said for centuries" (p. xxix) and – without argument or citation to support this claim – that textualism's "principal tenets have guided the interpretation of legal texts for centuries" (p. 16).

Reading Law frequently quotes and cites authorities from around the time of the framing of the US Constitution as supporting its views, but these examples cut both ways. For example, Scalia and Garner began their arguments against using legislative history with a block quotation from William Blackstone, the eighteenth-century British jurist whose *Commentaries* had a profound influence on judges for more than 100 years and which appeared in its first American edition shortly before the Revolution. The beginning of the Blackstone quotation says that the interpreter should look for legislators' intentions in "*signs* the most natural and probable" (Scalia & Garner, 2012, p. 369).[21] What seems surprising, however, is that Scalia and Garner continued the quotation: "these signs are either the words, the context, the subject matter, the effects and consequence, or the spirit and reason of the law." The consequences and spirit of the law, however, have no place in Scalia and Garner's interpretive scheme.

Scalia and Garner (2012) also needed to abjure certain judicial traditions that were current at the time of the framing, which *Reading Law* usually does without supporting argument. It admits, for example, that judges had both legislative and judicial powers in England and before the US Constitution. Scalia and Garner (2012, p. 4) complained that "[s]ome judges, however, refuse to yield the ancient judicial prerogative of making the law, improvising on the text to produce what they deem socially desirable results." To support their assertion that judges should only interpret and not make law, they pointed to Article III of the Constitution. But the Constitution says only that "[t]he judicial Power of the United States, shall be vested

[21] *Quoting* William Blackstone (1770, p. 59).

in one Supreme Court, and in such inferior Courts as the Congress may from time to time ordain and establish" and says nothing in derogation of the common-law equity or law-making powers of courts.

Reading Law supports the determinist imaginary by picking and choosing from among the forms of restraint and legal traditions only those that support its story.

* * *

Cicero (1949) on the one hand and Scalia and Garner (2012) on the other both counsel judges to explore thoroughly the intrinsic context of a text. Cicero and the Texas legislature also counseled interpreters to use rhetorical knowledge from broader, extrinsic contexts, such as legislative history and considerations of equity. The Texas Court of Appeals in the *Texas Health Presbyterian* case exhibited these characteristics of judging well, taking "perfect reason" as far as it could go with grammar and punctuation and then balancing considerations derived from broader contexts, intrinsic *and* extrinsic. Even if we set aside the extrinsic aid of legislative history, the appeals court could have concluded for either party based on its analysis. The Supreme Court, on the other hand – licensed by the determinist imaginary and by Scalia and Garner's rhetoric *about* legal reasoning – concluded based only on a questionable application of one canon and an erroneous application of grammatical rules that there was only one possible conclusion.

To be clear, I don't argue that either court could not reasonably have concluded as it did in *THP*.[22] The problem is rather that the Supreme Court, trying "to promise unequivocal, correct results" (Hohmann, 2006, p. 194), deprived the parties and the broader audience of citizens of Texas of a more thoughtful analysis, one that accounted for all the context that judging well requires. For fear of admitting the antinomy of "fiat" and "reason," the court dressed its opinion in the rhetoric of certainty. Judging well requires more.

The remedy to this concern is not in particular courts' opinions, but rather in the professional and public rhetoric surrounding judicial decision-making. Those who embrace Scalia and Garner's rhetoric *about* legal reasoning, without admitting the contingencies that even Scalia and Garner must acknowledge *within* legal reasoning – and its need for rhetorical invention – fail to embrace the legacy of judging well that the West can inherit from Cicero.

REFERENCES

Aristotle. (1934). *The Nicomachean ethics* (H. Rackham, Trans.; 2nd ed.). Harvard University Press. (Original work published fourth century BCE.)

[22] In 2019, the Texas legislature amended Section 74.153, and the relevant clause now reads "arising out of the provision of emergency medical care in a hospital emergency department, in an obstetrical unit, or in a surgical suite immediately following the evaluation or treatment of a patient in a hospital emergency department," apparently siding with the plaintiff here against the Supreme Court.

(2007). *On rhetoric: A theory of civic discourse* (G. A. Kennedy, Trans.; 2nd ed.). Oxford University Press. (Original work published fourth century BCE.)

Atmos Energy Corp. v. Cities of Allen, 353 S.W.3d 156 (Tex. 2011).

Balkin, J. (2009). Critical legal theory today. In F. J. Mootz, III (Ed.), *On philosophy in American law* (pp. 64–72). Cambridge University Press.

Bencze, M., & Ng, G. Y. (2018). Measuring the unmeasurable? In M. Bencze & G. Y. Ng (Eds.), *How to measure the quality of judicial reasoning* (pp. 1–23). Springer International. https://doi.org/10.1007/978-3-319-97316-6_1

Bishop, J. P. (1882). *Commentaries on the written laws and their interpretation*. Boston, Little, Brown. http://archive.org/details/cu31924018806764 [https://perma.cc/6GMJ-49Y9]

Bix, B. H. (2022). Practical reasoning and the communicative model of law. In T. Gizbert-Studnicki, F. Poggi, & I. Skoczen (Eds.), *Interpretivism and the limits of law* (pp. 12–22). Edward Elgar.

Blackstone, W. (1770). *Commentaries on the laws of England* (4th ed., Vol. 1). Clarendon Press.

Brannon, V. C. (2023). *Statutory interpretation: Theories, tools, and trends* (R45153). Congressional Research Service. https://crsreports.congress.gov/product/pdf/R/R45153 [https://perma.cc/JUX6-WXXC]

Burton, S. J. (1989). Law as practical reason. *Southern California Law Review*, *62*(3–4), 747–793.

Camper, M. (2018). *Arguing over texts: The rhetoric of interpretation*. Oxford University Press.

Cicero. (1949). *Cicero II: De inventione, de optimo genere oratorum, topica* (H. M. Hubbell, Trans.). Harvard University Press. (Original work published first century BCE.)

Connecticut National. Bank v. Germain, 503 U.S. 249 (1992).

D.A. v. Texas Health Presbyterian Hospital of Denton, 514 S.W.3d 431 (Tex. App. – Fort Worth 2017).

Eisgruber, C. L. M. (1988). Justice Story, slavery, and the natural law foundations of American constitutionalism. *University of Chicago Law Review*, *55*, 273–327.

Fuller, L. L. (1946). Reason and fiat in case law. *Harvard Law Review*, *59*(3), 376–395. https://doi.org/10.2307/1335588

Garner, B. A., ed. (2019). *Black's law dictionary* (11th ed.). Thomson Reuters.

Hohmann, H. (2006). Ciceronian rhetoric and the law. In V. Cox & J. O. Ward (Eds.), *The rhetoric of Cicero in its medieval and early Renaissance commentary tradition* (pp. 193–207). Koninklijke Brill.

Kant, E. (1909). *Kant's critique of practical reason and other works on the theory of ethics* (T. K. Abbott, Trans.; 6th ed.). Longmans, Green. (Original work published 1788.)

Kimble, J. (2017). The doctrine of the last antecedent: A case study in flimsiness. *Legal Communication & Rhetoric: JALWD*, *14*, 130–134.

Krishnakumar, A. S. (2024). Textualism in practice. *Duke Law Journal*, *74*(3), 573–679. https://scholarship.law.duke.edu/dlj/vol74/iss3/1

Larson, B. N. (2019). Law's enterprise: Argumentation schemes & legal analogy. *University of Cincinnati Law Review*, *87*(3), 663–721.

(2022). Endogenous and dangerous. *Nevada Law Journal*, *22*(2), 739–802.

Larson, B. N., & Tiscione, K. K. (2024). Classical rhetoric: Then and now. In F. J. Mootz, III, K. A. Davis, B. N. Larson, & K. Tiscione (Eds.), *Classical rhetoric & contemporary law: A critical reader* (pp. 11–25). University of Alabama Press.

Llewellyn, K. N. (1950). Remarks on the theory of appellate decision and the rules or canons about how statutes are to be construed. *Vanderbilt Law Review*, *3*, 395–406.

Mootz, F. J., III. (2018). Judging well. *Washington University Jurisprudence Review*, *11*(1), 1–37.

Moskal v. United States, 498 U.S. 103 (1990).
Plato. (2004). *Gorgias* (W. Hamilton & C. Emlyn-Jones, Trans.; Rev. ed.). Penguin. (Original work published fourth century BCE.)
Pollock, F. (1896). *A first book of jurisprudence for students of the common law*. Macmillan.
Roberts, J. (2005). *Chief Justice Roberts statement – Nomination process*. United States Courts. www.uscourts.gov/educational-resources/educational-activities/chief-justice-roberts-statement-nomination-process [https://perma.cc/DYM2-VREZ]
Robinson, W. C. (1893). *Forensic oratory: A manual for advocates*. Little, Brown.
Roe v. Wade, 410 U.S. 113 (1973).
Scalia, A., & Garner, B. A. (2012). *Reading law: The interpretation of legal texts*. Thomson West.
Solum, L. B. (2010). The interpretation–construction distinction. *Constitutional Commentary*, 27, 95–118.
Taylor, C. (2004). *Modern social imaginaries*. Duke University Press.
Texas Health Presbyterian Hospital of Denton v. D.A., 569 S.W.3d 126 (Tex. 2018).
Texas Government Code § 311.023.
Texas Medical Liability Act, Tex. Civ. Prac. & Rem. Code §§ 74.001–74.507.
The Greek Sophists. (2003). (J. Dillon & T. Gergel, Trans.). Penguin.
U.S. Constitution art. III, § 1.
Wal-Mart Stores, Inc. v. Forte, 497 S.W.3d 460 (Tex. 2016).

PART III

Façade of Neutrality

5

Deciphering *Dobbs*

Syllogism and Enthymeme in Contemporary Legal Discourse

Susan Tanner

The syllogism is at the heart of legal reasoning. Many law students have heard some variation of this claim. Many law professors have repeated it. So foundational is this concept that Justice Scalia and Bryan Garner (2008, p. 41) argue that "the most rigorous form of logic, and hence the most persuasive, is the syllogism." But the syllogism offers a very limited lens onto legal argumentation. The syllogism merely provides a framework for ascribing logical structure to propositional statements; the enthymeme serves as a bridge between logic and persuasion, playing a crucial role in how arguments are presented and understood in the legal context.

The syllogism, as Aristotle elaborates particularly in his *Prior Analytics* (1989), is a form of deductive reasoning where a conclusion is logically derived from two given premises. For instance, in a classic syllogism, from the premises "All humans are mortal" and "Socrates is a human," one deduces the conclusion "Socrates is mortal." This structure is key to formal logic, where the conclusion necessarily flows from the premises. The enthymeme, discussed in Aristotle's *Rhetoric* (2004), mirrors the syllogistic structure but with one key difference: One of the premises is implied rather than explicitly stated, relying on the audience's inference. For example, the statement "Socrates is mortal because he is human" implies the general principle that all humans are mortal, without stating it outright. Thus, the enthymeme is often characterized as a truncated or incomplete syllogism.

However, it is important to recognize that the enthymeme is not a deficient form of syllogism. Rather, it serves as a parallel construct in the domain of contingent truths and persuasive argumentation. While syllogisms are appropriate in environments of certainty or agreed-upon premises, enthymemes are appropriate for the domain of legal argumentation, where premises are often subject to interpretation and debate, and all the logically necessary premises cannot be fully articulated.

Understanding the enthymeme's role in legal argumentation is particularly important when examining cases like *Dobbs v. Jackson Women's Health Organization* (2022). This case provides a compelling study of how enthymematic reasoning shapes legal discourse and decision-making. The leaked draft opinion and the final decision, authored by Justice Alito, demonstrate how unarticulated societal values and assumptions underpin judicial reasoning. The majority opinion's reliance on a historical and originalist interpretation of the Constitution, while ignoring the historical lack of representation of women and minorities, demonstrates the rhetorical effect of implicit premises on judicial reasoning.

5.1 THE ENTHYMEME

In Aristotle's framework, enthymemes are closely related to syllogisms, sharing several key characteristics and a similar form, but inhabiting different domains. Aristotle's treatment of these forms in his works on logic and rhetoric reveals their complementary nature. While he categorizes "examples" as a rhetorical form of induction, he identifies the "enthymeme" as a variant of the syllogism, which he further characterizes as a "rhetorical syllogism." This distinction is crucial in understanding Aristotle's conception of enthymemes as not merely logical constructs but as tools adeptly suited for the art of persuasion.

Aristotle posits that the essence of rhetoric lies in its focus on modes of persuasion, which he equates to a form of demonstration (Aristotle, 2004). Persuasion, in his view, is most effective when an argument is not only formally valid but also perceived as having been demonstrably proven. This perspective is where the enthymeme's significance in rhetoric comes to the fore. Unlike the syllogism, which is primarily concerned with the logical structuring of premises leading to a conclusion, the enthymeme incorporates this logical framework within a rhetorical context. It is designed to persuade by presenting a logical argument where at least one premise is typically left unstated yet understood by the audience. This characteristic of the enthymeme makes it a powerful tool in rhetoric, as it engages the audience's own beliefs and knowledge to fill in the gaps, thereby making the argument more relatable and convincing.

Aristotle's emphasis on the enthymeme in rhetoric highlights its dual nature, combining the rigors of logical reasoning with the art of persuasive communication. This dual nature allows the enthymeme to be more adaptable and context-sensitive compared to the more rigid structure of the syllogism. In rhetorical discourse (including law), this adaptability makes the enthymeme particularly effective, as it can be tailored to the specific beliefs, values, and knowledge of a particular audience, thereby enhancing the persuasive impact of the argument. Thus, in Aristotle's view, the enthymeme stands as one of the most convincing modes of persuasion, embodying the intersection of logical reasoning and the art of persuasion in a manner uniquely suited to the objectives of rhetorical discourse (Aristotle, 2004). He goes on to say:

> The enthymeme is a sort of syllogism, and the consideration of syllogisms of all kinds, without distinction, is the business of dialectic, either of dialectic as a whole or of one of its branches. It follows plainly, therefore, that he who is best able to see

> how and from what elements a syllogism is produced will also be best skilled in the enthymeme, when he has further learnt what its subject-matter is and in what respects it differs from the syllogism of strict logic. The true and the approximately true are apprehended by the same faculty; it may also be noted that men have a sufficient natural instinct for what is true, and usually do arrive at the truth. Hence the man who makes a good guess at truth is likely to make a good guess at probabilities. (Aristotle, 2004, p. 3)

For those who teach legal reasoning through syllogism, it is reassuring to know that these processes are not entirely separate entities. According to Aristotle, understanding formal logic indeed aids in grasping quasi-logical reasoning. So, if the purposes are similar, the capacity for creating them is similar, and the form is similar, then why is Aristotle so careful to separate them in his taxonomy? In short, because syllogisms and enthymemes inhabit different domains. Syllogisms belong to the domains of philosophy and science, of dialectic and proof. Enthymemes belong to the domains of law and politics, of contingent truths and political philosophies.

But while Aristotle it careful to explain that the pursuits of man are not concerned with universal truths, he does not go so far as to accept a worldview that we would now categorize as postmodern – one where all truth is contingent and where all logical arguments are necessarily predicated on faulty understanding or deception and where emotional or manipulative arguments share the same status as arguments that attempt an internal logical consistency. He argues for the primacy of a particular mode of rhetorical argument, one that privileges logic above emotional appeals, at least for legal discourse. He says:

> Now, the framers of the current treatises on rhetoric have constructed but a small portion of that art. The modes of persuasion are the only true constituents of the art: everything else is merely accessory. These writers, however, say nothing about enthymemes, which are the substance of rhetorical persuasion, but deal mainly with non-essentials . . . It is not right to pervert the judge by moving him to anger or envy or pity – one might as well warp a carpenter's rule before using it. Again, a litigant has clearly nothing to do but to show that the alleged fact is so or is not so, that it has or has not happened. As to whether a thing is important or unimportant, just or unjust, the judge must surely refuse to take his instructions from the litigants: he must decide for himself all such points as the law-giver has not already defined for him. (Aristotle, 2004, p. 2)

It is this vision of the purpose of the enthymeme that many legal rhetoric scholars would readily adopt: an informal logic that aspires to logical certainty – one that avoids the dangers of undignified appeals to *pathos* and reproduces facts so that a judge may make a reasoned determination. A conservative reimagining of the structure of legal argumentation might acknowledge that, at the very least, legal arguments are advanced through enthymemes of the form described above, rather than through syllogisms. This acknowledgment would represent a significant shift in the understanding of legal reasoning, as it would move away from the purely logical and formalistic view of the law.

5.2 ENTHYMEME IN LEGAL ARGUMENTATION

The seemingly infallible logical and quasi-scientific structure of the syllogism is what has endeared it so deeply to those who seek to make legal argumentation seem a formalistic pursuit. This deep-rooted affinity for the syllogism in legal circles is not merely due to its logical rigor but also because it offers an appearance of objectivity in legal reasoning. By framing legal arguments within a syllogistic structure, there is an implication that judicial decisions are the product of a straightforward, almost mechanical, process of logical deduction. This perspective is attractive in the legal field as it suggests that conclusions in legal matters are derived from a clear, rational process, minimizing the perception of subjectivity or bias. The syllogism, in this sense, is seen as a tool that distills complex legal arguments into a format that is both logically sound and ostensibly impartial. This approach aligns well with the desire in legal practice to portray the law as a system based on reason and universal principles, rather than one influenced by the whims and biases of individuals.

When explaining legal reasoning, law professors often map the well-known IRAC model (Issue, Rule, Application, and Conclusion) onto the syllogistic structure. In this model, the "Rule" represents the general law or legal principle applicable to the case at hand, forming the major premise of the syllogism. The "Application" involves an analysis of how this rule pertains to the specifics of the case, serving as the minor premise. And the "Conclusion" provides a resolution to the issue at hand, effectively acting as the syllogism's conclusion. Brian Larson calls this brand of deductive reasoning "rule-based reasoning" (Larson, 2018) and found that these rule-based arguments make up the majority of legal arguments in a study of legal briefs and opinions (Larson, 2021).

Legal formalists often champion the syllogism as the correct method of legal reasoning, advocating the view that the application of case law is akin to a scientific process, capable of being encapsulated within formal models of logical reasoning. This perspective is further elaborated by Thomas F. Gordon and Douglas Walton in their work, "Legal Reasoning with Argumentation Schemes" (Gordon and Walton, 2009). Gordon and Walton discuss various methods of argumentation in legal reasoning, aligning more closely with philosophical concepts of argumentation. They describe their model of argumentation scheme as tuples of the type (list [premise], statement), where the list [premise] denotes a list of premises, and the statement represents the conclusion of the argument. In their framework, a premise can be a statement, an exception, or an assumption, offering a nuanced approach to understanding legal arguments.

This perspective on legal reasoning suggests that the judicial process can be structured and dissected into a series of definable elements that construct a logical argument. Just like solving a mathematical problem, each premise, statement, exception, or assumption is a variable in the equation that can either add, subtract, or modify the strength and direction of the argument. This means that the analytical rigor employed in the legal process goes beyond the mere presentation of facts and laws. It examines the underlying logical structure of the arguments and identifies the necessary conditions required to validate or negate a legal conclusion.

However, legal reasoning, unlike mathematics or natural sciences, requires significantly more than internal logical consistency or formal validity. It involves subjective factors such as human interpretation and judgment. Thus, while Gordon and Walton's approach provides a robust framework for breaking down the elements of legal reasoning into a systematic and methodical model, it also necessitates the acknowledgment of the inherent ambiguity and interpretative latitude within the law.

In response to the limitations of formal logic, there has been a shift, not only among critical legal scholars but also within the field of legal argumentation, toward a more rhetorical understanding of legal reasoning. This shift acknowledges the influence of rhetoric in legal discourse, challenging traditional legal thought that often underestimates the role of the enthymeme. João Maurício Adeodato (1999), for instance, critiques the traditional legal mindset that tends to view the enthymeme with skepticism, suggesting that the traditional approach is at odds with the inherently rhetorical and constructive nature of legal discourse. This evolving viewpoint underscores a growing recognition of the complexity and nuance in legal reasoning, beyond the confines of strict formal logic.

Adeodato's perspective represents a significant departure from the conventional legal formalist approach. He contends that the enthymeme, by acknowledging the unstated premises derived from shared values or beliefs, provides a more accurate representation of the real-world application of law. It captures the inherently rhetorical nature of law, where the decision-making process is not just a mechanistic application of pre-established rules but also involves interpretation and judgment, shaped by societal norms and values. His assertion that legal agents often unconsciously use enthymemes in their reasoning process underscores the inherently persuasive and interpretive nature of legal discourse.

But the rhetorical use of the enthymeme extends beyond just employing it when premises are universally understood; it also involves its use when the premises are controversial – in fact, sometimes *because* they are controversial. This more rhetorical understanding is explored in the work of Fabrizio Macagno and Giovanni Damele (2013), who investigate the role of implicit premises in argumentation, particularly when these premises are contentious or debatable. Their work provides insights into the rhetorical strategies used in selecting which premises to omit to lend legal arguments a veneer of being unassailable. Yet few legal scholars have engaged with the work of reconstructing implicit premises to understand their rhetorical force and to fully examine the internal logic of judicial opinions.

Rethinking the IRAC model as an enthymeme rather than a syllogism offers a more accurate reflection of the nuanced nature of legal reasoning. The syllogistic interpretation of IRAC suggests a rigid, linear progression from rule to application to conclusion, implying a level of certainty and predictability that often does not exist in legal contexts. In contrast, viewing IRAC through the lens of the enthymeme acknowledges the inherent uncertainties and interpretative elements in legal argumentation. The enthymeme, by its nature, allows for an unstated premise – often a normative or contextual assumption – which is crucial in legal reasoning. This perspective aligns more closely with the reality of legal practice, where judges and lawyers frequently rely on unarticulated principles, societal norms, or ethical considerations that are not explicitly stated but are nonetheless pivotal to the reasoning process. By conceptualizing IRAC as an enthymeme, we embrace a more realistic and flexible model of legal argumentation, one that better accommodates the complexities and subtleties inherent in the application of law to diverse and often unpredictable real-world situations. This approach not only provides a more accurate framework for understanding legal reasoning but also underscores the importance of critical thinking and interpretative skills in the practice of law.

In this light, I aim to examine the effect of the unstated premises on legal argumentation in *Dobbs*. For this examination, I use the following definition, tailored for legal analysis: An enthymeme is a rhetorical construct that connects premises to a conclusion in the realm of real-world, contingent truths, by strategically omitting certain premises and relying on the audience to fill these gaps. This omission is not a flaw but a deliberate technique that engages the audience's own beliefs and values, or obscures the omitted premises if they are controversial, making the argument more compelling and resonant within the specific context of legal reasoning and persuasion. Further, identifying legal reasoning as syllogistic not only overlooks the rhetorical dimension of legal argumentation but also mistakenly aligns it more with scientific discovery than with argumentation about pragmatic legal issues. This perspective erroneously positions legal reasoning in a domain akin to empirical science, where conclusions are drawn from established, objective facts through deductive and inductive reasoning. In contrast, legal argumentation is fundamentally about navigating and interpreting the complexities of human-made law, human behavior, societal norms, and ethical considerations. As Aristotle argues, legal argumentation involves a dynamic process of persuasion and interpretation, which necessarily operates through an enthymematic, rather than syllogistic, framework.

5.3 ENTHYMEME IN *DOBBS*

Dobbs v. Jackson Women's Health Organization (2022) highlights the difficulty of ascribing a to Supreme Court argument formal logic schemas, especially ones as rigid as the syllogism. Even though the argument does not map well to a rigorous logical test, the exercise in attempting to do so results in a better understanding of where the argument fails.

Numerous legal scholars have already pointed out some of the major failings of the decision – it purports to represent a history that most likely never existed, it misreads precedent, and it ignores decades of established legal precedent to get to its justification for its ruling. Dahlia Lithwick and Neil S. Siegel (2022) have argued that "*Dobbs* [is] not just wrong, but *lawless* . . . [b]ecause it is utterly unprincipled. It articulates a reason for overruling *Roe* out of one side of its mouth, then repeatedly protests that it will not be bound by this reason out of the other side of its mouth." But more insidious than these obvious examples of where the evidence or stated reasoning fails is where the majority opinion's reasoning is obscured by its reliance on unstated premises, a tactic that further complicates the application of formal logic schemas to its argument.

This elusiveness in the opinion's structure allows it to maneuver around certain logical and legal expectations. The decision, while overtly grounded in legal reasoning, subtly embeds its rationale in premises that are not explicitly articulated but are critical to its conclusion. These unstated premises include particular interpretations of history, assumptions about societal norms, or specific views on the role of the judiciary that would be controversial if stated overtly. This approach effectively conceals the full basis of its reasoning, making it challenging to dissect and critique the decision using traditional legal analysis. The concealment of these key premises not only contributes to the perceived failings of the decision, as noted by legal scholars, but also illustrates a strategic use of legal rhetoric. By not openly stating these foundational premises, the opinion avoids direct engagement with counterarguments and criticism, thereby shielding its reasoning from straightforward legal scrutiny. This method of hiding reasoning through unstated premises is not just a feature of this particular decision, but a broader tactic that can be observed in various judicial opinions, highlighting the complex interplay between legal argumentation, rhetoric, and logic.

Justice Alito's majority opinion employs enthymematic arguments within a quasi-logical framework to make its case for overturning *Roe v. Wade* (1973). By leveraging enthymematic arguments, Justice Alito aims to shape the Court's decision and persuade the reader, employing a structure that exhibits the appearance of logical coherence while concealing potential gaps in the reasoning. Moreover, its verisimilitude to the syllogism and the scientific rigor necessary to construct a syllogistic proof helps to give Alito's argument its rhetorical force.

Within this quasi-logical structure, Justice Alito strategically selects and presents arguments that encompass implicit premises, relying on the audience to fill in the missing elements. By leaving certain premises unexpressed, Justice Alito capitalizes on the persuasive force of these unspoken assumptions, thereby shaping the audience's perception and bolstering the strength of his argument.

To understand the rhetorical effect of Alito's enthymematic argumentation, let us first turn to those premises that are explicitly stated in the opinion. Alito says:

> We hold that *Roe* and *[Planned Parenthood v.] Casey* [(1992)] must be overruled. The Constitution makes no reference to abortion, and no such right is implicitly protected by any constitutional provision, including the one on which the defenders of *Roe* and *Casey* now chiefly rely – the Due Process Clause of the Fourteenth Amendment. That provision has been held to guarantee some rights that are not mentioned in the Constitution, but any such right must be "deeply rooted in this Nation's history and tradition" and "implicit in the concept of ordered liberty." *Washington v. Glucksberg*, 521 U.S. 702, 721 (1997) (internal quotation marks omitted).
>
> The right to abortion does not fall within this category. Until the latter part of the 20th century, such a right was entirely unknown in American law. Indeed, when the Fourteenth Amendment was adopted, three quarters of the States made abortion a crime at all stages of pregnancy. The abortion right is also critically different from any other right that this Court has held to fall within the Fourteenth Amendment's protection of "liberty." *Roe*'s defenders characterize the abortion right as similar to the rights recognized in past decisions involving matters such as intimate sexual relations, contraception, and marriage, but abortion is fundamentally different, as both *Roe* and *Casey* acknowledged, because it destroys what those decisions called "fetal life" and what the law now before us describes as an "unborn human being." (*Dobbs*, 2022, p. 5)

One might reconstruct the nested enthymemes that comprise the test for *Dobbs* thus:

First major premise: Abortion is not a right enumerated in the Constitution.
- **Implied premise:** This case is about abortion, not a more general right to privacy, nor a right to control medical decisions about our bodies.

Second major premise: Unenumerated rights exist only if they are deeply rooted in our nation's history.
- **Implied premise:** A right is deeply rooted in our nation's history only if it has been legally recognized in all circumstances across all time (or at least in all circumstances across a particular time period).
- **Minor premise:** Abortion has not always been legal in all circumstances across all time.
- **Minor conclusion:** Abortion is not deeply rooted in our nation's history.

Conclusion: Abortion is not a right enshrined in the Constitution; therefore, *Roe* and *Casey* must be overruled.

The enthymemes at the heart of the *Dobbs* decision operate through missing premises, which play a crucial role in shaping the argument's trajectory and conclusion. The major premises, while they rely on some shared values and assumptions, have support beyond the argument being made by Alito in *Dobbs*. However, the implied premises introduce significant nuances that direct the argument toward a predetermined conclusion.

5.3.1 *Major Premise: Abortion Is Not a Right Enumerated in the Constitution*

Choosing a major premise for an enthymeme in legal argumentation is a deeply rhetorical act, one that sets the tone and direction for the entire argument. This choice is far from arbitrary; it reflects the arguer's perspective, biases, and the intended message they wish to convey. In essence, the major premise serves as the foundation upon which the argument is built, guiding the logical progression and influencing the conclusions drawn. It is the lens through which facts are interpreted and through which the argument gains its persuasive power. For instance, in a legal context, selecting a major premise that aligns with a particular legal theory or interpretation can significantly shape the outcome of the case. This premise acts as a filter, determining which facts are relevant and how they are to be understood. It is not just a statement of fact, but a declaration of the argument's underlying assumptions and values.

Furthermore, the rhetorical choice of a major premise in an enthymeme also dictates the engagement of the audience with the argument. A well-chosen premise can resonate with the audience's beliefs or values, making the argument more persuasive. It can also challenge or provoke the audience, compelling them to reconsider their views. In judicial decision-making, the selection of a major premise is a critical step that shapes the entire framework of legal analysis. It goes beyond ensuring the logical coherence of the decision; it involves a careful consideration of the broader legal principles, ethical implications, and societal values that underpin the law. By selecting a particular major premise, a judge essentially determines the narrative through which legal facts are understood and contextualized, thereby guiding the legal discourse toward a certain trajectory that resonates with the judge's understanding of the law and its role in society. This decision is a constitutive act, one that not only applies the law but also shapes it, reflecting James Boyd White's (1973) view of the law's constitutive nature.

The majority opinion sets up the analysis of *Dobbs* through the lens of abortion rights. The first major premise *is* demonstrably true through a reading of the Constitution: Nowhere is abortion mentioned in the document. When Justice Alito centers his analysis on whether abortion is an enumerated right in the Constitution, he strategically bypasses the broader and more contentious debate about the existence of a fundamental right to privacy.

5.3.2 *Implied Premise: This Case Is about Abortion, Not a More General Right to Privacy, nor a Right to Control Medical Decisions about Our Bodies*

The implied premise, that *Dobbs* is specifically about abortion and not about a broader right to privacy or bodily autonomy, limits the argument's scope. By framing the issue narrowly around abortion, Alito effectively limits the discussion to the legality of abortion itself, rather than engaging with the wider constitutional principles that might underlie such a right. This strategic narrowing of the argument's scope is a key rhetorical move, as it shifts the focus of the debate and potentially influences how the audience, including the Court and the public, perceives and evaluates the issue.

Alito's approach sets up his narrow view of the historical development and understanding of privacy rights in American jurisprudence. While ideas about which privacy rights are fundamental has shifted over time, the argument that privacy is fundamental is not new. In their 1890 law review article, "The Right to Privacy," Warren and Brandeis initially characterized the right to privacy as an existing common law right that encompassed safeguards for an individual's "inviolate personality" (Warren and Brandeis, 1890, p. 205). According to their view, the common law ensured that each person had the right to determine the extent to which their thoughts, sentiments, and emotions would be communicated to others, establishing the boundaries of public disclosure. Their conception of the right to privacy emphasized that individuals possessed the choice to share or withhold information about their private life, habits, actions, and relationships.

The necessity for the legal system to recognize the right to privacy, as argued by Warren and Brandeis, stemmed from the potential impact of disclosing information about an individual's private life. They contended that such revelations had the capacity to influence and harm the very core of a person's personality, particularly their self-perception. In essence, they recognized that an individual's personality, including their self-image, could be affected, distorted, or even injured when private information became accessible to others. This original understanding of the right to privacy incorporated a psychological insight which, at the time, was relatively unexplored – an understanding that the disclosure of private aspects of an individual's life could have profound psychological consequences.

So, by the early part of the twenty-first century, the right to privacy had been enshrined as a fundamental right – one so foundational to understanding all our other rights that it can be left unsaid, thus forming a penumbra of constitutional protections. Alito strategically did not revisit the issue of whether a general right to privacy exists, instead limiting his focus to abortion more specifically. This allows him to find that abortion is not a fundamental right and skip the analysis of whether an anti-abortion law passes constitutional muster.

To determine whether such a fundamental right has been impermissibly infringed upon, courts generally apply the doctrine of strict scrutiny. Under this doctrine, which has been called one of "the most important and distinctive tenets … of modern constitutional law," the government must show that the law is narrowly tailored to achieve a compelling state interest (Siegel, 2006, p. 355). Strict scrutiny is a high standard that is difficult for the government to meet, and it often results in laws or policies being struck down as unconstitutional.

For instance, a state may enact a law that limits the exercise of free speech, but only if it can demonstrate that it has a compelling interest, such as safeguarding national security, and that the law is carefully tailored to achieve that interest. To pass constitutional scrutiny, the government must meet both prongs of the test: showcasing a compelling state interest and ensuring that the chosen means are narrowly tailored, meaning the law is the least restrictive way to accomplish the desired objective.

This is the test *Roe* applied to anti-abortion laws in 1973. The Court weighed a woman's right to make decisions about her pregnancy against a state's interest in protecting "potential life." The balancing test it applied came to an equilibrium at the time of viability of the fetus. It weighed the relative interests, stating:

> On the basis of elements such as these, appellant and some amici argue that the woman's right is absolute and that she is entitled to terminate her pregnancy at whatever time, in whatever way, and for whatever reason she alone chooses. With this we do not agree. Appellant's arguments that Texas either has no valid interest at all in regulating the abortion decision, or no interest strong enough to support any limitation upon the woman's sole determination, are unpersuasive. The Court's decisions recognizing a right of privacy also acknowledge that some state regulation in areas protected by that right is appropriate. As noted above, a State may properly assert important interests in safeguarding health, in maintaining medical standards, and in protecting potential life. At some point in pregnancy, these respective interests become sufficiently compelling to sustain regulation of the factors that govern the abortion decision. The privacy right involved, therefore, cannot be said to be absolute. In fact, it is not clear to us that the claim asserted by some amici that one has an unlimited right to do with one's body as one pleases bears a close relationship to the right of privacy previously articulated in the Court's decisions. The Court has refused to recognize an unlimited right of this kind in the past. *Jacobson v. Massachusetts*, 197 U.S. 11 (1905) (vaccination); *Buck v. Bell*, 274 U.S. 200 (1927) (sterilization).
>
> We, therefore, conclude that the right of personal privacy includes the abortion decision, but that this right is not unqualified and must be considered against important state interests in regulation. (*Roe v. Wade*, 1973, p. 154)

In this deductive argument, the Court considers a hypothetical syllogism: (i) "Rights of privacy are always absolute," (ii) "Reproductive decisions are subject to a right of privacy," and (iii) "Therefore, reproductive decisions are an absolute right." The Court then proceeds to demonstrate the falsity of premise (i) by presenting counterexamples that show privacy rights are not always absolute. This refutation of the first premise effectively undermines the conclusion (iii), demonstrating that reproductive decisions cannot be considered an absolute right in every circumstance.

Following this deductive reasoning, the Court's balancing test is reintroduced to provide a more nuanced explanation. The balancing test allows the Court to articulate why the conclusion (iii) is not universally true, particularly in the context of the case at hand. By employing this test, the Court can consider a range of factors, including societal values, legal precedents, and the implications of absolute rights, to arrive at a more comprehensive and context-sensitive conclusion.

A balancing test may be seen as a compromise, one that Alito is not willing to make when he revisits the idea almost fifty years later in *Dobbs*. Where certain "fundamental rights" are involved, the Court has held time and again that regulation limiting these rights may be justified only by a "compelling state interest." But, in *Dobbs*, Alito is careful to state that the right to an abortion is not a fundamental right. He says, "Even though the Constitution makes no mention of abortion, the Court held that it confers a broad right to obtain one" and goes on to question whether unenumerated rights exist and under what circumstances the Court should be willing to acknowledge them (*Dobbs v. Jackson Women's Health Organization*, 2022, p. 1).

The recognition of unenumerated rights within the constitutional framework has been a subject of considerable debate and interpretation. The courts have consistently acknowledged that the Constitution's protection extends beyond its explicit provisions, encompassing inherent and implied rights that are integral to individual liberty and justice. This understanding acknowledges that the Constitution operates as a living document, capable of evolving to address new challenges and societal expectations. But not all are willing to accept the Constitution as a living document. Originalism as a jurisprudential principle is rooted in the idea that we should seek to understand and apply the law as those living in the time it was written would have understood it. (See Hannah and Mootz, Chapter 2 in this volume, about the role of originalism in legal argumentation.) It has also been used to justify reactionary judicial rulings, as has the test applied in *Dobbs*.

When Alito focused his analysis on the specific question of whether abortion is an enumerated right in the Constitution, rather than exploring the broader concept of privacy, he effectively narrowed the scope of the legal debate. By concentrating solely on abortion, Alito implicitly underscores a widely held legal perspective: that abortion, in itself, is not typically regarded as a fundamental right. This framing contrasts with the broader and more complicated discussions surrounding privacy as a fundamental right, which might encompass a variety of personal decisions, including choices about one's body. Alito's decision to isolate abortion from this broader context of privacy rights thus shifts the legal discourse, focusing it on the enumeration of specific rights rather than on the exploration of underlying principles that might be considered fundamental to personal liberty and autonomy.

The argument then becomes: If the right in question is not a fundamental right, then it is not appropriate for the Court to apply a strict scrutiny test. This does two things for the argument, and hence the enthymeme. First, it allows Alito to apply a test that is much more favorable to the state. The government in the traditional analysis would be said to have an interest in protecting the rights of fetuses, and that interest would have to be a compelling one to overcome the burden of the law prohibiting abortion. And second, it removes the emphasis of competing rights from the discussion. Rhetorically, this is an important move. Rather than pitting the rights of women against those of fetuses (or those of the state in protecting fetuses), the court is now able to examine whether "potential life" should have *any* rights, not just whether those rights should overcome the rights of the woman.[1]

Thus, Alito further obscures the rationale through his choice of categorical analogy. When defining the fundamental right to privacy that *Roe* protected, he selected a narrow focus not of bodily autonomy over the medical procedures we choose to have (something that would apply to men and women equally) but the right to an abortion (something that only women could face). And in doing so he ensures that groups that have been historically marginalized will continue to be treated as a different class from those who have traditionally held power in the United States, heterosexual white men. Rather than asking "is this basic right something that we have recognized on a broad basis," he narrows his focus to be something that would only apply to women.[2] By choosing the category from which to define a class, Alito sets up a test that could only fail.

The dissent takes issue with this narrow categorization and contextualizes the line of cases that helped define privacy rights as being fundamental to personhood:

> *Roe* and *Casey* fit neatly into a long line of decisions protecting from government intrusion a wealth of private choices about family matters, child rearing, intimate relationships, and procreation. See *Casey*, 505 U. S., at 851, 857; *Roe*, 410 U. S., at 152–153 . . .). Those cases safeguard particular choices about whom to marry; whom to have sex with; what family members to live with; how to raise children – and crucially, whether and when to have children. In varied cases, the Court explained that those choices – "the most intimate and personal" a person can make – reflect fundamental aspects of personal identity; they define the very "attributes of personhood." *Casey*, 505 U. S., at 851. And they inevitably shape the nature and future course of a person's life (and often the lives of those closest to her). So, the Court held, those choices belong to the individual, and not the government. That is the essence of what liberty requires.
> (*Dobbs v. Jackson Women's Health Organization*, 2022, Breyer et al. dissent, p. 22)

The selection of rules and categorical definitions in legal arguments, as exemplified in the *Dobbs* decision, highlights the profound impact of the enthymeme and underscores the risk of equating legal arguments with syllogisms. If legal argumentation were purely syllogistic, its premises would be governed by natural law or intrinsic rules of the system, much like a geometric proof is bound by established

[1] In fact, it is this very pivot point that has led to much of the backlash about the decision from conservatives. A recent survey reveals that 90 percent of Americans think abortion should be legal if the woman's health is seriously endangered by the pregnancy. This view is shared by an overwhelming majority of Republicans, with 86 percent supporting this exception. Further, the survey found that two-thirds of Americans believe abortion regulations should be determined by public referendum rather than by elected officials or judges (Perry et al., 2022).

[2] It is also argued that abortion bans disproportionately affect women of color. See, e.g. *Attorney General Merrick B. Garland Statement*, 2022; Farge, 2022; Kirkegaard, 2021.

mathematical principles. In such a proof, the steps are dictated by predetermined rules; the person constructing the proof cannot arbitrarily dictate whether an acute angle is more or less than 90 degrees or whether a given angle is properly classified as acute or obtuse.

However, the realm of legal argumentation operates differently. A judge, unlike a mathematician, has the latitude to define the categories and rules applicable to a case. In the *Dobbs* decision, Alito exercises this discretion by narrowly defining the category of rule to specifically encompass abortion, excluding broader privacy rights. This strategic categorization sets up a test designed to fail under the parameters he establishes. Ironically, this approach not only allows him to apply the law as he has redefined it in *Dobbs*, which is narrowly tailored to abortion, but it also potentially paves the way for him to further restrict other privacy rights in the future, based on what he has decided in *Dobbs*.

5.3.3 *Major Premise: Unenumerated Rights Exist Only If They Are Deeply Rooted in Our Nation's History*

This premise comes with a rarely used test which, when applied, is likely to reduce individual rights: the *Glucksberg* test. The *Glucksberg* test sets forth the standard for evaluating substantive due process claims related to the recognition of new fundamental rights (Turner, 2020). Named after the 1997 Supreme Court case *Washington v. Glucksberg*, in which the Court upheld a Washington state law criminalizing assisted suicide, the test is used to determine whether a right is a fundamental right protected under the Due Process Clause of the Fourteenth Amendment of the United States Constitution. In its decision, the Supreme Court rejected the argument that there is a fundamental right to assisted suicide, and instead established a two-part test for determining whether a right is fundamental. The first part of the *Glucksberg* test requires that the right be "deeply rooted in this Nation's history and tradition" (*Washington v. Glucksberg*, 1997, p. 721). The second part of the test requires that the right be "implicit in the concept of ordered liberty" (p. 721), meaning that it is necessary for an individual's autonomy and dignity.[3]

Alito, in pages 11–13 of the *Dobbs* opinion, sets out to explain some of the history of the *Glucksberg* test. He specifically discusses the way that historical inquiries have been made when looking to confer a previously unrecognized right in *Timbs* and *McDonald*. He argues, "Historical inquiries of this nature are essential whenever we are asked to recognize a new component of the 'liberty' protected by the Due

3 There is also, arguably, another prong to the *Glucksberg* test, which was limited by its treatment in *Obergefell v. Hodges* (2015): the requirement of a "careful description" of the right under analysis. This prong was found to be inconsistent with an analysis of certain fundamental rights, especially those involving privacy.

Process Clause because the term 'liberty' alone provides little guidance" (*Dobbs v. Jackson Women's Health Organization*, 2022, p. 13).

If we accept his theory of *Glucksberg*, then we might reconstruct the "syllogism" thus:

Major premise: Historical inquiries are essential whenever we are asked to recognize a new component of the "liberty" protected by the Due Process Clause.

Implied premise: In *Dobbs*, we are now asked to recognize a new component of the "liberty" protected by the Due Process Clause.

Implied conclusion: A historical inquiry is essential for *Dobbs*.

Of course, when we re-create the implied premise here, it fails. Alito never claims to be conferring a new right with *Dobbs*. He is revisiting a clearly established right, one that he argues was conferred in the *Roe* decision, but one that Blackmun argued had predated *Roe*.

Perhaps Alito would argue that the part of the implied premise here is that when *Roe* was decided, it would have been appropriate to have evaluated the case using the *Glucksberg* test. If we reconstruct the premise in that way, then we have a bit of a timeline problem. The Court can no longer rely on *Glucksberg* to justify the rule it is applying, as *Glucksberg* was decided two decades after *Roe*. The problem lies in the fact that legal precedent, as a principle, is typically not applied retroactively. Therefore, using the *Glucksberg* test as a yardstick to measure the historical legitimacy of a right recognized in *Roe* contradicts the general legal principle that precedent should not be applied to past rulings. This approach essentially reevaluates *Roe* with a standard that did not exist at the time of its decision.

Perhaps Alito would argue that the principle that a court must engage in historical inquiry of the type that *Glucksberg* lays out predates its articulation in *Glucksberg* and would have still been an appropriate test when deciding *Roe*. But then, ironically, we have an enumeration problem. The Court would be relying on an unarticulated rule whose foundations predate its articulation in *Glucksberg*. It seems absurd to argue that a legal principle is so foundational that the Court should apply it, even though it has not been previously articulated, for the express purpose of striking down a constitutional protection that is so foundational that the Court should acknowledge it, even though it has not been previously articulated.

Alito is doing something unusual in *Dobbs*: He is essentially relitigating a prior case. *Roe* was wrongly decided, his logic goes. When one applies a 1997 test to the 1973 *Roe* case, the result is different.

Reconstructing the "syllogism" in Alito's argument sheds light on what Macagno and Damele (2013) propose as the rhetorical force of implied premises. The uncontroversial premises are stated overtly; the controversial ones are not articulated. Thus, audiences must first supply the premise before they can point out any flaws with it. More problematic still is the plausible deniability that gets built into the system because the speaker can respond to any such critique by reframing or rewriting their own argument. The enthymeme becomes a dialogical and living argument, capable of adapting to changing circumstances. And in this system, the speaker gets the benefit of the doubt: It seems unfair to put words into Alito's mouth and hold him to task for something he never said.

By carefully analyzing the argument as it is constructed, we can see that the application of *Glucksberg* is dubious at best. But what is a justice who wants to revoke a fundamental right to do in this situation? There is no corollary to the *Glucksberg* test when revoking rather than conferring a right under the Fourteenth Amendment. In fact, when the Court limits a fundamental right, it must do so with the restraint that the strict scrutiny test requires. Alito seems to be doing logical gymnastics to provide a basis for his argument that the right to an abortion is not a fundamental right.

5.3.4 *Implied Premise: "Deeply Rooted" Means Unwaveringly So*

The reconstructed, implied premise, "a right is deeply rooted in our nation's history only if it has been legally recognized in all circumstances across all time," though not explicitly stated in Alito's opinion, is essential for completing the "syllogism." It sets a remarkably high bar for any right to be considered fundamental and effectively narrows the scope of what can be considered a historically rooted right, excluding rights that may have evolved or been recognized over time.

This premise is arguably the most contentious, making its rhetorical omission advantageous, as it compels the audience to reconstruct it. Moreover, it is precisely this unspoken premise, along with the historical "evidence" Alito employs to support this aspect of his argument, that has attracted significant scrutiny and criticism.

The dissent critiques this narrow view of constitutional rights as failing to grasp how applications of liberty and equality can evolve with changing societal understandings, saying, "The Framers (both in 1788 and 1868) understood that the world changes. So they did not define rights by reference to the specific practices existing at the time. Instead, the Framers defined rights in general terms, to permit future evolution in their scope and meaning" (*Dobbs v. Jackson Women's Health Organization*, 2022, Breyer et al. dissent, p. 14).

> **Minor premise:** Abortion has not always been legal in all circumstances across all time.

In arguing that the right to abortion is not deeply rooted in the nation's history and tradition, Alito faces the challenge of proving a negative. It is notoriously difficult to prove the absence of something, especially a concept so nebulous as an unenumerated constitutional right. Instead of directly establishing the lack of historical entrenchment, he opts to provide evidence that abortion has, at various points, been illegal.

Alito asserts that "until the latter part of the [twentieth] century, there was no support in American law for a constitutional right to obtain an abortion. Zero. None. No state constitutional provision had recognized such a right" (*Dobbs v. Jackson Women's Health Organization*, 2022, p. 15). Here, he provides more evidence to support the major premise that if abortion is a right, it had not been enumerated until recently. But this evidence does not answer whether the right would pass the *Glucksberg* test. Whether the right claimed is "deeply rooted in this Nation's history and tradition" requires an inquiry beyond just whether there has always been a legal right recognized in official statutes and constitutions.

He further contends that "by the time of the adoption of the Fourteenth Amendment, three-quarters of the States had made abortion a crime at any stage of pregnancy, and the remaining States would soon follow" (*Dobbs v. Jackson Women's Health Organization*, 2022, p. 16). By highlighting instances and periods where abortion was criminalized, Alito seeks to undermine the notion that the right to abortion is historically entrenched. However, this approach is logically flawed. As the dissent points out, "the right to an abortion emerged not recently, but as part and parcel of two centuries of jurisprudence grappling with the protection of the individual's liberty and dignity" (*Dobbs v. Jackson Women's Health Organization*, 2022, Breyer et al. dissent, p. 12). The dissent argues that the majority's focus on specific historical instances of abortion criminalization fails to account for the broader evolutionary arc of rights related to personal autonomy and reproductive freedom.

Moreover, the majority's reliance on historical abortion laws as evidence against a deeply rooted right is problematic because it assumes a static view of rights. As the dissent notes, "The Framers defined rights in general terms, to permit future evolution in their scope and meaning" (*Dobbs v. Jackson Women's Health Organization*, 2022, p. 15). The fact that abortion had been criminalized in the past does not necessarily preclude the recognition of a constitutional right in the present, consistent with a modern interpretation of a foundational right. The historical legality of a practice is just one factor in a broader, more nuanced analysis. The *Glucksberg* test requires a deep dive into the historical context, societal values, and legal traditions surrounding the practice. For instance, a practice might have been criminalized due to historical misconceptions, cultural biases, or lack of scientific understanding, which have since evolved. Therefore, the mere fact of past criminalization does not definitively determine a practice's alignment with deeply rooted national traditions or its place within the concept of ordered liberty. The *Glucksberg* test calls for a more comprehensive historical and cultural understanding to assess whether a right is fundamental.

> **Minor conclusion:** A right to abortion is not deeply rooted in our nation's history.

The minor conclusion in the *Dobbs* decision, that abortion is not deeply rooted in our nation's history, emerges as a logically consistent outcome based on the major and minor premises previously established in the argument. However, it's crucial to distinguish between the formal logical validity of this conclusion and its rational soundness, as these are two distinct concepts in logical and legal reasoning.

Formal logical validity refers to the coherence within the structure of an argument. It evaluates whether the conclusion follows logically from the premises, without any internal contradiction, assuming the premises are true. In the case of the *Dobbs* decision, the argument is constructed in a way that the conclusion – that abortion is not deeply rooted in our nation's history – logically aligns with the premises laid out. The major premise, that unenumerated rights must be deeply rooted in our nation's history to be recognized, combined with the minor premise, that abortion has not always been legal in all circumstances, leads to the minor conclusion in a manner that is internally consistent. This formal validity is crucial for the argument to be seen as rational and coherent within its own framework.

However, rational soundness is a broader concept. It concerns not just the formal structure of the argument, but also the truthfulness or factual accuracy of the premises and the relevance and sufficiency of these premises in leading to the conclusion. An argument can be formally valid yet still be unsound if its premises are false or if they do not adequately support the conclusion. In the context of the *Dobbs* decision, questioning the rational soundness of the conclusion involves scrutinizing the historical and legal assumptions underlying the premises.

The major premise assumes that for a right to be constitutionally protected, it must have a deep historical root. This premise can be contested on several grounds. First, the interpretation of what constitutes "deeply rooted" is subjective and open to debate. History is not a static or objective narrative but is subject to interpretation and reevaluation. Second, the premise seems to ignore the dynamic nature of societal values and legal interpretations, which evolve over time. Rights that were once unrecognized or even unthinkable can become fundamental as societal norms and understandings progress. Finally, as explained above, the retroactive application of this principle, the *Glucksberg* test, is dubious at best.

Similarly, the minor premise, that abortion has not always been legal in all circumstances, while factually accurate, may not be sufficient to support the conclusion. The legal status of abortion throughout history is complex and varied, influenced by cultural, religious, and social factors. The premise oversimplifies this history and does not account for the nuanced ways in which abortion rights have been understood and exercised in different contexts.

Therefore, while the conclusion that abortion is not deeply rooted in our nation's history may follow logically from the premises in the argument, its soundness is questionable. It relies on premises that are either debatable or insufficiently robust to support the conclusion. This distinction between formal logical validity and rational soundness is crucial in legal reasoning. It highlights the importance of critically examining not just how conclusions follow from premises, but also the soundness of those premises and their capacity to genuinely support the conclusions drawn. The enthymematic structure, complete with unstated but necessary premises, allows for the appearance of logic amidst an invalid argument.

> **Conclusion:** Abortion is not a right enshrined in the Constitution; therefore, *Roe* and *Casey* must be overruled.

This conclusion is controversial, not just because of its effects, but also because of the method by which Alito supports it. He is ignoring *stare decisis*, which he justifies through the lens of a respect for the history of the United States and its legal system. The *Glucksberg* test allows him to do so.

The use of the *Glucksberg* test by Justice Alito in this context serves as a strategic tool, enabling him to reject longstanding legal precedent while framing his argument within a historical and traditionalist perspective. By applying this test, Alito positions his reasoning as a reflection of a deep respect for historical legal principles, rather than a departure from them. This approach provides a veneer of continuity and respect for legal tradition, even as it facilitates a significant shift in the interpretation of constitutional rights.

Alito's approach was carefully crafted to circumvent the label of an activist judge, a term often used to describe justices who are perceived as using their judicial power to promote personal ideologies rather than adhering to established legal principles and precedents. In his opinion, Alito could have explicitly stated his disagreement with the past fifty years of legal precedent regarding abortion rights and his consequent desire to overturn it. Such a direct approach, however, would have starkly positioned him as a judicial activist, openly challenging established legal norms and the Supreme Court's tradition of respecting precedent. And so, he refrains from such directness, opting instead for a more subtle approach that masks the radical nature of his decision.

The opening of Alito's opinion in *Dobbs* is particularly telling in this regard. Alito begins his opinion with the declaration, "Abortion presents a profound moral issue on which Americans hold sharply conflicting views" (*Dobbs v. Jackson Women's Health Organization*, 2022, p. 1). Rather than beginning with the law, he begins with a discussion of morals and politics. Here, he tips his hand that he will not be "following the law" in the way we generally assume the Court will follow its own precedent, according to long-held standards of *stare decisis*.

Compare the first line of *Dobbs* with that of *Roe v. Wade* (1973, p. 116): "This Texas federal appeal and its Georgia companion, *Doe v. Bolton*, . . . present constitutional challenges to state criminal abortion legislation." Blackmun, in *Roe*, begins with a focus on the law and the legal issues. He does this, ostensibly, because he will argue that Doe is not entirely new law, that it is well-founded based on entrenched constitutional principles of privacy and personal autonomy. The opening line of *Dobbs* shows Alito's cards. He will be overturning a legal rule that has been on the books since *at least* 1973.

The departure from *stare decisis* in the *Dobbs* decision represents more than just a deviation from established legal precedent; it also signifies a divergence from the traditional functions attributed to the courts by legal theorists. Typically, the judicial branch is primarily viewed as an interpreter of the law, tasked with applying established legal tests. However, in cases like *Dobbs*, the Supreme Court transcends this conventional role, notably engaging in the creation and endorsement of legal tests, especially in matters involving constitutional questions, such as the right to privacy. A significant portion of the rhetorical effort in the *Dobbs* decision lies in how the Court selects the appropriate test to apply.

The Supreme Court's role in formulating and endorsing legal tests underscores its influential position in the constitution of legal norms and the shaping of societal values. By engaging in this process, particularly in constitutional matters, the Court actively participates in the development of legal doctrine, sets precedents, and influences societal perceptions of rights and responsibilities. Consequently, the Court's decision-making process inherently involves enthymematic reasoning and argumentation. Each time it selects a rule to apply in a case, the Court implicitly engages in an argumentative process, where the choice of the rule serves as a premise, but the rationale for applying that rule often remains unstated.

5.4 CONCLUSION

The application of the *Glucksberg* test in the context of *Dobbs* underscores the challenges inherent in viewing legal reasoning purely through a syllogistic lens. Such an approach fails to fully grasp the rhetorical nature of legal argumentation, which goes beyond the rigid structure of deductive reasoning. While legal "syllogisms" can maintain internal consistency, they are unable to encompass the entirety of a legal argument. Invariably, there will be missing premises or unexpressed assumptions that shape the reasoning process.

The *Dobbs* decision reflects the inherent complexity of judicial decision-making, where the Court must balance fidelity to legal precedent with responsiveness to evolving societal values. By overturning *Roe* after almost fifty years, the *Dobbs* majority engaged in a quasi-logical argument that, while exhibiting a veneer of deductive reasoning, ultimately relied on unstated assumptions and controversial premises reflecting the particular worldview of the justices who joined it. Justice Alito's opinion models an enthymematic form of persuasive rhetoric in which the formal application of judicial tests obscures controversial moral and philosophical principles regarding privacy rights and bodily autonomy.

This strategic ambiguity is characteristic of skilled legal advocacy, allowing the audience to project their own values onto the gaps in logical reasoning. As a method for enacting this strategic ambiguity, the enthymeme represents not merely an abbreviated syllogism but a sophisticated rhetorical device for subtly encoding judicial activism in a framework resembling objective formal deduction. It enables the veiling of ideological assumptions within a superficially neutral analytical approach.

Critiquing legal opinions like *Dobbs* hence necessitates disentangling complex layers of rhetorical technique, including the decoding of strategic enthymemes. This more comprehensive orientation attunes legal scholars to the multifaceted interplay between persuasive communication and argumentation schemes in judicial decision-making. Ultimately, interpreting high-stakes rulings requires both rigorously assessing logical coherence and uncovering the symbolic meanings implicitly embedded within the Court's enthymematic rhetoric.

Acknowledging the rhetorical nature of legal argumentation prompts a deeper understanding of the complexity and nuance involved in legal decision-making. It emphasizes that legal reasoning is not a simple exercise in deductive logic but rather a dynamic process shaped by legal precedent, statutory interpretation, policy considerations, and societal values. And recognizing the limitations of a purely syllogistic approach to legal reasoning encourages a broader appreciation of the multifaceted nature of the law. It invites a more comprehensive exploration of the interplay among legal doctrine, persuasive communication, and the social and political factors that influence judicial decision-making.

By embracing the rhetorical dimension of legal argumentation, we gain insight into the art of persuasion within the legal sphere. This perspective highlights the importance of effectively engaging with the audience, presenting compelling narratives, and deploying persuasive techniques to shape legal outcomes. It underscores that legal reasoning is not merely an exercise in logical deduction but also a means to influence and persuade, recognizing the significant role of rhetoric in shaping legal decisions.

Ultimately, a holistic understanding of legal reasoning goes beyond the confines of a rigid syllogistic structure. It requires an appreciation of the interplay among logic, rhetoric, precedent, and the broader social and political context in which legal decisions are made. By embracing this complexity, we can engage in more nuanced discussions about the nature of legal argumentation and its implications for the development of the law.

REFERENCES

Adeodato, J. M. (1999). The rhetorical syllogism (enthymeme) in judicial argumentation. *International Journal for the Semiotics of Law*, 12(2), 133–150. https://doi.org/10.1023/A:1008998121097

Aristotle. (1989). *Prior analytics* (R. Smith, Trans.). Hackett.

(2004). *Rhetoric* (W. R. Roberts, Trans.; Dover Thrift edition). Dover Publications.

Attorney General Merrick B. Garland statement on Supreme Court ruling in Dobbs v. Jackson Women's Health Organization. (2022, June 24). Department of Justice. www.justice.gov/opa/pr/attorney-general-merrick-b-garland-statement-supreme-court-ruling-dobbs-v-jackson-women-s [https://perma.cc/R2MS-HZXZ]

Dobbs v. Jackson Women's Health Organization, 597 U.S. 215 (2022), No. 19-1392, slip op. www.supremecourt.gov/opinions/21pdf/19-1392_6j37.pdf [https://perma.cc/K6MJ-SXBJ]

Farge, E. (2022, August 30). UN racism body calls for U.S. to do more on abortion access. *Reuters*. www.reuters.com/world/us/un-racism-body-calls-us-act-mitigate-dobbs-effects-2022-08-30/

Gordon, T. F., & Walton, D. (2009). Legal reasoning with argumentation schemes. *Proceedings of the 12th International Conference on Artificial Intelligence and Law*, 137–146. https://doi.org/10.1145/1568234.1568250

Kirkegaard, D. (2021, November 29). *The disproportionate harm of abortion bans: Spotlight on Dobbs v. Jackson Women's Health*. Center for Reproductive Rights. https://reproductiverights.org/supreme-court-case-mississippi-abortion-ban-disproportionate-harm/ [https://perma.cc/H4N4-K7T9]

Larson, B. N. (2018). Law's enterprise: Argumentation schemes & legal analogy. *University of Cincinnati Law Review*, 87, 663.

(2021). Precedent as rational persuasion. *Legal Writing: The Journal of the Legal Writing Institute*, 25, 135.

Lithwick, D., & Siegel, N. S. (2022, June 27). The lawlessness of the *Dobbs* decision. *Slate*. https://slate.com/news-and-politics/2022/06/dobbs-decision-glucksberg-test-lawlessness.html [https://perma.cc/Y4SD-GSHZ]

Macagno, F., & Damele, G. (2013). The dialogical force of implicit premises. *Presumptions in Enthymemes. Informal Logic*, 33(3), 361–389.

Obergefell v. Hodges, 576 U.S. 644 (2015).

Perry, S., Trussler, M., Clinton, J., & Lapinski, J. (2022, October 17). A *vast majority of Republicans support abortion exceptions for rape, incest, and the woman's health*. NBC News. www.nbcnews.com/politics/2022-election/vast-majority-republicans-support-abortion-exceptions-rape-incest-moth-rcna52237 [https://perma.cc/YS82-RJ4U]

Planned Parenthood v. Casey, 505 U.S. 833 (1992).

Roe v. Wade, 410 U.S. 113 (1973).

Scalia, A., & Garner, B. A. (2008). *Making your case: The art of persuading judges*. Thomson/West.

Siegel, S. A. (2006). The origin of the compelling state interest test and strict scrutiny. *American Journal of Legal History*, 48(4), 355–407.

Turner, R. (2020). W(h)ither *Glucksberg*. *Duke Journal of Constitutional Law & Public Policy*, 15, 183–216.

Warren, S. D., & Brandeis, L. D. (1890). The right to privacy. *Harvard Law Review*, 4(5), 193–220.

Washington v. Glucksberg, 521 U.S. 702 (1997).

White, J. B. (1973). *The legal imagination: Studies in the nature of legal thought and expression*. Little, Brown.

6

Eradicating Ethos

Language, Circumstances, and Locke's Empirical Language Ideology in the Anglo-American Hearsay Principle

Jennifer Andrus

6.1 INTRODUCTION

On August 5, 1999, in the state of Washington, Kenneth Lee was stabbed in his apartment by Michael Crawford, who was accompanied by his wife, Sylvia Crawford. According to court records, Crawford believed that Lee had attempted to rape Sylvia at some earlier time, and the Crawfords were in Lee's apartment to confront him. In an altercation, Lee was stabbed. When the police arrived, they arrested Crawford after Mirandizing both Crawford and Sylvia and interviewing them both twice. Because of Washington's marital privilege which states, "a spouse or domestic partner shall not be examined for or against his or her spouse or domestic partner, without the consent of the spouse or domestic partner" (Washington Revised Code Annotated § 5.60.060(1)), Sylvia did not testify at Crawford's trial. Instead, her tape-recorded police interviews were admitted (over objection by the defense) as (hearsay) evidence at trial. Such tape-recorded statements are considered hearsay, because there is no physical person – the person (Sylvia) who witnessed the event – to take the stand, swear an oath, testify in court, and be subjected to cross-examination.

Because the original witness, Sylvia, was not present and because Sylvia's prior statements "asserted the truth of the matter asserted" (Federal Rules of Evidence, 2023), they are considered hearsay and are therefore objectionable. Further, because the tape-recording was played rather than having Sylvia take the stand and swear an oath to tell the truth, the defense had no opportunity to question the truth of her testimonial evidence in what Justice Scalia has called "the crucible of cross-examination" (*Crawford v. Washington*, 2003, p. 61). The Confrontation Clause of the Sixth Amendment (U.S. Const. amend. VI) promises the accused the right to confrontation. Because all those measures were not in place, Sylvia's recorded interviews, though admitted through an exception in this case, were hearsay.[1]

[1] There are other types of out-of-court speech not governed by the hearsay rule because they don't assert truth regarding evidence central to the circumstances of the alleged crime. Those

Hearsay is defined extensively throughout this chapter. For now, suffice it to say that hearsay is the process of repeating during in-court testimony a story that somebody else (not in court) told the witness on the stand and in which the repeated account is presented as substantive evidence of truth regarding the legal matter at hand. Hearsay is an account of an account, a story about an event that the witness on the stand did not themselves witness. In the case of *Crawford v. Washington* (here meaning the trial), Sylvia's recorded testimony given to police in a prior context was hearsay because it was played outside of the context of sworn in-court testimony, rendering it impossible to cross-examine the truthfulness of the evidentiary statements in that recording. Though hearsay is typically inadmissible, there are many exceptions – occasions when hearsay can be admitted during a trial – such as was used in the *Crawford* trial. When these exceptions are applied, legal discourse and debate such as the ones analyzed here arise regarding when and how any hearsay may be admissible.

At trial, Crawford was found guilty. On appeal, the intermediate court upheld that verdict. The Washington Supreme Court upheld Crawford's conviction after determining the hearsay evidence was both properly admitted and reliable. *Ohio v. Roberts* (1979) (hereafter *Roberts*), which was the US Supreme Court precedent when Crawford was tried, opined that hearsay may be admitted in line with the rights promised by the Sixth Amendment as long as the statements in question "bear adequate indicia of reliability" (p. 5) and "particularized guarantees of trustworthiness" (p. 66). Using a nine-factor test it had developed in line with this reasoning, the Washington Supreme Court upheld Crawford's conviction, agreeing with the trial court that Crawford and Sylvia's statements were "virtually identical" and "interlocking" (*Crawford v. Washington*, 2003, p. 66) and thus reliable and trustworthy enough to admit as hearsay. Crawford then appealed to the US Supreme Court. The US Supreme Court agreed to hear the case, citing the so-called Confrontation Clause of the Sixth Amendment when writing that "the question presented is whether this procedure complied with the Sixth Amendment's guarantee that, '[i]n all criminal prosecutions, the accused shall enjoy the right . . . to be confronted with the witnesses against him'" (*Crawford v. Washington*, 2003, p. 38).

Ultimately, hearsay is about language – when and how language can be/is trustworthy. The law is constituted in and of language, whether it be documents, statements, transcripts, testimony, precedent, or statute. Hearsay is a moment in the law where we hear the law talk about, discuss, and explain language in its own words. In legal precedents and treatises about hearsay, we hear the law asking many of the same questions about language that rhetoric does: How do we recognize an

types of reported speech are not hearsay and are not a part of this chapter. Only the hearsay rule, which oversees reported speech that does make assertions with regard to the central legal issue in a trial, is evaluated in this chapter. Further, although the hearsay rule applies in criminal and civil courts, this chapter deals only with criminal courts.

accurate account? What contextual parameters create a (perfectly accurate) linguistic account of an event? What role does the witness/speaker play in the creation of an account? And, ultimately, can we ever really trust language? Because law and rhetoric come up with wildly different answers to these questions, it's important to dig into legal rhetoric and to understand how law's view of language impacts all of us. In what follows, I argue that one of the things that happens when a statement is evaluated as potential hearsay is that the rhetorical consequences to the ethos of the speaker are ignored and scrubbed from the statement. Instead, the truth of the statement is linked to the circumstances under which it was spoken and the contexts to which the statement refers, positioning *logos* as the key, and, in the end, nearly only thing on which truth rests. In his *Essay Concerning Humane Understanding*, (hereafter, *Essay*) John Locke (1690) asserts that truth is objective, resting on the empirical, that which can be confirmed by material proof, or what I am referring to as logos. In hearsay legal discourse, the law sees truth in the same way. In this chapter, I put Locke, Aristotle, and the law into conversation to better understand the consequences that such a fetishization of logos has for ethos and ultimately the speaker in legal contexts where the stakes are high.

In the traditional, Aristotelian rhetorical structure, three rhetorical components operate together in the process of making nearly any argument: *ethos*, *pathos*, and *logos* (Aristotle & Kennedy, 2006). For Aristotle (and this is by no means a definitive or comprehensive description), the appeals to ethos, pathos, and logos have to do with the relationship between an audience and a speaker discoursing about a particular topic. These so-called appeals are used by the speaker to persuade the audience of a particular truth and win the argument. For Aristotle, ethos is a feature of the text itself; ethos functions within the speech or document. Ethos is formed and performed through the discursive structure of the argument. Over time, the notion of ethos has been developed to encompass a sense of the credibility of the speaker; the reasons why they are believable; their standing in the community; their potential to speak the truth; and their trustworthiness in word and deed (Carlo, 2020; Hyde, 2004; Sullivan, 1993). In other words, over time, ethos has been linked instead to the speaker's credibility and character. Logos has to do with logic and proof, the argument's evidence and logical structure. Pathos is the emotional thrust of the argument, its ability to resonate with and move the interlocutor.

For Aristotle, in order for an argument to be persuasive, it must leverage these three appeals in a more-or-less balanced way depending on the needs, opportunities, and constraints of the situation, and therefore perhaps focusing on one aspect more than the others, but still operationalizing the three. This typical relationship between ethos, pathos, and logos, or at least typical in rhetorical theory, is disrupted in evaluations of hearsay evidence. Pathos is disregarded nearly completely, and ethos and logos are sent into a dance in which logos is assumed to be objective and far superior to and more trustworthy than anything so closely related to subjectivity, which is situated in (and linked to) the ethos of the speaker.

In hearsay legal debates, the disruption of ethos/pathos/logos appears in discussions about the relationship between a statement and a speaker and how to identify an objectively true account, which the law believes exists, and which would be admissible hearsay. A key argument made in this chapter is that the legal reasoning circulated in hearsay statutory and case law works to disrupt the typical rhetorical relationship between a statement and a speaker, in which a speaker makes a statement for an audience with particular rhetorical goals, embedded in a particular context, stocked with constraints, actors, and actions. This disruption happens whether the hearsay statement is deemed inadmissible or admissible. The other argument in this chapter shows that this legal line of reasoning, which overemphasizes logos, is affiliated with Locke's notions about truth and empiricism. Indeed, Locke had great influence on Anglo-American law in its early stages of development.

I will focus my discussion of Locke on the ideas and concepts that he presents in his *Essay* (1690), where he places high value on sensory experiential learning and the physical world that can be experienced with the senses. Language, for Locke, comes after sensing and is thus essentially less reliable. According to Locke, language is mere representation, only ever pointing, always secondarily, at the empirical. In his description, sensory experience and the empirical are truth's only sources, which language is always lacking. Language is wholly removed from the empirical world and merely indexes that which is empirically grounded in knowledge, rooted in experience. The way to control and manage the unruliness of language, in Locke's philosophy, is empiricism, a turning to the real world of experience and circumstances to locate truth, which puts pressure on ethos.

In this chapter, I trace and describe the ever-evolving (but remarkably consistent) historical, legal positioning of ethos and logos by analyzing hearsay statute, historical treatise, and precedential structure. I focus a significant part of this chapter on the US Supreme Court's decision in *Crawford v. Washington* (2003), which provides us with a close look into the language ideology and rhetorical legal structures that are at the center of questions surrounding the trustworthiness of language. I also analyze the Lockean language ideology circulating in *Ohio v. Roberts* (1980) (hereafter, *Roberts*) and *Davis v. Washington* (2006), which the Court consolidated with *Hammon v. Indiana* (hereafter, *Davis/Hammon*). What it means to be a witness; what it means for an utterance to be reliable and trustworthy; what it means to give testimony – all of these concerns about language have deep roots in the crucial period of high modern thought during which Locke wrote.

In what follows, I demonstrate that Lockean thinking about language, empiricism, and truth is present and circulating in hearsay law. I use the discussion of high modern language ideology to argue that in hearsay legal discourse, the rhetorical structure of ethos/pathos/logos is altered to apply and accommodate the empiricism that is linked to objective truth for both Locke and law. This accommodation delinks the speaker from their statement, reducing ethos to nearly nothing and extending the role of logos to an extreme degree. The process of evaluating hearsay in judicial opinions renders the circumstances surrounding a statement into proof (logos). This process has the effect of pushing aside ethos, because it is always potentially untrustworthy and would need to be tested via cross-examination. By delinking the statement from the speaker through a process that exalts the circumstances surrounding the production of a statement, the statement is transformed into something that is indelibly linked to circumstances and therefore infinitely repeatable without (it is assumed) altering the statement or its relationship to empirical truth. In the law there is a "translation of people and events into legal categories so that they can be used strategically in a struggle for the dominant interpretation" (Mertz, 2007, p. 159). In the case of hearsay, the statement and speaker are hypostatized in isolation from each other, flattened and translated into legal artifacts. This odd diminished and diminishing account of the speaker and their statement relies on Lockean ideas about language, empiricism, and context that have been woven into hearsay law for over 400 years.

6.2 CREATING A HIGH MODERN RULE AGAINST HEARSAY

The story of hearsay is long, beginning in England in the late 1600s (*Thompson v. Trevanion*, 1694). Our modern version of hearsay is closely tied to its historical developments through precedent and the continued reference of legal texts that are used as though there are direct, clean lines between historical precedent and modern-day applications of law. *Crawford v. Washington* (2003) and *Davis/Hammon* (*Davis v. Washington*, 2006) are riddled with historical legal arguments from the early 1700s. Hearsay is a product of case law, organized systematically, indexed, and handed down through the ages in judicial opinion and historical legal texts such as the treatises, abridgements of philosophical texts, and abstracts of legal and philosophical texts, which present legal process, procedure, and expectations. Recent US Supreme Court opinions reference legal rulings and treatises from across the seventeenth, eighteenth, and nineteenth centuries.

Hearsay erupts in a time when the relationship between law and community was changing. In the early seventeenth century, most members of a jury were likely to already know each other and have knowledge of (and even discussed) what had happened in their communities. Communities were small enough for there to be more intimate knowledge of the goings on of its members (Landsman, 1992; Langbein, 1996). Hearsay rules were unnecessary, even in jury trials, because the jurors likely already had prior knowledge of and were connected more closely to all aspects of the legal situation and actors – the accused, witnesses, events, and so forth (Landsman, 1992; Langbein, 1996). As communities grew and diversified, the intimate aspects of community knowledge began to break down. Changes in the language theories and philosophies were also evolving. Out of these changes grew a need to control statements in legal settings. Witnesses were expected to give accounts based on what they *knew* (had seen) from first-hand interaction with the empirically grounded world (Landsman, 1992; Langbein, 1996). They were not allowed to give accounts of what they had *heard* second-hand.

At the same time that laws and communities were changing, so were views about language. During the eighteenth century, language became a "mere" medium, only a conduit for information and experience, functioning through mimicry and representation (cf. Foucault, 2001). Locke's *Essay* (1690) takes up questions of human knowledge, experience, and reasoning, considering the ways humans learn from sensory experience and learn to reason and use language both individually and socially. Locke argues that the knowledge of things and words was not innate but rather developed through sensory experience. He writes:

> The Idea's [sic] themselves, about which the Proposition is, are not born with [individuals], no more than their Names, but got afterwards. So, that in all propositions that are assented to, at first hearing the Terms of the Proposition, their standing for such Idea's [sic], and the Idea's themselves that they stand for, being neither of them innate. (Locke, 1690, p. 11)

According to Locke, neither ideas nor words are innate. Ideas and words are learned, laid down through experience, in an indexical, rhetorical relationship in which ideas and words point at experience, which provides the foundation of the true. Words are an impression of the empirical world on the so-called *tabula rasa* of the human mind. As Locke put it, "the Mind" is a "white Paper, void of all Characters, without any Ideas" (p. 37). According to Duschinsky (2012, p. 513), "in the immediate context in which Locke was writing, the term *tabula rasa* was a familiar image," likely due to the Aristotelian revival of the early seventeenth century. In *On the Soul*, Aristotle writes, "what [the mind] thinks must be in it just as characters may be said to be on a writing tablet on which as yet nothing actually stands written" (Aristotle, n.d., III.4). That is, the mind only has in it that which was written down in it via experience with the world. Nothing is innate.

Circulating in the late eighteenth century were ideas about the relationship between word and world. Some argue that before this time period, people considered the world and the world to be seamlessly connected, even entirely integrated (Foucault, 2001). In the modern period, when Locke was writing, language became separated from the world such that the word merely indexed the world, which is more real and credible than its representation in language. At the end of Book IV of the *Essay*, Locke asserts a division between language and empirical experience explicitly, categorizing the objects of understanding as: (1) "things as they are in themselves knowable" (physica); (2) "Actions as they depend on us in order to [achieve] Happiness" (practica); and (3) methods for interpreting the signs of what is, and of what ought to be, that are presented in our ideas and words (logica) (Locke, 1690, p. 362). This short extract divides nature, language, and human behavior into three distinct categories: "things," "actions," and "methods." These elements are sharp, operating separately and rationally. "Things," or "physica," are knowable through sensory experience. "Actions" are what humans do to manage a practical and productive life, operationalizing both "things" and "methods." "Methods" are directly related to language and the interpretation of signs and words. In this construction, methods and language are removed from things. They are not overlapping. Their boundaries are clear. "Things" are knowable. "Methods" are merely interpretational.

One place where we see tight linkages between eighteenth-century philosophy and eighteenth-century law is in Sir Geoffrey Gilbert's 1752 abridgement of Locke's *Essay*. Gilbert is adamantly against the admission of hearsay, and he structures his arguments in ways that reference Locke both directly and indirectly. Relying on Locke, for Gilbert, hearsay is language and not empirical experience; language is distant from the empirically grounded world; language is not truth. Truth resides in empirical experience. Hearsay is repetition, too far removed from the empirical world of experience to be tolerated by the burgeoning young law with its links to Locke.

In Gilbert's abridgement of Locke's *Essay*, the two scholars collaborate in a claim that what is knowable is the "being and existence of things not language" (Gilbert & Locke, 1752, p. 264). Sounding very much like Locke, Gilbert asserts that "language is nothing else but the connection of sounds to ideas" (p. 264). In eighteenth-century empiricist theory (readily translatable to law), knowledge lives in things, the material world. Language is disconnected from the material, from "things," from knowledge. According to this theory, language functions through representation, doing little more than indexing what is true and knowable in the material world.

The rule prohibiting hearsay is related to a set of ideas that cross paths with, reproduce, and reimagine those presented by Locke in the *Essay*, namely the high value placed on first-hand empirical knowledge – the eyewitness. The heavy emphasis on the empirical creates space for logos to be elevated and ethos to be diminished. Logos is where truth resides. Ethos is irrelevant because of its links to subjectivity, which can never be trusted on its own. The earliest legal documentation of hearsay, the English case *Thompson v. Travanion*, dates to 1694, only four years after Locke's *Essay* was published in 1690. Arguments about hearsay going back to at least 1785 conceive of hearsay as nothing more than speaking, which is inferior, not to be trusted. John Pitt Taylor, quoting English Justice Francis Buller, called hearsay "a mere speaking" (Taylor, 1872, p. 521). Put quite succinctly in another English case, *Chettle v. Chettle* (1821): "What is the evidence here? Mere hearsay. Nothing seen"; evidence that is visually witnessed prevails. In this construction, statements are clearly connected to the speaker through sensory experience, but they come after sensory experience. Statements are lesser. The tight focus on sensory experience puts the thing that happened, logos, at center stage of the "true." That is, truth can only be considered truth when it is directly related to empirically derived experience and knowledge. The speaker, their ethos, and their linguistic account are a deterioration of sensory experience. Hearsay further degrades the empirical because it is doubly removed from Locke's notion of "things." Hearsay rests only on the precarious and unsteady foundation of language rather than the empirical steadiness of "things."

Locke makes a claim about language, empiricism, and truth directly when he writes: "Any Testimony, the farther of it is from the original Truth, the less force and proof it has. The Being and Existence of the thing itself, is what I call the original Truth. ... [I]n traditional Truths, each remove weakens the force of the proof" (Locke, 1690, p. 338). That is, language is a weak proof. Indeed, language mutes the material proofs because they are distant from "the original truth":

> Hearsay is no Evidence ... if a Man had been in Court and said the same Thing and had not sworn it, he had not been believed in a Court of Justice; for all Credit being derived from Attestation and Evidence, ... such a Speech makes it no more than a bare speaking. (Gilbert, 1791, quoted in *Crawford v. Washington*, 2004, p. 70, note 2)

Hearsay is not evidence because it is "bare speaking" – nothing more than language divided from those aspects of the material world that might make it trustworthy, namely the speaker (to cross-examine) and the material world that it references (circumstances). In *Crawford v. Washington* (2003), Justice Scalia connects to this eighteenth-century concern with language, referencing Gilbert directly.

Language is only ever "a bare speaking" in the law unless the gap between the empirical and the linguistic is tightened and controlled. In *The Law of Evidence*, Gilbert writes:

> The *Attestation* of the *Witness* must be to what he *knows*, and not to that only which he has *heard*; for a *mere hearsay is no Evidence*: for it is his *Knowledge* that must direct the Court and Jury in the Judgement of the Fact. ... If the first speech was without Oath, an Oath that there was such a Speech makes it no more than a bare speaking. (Gilbert, 1791, p. 889)

By repeating full phrases from his earlier works, Gilbert reasserts a ban on hearsay. The goal of the rule against hearsay is to determine what can count as evidence. As Gilbert puts it elsewhere, "nothing can be more 'indeterminate' than loose and wandering '*Testimonies*' taken up on the uncertain Report of the Talk and Discourse of others" (Gilbert, 1791, p. 890). Here, wandering testimonies, reports, talk, and discourse are presented as synonyms for bad evidence. Hearsay rests on the unsteady ground of language. Thus, hearsay does not meet the requirements of logos – it has no substance – which is demanded by the law. Because of this emphasis on empirical evidence, logos, in debates about whether a hearsay statement may be admissible, the law misunderstands the full rhetorical structure of a statement, rendering ethos moot at best and dangerous (read subjective) at worst.

6.3 A CONTEMPORARY HEARSAY RULE

Essentially a product and representation of legal language ideology, the rule against hearsay (and all of its exceptions) is developed in the US Federal Rules of Evidence (2023), officially adopted in 1972 and most recently reviewed, revised, and re-ratified in 2023. Rule 801 (Federal Rules of Evidence, 2023) in the US Federal Rules of Evidence defines the rule this way:

> The following definitions apply under this article:
> (a) Statement. "Statement" means a person's oral assertion, written assertion, or nonverbal conduct, if the person intended it as an assertion.
> (b) Declarant. "Declarant" means the person who made the statement.
> (c) Hearsay. "Hearsay" means a statement that:
> (1) the declarant does not make while testifying at the current trial or hearing; and
> (2) a party offers in evidence to prove the truth of the matter asserted in the statement.

A statement, in this configuration, is an assertion, whether written, verbal, or gestural, given as evidence toward and about the truth of the statement inasmuch as it indexes the legal matter at hand – the evidence asserted as a true account of what happened. A statement is made by a declarant. A declarant would typically be the person who witnessed the crime; in hearsay law the declarant is the person who made the *original* statement, a witness to the crime, the person who witnessed the event in question. The declarant is not the person on the stand who merely parrots the words of some other person. Hearsay is a statement of evidence that speaks directly to the alleged crime under legal evaluation, asserting the truth of what happened, and offering evidence about the crime. It is made in court by somebody who did not themselves witness the events about which the claims are made. Hearsay, then, always involves a speaker on the stand who narrates a prior statement about a prior event that they only heard about secondarily but did not witness themselves. Typically, such an evidentiary statement that "asserts the truth of the matter" would be given only in the context of testimony about the declarant's first-hand experience, which would then be subjected to direct and cross-examination. In court, such a declarant bears witness to that which they have seen with their own eyes. When hearsay is involved, the person who takes the stand is not the original speaker who saw the event and who can be cross-examined, as per the Sixth Amendment (U.S. Const. amend. VI), but rather it is another person, the person to whom the declarant spoke after the fact (or was recorded and replayed after the fact), and their testimony is typically not admissible (Federal Rules of Evidence, 2023, Rule 8.2). Therefore, the admission of hearsay (potentially) runs afoul of the US Constitution, and it is that exact relationship – between hearsay and the Sixth Amendment – that is debated in criminal courts and especially in this argument, by the US Supreme Court.

There are some twenty-three exceptions to the hearsay rule (Federal Rules of Evidence, 2023, Rule 803), and therefore, there can be long and extensive analyses of which types of out-of-court, truth-bearing utterances may be admitted. I am arguing that the hearsay rule is structured and worded as though it is about the utterance, the hearsay statement presented in court, when in fact it assesses the original speaker in many different ways, more, in fact, than it assesses the utterance. This legal deconstruction of the hearsay rule, which displaces the utterance in favor of a discussion of the speaker, envisions a relationship between ethos (the credibility and trustworthiness of the speaker) and logos (empirical proofs that work against the speaker).

6.3.1 Ohio v. Roberts *(1980) and Its Demise*

In the mid-to-late twentieth century, a number of cases take up the issue of hearsay. Our more recent story about hearsay begins with *Roberts* (*Ohio v. Roberts*, 1979). *Roberts*' rhetorical structure helps shift the analytical focus away from ethos – the credibility of the speaker – and toward logos – empirical evidence presented as truth. In so doing, *Roberts* surreptitiously dismisses ethos from the equation, just as Locke and Gilbert would have it. The analyses of hearsay in the Supreme Court evident in reading the precedent in the law itself, including *Roberts*, regularly push off accounts that can be linked to individual subjectivity as fallible and thus inadmissible. Only those linked to the empirical world that somehow circumvent the now dismissed ethos of the speaker are found to be admissible.

There are a number of heuristics circulating in case law that operationalize the rulings of the US Supreme Court. They are used in lower courts to evaluate and measure a proposed hearsay statement. According to *Crawford v. Washington* (2003), the well-used heuristics established in *Roberts* (*Ohio v. Roberts*, 1979), written by Justice Blackmun, run afoul of the Sixth Amendment. In *Roberts*, Roberts was accused of forging a check and possessing stolen credit cards belonging to Bernard Isaacs and his wife. Roberts claimed that Issacs' daughter, Anita, had given him the check and credit cards to use. During long and extensive questioning at a preliminary hearing, Anita denied Roberts' claim that she had given him the stolen items. Though she was subpoenaed several times, Anita did not appear at Roberts' trial. Because Anita could not be found and against the hearsay objections of the defense, Anita's prior testimony from the preliminary hearing was admitted as hearsay during the trial. Roberts was found guilty based on the admission of Anita's hearsay evidence. The case was nearly immediately appealed, with the appellate court finding that the trial court had not tried hard enough to find Anita and that they erroneously admitted her prior testimony. The Supreme Court agreed to hear *Roberts* (*Ohio v. Roberts*, 1979) and take up, again, the issue of hearsay.

The test developed by the Supreme Court in *Roberts* relies heavily on two sociolegal constructions. First, hearsay can be admitted if it fits within a "firmly rooted hearsay exception" (*Ohio v. Roberts*, 1979, p. 66) This component of the hearsay test points directly back to the framing of the US Constitution – any hearsay exception in place when the Sixth Amendment was conceived is typically deemed valid. If the exception was not a part of longstanding tradition, according to *Roberts*, admissible hearsay must be shown to bear "particularized guarantees of trustworthiness" (*Ohio v. Roberts*, 1979, p. 66). *Roberts*' formulation rests heavily on a largely under-defined conception of "trustworthy" and the related concept "reliable."

Relying heavily on the 1895 opinion *Mattox v. United States* (1895, hereafter *Mattox*), *Roberts* (*Ohio v. Roberts*, 1979) affirms the requirements of confrontation. According to *Mattox*,

> a personal examination and cross-examination of the witness in which the accused has an opportunity, not only of testing the recollection and sifting the conscience of the witness, but of compelling him to stand face to face with the jury in order that they may look at him, and judge by his demeanor upon the stand and the manner in which he gives his testimony whether he is worthy of belief. (*Mattox v. United States*, 1895, p. 242)

In this late nineteenth-century precedent, *Mattox* focuses attention on the declarant. For our purposes, there are two important concepts in *Mattox* that interlock: "conscience of the witness" and "worthy of belief." In 1895, when watching a person give testimony, the jury was looking for imperfections and inconsistencies in the testimony, but they were also required to assess the conscience of the witness: their trustworthiness and believability. Their ethos. By analyzing the conscience of the witness, the jury can determine whether that person was "worthy of belief," that is, trustworthy. Hearsay in *Mattox* is inadmissible because it disallows the jury from evaluating the witness' ethos.

The requirement for hearsay to match the requirements of in-court, on-the-stand testimony as explained in *Mattox v. United States* (1895) positions ethos as an important feature of law at that time. *Mattox* asserts that only hearsay that meets the standards of an in-court performance of ethos tested in cross-examination is admissible. In at least this one iteration of hearsay (*Mattox*), the relationship between the speaker and the audience somewhat follows typical rhetorical lines of logic: The speaker makes assertions of truth to which legal rules and procedures are applied and, in the process, the speaker's worthiness, conscience, and trustworthiness (ethos) are assessed by the audience, in this case a judge and jury (pathos), in order for the evidence (logos) to be presented and accepted as true.

Because *Mattox v. United States* (1895) places so much emphasis on the witness on the stand, when hearsay is admitted, the speaker's ethos is positioned in such a way as to be open to peril and ultimately to erasure. In demanding an original witness, *Mattox* asserts extra weight on the importance of empirically grounded, experiential truth in relationship to arguments about the speaker. In discussions about hearsay and their heightening attention to the ethos of the speaker on the stand as they are related to the truths found in the material world, *Mattox* opens room for the ethos of the speaker who is not on the stand to be suppressed when the speaker is unavailable. This is because the person with empirical knowledge is not testifying. This assertion ultimately lays the groundwork for ethos to be suppressed altogether. Let me explain. When the spotlight is put on ethos and logos as they are in *Mattox*, logos is isolated from the speaker, seeming to work independently from ethos. Logos refers to the world of lived experience, while ethos refers back to the speaker of the utterance in question, alone. Here as well as elsewhere in the law, then, ethos is disparaged precisely because it is unique to the individual and must be assessed as such. The relationship of logos to objectivity is wildly preferred.

In its application of *Mattox v. United States* (1895) and other precedents, *Roberts* (*Ohio v. Roberts*, 1979) works to isolate logos in order to render it open to evaluation on its own. For example, *Roberts* applies *Mancusi v. Stubbs* (1972, hereafter, *Mancusi*) (which itself quotes from precedents, which also quote from precedents, and so on *ad infinitum*). According to *Roberts*: "The focus of the Court's concern has been to ensure that there 'are indicia of reliability which have been widely viewed as determinative of whether a statement may be placed before the jury though there is no confrontation of the declarant...'" (*Ohio v. Roberts*, 1979, pp. 65–66, quoting *Mancusi v. Stubbs*, 1972).

Using *Mancusi v. Stubbs* (1972), *Roberts* (*Ohio v. Roberts*, 1979) ultimately shifts from an evaluation of the ethos of the speaker/witness (*Mattox*) to an evaluation of the statement, isolating the statement and assessing it only in terms of logos – empirical proof. In *Mancusi*, the statement is "placed," passive voice, before the jury with the speaker of the statement grammatically removed. This grammar makes it seem as though there was no speaker behind potentially admissible hearsay at all, which, in fact, resonates throughout this case law. Only delinked from a speaker and their ethos can a statement bear the so-called indicia of reliability and be admitted as hearsay. This procedure is possible *because* the speaker (ethos) has been first isolated and then excluded in legal discussion and debate.

The shift away from the speaker and toward the statement makes one further shift in *Roberts* (*Ohio v. Roberts*, 1979) away from an evaluation of ethos. The notion "indicia of reliability" that *Roberts* relies on uses precedential chains that reach backward to eighteenth-century ideas about reliability. *Dutton v. Evans* (hereafter *Evans*) also cited in *Roberts*, argues: "circumstances under which [the out-of-court speaker] made the statement were such as to give reason to suppose that [the out-of-court speaker] did not misrepresent [the accused's] involvement in the crime" (*Dutton v. Evans*, 1970, p. 10). This reliance on circumstances to indicate the trustworthiness or reliability of the statement is one place where we see Locke's language ideology peek through. Indeed, when the speaker is divided from the statement, circumstances – material conditions – become even more important and ethos is rendered immaterial, in every way that word can mean. The reliance on circumstances to provide assurance of truth when the speaker is unavailable to take the stand and be assessed is operational precisely because circumstances are empirical rather than linguistic, therefore placing such a statement closer to the truth. According to the logic of the law, "circumstances" (we can call them events and contexts) can render some statements inherently true. "Circumstances" are truths from the empirical, material world, and, as such, the law proposes, they control, even counter, the natural subjectivity of the speaker, creating space to push the speaker out of the equation completely.

6.3.2 *Enter* Crawford *(2004) and the Redefinition of Hearsay*

I turn attention now back to *Crawford v. Washington* (2003) and to *Davis/Hammon* (*Davis v. Washington*, 2006), both of which were written by Justice Scalia. For Justice Scalia, when analyzing a case and writing a Supreme Court opinion, "historical inquiry" is entirely relevant, if not required, in order to accurately understand the original meaning of any document, but especially a legal document (see Hannah & Mootz, Chapter 2 in this volume). In *Crawford* and *Davis/Hammon*, Justice Scalia uses historical research and performance when he insistently relies on (his interpretation of) the lexical and legal knowledge of the Framers. When Justice Scalia writes the following in *Crawford*, he is very clearly presenting a seventeenth-century-language ideology: "Where testimonial statements are involved, we do not think the Framers meant to leave the Sixth Amendment's protection to the vagaries of the rules of evidence, much less to amorphous notions of 'reliability'" (*Crawford v. Washington*, 2003, p. 61). Justice Scalia very obviously and purposefully inserts and applies his linguistic and legal language ideology about original intent in his opinions about hearsay. As he said in an interview, "words have meaning. And their meaning doesn't change" (Senior, 2013).

Crawford v. Washington (2003) overturned *Ohio v. Roberts* (1979) by operationalizing new terms, definitions, and rhetorics that have tighter restrictions and more stringent methods for evaluating hearsay, but that, nevertheless, share its language ideology, relying heavily on empiricism and further eradicating the desirableness of speaker ethos. As Justice Scalia presents them, the terms and concepts in hearsay discourse are defined in ways that explicitly and directly link present case law to historical texts and definitions through the copious use of eighteenth-century precedents and legal treatises.

Recall that *Crawford v. Washington* (2003) was a case in which a man, Lee, had been stabbed by Crawford, and in which Sylvia Crawford's police interrogation was admitted as hearsay when Crawford invoked his marital privilege (explained further above). In *Crawford*, Scalia begins his arguments with a reference to a dictionary definition of the term "witness" published in 1828. *Crawford* states,

> The text of the Confrontation Clause reflects this focus. It applies to "witnesses" against the accused – in other words, those who "bear testimony." 2 N. Webster, An American Dictionary of the English Language (1828). "Testimony," in turn, is typically "[a] solemn declaration or affirmation made for the purpose of establishing or proving some fact." (*Crawford v. Washington*, 2003, p. 51)

First, note that the dictionary referenced in *Crawford* is as close to the time of the Framers of the Constitution as Justice Scalia could find – the 1828 edition. In that 1828 dictionary, a "witness" is a person "who bear[s] testimony." This is not controversial. In the context of the law, it gestures quite obviously to in-court testimony. A witness, according to this dictionary from the early nineteenth century, "bears testimony." According to the same edition of Webster's dictionary, "testimony" is a "declaration or affirmation made for the purposes of establishing or proving some fact." The passive construction of this definition excises the speaker of the declaration. Locke would be proud.

The concept of witness is the central concern of the Confrontation Clause of the Sixth Amendment (U.S. Const. amend. VI) (even though most of the discussion in hearsay case law in the twenty-first century has been about the statement), and so the Supreme Court must begin with the "witness." However, the real work in this reframing of hearsay is with "testimony." This case law presumes that testimony comes prior to the act of being a witness in the process of giving what the court deems inherently testimonial; in this process, the declarant is automatically transformed into a *witness*, who must always have been acting as a *witness*, regardless of whether they were on the stand, under oath, or are even aware of their witnessing. The involvement of a witness animates the requirements of the Confrontation Clause. (In the Sixth Amendment, the accused is promised the right to confront their accusers, so the witness must be present in the equation of hearsay.) The process of evaluating hearsay within this definition's structure – the one that puts testimony in front of witnessing – removes the statement from the real, in-the-world speaker (Sylvia and others) and relinks it instead to a legal abstraction, *witness*, and ultimately to the circumstances in which and about which the statement is made. It is these circumstances that indicate whether a statement is testimonial, and it is testimony which proves the presence of a witness. With these legal acrobatics, the statement is transformed into evidence (or hearsay) that has nothing to do with the speaker or their ethos; it has to do only with the legal formation, *witness*. These statements are constructed out of logos – the empirical. *Testimony* relies only on circumstances for its relationship to real knowledge and truth. The formation of *witness* follows the identification of *testimony*. It is the empirical world, the circumstances, that can verify the truthfulness of *testimony*. It is no longer the "conscience" of the witness (*Mattox v. United States*, 1895). Moreover, it is testimony that produces a *witness*, which functions as sort of an abstract for anybody, not only the person whose utterance is in question.

To restate my argument, legal discourses transform a statement made in the world into legally recognizable *testimony*, by overemphasizing logos and censoring ethos. This takes the statement functionally away from the speaker by transforming the speaker into the legal abstraction, *witness*, which is equated with a speaker on the stand but should not be confused with an embodied person. In this way, *Crawford v. Washington* (2003) delinks the speaker from the statement, because *testimony* is always spoken by a *witness*, but testimony is proved not through reference to the witness but rather through reference to circumstances. However, in evoking the abstraction, *witness*, the Sixth Amendment to the Constitution is called into play. If the speaker is a *witness* (in or out of the courtroom and whether or not they know they are a witness), then the requirements of the Confrontation Clause must be satisfied. Any utterance deemed testimonial must be cross-examined.

It is the circumstance, the logos, that proves the testimonial*ness* of a statement, and, in the process, an abstract *witness* is produced who has no ethos. According to the Supreme Court, Sylvia Crawford's recorded police interrogation was *testimony* and thus Sylvia was acting as a *witness* even though she was not in court and had not sworn an oath, and even though she likely had no idea that she was acting as a witness in the legal sense. These two paired concepts have the power to reach through time, pulling people into their abstracting capabilities – turning real people into abstractions – and altering their relationship with their own speech.

After giving the dictionary definitions discussed above, *Crawford* goes on to say:

> An accuser who makes a formal statement to government officers bears testimony in a sense that a person who makes a casual remark to an acquaintance does not. The constitutional text, like the history underlying the common-law right of confrontation, thus reflects an especially acute concern with a specific type of out-of-court statement. (*Crawford v. Washington*, 2003, p. 51)

In other words, some declarations are testimonial in the legal sense, even if they are produced out of court, while others are *objectively* not testimonial. And importantly, statements are testimonial not because the speaker was an in-court witness, but because of the circumstances surrounding the production of the statement, even those outside of the courtroom, indicated that the speech was testimonial. The trustworthiness of *testimony* is a feature of logos alone.

6.3.3 *Enter* Davis/Hammon (2006)

Davis/Hammon (*Davis v. Washington*, 2006), also written by Justice Scalia, supplies a single opinion for two cases as a way of rectifying perceived misapplications of law in lower courts. In one case (*Davis*), the Supreme Court admits hearsay as constitutionally sound, and in the other (*Hammon*), the Supreme Court determines that the hearsay is not admissible. *Davis* and *Hammon* are both domestic violence cases. In *Davis*, Michelle McCottry called the police when she was being assaulted by her former boyfriend, Davis. On the phone with 911, McCottry exclaimed, "he's here, jumping on me again" (*Davis v. Washington*, 2006, p. 877). Police arrived four minutes after she called 911 and observed that McCottry was "frantic." The excited utterance exception to hearsay, which was used in *Davis*, hinges on the emotional state of the speaker; the speaker must be shown to be "frantic," "hysterical" (cf. Andrus, 2015). McCottry did not appear at Davis' trial, and so her statements to 911 were admitted using the excited utterance exception to hearsay. These statements are hearsay because the person who said them – McCottry – was not available in court to be cross-examined. McCottry's "excited utterance" is nevertheless determined admissible by the Supreme Court because it is inherently "nontestimonial," that is, not spoken by a *witness*.

Hammon (*Davis v. Washington*, 2006) involves an assault by Hershel Hammon on his wife, Amy Hammon, resulting in a call to police, who responded to a "domestic disturbance" (p. 819). When they arrived, police found Amy sitting outside on the front porch. She appeared "somewhat frightened" but told them that "nothing was the matter" (p. 819). She gave police permission to enter the home, where they found a broken heater and other broken household objects. As is usual, officers separated Amy and Hershel and questioned them individually. After hearing Amy's account of what happened, the police officer questioning her had her fill out a battery affidavit. Amy did not appear when she was subpoenaed to Hershel's bench trial. Her statements to police when they arrived at her house were not admitted at trial as excited utterances because Amy appeared too calm when officers spoke with her. The battery affidavit, however, was admitted at trial. The Supreme Court disagreed with this decision. Amy's statements were determined "testimonial" and were thus excluded because Amy had been acting as a *witness* when she spoke with police.

The arguments in *Davis/Hammon* (*Davis v. Washington*, 2006) compare and contrast the two cases, using the newly minted *Crawford v. Washington* (2003). At the center of the arguments in *Davis/Hammon* is the renewed p/re/conception of what it means to give *testimony* and act as a *witness*. Ultimately, *Davis/Hammon* reinforces the arguments in *Crawford* that some hearsay statements can be admitted without cross-examination, using the reasoning that they are obviously legally and semantically stable, reliable, and trustworthy because of their close relationship to the empirical world and the absence of speaker subjectivity/ethos. Some statements do not give *testimony*, they are not spoken by a *witness*, and therefore they don't need to be cross-examined. Others are *testimonial* and as spoken by a *witness*.

In the recapitulation of the legal reasoning established in *Crawford v. Washington* (2003), *Davis/Hammon* makes the following argument:

> A critical portion of this holding, and the portion central to resolution of the two cases now before us, is the phrase "testimonial statements." Only statements of this sort cause the declarant to be a "witness" within the meaning of the Confrontation Clause. ... It is the testimonial character of the statement that separates it from other hearsay that, while subject to traditional limitations upon hearsay evidence, is not subject to the Confrontation Clause. (*Davis v. Washington*, 2006, p. 821)

The Supreme Court therefore determines that McCottry's statements to 911 were nontestimonial (*Davis*), while Amy Hammon's affidavit were testimonial. *Davis/Hammon* explicitly states that a testimonial statement "*cause[s]*" a person to become a *witness*. This is some kind of legal magic. According to *Davis/Hammon*, legal procedure and evaluation transform a person into a *witness* and in that process, the speaker is divested of their subjective, rhetorical link to their own language, cutting off ethos in perpetuity. Indeed, it is presumed that such a link never existed. The admissible statement is the product of the circumstances in which the statement is uttered. The speaker in this rhetorical construction is positioned as a sort of legal, vestigial tail.

Davis/Hammon goes on to further clarify the distinction between testimonial and nontestimonial:

> Statements are nontestimonial when made in the course of police interrogation under circumstances objectively indicating that the primary purpose of the interrogation is to enable police assistance to meet an ongoing emergency [*Davis*]. They are testimonial when the circumstances objectively indicate that there is no such ongoing emergency, and that the primary purpose of the interrogation is to establish or prove past events potentially relevant to later criminal prosecution [*Hammon*]. (*Davis v. Washington*, 2006, p. 822)

Notice in this quotation that the use of the word "objectively" (again) relates us directly to Locke and his theory of truth, rooted in high modern notions of the relationship between language and the world of experience. In *Crawford*, "objective speakers" such as Amy Hammon, who was sitting on her front porch having just been assaulted, should know, according to legal logic, that her words were likely to be used in court. In that moment, as a reasonable person, she must have known that in talking to police, she was bearing *witness*. Or so the legal reasoning goes. *Davis/Hammon* further develops the distinction between testimonial and nontestimonial by introducing the concept "primary purpose" (*Davis v. Washington*, 2006, p. 822). In the "primary purpose" assessment, it is the "circumstances" that behave objectively. These objective circumstances – not the speaker – indicate what kind of statement it is: testimonial or nontestimonial. To be clear, hearsay is not a statement existing in some accessible past event, waiting to be located in the world and simply plucked out of the circumstances. What I am showing in this analysis is that these statements – testimonial or nontestimonial – are framed, constrained, and produced *in the law*; their supposed objectivity is a legal construct that the law itself refuses to see.

The rhetorical force of the statement in this legal context is established by analyzing the circumstances and the "primary purpose" (*Davis v. Washington*, 2006, p. 822) for which the statement was elicited. Circumstances such as an ongoing emergency produce a statement that can be considered nontestimonial, while a discussion with police would be considered (always and already) testimonial. Amy Hammon's statements are excluded, labeled hearsay, because their primary purpose was to answer police questions, which an "objective speaker" would have known could be used later in court. Michelle McCottry's statements, on the other hand, were a cry for help, and were therefore admissible as objective accounts of what *really* happened. McCottry's speech was nontestimonial because she was asking for help. The "primary purpose" in both cases is determined by the context, the circumstances (i.e., the logos), surrounding the production of the statement, not by assessing the speaker, who is of course structurally absent.

The *Davis/Hammon* court therefore asserts that Amy's statements given "under official interrogation are an obvious substitute for live testimony, because they do precisely *what a witness does* on direct examination; they are inherently testimonial" (*Davis v. Washington*, 2006, p. 830). Because police ask questions in similar ways as lawyers in court do, the resultant statements are assumed to function identically to in-court testimony. Not to get into the virtually innumerable ways that police and lawyer questioning are different. Circumstances, not the speaker, have discursive agency in both testimonial and nontestimonial configurations; they are two sides of a coin, proving each other correct. The speaker of a testimonial statement is translated into an *always witness*, a linguistic, rhetorical construction that places empirical circumstances at the helm of identifying the truth. And with that, the delinking of the statement from ethos is complete.

6.4 CONCLUSIONS

The legal language ideology apparent in the hearsay rule, along with its exceptions, uses a Lockean language ideology to re/organize and re/structure the relationship among ethos/pathos/logos, subjectivity/void/objectivity, and speaker/void/empirical evidence. In *Crawford v. Washington* (2003) and *Davis/Hammon* (*Davis v. Washington*, 2006), *testimony* is moved out of the courtroom to any place that a person could be speaking in circumstances that indicate that the statement is empirically true and that the person would necessarily know that their speech may be used later in court as *testimony*. When *testimony* is placed out in the world like this, the speaker is forced to bear witness without a connection to their own ethos, regardless of their discursive, rhetorical desires, and without the trappings of the courtroom context. The heavy reliance on logos transforms ethos into a forced, empty position. *Witnessing* becomes a product of legal reasoning, rather than an in-court, visible, literal procedure, and, as such, it can be applied to any speaker, speaking in circumstances that empirically proclaim that the statements produced therein are always already *testimony*. The orphaned statements that result from and are produced in hearsay discourse are hypostatized. They are diminished rhetorically, reduced to a subjective/objective dichotomy.

When hypostatized, statements lose their rhetorical flux and semantic flexibility. Speakers, too, suffer rhetorically and semantically through legal sedimentation. They are either *witnesses* or not, objectively. In either case, the speaker's relationship to their own speech is weakened if not dissolved. To be clear, I don't necessarily think a statement belongs to a speaker in a totalizing way. From a postmodern rhetorical approach, statements are produced by a broad set of actors, events, social discourses, and the like, all engaged in interaction. The ways in which the rule against hearsay dismisses human agency and instead positions it on the text may seem aligned with postmodernity. However, this dismissal of the speaker and their agency doesn't disbelieve in sovereign agency; it merely rearranges the position of agency in the rhetorical situation. What interests me in this discourse is the fact that the law does not take into account the effects of social discourses, interaction, the productive effects of cultural values, the broader relationship between events, or the like, on things such as testimony (logos/language) and witnessing (ethos/embodied person).

I have argued that legal reasoning, similar to Lockean theories of language, identifies reality in events which are considered to be finite, real, and identifiable. *Witnesses* are instrumentalized such that they are legally useful. And this is the problem. Not only is semantic and rhetorical access to the statement undone in the evaluation of hearsay, but it is also undone in such a way as to instrumentalize the speaker and erase their ethos. Such a structuralist language ideology idealizes and obsesses over the empirical. Buried within the legal contest between "testimonial" and "nontestimonial" is the idea that signification and meaning are only the product of sensory experience that is translated into words and that are only true when they mean the same thing for everyone forever because of their relationship to the "real" world.

I have shown that the dismissal of ethos in favor of all logos all the time is more closely related to high modernity, structuralism, and a Lockean language ideology. Language is always problematic in a Lockean rhetoric, because, in his representational model of language, language is merely indexical and lesser than the empirical world of experience. Language is itself not real. Language is merely a channel for the empirical. Perhaps unexpectedly, a byproduct of this view of language is the dismissal of not only the important work that language does for and in the law (in a set of laws about language, no less), but also the dismissal of the pivotal role that speakers play in the rhetorical production of their speech. According to the legal reasoning circulating in hearsay legal discourse, if language is built on the unknowns that speakers bring to the rhetorical equation (motive, intention, emotion, etc.) rather than on a foundation of sensory experience, if language is not moored to something empirical, then it will float away into semantic chaos where it will not be legally useful.

REFERENCES

Andrus, J. (2015). *Entextualizing domestic violence: Language ideology and violence against women in the Anglo-American hearsay principle*. Oxford University Press.

Aristotle. (n.d.). *On the soul*. The Internet classics archive. (J. A. Smith, Trans.). http://classics.mit.edu/Aristotle/soul.html (Original work published ca. 350 BCE.)

Aristotle, & Kennedy, G. A. (2006). *On rhetoric: A theory of civic discourse*. Oxford University Press.

Carlo, R. (2020). *Transforming ethos: Place and the material in rhetoric and writing*. University Press of Colorado.

Chettle v. Chettle, [1821] 161 English Reporter 1399.

Crawford v. Washington, 541 U.S. 36 (2003).

Davis v. Washington, 547 U.S. 813 (2006).

Duschinsky, R. (2012). Tabula rasa and human nature. *Philosophy*, 87(4), 509–529. https://doi.org/10.1017/S0031819112000393

Dutton v. Evans, 400 U.S. 74 (1970).

Federal Rules of Evidence (2023).
Foucault, M. (2001). *The order of things*. Routledge. https://doi.org/10.4324/9780203996645 (Original work published 1975.)
Gilbert, J. (1791). *The law of evidence*. A. Strahan & W. Woodfall. Available at archive.org/embed/bim_eighteenth-century_the-law-of-evidence-by-_gilbert-geoffrey-sir_1791_1
Gilbert, J., & Locke, J. (1752). *An abstract of Mr. Locke's essay on human understanding*. Available at archive.org/embed/bim_eighteenth-century_an-abstract-of-mr-locke_locke-john_1752
Hyde, M. J. (2004). *The ethos of rhetoric*. University of South Carolina Press.
Landsman, S. (1992). The civil jury in America: Scenes from an unappreciated history. *Hastings Law Journal*, 44(3), 579–620.
Langbein, J. H. (1996). Historical foundations of the law of evidence: A view from the Ryder sources. *Columbia Law Review*, 96(5), 1168. https://doi.org/10.2307/1123403
Locke, John. (1690) *An essay concerning humane understanding*. Available at archive.org/embed/bim_early-english-books-1641-1700_an-essay-concerning-huma_locke-john_1690
Mancusi v. Stubbs, 408 U.S. 204 (1972).
Mattox v. United States, 156 U.S. 237 (1895).
Mertz, E. (2007). *The language of law school: Learning to "think like a lawyer."* Oxford University Press.
Ohio v. Roberts, 448 U.S. 56 (1979).
Senior, J. (2013, October 4). In conversation with Antonin Scalia. *New York Magazine*. https://nymag.com/news/features/antonin-scalia-2013-10/ [https://perma.cc/AD3Z-GBUF]
Sullivan, D. L. (1993). The ethos of epideictic encounter. *Philosophy & Rhetoric*, 26(2), 113–133.
Taylor, J. P. (1872), A *treatise on the law of evidence* (6th ed.). William Maxwel & Son.
Thompson v. Trevanion, 90 Eng. Rep. 179 (K.B. 1694).
U.S. Const. amend. VI.
Washington Revised Code Annotated § 5.60.060.

PART IV

Permeable Boundaries

7

Searching for Legal *Topoi* in the Shadow Docket

M. Kelly Carr

7.1 INTRODUCTION

On February 7, 2022, the US Supreme Court issued a stay of an Alabama district court's ruling blocking that state's redrawn congressional map. The district court had found that the redrawn map likely violated Section 2 of the Voting Rights Act, and it ordered the Alabama legislature to redraw the map before the state's 2022 midterm elections. In *Merrill v. Milligan* (2022), the Supreme Court sidelined that order until it could hold a full hearing, thus guaranteeing that the original map in question would represent the voting districts in 2022.

Justice Kagan dissented from granting that stay, and, in so doing, articulated her long-standing concerns about similar emergency actions that her colleagues had taken and their impact on the Court. "Today's decision is one more in a disconcertingly long line of cases in which this Court uses its shadow docket to signal or make changes in the law, without anything approaching full briefing and argument," wrote Kagan (*Merrill v. Milligan*, 2022, p. 11). The Court's stay decision "does a disservice to our own appellate processes, which serve both to constrain and to legitimate the Court's authority" (p. 12).

William Baude argues that emergency orders and summary decisions – a series of judicial actions that Baude collectively dubbed the "shadow docket" – lack the transparency and consistency of cases granted and decided on their merits (Baude, 2015, p. 12). Cases such as these have increased over the past decade, however, and the stakes of the decisions have been more far-reaching. Moreover, they have increasingly attached rather lengthy and combative holding opinions, concurrences, and dissents. Even more significant: They have asked lower courts to treat these emergency declarations as precedent in deciding newer cases, vacating subsequent lower court decisions and remanding them for further consideration in light of emergency stay opinions.[1]

[1] The Supreme Court received a rare petition for writ of certiorari before judgment in *Harvest Rock Church, Inc. v. Newsom* (2020). Eight days after *Roman Catholic Diocese of Brooklyn NY*

This confluence of changes subverts the typical appellate court dialectical process, to the detriment of legal argumentation within a democracy. This is true for several reasons. First, emergency stays and injunctions rely solely on party briefs, denying third-party or public arguments before the Court. These cases sometimes do substantive doctrinal work or claim broader precedential power without the substantive merits-docket process of briefing, oral arguments, and circulating drafts of opinions, each of which holds important internal – between the Justices' chambers – and external – to legal, political, and lay audiences – rhetorical functions.

Second, their holdings turn the rhetorical audience of their discourse inward, toward other legal actors, ignoring the public(s) that they are obligated to engage with in the public sphere. The insulated and quick nature of emergency stays and injunctions leads to opinions that fail to engage fully with the important audiences and starting points of argument.

Third, the truncated review process and lack of established norms for the published opinions (since no opinions are required) means that Justices can shorthand or even skip elements of the rhetorical invention process that are crucial to both the reasoning and justification of their opinions. This means that lawyers are left to read the tea leaves when crafting new arguments, and Justices are making decisions without the full scope of the implications available to them.

Moreover, the constrained vision of the Supreme Court's rhetorical audience neglects public audiences and diminishes the characterological integrity of the Justices, who take pains to repair their image absent the full performance of instructional process that full merits opinions engage in.

In this chapter, I attend to the implications of shadow docket opinions for both public and legal argument by analyzing a COVID-restriction shadow docket case: *Roman Catholic Diocese of Brooklyn NY v. Cuomo* (2020) (hereinafter *Roman Catholic Diocese v. Cuomo*). First, I review the origins of the shadow docket and its significance in contemporary legal culture. Next, I outline how elements of classical and contemporary rhetorical theory form the foundation for contemporary Supreme Court opinion writing and reasoning, addressing in particular the implications for both public and legal argument more generally. I use this section as a roadmap for analyzing *Roman Catholic Diocese v. Cuomo*, highlighting the missing commonplaces – or *topoi* – of argument that stem from the expediency and lack of public access inherent in shadow docket decisions.

7.2 DEFINING THE SHADOW DOCKET

Typically, the Supreme Court cases that garner attention are those on the merits docket, wherein parties are granted a full hearing and consideration before the

v. Andrew Cuomo (2020), the Court issued a GVR: an order that grants the petition (G), vacates the district court's order denying injunctive relief (V), and remands the case for reconsideration in light of a recent development (R) (Vladeck, 2022; see also McFadden & Kapoor, 2021).

Supreme Court, a process that includes a full spate of briefings, oral arguments, and publicly issued decisions of the Justices' votes, including lengthy opinions explaining the reasoning and justifications for their conclusions (Black & Brannon, 2022; Vladeck, 2023, p. 3). The Court's merits docket is published and accessible, as are all the briefs filed in relation to the cases.

In contrast, Baude, a law professor and former law clerk to Chief Justice Roberts, defined the Court's shadow docket as "a range of orders and summary decisions that defy its normal procedural regularity," including summary decisions, emergency stays (of a lower court's ruling), and injunctions (wherein the Court restrains a party instead of a court) (Baude, 2015, p. 1). The shadow docket encompasses the large amount of Supreme Court work that issues a ruling without full briefings or oral arguments (Vladeck, 2019, p. 123). Such decisions are often unsigned and without reasoning attached. These non-merits judicial acts are not new, but the frequency, scope, and significance of their orders has grown exponentially over the past decade, as well as the frequency of publicly issued dissents from Justices regarding the decisions made. The American Bar Association reports that while only eight emergency relief applications were filed during the Bush and Obama administrations combined (2001–2017), averaging about one every other year, thirty-six applications were filed during the four years of the Trump administration (O'Connell, 2021).

The potential harms of non-merits Supreme Court decisions have been criticized for decades (Hartnett, 2016). Legal scholars have warned about the "managerial or executive character" of summary decisions, rather than the dialectical character of judicial tribunals, since at least the 1950s (Brown, 1958, p. 94). Steve Vladeck makes it clear that recent concerns over the shadow docket are not so much about their procedural illegitimacy – the Supreme Court has broad authority to intervene without having to await any rulings. Rather, the concern lies with the increasing frequency with which Justices use it for constitutionally significant questions; the Court's disregard for restraint, a primary source of this non-elected institution's credibility; the lack of respect for lower courts, which are more in touch with local goings on; and the abandonment of the legal reasoning that provides decision-making tools for lower courts, policymakers, and future merits cases (Vladeck, 2019, pp. 127–128). Emergency applications provide a way for litigants to bypass the sometimes years-long process of gaining a full merits hearing before the Supreme Court, or to freeze a lower court's ruling, either skipping stages of appeal or running out the clock on time-sensitive issues such as elections and death penalty cases. Finally, and most importantly to this chapter, the trust and legitimacy of the Supreme Court is undermined when controversial or far-reaching cases are decided in private and without full briefing. McFadden and Kapoor (2021, p. 828) argue that we are in a "new era of litigation, in which securing emergency interim relief can sometimes be as important as, if not more important than, an eventual victory on the merits." The lack of transparency innate in these cases, as well as the capacity to drastically change the trajectory of public policy or even electoral processes without hearings or deliberations, led the House Judiciary Committee to hold a hearing on shadow docket practices in February 2021.

Shadow docket decisions have the potential to alter existing doctrine and the scope of the Constitution without the substantive reasoning that normalizes doctrinal change through acceptable legal reasons. This is true even when Justices attach reasoning to their decisions in a *per curiam* opinion – meaning the unsigned, collective ruling of an appellate court. A brief review of an important shadow docket case shows how. This analysis will foreground the truncated or missing topoi of legal argumentation, as well as impoverished or missing artifacts that merits-based Supreme Court opinions offer. Perhaps because the norms of legal opinion writing are not binding on these cases, Justices writing the per curiam holding are liberated from the constraints that bind them in signed, merits-based decisions. Yet the liminal space created between a summary judgment without opinion and a full merits decision raises several rhetorical problems, especially in cases of controversy: a lack of transparency on why it was granted, raising the specter of political motivations; a notable and contentious lack of agreement between Justices on both the holding and the interpretations; and the pseudo-precedential treatment of the resulting shadow docket decisions, both by lower courts and the Justices themselves.

7.3 CLASSICAL ROOTS OF CONTEMPORARY LEGAL WRITING

The art of finding all the available means of persuasion in order to fruitfully choose the best tools to craft the best messages to suit the particular moment, audience, and context is broadly known as the rhetorical invention process. Accomplished rhetors consider the knowledge levels and existing beliefs of key audience members, useful analogues to the present situation, expectations of institutions and culture, and existing starting places of similar arguments, or topoi, before crafting messages that best appeal to audience and moment.

Rhetorical invention has formed the basis of legal decision-making for centuries. Justices examine the inventional topoi, or rhetorical starting places of argument (*topoi* literally translating into "places"), both as the bases for original solutions to unique problems and for their value as legal precedent. In doing so, they blend utilitarian and creative qualities of rhetoric into their written opinions. Those opinions include both the legal conclusion itself "so ordered" and the corresponding reasoning that supports it (Scallen, 1995, p. 1722). Justices "showing their work" can also be seen as an act of deliberative fidelity – both voluntary and important to our belief in democratic processes, wherein political actors are guided by "good reasons" and beholden to their publics, at least rhetorically (Fisher, 1987; Perelman & Olbrechts-Tyteca, 1969). Judicial opinions are more than just holdings: They are "claims of meaning," constitutive documents that characterize both speaker and auditor (White, 1995, p. 1363). Judicial opinions are part of a centuries-long tradition of legal decisions, and contemporary legal discourse builds on classical traditions for inventional topoi, self-deliberation and dialectic reasoning, and reliance on input from non-technical audiences.

Aristotle's *Rhetoric* (1991), and subsequently Cicero's *On Invention* (1949), mapped a complex relationship between philosophical dialectic and situation-specific rhetoric that held heavy implications for legal rhetoric then, and now. Aristotle defined rhetoric not merely by its persuasive effect but also by its inventional tools to aid in discovery and judgment. Abstract principles of justice established by laws may, in their abstraction, become incapable of speaking to the nuance of specific situations if one does not allow for the situation-specific argumentative forms of rhetoric, which bring equity to the justice of laws. Topoi were at the situational center of rhetorical reasoning: The rhetorical commonplaces both reflected cultural habits of knowing, reasoning, and believing and motivated new forms of knowing through their combinations and application to novel situations.

As common laws became codified and the principles behind them came into question, Roman legal arguments focused on the dialectical features of argument (Scallen, 1995, pp. 1728–1729). With the changes in the law courts came early judicial writing, which divided between a *praetor*, who would craft the pleadings into a formula similar to jury instructions; a *iudex*, a lay arbitrator who would decide questions of both law and fact; and jurists, who rendered advice to both litigants and praetors and published treatise-like commentaries describing the resolution of real and hypothetical problems (Wald, 1995, p. 1371).

The contemporary US analogue is more symbiotic; temporally, between past and present opinions of a longstanding magistrate body (the Supreme Court), where current Justices turn to earlier opinions (precedents) and doctrinal principles established over time and multiple cases; hierarchically, between the Supreme Court and lower appellate courts, where the former offers rules and advice on how to interpret and apply existing laws; and finally, between spheres of argument, through dialectic engagement between Supreme Court Justices, the parties to the case, interested third parties who may also file briefs (called amicus briefs), and public arguments that serve as the cultural and linguistic tapestry from which legal discourse draws its threads.

7.4 INVENTIONAL TOPOI IN SUPREME COURT ARGUMENTS

When the Supreme Court grants certiorari to review a case, it proceeds through an inventional process that mirrors classical rhetorical invention in many ways. Individually and collectively, Justices search for appropriate starting places – or topoi – on which to build an acceptable justification for the final opinions. The topoi will vary in significance and applicability depending on the specifics of the case, and successful topoi will generally reflect the audiences' values and beliefs, the institutional parameters for argument, and the particulars of the situation surrounding the controversy.[2] These topoi include facts of the case (as asserted by parties, amici, and external sources); constitutional principles and doctrines, both previously used and newly interpreted; important precedents based on previous decisions of the Court; and legislative and regulatory histories (Alexy, 1989, pp. 18–19; Carr, 2018, pp. 113–119).

Before the written decisions are published, Justices' chambers also consider the contemporaneous arguments of fellow Justices and various publics as essential topoi, providing important context, meritorious counter-arguments, and pathways to acceptable arguments both inside and outside the Court. They do so because, for all of its jurisprudential-specific topoi, Supreme Court decisions lose their rhetorical power and moral force when they fail to take in, and address, *public arguments*. Perelman (1963) posits that all successful argument – legal and non-legal alike – proceeds from "that which is accepted, that which is acknowledged as true, as normal and probable, as valid agreement"; and because of that, it thereby "*anchors itself in the social*, the characterization of which will depend on the nature of the audience" (Perelman, 1963, p. 156). Studies on judicial reasoning indicate that "Supreme Court inventional strategies both reflect and help create cultural norms, particularly those that govern institutional ethics and the ostensible grounds for institutional decision making" (Makau & Lawrence, 1994, p. 191). Public audiences expect more than merely legally valid decisions; they expect the Court to speak to urgent social needs and questions, and to protect nonlegal interests (Makau, 1984, p. 382).

For all of the particularities and field-specific topoi of legal argumentation, then, these features do not separate the practice entirely from general practices of argument; nor does the focus on legal audiences negate the need to consider more general audiences. Even given the constraining features of legal justification, "the actual process of justification or deliberation should proceed (and in ideal cases does indeed proceed) according to the criteria of general practical discourse, and that legal justification only serves as a secondary legitimation of any conclusions arrived at in this way" (Alexy, 1989, p. 19).

Even as they write their final opinions, Justices do more than answer the question (s) before them; they also construct the rhetorical resources necessary to form an acceptable legal judgment. These include the building and maintenance of the Court's authority; specific constructions of history that support and even naturalize the outcomes that the opinion argues for; and maintaining and building upon certain features of legal culture that confer institutional legitimacy and legal decision-making (Carr, 2018). This is where the increasing number of, and more substantive, cases taken up in the shadow docket are particularly damaging to legal discourse. Shadow docket decisions fail both to show their work – demonstrating for audiences which

[2] Portions of this section are paraphrased from my book on the Supreme Court's rhetorical invention (Carr, 2018).

topoi most significantly shaped the decision, and *why* – and fail to build and affirm legal topoi for future Supreme Court decisions and for lower courts.

An important consideration of all Supreme Court decisions – merits cases and shadow docket alike – is what, exactly, the Court is trying to produce. Producing a cogent written decision about a particular case is not the only goal of Supreme Court invention. Of the same inventional tools, the Supreme Court uses written opinions to construct and maintain its own authority and to maintain the forms, authority, and logic of the broader legal culture. These constructions are necessary to the internal logic of the opinions, and they form the basis for public acceptance of the Court's decisions in particular cases as well as the Court's legitimacy on the whole. Justices construct these artifacts through both showing and doing. That is, they construct these resources both through their particular arguments and through the performative display of their roles through the form, structure, and institutional expectations of written opinions.

7.4.1 *Authority and Credibility*

Because the Supreme Court has no enforcement body, a key rhetorical feature for the Court is its need to motivate support for its decisions in lieu of forcibly imposing them. Thus, written opinions must continuously invest time explaining or constructing the sphere of authority within which Justices can make legitimate their decisions. Perelman (1980, p. 121) notes that, in democratic societies, "the role of the judge, servant of existing laws, is to contribute to the acceptance of the system. He shows that the decisions which he is led to take are not only legal, but are acceptable because they are reasonable." Although Justices serve appointed life terms as of this writing, the Supreme Court is nonetheless constrained by broader social conditions, including matters of public opinion (Rosenberg, 1991). In cases of public interest, the need to sound reasonable extends beyond legal practitioners involved with the case to a wider audience that may not know the legal precedents or doctrinal habits relating to the subject area. In cases such as this, "the authority of the court opinion is not a given – it must be earned; and the audiences from which assent must be won are often multiple" (Brooks, 1996, p. 21).

Audiences' perception of the Justices' character cannot be separated from the message they send. This is particularly true in the highly secretive, unelected branch of federal government that is the Supreme Court. Drawing from the Constitution's concern for the characters of individuals who hold office and characterologically embodying the Constitution as its primary interpreters, Justices are scrutinized by the public from their nominations through their retirements (Parry-Giles, 1996, pp. 367–369). Especially when public audiences are largely unfamiliar with legal vocabulary and doctrine, the character of political actors is rightfully scrutinized as "the only 'issue' upon which a voter is competent to judge" (McGee, 1978, p. 153).

7.4.2 *Legal Culture*

Another inventional artifact of legal discourse is American legal culture itself. The field of law is more than just a place where disputes are resolved. It is an institutional culture, crafted through formal and informal rules, organizational hierarchies, traditions, vocabularies, and habits of mind. Valued precedents and doctrine will structure the Court's reasoning and provide support for decisions. Dissents provide the foundations for future arguments. Both explicitly, through its opinions, and performatively, through its modeling, the Supreme Court provides guidance to lower courts, defining acceptable standards of evidence, levels of scrutiny, treatments of groups and categories, the pace and structure of lawsuits and decisions, and the relative value of established doctrines and conflicting precedents.

Similarly, legal discourse is more than a discipline and a vocabulary; it also constructs social norms, characters, standards of judgment, and particular worldviews. One characteristic of the constructed legal culture, then, is the composition of particular characters within the framework, language, and logic of the legal culture. Justices construct the Supreme Court's own character through their performative enactment of legal norms such as the form and structure of legal opinions; their tone toward each other, the appellants, and the other institutions they engage with; and the performance of their responsibility to guide lower courts in consistent and sound decision-making. Opinions also constitute the publics and actors evoked within the legal drama, thus serving "to create – and rank – communities of competing voices" (Conway, 2003, p. 489). Judicial constructions of themselves, each other, the parties, and the publics that the decision impacts are inevitable byproducts of Supreme Court opinions.

In summary, Supreme Court Justices make their final opinions consonant with accepted forms of legal decision-making, but that does not mean that the reasons given in the opinions were the only factors considered when deciding how to vote in the first place. The process of writing is in itself an inventional tool, because it requires engagement among author, topoi, and audiences in ways that alter the direction of the result. Decades before the rising frequency of Supreme Court shadow docket stays and injunctions on decisions of constitutional import, Judge Patricia Wald (1995) lamented the move of some appellate judges away from written opinions.[3] The process of opinion writing brings to the surface potential problems with the decision, asserts Wald. The process of writing,

> more than the vote at conference or the courtroom dialogue, puts the writer on the line, reminds her with each tap of the key that she will be held responsible for the logic and persuasiveness of the reasoning and its implications

[3] Wald asserts that "there is indeed a worrisome 'lost horizon' aspect to no-opinion dispositions. Even when judges agree on a proposed result after reading briefs and hearing argument, the true test comes when the writing judge reasons it out on paper (or on computer)" (Wald, 1995, pp. 1374–1375).

> for the larger body of circuit or national law. Most judges feel that responsibility keenly; they literally agonize over their published opinions, which sometimes take weeks or even months to bring to term. It is not so unusual to modulate, transfer, or even switch an originally intended rationale or result in midstream because "it just won't write." (Wald, 1995, p. 1375)

Judicial writing choices are complicated by the fact that audiences to which the Supreme Court must appeal are multiple, including other present and future Justices, lower courts, legal administrators, legislators, litigants, legal scholars, and the nonlegal public (Makau, 1984, pp. 379–396). The possibility of disagreement by some of these audiences can have varying impacts, from constitutional or structural changes to law, to confusion when applying the decision with the lower courts, to general dissatisfaction with the Supreme Court among the general public (Christie, 2000, p. 19).

As we will see in *Roman Catholic Diocese v. Cuomo* (2020), opinions unmoored from these constraints, if only for the proclaimed sake of expediency, render the judgments problematic. Previous research had pointed out the harms of truncated shadow docket decisions on legal culture: namely the lack of precedent, with the result of throwing lower courts into disarray. This chapter complicates that concern. The Court has begun mirroring the form and structure of a full Supreme Court opinion within some of these decisions – long opinions and multiple concurrences and dissents – while depriving the record of any substantive public argument: no oral arguments, no amicus briefs, and no time for Justices and law clerks to gather additional public resources. The resulting "opinions" do substantive doctrinal work without full consideration of its audience's premises of argumentation.

7.5 ANALYSIS OF *ROMAN CATHOLIC DIOCESE OF BROOKLYN V. CUOMO* (2020)

Roman Catholic Diocese of Brooklyn v. Cuomo (2020) challenged COVID-related restrictions on gatherings based on the prevalence of cases in neighborhoods, which included limitations on houses of worship. The applicants posited the constitutional harm in question as the Free Exercise Clause of the First Amendment. The Court had previously rejected a COVID-restriction injunction application from California – *South Bay United Pentecostal Church v. Newsom* (2020) – on similar grounds. In *South Bay*, plaintiffs asked the Supreme Court to stop an executive order that temporarily placed restrictions on public gatherings, including limiting places of worship to 25 percent building capacity or 100 attendees, whichever was less. In a 5–4 vote, the majority of the Court declined to intervene in *South Bay*. Chief Justice Roberts penned a two-page concurrence with the denial order, finding that the executive order treated places of worship similarly to other secular gatherings that held similar risk, that local governments need flexibility to rapidly address the (still very new) pandemic which had no cure or vaccine, and finally that the application did not meet the very high standards for injunctive relief, including "indisputably clear" unconstitutionality. Three of the four Justices who would have granted the injunction (Kavanaugh, Thomas, and Gorsuch) joined for a three-page dissent from the Court's denial of relief, asserting that because some secular businesses, less constitutionally protected than places of worship were, were subject to looser restrictions, then the executive order clearly violated the Constitution and was furthermore irreparably harmful to worshippers.

Months later – after Justice Ruth Bader Ginsburg died and was replaced by Justice Amy Coney Barrett – the Court granted the emergency injunction application regarding a COVID-restriction executive order in New York. The New York order established rules based on prevalence of COVID cases in neighborhoods. In high-infection "red" zones, houses of worship were limited to 25 percent or ten people, whichever was fewer. Other "non-essential" secular businesses were closed altogether, treating religious gatherings more leniently than other non-essential organizations, but more strictly than "essential" secular businesses. The Roman Catholic Diocese of Brooklyn and the Agudath Israel Synagogue filed separate suits, asking for an emergency injunction against the order, and arguing that the order violated the Free Exercise Clause by singling out religious gatherings. Both the district court and the Second Court of Appeals declined, citing Roberts' reasoning in *South Bay* for declining injunctions of this sort amid COVID – except for lower court dissenters, who argued that the executive order violated the Free Exercise Clause because it was more restrictive on houses of worship than on essential secular businesses. The Supreme Court dissenters from *South Bay* maintained their same positions in *Roman Catholic Diocese v. Cuomo*, and this time Justice Barrett joined them to form a majority.

The following analysis will explore the fault lines that appear in rhetorical output when Justices attempt to mirror the form and structure of a merits opinion without the full inventional process that supports it.

7.5.1 *Diminishing Legal Culture in* Roman Catholic Diocese v. Cuomo

As previously noted, Justices pursuing the merits docket engage in topoi that include arguments from many different origins: past arguments from the same Court, via precedents, important dissents, and established doctrine; from legislative histories as they search for the intentions of the laws in question; from the lower courts, part of their own system of decision-making; from the parties; from the public, via amicus briefs; and from each other. They engage these arguments at several stages. First, in granting or denying certiorari; next, through a system of party and amicus briefs; substantively and live via oral arguments; privately, through memos and draft opinions circulating between the chambers; and finally, during the majority, concurrence, and dissenting opinions that are released to the public. At each of these argumentative touchpoints, Justices' own arguments have the chance to be molded and tempered through their engagements; at the very least, they remind the Justices of the myriad audiences and artifacts to which they must tailor their decisions. In shadow docket decisions, Justices are liberated by expediency from these high demands.

Shadow docket opinions, when released at all, do not carry the same institutional expectations for form, structure, length, and scope of argument that full Court opinions do. This is true in part because of the "emergency" nature of these cases, and in part because of the limited temporal orientation. That is, there is an expectation that emergency stays and injunctions will only hold until a fuller review occurs. Justice Barrett, the author of the Court's per curiam holding, expressed the limited nature of *Roman Catholic Diocese v. Cuomo*'s holding granting injunctive relief to its applicants: "Should the petition for a writ of certiorari be denied, this order shall terminate automatically. In the event the petition for a writ of certiorari is granted, the order shall terminate upon the sending down of the judgment of this Court" (*Roman Catholic Diocese of Brooklyn, NY v. Cuomo*, 2020, p. 15).

At first blush, this holding seems to perform the conservative ethos of Supreme Court jurisprudence – and a common starting place of argument – by articulating its limited scope and circumstances for its termination. Yet considering this application in its historical moment, together with two similar applications for emergency injunctions that had been declined mere months before, the decision to grant injunctive relief itself represented a significant departure from the coveted status quo upon which the Supreme Court builds it character and authority.

The reasons offered to grant relief are incommensurate with careful inventional discovery and selection as well. Long-standing precedent and attendant legal culture set the threshold for granting an injunction incredibly high, and for good reason: Through injunctions, Justices substitute their judgments for the judgments of lower courts, and intervene directly upon the parties themselves, rather than merely delaying a court's ruling from taking place. For these reasons, the settled Supreme Court standard, established in the All Writs Act of 1789, holds that in order for the Court to intervene, the party's claim to relief needs to be "indisputably clear."

Former Justice Antonin Scalia believed that "an emergency injunction 'demands a significantly higher justification' than stay; appellate courts need a stronger case for restraining the *parties* than for restraining the *courts* from which those parties are appealing" (Vladeck, 2022, p. 712). In addition to the direct intervention at the party level, injunctions also supersede their usual supervisory role on the lower courts. For this reason, the Court held in 2010 that an injunction request "demands a significantly higher justification than a request for a stay because, unlike a stay, an injunction does not simply suspend judicial alteration of the status quo but grants judicial intervention that has been withheld by lower courts" (*South Bay United Pentecostal Church v. Newsom*, 2020, 1; Roberts, CJ, quoting *Respect Maine PAC v. McKee*, 2010).

In the per curiam decision, however, the majority applied a much less aggressive standard, designed for use by trial courts (rather than appellate courts) deciding to issue a preliminary injunction at the beginning of a new lawsuit: whether there is a reasonable expectation that the party will succeed on the merits, and whether they would suffer irreparable harm if restrictions remained. Vladeck (2022, p. 719) argues that such a move re-envisions the All Writs Act in ways that vastly expand the reach of Supreme Court injunctions.

In such high-stakes cases, ones departing from long-standing precedent, or on controversial issues where Supreme Court interference could be construed as overreaching, institutional expectations require that great care be taken to craft a justification that aligns the proposed change to the status quo with a strong performance of juridical neutrality. In a merits opinion, the decision to ignore or alter the application of an important legal standard would motivate Justices to call on applicable topoi to justify their move – to balance the change with the appearance of consistency, for credibility's sake, by painstakingly laying out existing precedents, doctrine, or past opinions that justified the current deviance from legal norms, or perhaps facts that make this case wholly unique. In the shadow docket, however, expediency reins, leading Barrett to pen: "Because of the need to issue an order promptly, we provide only a brief summary of the reasons why immediate relief is essential" (*Roman Catholic Diocese of Brooklyn, NY v. Cuomo*, 2020, p. 16).

Further eroding the standard of "indisputably clear" relief, the red zone restrictions in question had been lifted on the neighborhoods that the applicants' houses of worship resided in, making the alleged harm moot at the time that the Court issued its injunction. By the time the Supreme Court issued a decision, the parties to the case were no longer in high infection zones, and so were not suffering the harms that the Court granted as urgent and irreparable, calling into question their standing. Nevertheless, the majority and concurrent opinions argued, this was a preemptive injunction meant to preclude any irreparable harm that would arise if the zone levels rose again.

Next, *Roman Catholic Diocese v. Cuomo*'s (2020, p. 19; Barrett, J) per curiam holding asserts that "There can be no question that the challenged restrictions, if enforced, will cause irreparable harm." To justify this assertion, Barrett's opinion offers a brief analysis of disparate treatment based on religion, an established standard for violating the Free Exercise Clause. Here, Barrett walks the reader through the restrictions that the red and orange zones would impose on places of worship and how they differ from designated essential, and some non-essential, businesses. Barrett evokes the precedent of *Elrod v. Burns* to support this interpretation: "The loss of First Amendment freedoms, even for minimal periods of time, unquestionably constitutes irreparable injury" (*Elrod v. Burns*, 1976, p. 5, full internal citation omitted). Again, precedent is a hallmark building block for Supreme Court opinions, mirroring the logic and legitimacy of a full merits opinion. The cited case, however, is not the most recent binding precedent – 1990's *Employment Division, Department of Human Resources of Oregon v. Smith* (hereinafter *Employment Division v. Smith*) – but a 1976 case from which current Free Exercise Clause doctrine has long since evolved.

A review of the missing topoi evidenced in the holding opens a window into the radical doctrinal move that this decision made. In 1990, Justice Scalia wrote the majority opinion for the Court in *Employment Division v. Smith* (1990). In it, Scalia argued that laws burdening religious practice are not immediately or inherently unconstitutional; rather, it is only if they are singled out. Vladeck (2022, p. 705) summarizes the thrust of the holding in *Smith*: "The Free Exercise Clause is not offended merely because a law impacts religious practice. Rather, the Constitution is violated only *if that was the point*" (emphasis added). In the merits docket, the Supreme Court continued to uphold *Smith* whilst chipping away at its edges, and Thomas, Alito, Gorsuch, and Kavanaugh hinted that *Smith* was ripe for revisit in 2019 (Vladeck, 2022, p. 709). The Court had yet to revisit it on the merits docket, however, when *Roman Catholic Diocese v. Cuomo* was taken up.

If *Roman Catholic Diocese v. Cuomo* had been a full merits opinion, then the norms of opinion writing (and of its precedential affects) would have forced the majority to engage with the full doctrinal history. Law clerks and Justices alike would have centered on the ways in which *Smith* supersedes *Elrod* as precedent and, through the draft opinion circulation process between chambers, Barrett would have been forced to expound on why her chambers found an older case, a predecessor in the since evolved standard of Free Exercise Clause interpretation, to be the appropriate case to rest her decision upon.

Under the guise of emergency and the shadow of per curiam anonymity, however, shadow docket opinions can truncate the full argumentation process that produces essential artifacts of legal and public culture. In this case, Barrett's per curiam opinion shifted the Court's approach to the Free Exercise Clause without the constraints of a typical Supreme Court opinion.[4] Absent a detailed building of legislative and jurisprudential histories that bring the Court to this moment, any reference to public concerns via amicus briefs, or broader constitutional questions put before it (parties to this injunction ask only about the immediate question at hand), the majority holding in *Roman Catholic Diocese v. Cuomo* rejected the longstanding precedent established in *Employment Division v. Smith* (1990) regarding the application of the Free Exercise Clause.

Some may argue that the expediency and limited scope of shadow docket decisions mediates against the harms of these truncated arguments and justifications. After all, these cases are meant to be temporary and party-specific, holding no precedential value. This is untrue for several reasons. First, shadow docket opinions such *Roman Catholic Diocese v. Cuomo* deprive lower courts of reliable guidance on how to decide related cases. The increased frequency and reliance upon shadow docket summary judgments and sparse opinions halts a meaningful appellate

[4] In his chapter, Stephen I. Vladeck (2022) makes this argument brilliantly and in more detail than I do. The goal of this chapter is to focus on the missing inventional topoi and artifacts that make this shadow docket constitutional shift particularly problematic.

process that produces merits-based opinion writing. By truncating the usual multiple layers of review by law courts, the Supreme Court, other legal actors, and public audiences do not receive the benefit of the multiple rounds of briefing, arguments, and rulings that result from a full appeals process (Vladeck, 2019, p. 127).

Secondly, increasing numbers and import of shadow docket decisions have left appellate lawyers attempting to extrapolate which topoi might be successful, even as they ponder the precedential value of shadow docket cases. McFadden and Kapoor (2021) attempted to craft a structure by which lower courts could sort the precedential value of various types of emergency stays, in order to better weigh the significance of those stays as guiding decisions for lower courts. Arguing that the Supreme Court has no set standards of review, thus "complicating the question of the precedential weight of stay rulings," the authors suggest that attorneys and judges consider the similarities of their underlying merits disputes, as well as the length and detail of any attached opinions (McFadden & Kapoor, 2021, p. 838). Even on the shadow docket, the authors recommend proceeding with deference to the emergency holdings if it seems clear that the Court's majority expressed its views on the merits of the case, or else lower courts should explain why they do not defer. The main reason McFadden and Kapoor offer: the fact that the Supreme Court itself has taken to referring in other cases to their summary judgment in *Roman Catholic Diocese v. Cuomo.*

7.6 CONCLUSION

At first read, *Roman Catholic Diocese v. Cuomo* (2020) offers substantive engagement between Justices about matters of public import, referencing judicial topoi of facts of the case, precedents, and established doctrine. The structure of the injunctive holding allows for both concurrences and dissents, allowing engagement between the Justices. The proclaimed temporal orientation is temporary in nature, to be negated after a full-court merits review, should that come to be. So what's missing, and what are the consequences for the artifacts of legal invention?

First, we miss public arguments. Shadow docket cases do not solicit amicus briefs, do not hold oral arguments, and rarely even have time for meaningful conferencing and rounds of draft opinion between the Justices and their clerks. The public is invited take the Court's word for it, because it isn't required to consider or answer to public arguments. In cases like *Roman Catholic Diocese v. Cuomo*, where regional contexts make the appellate court the appropriate body to hear the case, granting emergency injunctions and stays usurp local voices in favor of federal dictate. Because of the proclaimed need for expediency, Justices can wave off the need to fully articulate the arguments of the parties – as Justice Sotomayor critiqued Justice Gorsuch for, when he chose not to engage with what makes houses of worship different, based on scientific evidence provided in the party record – namely that shouting and singing while gathered together for lengths of time was a leading cause of group COVID spread.

The Supreme Court always has greater responsibilities than the case at hand, even when those cases are urgent and time specific. It must consider the impact of its decisions on future similar cases and provide a roadmap for lower courts and policymakers. And it needs to show that it fully considered them, especially if it is altering its approach to future similar cases in any way. Here, the new majority of the Court used a non-live emergency injunction to move the doctrine of the Free Exercise Clause in ways that it refused to do on the merits docket. And in the immediately following shadow docket cases, the Court has also demanded that lower courts treat its per curiam decision as the same level of precedent as a merits case. Vladeck traces the sequence of shadow docket cases to conclude that the Justices seem to have "*preferred* to make significant new constitutional law on the shadow docket rather than through the regular – if laborious – procedure of a merit case" (Vladeck, 2022, p. 737, emphasis in original). Regardless of the Court's intent, the impact lowers the inventional burden of the Justices and impoverishes its results for legal and public audiences alike.

Such a system also loses several important artifacts of legal opinions, with grave implications. The first, and probably the most important, is authority. Lawyers and lower appellate court judges could not evoke the past as authority, an act which "seems to require the existence of a judicial opinion, or something like it" (White, 1995, p. 1366). One might intuit the Court's thinking, but one cannot explicitly model it on the Court's reasoning. Opinions "invite lawyers and judges in the future to think and speak as it does" (White, 1995, p. 1366). Opinions characterize. Through their characterizations, audiences (legal and public alike) can judge those characterizations, can trace the contours of the reasoning and decide whether the reasons are generous, dubious, well-supported, or contrary. They engage in a conversation with a reader, and invite the reader to follow them. Future auditors can cite moments of characterization as reasons that they, too, characterize the law in particular ways, and they are evoking a foundational premise of legal argumentation when they do so: an appeal to authority.

The lack of opinion also silences critique in ways that impoverish legal reasoning. White argues, "the criticism of opinions, on all grounds – rational, political, moral – is an essential part of law" because it is the only way that others can "argue for or against the continued authority of a particular opinion or line of opinions" (White, 1995, p. 1368). Of course, the goal of a judicial opinion is to issue a result. But White emphasizes the importance of having both, for it matters that both the reasoning and result be sound: "There is a profound relation between them, because the right 'style' or the right mode of reasoning will over time lead to the best results" (White, 1995, p. 1368).

Herein lies the concern with contemporary shadow docket cases that engage substantively with constitutional decision-making, without the expectation of oral argument, conference meetings, draft opinions wherein Justices wrestle with complexities, and a full-throated opinion of the Court sturdy enough to build doctrine upon. White used the Greek legal system as an example of what the law would look like if it were something that judges just performed, and did not explain: as in Athens, with no judges, juries of hundreds, no deliberation, no reliable way of evoking precedent, and no appeal. What the Greek legal system had lacked in material law, it compensated for with the "cheerful simplicity of the infant state" (Greenidge, 1971, pp. 3–4). Supreme Court shadow docket opinions behave similarly, assuming a "because I said so" model of jurisprudence that does nothing to further legal reasoning, instead asking lower courts to behave as Greek citizens did before juries – adopting arguments that seem to work, without knowing or concerning themselves with the reasons.

REFERENCES

Alexy, R. (1989). *A theory of legal argumentation: The theory of rational discourse as theory of legal justification* (R. Adler & N. MacCormick, Trans.). Oxford University Press.

Aristotle. (1991). *On rhetoric: A theory of civic discourse* (G. Kennedy, Trans.). Oxford University Press. (Original work published fourth century BCE.)

Baude, W. (2015). Foreword: The Supreme Court's shadow docket. *NYU Journal of Law & Liberty*, 9, 1–63.

Black, H. I., & Bannon, A. (2022, July 19). *The Supreme Court "shadow docket."* Brennan Center for Justice. www.brennancenter.org/our-work/research-reports/supreme-court-shadow-docket [https://perma.cc/H3SP-FYU7]

Brooks, P. (1996). The law as narrative and rhetoric. In P. Brooks & P. Gewirtz (Eds.), *Law's stories: Narrative and rhetoric in the law*. Yale University Press.

Brown, E. J. (1958). The Supreme Court, 1957 term. *Harvard Law Review*, 72(1), 77–198. https://doi.org/10.2307/1338364

Carr, M. K. (2018). *The rhetorical invention of diversity: Supreme Court opinions, public arguments, and affirmative action*. Michigan State University Press.

Christie, G. C. (2000). *The notion of an ideal audience in legal argument*. Kluwer Academic.

Cicero (1949). *On invention*. (H. M. Hubbell, Trans.). Harvard University Press.

Conway, G. (2003). Inevitable reconstructions: Voice and ideology in two landmark U.S. Supreme Court opinions. *Rhetoric & Public Affairs*, 6(3), 487–507. www.jstor.org/stable/41939845

Elrod v. Burns, 427 U.S. 347 (1976).

Employment Division, Department of Human Resources of Oregon v. Smith, 494 U.S. 872 (1990).

Fisher, W. (1987). *Human communication as narration: Toward a philosophy of reason, value, and action*. University of South Carolina Press.

Greenidge, A. H. J. (1971). *The legal procedure of Cicero's time*. Augustus M. Kelley.

Hartnett, E. A. (2016). Summary reversals in the Roberts Court. *Cardozo Law Review*, 38, 591–621.

Harvest Rock Church, Inc. v. Newsom, 141 S. Ct. 889 (2020).

Makau, J. (1984). The Supreme Court and reasonableness. *Quarterly Journal of Speech*, 70, 379–397.

Makau, J., & Lawrence, D. (1994). Administrative judicial rhetoric: The Supreme Court's new thesis of political morality. *Argumentation and Advocacy*, 30, 191–205.

McFadden, T. N., & Kapoor, V. (2021). The precedential effects of the Supreme Court's emergency stays. *Harvard Journal of Law & Public Policy*, 44(3), 828–915.
McGee, M. C. (1978). "Not men, but measures": The origins and import of an ideological principle. *Quarterly Journal of Speech*, 64(2), 141–154.
Merrill v. Milligan, 595 U.S. ___ (2022), Nos. 21A375 (21-1086) & 21A376 (21-1087).
O'Connell, S. (2021, April 14). Supreme Court "shadow docket" under review by U.S. House of Representatives. American Bar Association. www.americanbar.org/groups/committees/death_penalty_representation/publications/project_blog/scotus-shadow-docket-under-review-by-house-reps/
Parry-Giles, T. (1996). Character, the constitution, and the ideological embodiment of "civil rights" in the 1967 nomination of Thurgood Marshall to the Supreme Court. *Quarterly Journal of Speech*, 82(4), 364–382. https://doi.org/10.1080/00335639609384163
Perelman, C. (1963). *The idea of justice and the problem of argument* (J. Petrie, Trans.). Routledge & Kegan Paul.
(1980). *Justice, law, and argument: Essays on moral and legal reasoning*. (J. Petrie, Trans.). Reidel Publishing.
Perelman, C., & Olbrechts-Tyteca, L. (1969). *The new rhetoric: A treatise on argumentation*. University of Notre Dame Press.
Respect Maine PAC v. *McKee*, 562 U.S. 996 (2010).
Roman Catholic Diocese of Brooklyn, NY v. Cuomo, 592 U.S. 14 (2020).
Rosenberg, G. (1991). *The hollow hope: Can courts bring about social change?* University of Chicago Press.
Scallen, E. A. (1995). Classical rhetoric, practical reasoning, and the law of evidence. *American University Law Review*, 44(5), 1717–1816.
South Bay United Pentecostal Church v. Newsom, 140 S. Ct. 1613 (2020).
Vladeck, S. (2019). The Solicitor General and the shadow docket. *Harvard Law Review*, 133(1), 123–163.
(2022). The most-favored right: COVID, the Supreme Court, and the (new) free exercise clause. *New York University Journal of Law & Liberty*, 15, 699–750.
(2023). *The shadow docket: How the Supreme Court uses stealth rulings to amass power and undermine the Republic*. Basic Books.
Wald, P. (1995). The rhetoric of results and the results of rhetoric: Judicial writings. Special issue: Judicial Opinion Writing. *University of Chicago Law Review*, 62(4), 1371–1419.
White, J. B. (1995). What's an opinion for? Special issue: Judicial Opinion Writing. *University of Chicago Law Review*, 62(4), 1363–1369.

8

Sensus Communis, Voter-Inflicted Harms, and *Schuette v. BAMN*

Laura J. Collins

8.1 INTRODUCTION

Appellate court opinions are often criticized for establishing difficult or shaky precedent as a result of imperfect reasoning. These sorts of criticisms rest on the assumption that had the judges or Justices considered possible implications more fully, they could have crafted an opinion more easily applied and more immune to manipulation by future courts. While there certainly are opinions whose reasoning could have been more thorough or more thoroughly explained, there are also those whose reasoning has become difficult to follow not because of any error or ineptitude on the part of those who authored them but because the very foundation of judgment, the *sensus communis*, has shifted. In this chapter, inspired by eighteenth-century rhetorician and philosopher of law Giambattista Vico, I explore the role that prerational judgment, embodied in the sensus communis, plays in the authoring and interpretation of what will become unintentionally difficult precedent, using the 2014 United States Supreme Court case *Schuette v. Coalition to Defend Affirmative Action, Integration and Immigrant Rights and Fight for Equality by Any Means Necessary (BAMN)* and its relevant precedent as my example.

In *Schuette v. BAMN* (2014), a plurality of the Court ruled that Michigan's 2006 voter-approved constitutional amendment removing the power to implement affirmative action plans from universities and government entities was not a violation of the Equal Protection Clause. Critical to the judgment was the plurality's insistence that *Schuette* was unlike earlier cases where voters had restricted the state's ability to implement race-conscious policies because, unlike in those cases, the voters' action in *Schuette* didn't implicate "injury by reason of race" but mere policy preference (an argument the losing side had made in each of those earlier cases) (*Schuette v. BAMN*, 2014, p. 314).

I argue that Vico's sensus communis helps explain both why those earlier cases didn't anticipate *Schuette* and why the *Schuette* plurality could discern a stark line between those historical cases and the one before it. Vico (2020, p. 142) defines sensus communis as "judgment without reflection," shared by an entire community, which evolves but endures. Importantly, sensus communis is "sedimented in language itself," such that a community's values and judgments are confined and animated by its language (Schaeffer, 2019, p. 35). Vico stresses that in confronting pressing issues, communities necessarily rely upon the sensus communis and, in so doing, simultaneously revise it. Vico's sensus communis is particularly useful when thinking about judicial precedent in a common-law system because it reminds us that law is inherently rhetorical and necessarily responsive to and rooted in its own historical context. But beyond that, if sensus communis is indeed embedded in our language, the concept reminds us that a court's precise use of language and careful reasoning cannot possibly guard against shifts in the sensus communis that will render past opinions "inadequate" because it is both the values and the language itself that have shifted. While it's not particularly novel to suggest that language changes (appellate courts agonize over this regularly), Vico's sensus communis helps us to see not only how the meaning of particular words and phrases shifts but that the "standard of judgment" embedded in language does too. Law and eloquence do not stand still.

In what follows, I begin by describing Vico's notion of sensus communis and the conflict that helped forge it, relying heavily on Vico scholar John Schaeffer's extensive body of work on the subject. I then suggest how Vico's sensus communis might aid legal and rhetorical scholars in appraising judicial precedent. I proceed to apply these insights to my analysis of *Schuette* and the precedent the Court uses to decide the case. I argue that in the opinions that preceded *Schuette*, the Court was accustomed to the evils the majority could undertake to preserve white dominance and maintain the status quo. Those Courts could not have anticipated the extent to which the future Court would understand that dynamic as a problem of another time. Further, I demonstrate how critics of that precedent similarly fail to account for the role of sensus communis in those earlier cases (and in their own appraisal of them) through their insistence that those opinions should have anticipated our controversies and the shifts in language that accompanied them. Vico's sensus communis, then, not only helps us to understand court opinions as rhetorical struggles that respond to and articulate the sensus communis but also reminds us how interpreting precedent is always an act of forging our current sensus communis.

8.2 VICO'S SENSUS COMMUNIS: COMMUNAL, RHETORICAL, AND PRERATIONAL

Giambattista Vico was a professor of eloquence at the University of Naples from 1699 to 1741. There he trained university students to qualify in law, the practice of which was markedly different from our own. During Vico's time, Naples' legal system did not have a written code and wouldn't until 1806. Thus, for Vico's students the practice of law would have required arguing from precedents and customs that were predominantly preserved in oral tradition (Schaeffer, 1990, p. 47). Beyond being able to recall and draw on copious amounts of information to make connections and argue for their clients, legal practitioners had to be able to think quickly, as criminal trials often occurred within twenty-four hours of arrest. To prepare students for this oral, adversative practice, Vico trained them in eloquence, modeled after the ancient Romans. Vico saw the ability to invent arguments, drawn from tradition and common opinion, as critical not only to the practice of law but also to participation in public life.

Though this was the tradition in which Vico taught and his students practiced, Cartesian thought was challenging that tradition and the constitution of Naples's legal system. Reformers sought to enact a legal code based on abstracted reason, unencumbered by common opinion and history. As John Schaeffer (1990, p. 52) relates, in "substituting Cartesian rationality for consensus the reformers were able to shift the whole basis of legal theory from tradition to the present." Vico was concerned with the way the Cartesian method, as employed in the push to codify law, would vacate the communal and historical aspects of law. He feared that the more specific and detached the legal codes, the less those arguing legal cases would have to reference general values and public interest. When law is a highly technical matter in which each particular instance is contemplated and addressed by code, there is no need to refer to community values or to history, as all is spelled out and available for private manipulation. In his version of Roman history, Vico (2018, p. 69) decries the point when the citizens came to realize that "law was nothing but their private self-advantage, and stopped taking an interest in the common welfare." It was because Vico saw codification as abstracting law and removing it from the realm of public good that he resisted it.

Thus, under pressure from Cartesian reformers, Vico set out to defend his method of education and the common law system currently in place in Naples. It was in the midst of this conflict that Vico formed and refined his unique conception of sensus communis. While sensus communis translates to "common sense," Vico's understanding of the term far outstrips that translation and is in stark contrast with notions of common sense circulating at Vico's time (Bayer, 2008; Schaeffer, 2004). Vico's sensus communis is inherently rhetorical, communal, and prerational. In contrast, Descartes' *bon sens* (good sense) is the individual's faculty for directing the mind from simple to more complex ideas, using binomial thinking to get there. While with Descartes' bon sens, history, common opinion, and the thinker's embeddedness in these things falls away, Vico's sensus communis is wholly dependent on them.

Vico (2018, p. 13) first defined sensus communis as "the standard of practical judgment" and "the guiding principle of eloquence." When he says that sensus communis is the standard for practical judgment, he means that this common fund of values is that from which we "make sense" of the new. Presented with a new case, the orator must draw comparisons and craft metaphors that ring true and that are rooted in the community and its past. This is because the audience is necessarily embedded in the sensus communis and so too is the rhetor.

While Aristotle's *doxa*, understood as common opinion, bears some resemblance to Vico's sensus communis, Vico's later elaboration of sensus communis as historically bound, linguistically embedded, and inescapable distinguishes it from that earlier concept. For Vico, sensus communis is foundational to human affairs. Indeed, in *The New Science*, Vico sought to explain the historical origins of the sensus communis and what we take to be natural law, which, for him, was a rhetorical phenomenon, not a philosophical one (Schaeffer, 2019). Vico writes in *The New Science* that sensus communis is "judgment without reflection, sensed in common by a whole order, a whole people, a whole nation, or the whole of humankind" (Vico, 2020, p. 142). He posits that the sensus communis emerges from a community's historical and ongoing confrontation with "human necessities and advantages" (p. 141). As the community confronts these circumstances, it necessarily develops new assumptions, decisions, institutions, and values (sensus communis). Notably, these things are not the product of isolated philosophic consideration but are developed ad hoc, out of necessity and in response to pressing needs. As new "necessities and advantages" present themselves, the sensus communis continues to be both the basis of judgment and the result of the struggle. Thus, the sensus communis is a force for measured, history-bound change. As Schaeffer explains, when communities confront novel circumstances, they must engage in both "linguistic inventiveness [and] social innovation so that new solutions [are] acceptable within the terms of the sensus communis" (Schaeffer, 2019, p. 100). Importantly, then, common values aren't merely *conveyed* through language, they are embedded in language and its rhythms and affective force. And those values aren't derived from philosophical confrontation but from necessity. For Vico, as Schaeffer (2019) understands him, a community doesn't set out to determine and define its values. Those values (the sensus communis) are forged through necessity – through confronting complications and attempting to resolve them. Thus, they form before rational judgment (and become, themselves, the basis for judgment). As Schaeffer (2019, p. 74) writes, for Vico "values and assumptions [are] sedimented in language itself, even beyond conscious apprehension." So, language, custom, and institutions arise from a community's perceptions, its needs, and its responses to those things. What has been created must always control future perception and response, though literacy – the ability to reference and analyze the thoughts of the past – opens all of that up to more reflection and contemplation.

8.3 SENSUS COMMUNIS AND OUR LAW

Vico's insights about sensus communis are helpful in situating legal texts and their authors. Generally, a rhetorical orientation toward law presumes that law itself is rhetorical (neither an isolated system of rational thought nor an impenetrable exercise of power) and that law and culture necessarily inflect each other (and, in some ways, cannot be neatly separated) (Hasian Jr. et al., 1996). It rejects the notion that law can be scientized in the way the reformers of Vico's time had hoped it could be. What Vico's notion of sensus communis adds is a particular appreciation for the way that any given legal claim, creation, or resolution (for example, a citizen's invocation of their constitutional rights, legislation, a court opinion) is a product of history and of its time and that the very language used is necessarily derived from and directed toward the sensus communis. Law is communal and reactive. Legal thought, reasoning, and language are necessarily tied to the histories and conflicts that forged them. There is no legal thought, no legal principle outside the sensus communis. The sensus communis is the metric by which we wage and evaluate legal claims, and the resolution of those claims is subsumed into that sensus communis. Thus, Vico's sensus communis reminds us that law and its language are not "above" the conflicts that emerge in and over the sensus communis; to the contrary, they are necessarily a part of them. Law is bound to and bound up in the sensus communis not just in terms of values but in language and expression – eloquence itself.

Of course, Vico's sensus communis poses some difficulties if we understand him to mean that the values embedded in the sensus communis are universal, settled, and durable. Given Vico's preoccupation with the evolution of sensus communis and the linguistic inventiveness required to evolve that sensus communis, I don't take that to be his meaning. Rather, I understand him to be relating something similar to what Marianne Constable (2014) does when she writes that law's language binds us. Constable, in contrast to those who would construe legal speech as directed at a distant state, argues that all legal claims are directed to the *we* of law. Law is fundamentally about our being and living together; its language binds *us* together and is a means by which we shape (and contest the shape of) that communal undertaking. It is precisely for this reason that people turn to law to consider and challenge the assumptions and values which seem to undergird our living together (as Vico would have it, our sensus communis). Law is the official language of our communal enterprise and is invoked and contested on these grounds. Constable (2014, p. 134) writes, "Claims of injustice or of justice made in the name of law recall hearers to what a speaker takes, perhaps mistakenly, to be the common practices and judgments of the two or, rather, of the 'community' to which they both belong." This certainly doesn't mean that law is always reflective of community values. Rather, because law, by design, binds us together, it is necessarily a powerful avenue for contesting the substances of those bonds.

Law does, in its way, acknowledge that it is a site and means of contest. But the scientized notion of law, which infects law now just as it did in Vico's time, suggests that law already contains all the answers when, in fact, Vico's notion of sensus communis shows us that this isn't true. There are always new "necessities and advantages," and this is why the sensus communis necessarily evolves. That we share this law in common and that it is supposed to address our universal principles and values binds us together and requires our constant negotiation of our law and our world. Legal pleas and resolutions are directed toward the sensus communis from the sensus communis. This doesn't mean that everybody agrees. It means that we have a sense of shared institutions and values. The assessment of what those are may be faulty, but the sense of them and the drive to cohere those shared values is still there, as is the language in which they are embedded. Thus, at the point of legal contest, we find ourselves both awash in the sensus communis and engaged in the negotiation of it.

Like the rest of us, judges are not above the sensus communis in which we find ourselves and toward which we direct our arguments. Judges and Justices can guess at, but cannot know, what will seem common, fanciful, or banal decades from now. Relatedly, they cannot predict the turns in language, as the standard of judgment, that will accompany those changes. They, like we, inhabit the sensus communis and its attendant language. According to Vico, we cannot escape the sensus communis in which we find ourselves. In fact, we aren't even able to see how common it is until after the fact. That poses a difficulty for those writing precedent with the idea that it will be precedent. Authors cannot know the new cases that will arise or the shifts in the sensus communis that will have occurred by the time those conflicts arise. Similarly, while judges and Justices can be attentive to and precise with their language, they cannot predict how language will shift to accommodate new values and necessities. If the sensus communis is embedded in language itself, authors of judicial opinions are hopelessly bound to that standard and its historical context. Those who author appellate opinions know they are in the midst of a struggle and that the opinion they issue will resolve the immediate issue before the court. What they don't know is how their resolution of the immediate issue will eventually settle into the sensus communis – what elements from the opinion and the context in which it arose will be sedimented into the sensus communis and what will be cast along the wayside. They cannot anticipate how future conflicts will necessitate linguistic inventions that change the very standard of judgment.

Vico reminds us that while the Supreme Court picks its cases, it doesn't pick our struggles (what Vico calls our "necessities and advantages"). Law is forged through inevitable confrontation of the novel, the unaccounted for, not the places where we simply apply the apparent and uncomplicated sensus communis but those where we struggle to do so. This insight is particularly helpful in appraising judicial precedent from the present. It reminds us that our common law system isn't just about consistency and predictability; it is about a history of which we are inevitably a part. It requires that we confront and contemplate the sensus communis of those who preceded us to *make sense* of what is now before us and that we be humbled by the knowledge that we inevitably inhabit our current moment. Judges and Justices engage the sensus communis in the process of issuing opinions and deciding cases (with varying degrees of attention to those histories and struggles). And we do this every time we evaluate or analyze an opinion. Vico reminds us that in that evaluation we must be mindful of our own position and historical location. Vico (2020, p. 127) writes in *The New Science* of the "vanity of the learned, who want what they know to be as ancient as the world." Schaeffer (2001, p. 15) summarizes that Vico is here implying that "the understanding which moderns bring to a text cannot be retrojected into its past." Vico's sensus communis, then, helps us to reject an uncomplicated originalism that seeks to project from the present a certainty about the struggles of the past. It reminds us that appellate opinions arise amidst conflict; they sediment into certainty but do not begin there and cannot predict what uncertainties and necessities will arise in the future. Generally, then, Vico's sensus communis can help us to appraise court opinions more fairly – not only to situate them within their time but also to consider them as wrestling in and over the sensus communis. Rather than assuming that they should be *above* the common sense of the time or that they should have anticipated *our* conflicts and their attendant language, we can understand appellate opinions as confronting the needs and necessities of their time and, in so doing, revising communal values without full appreciation of the extent to which they would do so. In particular, Vico's sensus communis can help us to remember that it is not only values and conflicts that shift, but the very language that encapsulates and animates them.

8.4 SITUATING *SCHUETTE*'S PREDECESSORS

I turn now to *Schuette v. BAMN* (2014) and its predecessors to demonstrate how we might employ Vico's insights about sensus communis when analyzing and evaluating judicial precedent. I begin by describing the facts of the *Schuette* case. I then describe the precedent upon which the plurality relies to decide *Schuette*, discussing those decisions in their historical context and in relation to each other. I then analyze how the *Schuette* plurality reads this precedent as well as how commentators have criticized the earlier decisions for their failure to provide clear guidance to the *Schuette* Court. I argue that previous opinions could not have anticipated the degree to which the future Court would reject the notion that individuals could be discriminated against as members of a group; I also argue that previous opinions could not have anticipated a time when, to find discrimination by the majority, you'd have to locate intent with respect to each voter. Critics of this precedent miss the extent to which this assumption – that it was commonplace that the majority would work to preserve its superiority at the expense of minorities and that this work needn't necessarily be motivated by overt and conscious bias to be understood as discriminatory – was embedded in the sensus communis, the very standards of language, of those earlier opinions.

In 2006, Michigan voters adopted, with 58 percent of the vote, a constitutional amendment (Proposal 2) that barred Michigan's public universities from using race-conscious admissions policies. While other states had already enacted voter-supported bans on affirmative action, the Michigan ban was legally distinct in that, per the Michigan state constitution, the universities' boards of trustees are invested with authority over the universities, including admissions policies. Thus, the voters had singled out race-conscious admissions, and only race-conscious admissions, as outside the scope of the boards' constitutionally mandated discretion. The plaintiffs challenged Proposal 2 on Equal Protection grounds, arguing that, by removing race-conscious admissions decisions and no others from the boards' purview, the state was discriminating on the basis of race. While the Sixth Circuit Court of Appeals determined that Proposal 2 did violate the Fourteenth Amendment's Equal Protection Clause, in *Schuette v. BAMN* (2014) the United States Supreme Court upheld Proposal 2, with six Justices concurring in the judgment and two dissenting. The plurality opinion, authored by Justice Kennedy, was joined by Justices Roberts and Alito. In total, there were five separate opinions authored in the case. The fractured opinions suggest the difficulty the Justices had in reasoning the outcome of the case. We might, then, suspect that this difficulty was caused by either the relative novelty of the question presented by *Schuette* or the lack of clarity provided by the precedent. My analysis, however, demonstrates something different – that the Court's difficulty in deciding *Schuette* is, in part, attributable to the dramatic shift in sensus communis around majority-inflicted racial injury that occurred between when the last relevant precedent was authored and when *Schuette* was decided.

Indeed, *Schuette* was not the first time the Court had been asked to review voters' concerted efforts to roll back a state's attempts to address racial discrimination and inequity. Against the immediate and then fading backdrop of the civil rights movement, the Court had been asked to consider such efforts from the late 1960s on. Three decisions consume the bulk of the *Schuette* plurality's opinion: *Reitman v. Mulkey* (*Mulkey*) (1967), *Hunter v. Erickson* (*Hunter*) (1969), and *Washington v. Seattle School District No. 1* (*Seattle*) (1982). Like *Schuette*, each case confronts what were, at the time, controversial state actions designed to combat racial oppression and subordination. *Mulkey* and *Hunter* consider fair housing and *Seattle* integrative busing. By the time of *Schuette*, however, the controversy around those actions had receded – the wisdom of fair housing and the impracticality of integrative busing had settled into the sensus communis. This enabled the *Schuette* plurality, situated within its contemporaneous sensus communis, to understand its case, concerning affirmative action, as something entirely different from the precedent.

Schuette and these earlier cases are unique in the Court's Equal Protection jurisprudence in that they concern actions that *would not* have raised any potential Equal Protections violations had they concerned mere state inaction rather than voter-led efforts to single out state-led policies aimed at stemming the effects of discrimination for differential treatment. In the case of *Schuette*, for example, the claim was not that Equal Protection *required* the state to implement affirmative action in their university admission policies; rather, the Equal Protection claim was based on the notion that voters could not single out race-sensitive admissions policies for differential treatment while otherwise leaving the board's discretion, which was mandated by state constitution, untouched. The allegation of racial discrimination lay in the differential treatment of race-based policies, not in the state's drawing of racial distinctions itself. The decision in *Students for Fair Admissions v. Harvard* (2023), in which the Court held that university affirmative action policies are unconstitutional, is a more typical example of an Equal Protection claim. There, the plaintiffs claimed that affirmative action policies violated Equal Protection because they drew impermissible distinctions on the basis of race.

The Equal Protection clause of the Fourteenth Amendment, ratified in the wake of the Civil War, declares that no state may "deny to any person within its jurisdiction the equal protection of the laws" (US Constitution Amendment XIV, § 2). While the Court refused to understand the clause as banning racial segregation in *Plessy v. Ferguson* (1896) (upholding the notion of "separate but equal"), it overturned that decision in *Brown v. Board of Education of Topeka* (1954). It has since then applied what has come to be known as "strict scrutiny" to any state action that draws distinctions on the basis of race. That standard requires that a state narrowly tailor race-based distinctions to further a compelling governmental interest. In essence, this has meant that a state is not permitted to draw distinctions on the basis of race unless it has an exceedingly convincing, nondiscriminatory reason for doing so and unless it can show that any race-neutral measure would not suffice to accomplish the same ends. As the Court's Equal Protection jurisprudence regarding race-based distinctions has developed, it has held that the Equal Protection Clause prohibits state actions that are demonstrably racially motivated or engineered (*Washington v. Davis*, 1976). In other words, the Court has understood the Equal Protection clause to prohibit states from drawing unjustifiable race-based distinctions, not to proactively require the end of racial inequity.

In a sense, *Schuette* and its predecessors concern whether the voters of a state may work to rescind a state's proactive steps to address racial inequity (steps that are neither constitutionally mandated nor constitutionally prohibited). These cases demonstrate the tension between the state's duty to right racial wrongs and the majority's prerogative to maintain the racial status quo. Through understanding *Schuette* and its predecessors – *Mulkey*, *Hunter*, and *Seattle* – not as mere reflections of common opinion but manifestations of the struggle over sensus communis, we are able to appraise all four more fairly. I now turn to each of those opinions.

In the 1960s, in *Mulkey* and *Hunter*, the Court twice, and in quick succession, reviewed voter actions designed to roll back fair housing legislation, finding them in violation of the Equal Protection Clause both times. The debate over the impacts of neighborhood segregation and the wisdom of prohibiting discrimination in housing was ripe at the time. In July 1967, President Lyndon Johnson commissioned the

National Advisory Commission on Civil Disorders (more commonly known as the Kerner Commission) to investigate the causes of urban riots in Black and Latino neighborhoods across the country. The commission's report famously declared: "Our nation is moving toward two societies, one black, one white – separate and unequal" (The National Advisory Commission on Civil Disorders, 2016, p. 1). It found that white racism, which led to segregated neighborhoods and lack of economic opportunity in those neighborhoods, was a primary cause of the riots. The report argued that ending neighborhood segregation was the only way to address the underlying inequities that inspired unrest and violence. About a month after the report was released, Dr. Martin Luther King Jr. was assassinated; days later, the Fair Housing Act, barring discrimination in the provision of housing, was signed into federal law.

The Supreme Court's decisions in *Mulkey* and *Hunter* came in the midst of these riots and the simmering debate over pursuing fair housing. The sensus communis over the wisdom of fair housing legislation had not yet settled, but the existence of segregated housing patterns (and the desire of many to maintain that system) was well known. *Mulkey*, decided in May 1967 by a margin of 5–4, concerned California's voters' enactment of a constitutional amendment that made it illegal for the state to abridge the right of property owners to exercise "absolute discretion" in the lease and sale of real estate. The Court found the amendment violated the Equal Protection Clause. Prior to the passage of the amendment, the California legislature had enacted one law that forbade restrictive covenants and another that prohibited racial discrimination in the sale or rental of residential real estate with more than four units. The amendment, then, was a reaction to the legislature's efforts to pursue fairer housing. Like *Schuette*, then, *Mulkey* concerned *not* the constitutionality of legislative inaction, but the constitutionality of voters' efforts to roll back legislative action. Because there was, as of yet, no federal law requiring fair housing, California wasn't compelled to ensure it. Had the California legislature failed to pass fair housing laws, California citizens would have been free to continue to discriminate in the sale and lease of housing. The question, then, was not whether federal law prohibited Californians from discriminating in the provision of housing; it was whether the State of California itself had violated the Equal Protection Clause, had itself engaged in invidious discrimination, by passing a constitutional amendment that proclaimed and protected the right to discriminate in the provision of housing. In reaching its decision, the Court stressed the necessity of "asses[ing] the *potential impact* of official action in determining whether a State has *significantly involved* itself with invidious discrimination" (*Reitman v. Mulkey*, 1967, pp. 379–380). In so doing, it relied on a line of case law in which the Court had struck down subtle state actions that were designed to distance the state from "official" discrimination while, nonetheless, promoting it. The *Mulkey* majority opinion breezes through five previous opinions without spending much time parsing the discriminatory action at work. Among the unconstitutional actions it cites are when New Orleans city officials made public statements about not permitting Black patrons to seek desegregated service in restaurants though they never passed an official ordinance to that effect and when a state statute gave a state political party's executive committee power to "prescribe the qualifications of its members for voting" in primaries, effectively restricting primary voting to white party members (*Reitman v. Mulkey*, 1967, pp. 379–380). Through these citations, the Court seemed to be intimating that either a narrow view of state action or the abstracted application of a "neutrality principle" might miss pernicious discriminatory state action. At the same time, it was conveying the many creative ways states had worked to promote discrimination while attempting to skirt constitutional scrutiny. In spending relatively little time discussing each opinion, the Court also seemed to be suggesting how commonplace and predictable this behavior was. The Court situated California's voters' actions squarely in this history, finding that the amendment "was intended to authorize, and does authorize, racial discrimination in the housing market. The right to discriminate is now one of the basic policies of the State" (*Reitman v. Mulkey*, 1967, p. 381). The majority opinion in *Mulkey*, then, reflects the common sense of the time (supported by social and judicial history) that state promotion of racial discrimination emerges in diverse and insidious forms and that such actions are regrettably common.

Justice Harlan's dissent provides further insight into the debates of the time and the contests over the sensus communis. Harlan rejected the majority's analysis, finding that the amendment was neutral on its face and that its constitutionality was to be determined "by what the law does, not by what those who voted for it wanted it to do" (*Reitman v. Mulkey*, 1967, p. 391). Harlan began and ended his dissent by stressing his concern that the majority's decision would impede racial progress. He opened by fretting that the decision would "actually serve to handicap progress in the extremely difficult field of racial concerns" in the long run (p. 387). And he closed by predicting that "the doctrine underlying this decision may hamper, if not preclude, attempts to deal with the delicate and troublesome problems of race relations through the legislative process" (p. 395). Harlan's dissent is reminiscent of the refrain "go slow" and reflects an ongoing and contentious debate at the time, as memorialized in King's "Letter from Birmingham Jail" (1963) and Nina Simone's "Mississippi Goddamn" (1964), among many others. It shows how there seemed to be a settling, though not yet settled, consensus that fair housing *was* an issue of racial equity ("go slow" suggests a recognition of a problem and a refusal to pursue it promptly) and how contentious the pursuit of that goal was. The rhetorical conflict surrounding *Mulkey* and the as yet unsettled sensus communis around the wisdom of guaranteeing fair housing would later be elided by the *Schuette* plurality, flattened into the ahistorical, uncontested notion that ensuring fair housing is common sense.

The Court's 8–1 decision in *Hunter v. Erickson*, decided in January 1969, concerned a similar effort to roll back fair housing protections. Though it was decided only two years after *Mulkey*, there had been significant national developments in the discussion around fair housing in the interim. *Hunter* came on the heels of the release of the Kerner Report and the passage of the Fair Housing Act. The case concerned voters' efforts to thwart a city council's fair housing ordinance and any future efforts to pass a similar ordinance. In 1964, the city of Akron, Ohio, passed a fair housing ordinance. Voters subsequently passed an amendment to the Akron city charter which vitiated the fair housing ordinance and required that any ordinance that regulated the sale or lease of real estate on the basis of "race, color, religion, national origin or ancestry" be approved by the voters in a regular or general election (not a special one). While the city argued that the case was distinct from *Mulkey* because the voters' amendment didn't declare a right to discriminate, the Court found that because the amendment "treat[ed] racial housing matters differently from other racial and housing matters" (by requiring that these matters be subjected to a special procedure outside the normal referendum process), it created a suspect racial classification (*Hunter v. Erickson*, 1969, p. 389). The Court was unimpressed with the city's argument that the amendment reflected a "public decision to move slowly in the delicate area of race relations" (p. 392), noting that the voters adopted a more "complex system" than a broadly applicable system for considering ordinances and insisting that "the State may no more disadvantage any particular group by making it more difficult to enact legislation in its behalf than it may dilute any person's vote or give any group a smaller representation than another of comparable size" (p. 393). The opinion presumes, without elaboration, that fair housing legislation benefits minorities, which is why the Court was able to find that the city's efforts to treat racial housing matters differently than all others was necessarily a "meaningful and unjustified distinctio[n] based on race" (p. 391). This was a reasonable presumption, though it was not without detractors, as white Southern politicians had spent decades claiming that segregation was to the benefit of both white and Black Americans (Epps-Robertson, 2016). Though it's now relatively uncontroversial to suggest that racial discrimination in the provision of housing is to the detriment of people of color – despite evidence of the continuing prevalence of the practice (United States Department of Justice, 2021) – *Mulkey* and *Hunter* themselves remind us that the sensus communis around the issue was still unsettled at the time of those decisions.

In a concurrence, Justice Harlan noted that the "city's principal argument in support of the charter amendment relies on the undisputed fact that fair housing legislation may often be expected to raise the passions of the community to their highest pitch" (*Reitman v. Mulkey*, 1967, p. 395). Rather than a justification for the amendment's differential treatment of fair housing matters, Harlan saw the obviousness of the controversy as proof of the amendment's discriminatory purpose, reasoning that "the charter amendment [would] have its real impact only when fair housing [did] not arouse extraordinary controversy" because it would tip the scales against fair housing *even* when majority support had shifted in favor of it (pp. 395–396). Harlan, then, takes the sensus communis that communities must "go slow" in pursuing fair housing to show how voters had leveraged that common opinion to preclude future progress, even when (and if) public opinion (the sensus communis) had shifted.

The next time the Court heard a case concerning voters' efforts to frustrate a state's attempts to address racial discrimination was in 1982 in *Washington v. Seattle School District No. 1*. The case concerned a statewide initiative to ban mandatory busing for the purposes of integration and was targeted, specifically, at the Seattle school district's voluntary efforts to desegregate its schools. The Court held the state's action in violation of the Equal Protection Clause by a 5–4 margin. Busing for the purposes of desegregation had been controversial since courts had first imposed it as a remedy to school districts' Equal Protection violations. Like the controversy around fair housing, that controversy has largely receded into the background. Unlike fair housing, the reason it has done so is because the practice has largely been abandoned (in part because of the Supreme Court's 2007 opinion in *Parents Involved in Community Schools v. Seattle School District No. 1* (*Parents Involved*), which I discuss later) and is regarded by many as a relic of history. This sentiment is well reflected by an exchange between Kamala Harris and Joe Biden during a 2019 Democratic presidential primary debate. In that debate, Harris attacked Biden for his history of opposing desegregative busing in the 1970s and 1980s, noting that she had been a beneficiary of the practice (Paz, 2019). However, when pressed after the debate about her current position on busing, she demurred, locating the practice and the controversy over it in the past: "I have asked [Biden] and have yet to hear him agree that busing that was court-ordered and mandated in most places and in that era in which I was bused, was necessary" (Martin & Glueck, 2019). In positioning their quibble over the past practice of busing, Harris locates the practice and its necessity in the past. Though the controversy over busing has receded, at the time of *Seattle* it was ripe; busing, both court-ordered and district-adopted, was still a primary way of addressing the racial segregation that plagued – and still plagues (United States Government Accountability Office, 2022) – many schools across the country.

In 1978 the Seattle school district implemented a desegregation plan that included busing and reassignments which resulted in "the reassignment of roughly equal numbers of white and minority students, and allow[ed] most students to spend roughly half their academic careers attending a school near their homes" (*Washington v. Seattle*, 1982, p. 461). As the program was being developed, disgruntled Seattle residents formed the Citizens for Voluntary Integration Committee (CiVIC) which sought, first, to enjoin enforcement of the desegregation plan and, after that failed, to pass a *statewide* initiative banning mandatory busing for the purposes of integration. The initiative passed with 66 percent of the vote. While the general facts appear similar to *Hunter* (voters overturning and creating a more arduous process for reinstituting a measure designed to pursue racial equality), the

Court obviously struggled with how divided public opinion about integrative busing was. A 1981 Gallup poll found 17 percent of white respondents in favor of desegregative busing (with 78 percent opposed) and 60 percent of Black respondents in favor (with 30 percent opposed) (Steadman, 1981). The Court was presented with a clear rupture in the sensus communis. If it was to find an Equal Protection violation, it would have to find that the voters' action discriminated on the basis of race even though it could not say that minorities were universally invested in integrative busing or that everybody who opposed integrative busing did so for racially motivated reasons. Accordingly, the Court noted that while "proponents of mandatory integration cannot be classified by race," its own cases "suggest that desegregation of the public schools, like the Akron open housing ordinance, at bottom inures primarily to the benefit of the minority, and is designed for that purpose" (*Washington v. Seattle*, 1982, p. 472). Its reasoning, then, rested not on assigning preference for integrative busing to minorities but on the Court's own, at that point, relatively uncontroversial conclusions (dating back to *Brown v. Board of Education*) that desegregated schools benefit minority students, and that segregation harms them. Essentially, the Court focused on the racial *injury* of segregation rather than the particular remedy (integrative busing) to reach the conclusion that the voters' initiative "burden[ed] minority interests" (*Washington v. Seattle*, 1982, p. 474). Rooting its opinion in the established sensus communis over the harms of racial segregation in education, the Court was able to assign race-based intent and effect to the voters' action.

As had the *Hunter* Court, the *Seattle* Court focused on the complicated process voters had devised to insulate integrative busing from school boards' control. It stressed that by removing the option of integrative busing from school boards' discretion, the voters had "expressly require[d] those championing school integration to surmount a considerably higher hurdle than persons seeking comparable legislative action," as they would have to appeal to the voters or legislature of the entire state rather than the school board about this, and only this, school assignment matter (*Washington v. Seattle*, 1982, p. 474). It noted that the voters' initiative to ban integrative busing singled out "racially-conscious legislation" for "peculiar and disadvantageous treatment" (p. 485) and stressed that "when the State's allocation of power places unusual burdens on the ability of racial groups to enact legislation specifically designed to overcome the 'special condition' of prejudice, the governmental action seriously curtails the operation of those political processes ordinarily relied upon to protect minorities" (p. 486). Again, the Court's analysis rests on the harm – prejudice that led to highly segregated schools – and not so much the remedy – integrative busing – to reach the conclusion that, in singling out integrative busing for differential treatment, the voters' action discriminated against minorities. For the Court to have concluded otherwise and imply that minorities were universally in support of integrative busing would have been to willfully ignore what it knew about the sensus communis and the controversy aroused by integrative busing; it also would have imposed a favorable opinion of integrative busing on an entire class of people. As it had in *Mulkey* and *Hunter*, the *Seattle* Court understood the measure voters sought to eviscerate as addressing the effects of racial prejudice. Its analysis assumed the continued and significant impacts of that prejudice (something the *Schuette* plurality would reject). Though integrative busing was, as described in *Seattle*, widely controversial at the time of the decision, that controversy wasn't a reason for the court to uphold the voters' action. The opinion looked to the Court like *Mulkey* and *Hunter* before it because it was yet another example of voters seeking to preserve the racial status quo and to prevent the state from addressing race-based injury. School segregation was a well-established injury. What to do about that injury was less well established and less sedimented in the sensus communis. The *Seattle* court was attempting to navigate these realities.

Mulkey, *Hunter*, and *Seattle* can be characterized as cases in which the Court confronted voter-enacted impediments to addressing racial injury; they each involve a state action that would otherwise be constitutionally permissible but was not because the majority of voters singled out that racial issue for special treatment. The facts of *Schuette* would seem to fit this pattern well, but the Court's inability to understand affirmative action as anything other than the infliction of harmful racial categories would be the difference in the outcome. As I explain below, this inability is attributable both to the plurality's flattening of the struggles over sensus communis memorialized in the precedent it cites as well as its inability to understand the *Schuette* case itself as being about the sensus communis over Equal Protection.

8.5 MAKING SENSE OF *SCHUETTE V. BAMN*

As I've indicated, *Mulkey*, *Hunter*, and *Seattle* are the primary precedents with which the *Schuette* plurality opinion wrestles. In comparison to the amount of time it spends discussing *Seattle*, the *Schuette* opinion (*Schuette v. BAMN*, 2014) devotes relatively little text to distinguishing *Mulkey* and *Hunter*. In its brief review of these two opinions, the *Schuette* plurality casts them as uncomplicated cases where the voters had sanctioned the racist practices of individuals. This characterization flattens the historical struggle over fair housing and abstracts the opinions from the sensus communis in which they were formed. The *Schuette* plurality mentions the plaintiffs' particular circumstances in both cases (specific acts of racial discrimination in the provision of housing) and finds that in *Mulkey* and *Hunter* "there was a demonstrated injury on the basis of race that, by reasons of state encouragement or participation, became more aggravated" (*Schuette v. BAMN*, 2014, p. 304). Interestingly, this construction locates the primary harm and action with individuals (those who would discriminate in the provision of housing) and assigns the state the role of "aggravating" the underlying problem. This is a markedly different characterization than that of earlier courts who declared in *Mulkey* that the voters' action had rendered the "right to discriminate" "one of the basic policies of the State"

(*Reitman v. Mulkey*, 1967, p. 381) and in *Hunter* that the voters' action "constitute[d] a real, substantial, and invidious denial of the equal protection of the laws" (*Hunter v. Erickson*, 1969, p. 392). By eschewing the opinions' own characterizations of the evils at work and locating the action with those who would discriminate in the provision of housing, the *Schuette* plurality abstracts those opinions from the sensus communis in which they were formed, minimizing the common opinion of those times that the majority was regularly and perniciously involved in preserving white supremacy. In the *Schuette* plurality's characterization, racism is wrought by individuals, not the majority or the state. This depiction also buttresses the *Schuette* plurality's tortured description of *Seattle* and serves to distinguish all three cases from how the plurality understands the Michigan voters' actions, which it sees as neutral democratic policymaking in action.

The *Schuette* plurality opinion describes *Seattle* as a case in which the "state action in question (the bar on busing enacted by the State's voters) had the serious risk, if not purpose, of causing specific injuries on account of race" (*Schuette v. BAMN*, 2014, p. 305). That determination poses some difficulty for the plurality because the Court ruled in *Parents Involved in Community Schools v. Seattle School District No. 1* (2007) that the Seattle district's integrative plan was unconstitutional because, in its determination, the district had not been subject to de jure segregation and, absent that determination, its plan failed to advance a compelling state interest in a way that was narrowly tailored. *Parents Involved*, then, rejected the *Seattle* Court's underlying premise that integrative busing was to the benefit of minority students by declaring that to classify students by race for the purpose of school assignment was, absent a finding of de jure segregation, presumptively to inflict injury on the basis of race. In other words, where the *Seattle* Court had found that integrative busing was to the benefit of minority students, the *Parents Involved* Court found that it harms all students (including minority students). The *Schuette* plurality opinion attempts to confront this complication by declaring that "we must understand *Seattle* as *Seattle* understood itself," as a case in which neither party "challenged the propriety of race-conscious student assignments for the purposes of achieving integration" (*Schuette v. BAMN*, 2014, p. 306). From there, the plurality concludes that, in *Seattle*, "the State's disapproval of the school board's busing remedy was an aggravation of the very racial injury in which the State itself was complicit" (p. 306). The *Schuette* plurality, then, seems to accept that, in the *Seattle* past, schools that were segregated through state action harmed minority students and that Seattle had such schools. In this way, the *Schuette* plurality assigns discriminatory action to specific actors – in *Mulkey* and *Hunter*, those who would discriminate in the provision of housing and in *Seattle*, the Seattle school district itself – and assigns to voters the role of "aggravating" racial injury. This move works to emphasize the role of individual bad actors in inflicting discrimination and to distance the states' and voters' roles in that work, abstracting those earlier opinions from the sensus communis of the time that the majority will often work to preserve white dominance and that the courts should be attuned to this danger. It also draws a distinction between historic, specific racial injuries that must be remedied (housing discrimination and state-sponsored school segregation) and racial disparities whose root causes are less easily assigned. This distinction aids the plurality in its aim of articulating a sensus communis that both majority-imposed and state-sponsored racial injuries are things of the past.

The *Schuette* plurality's selective historical contextualizing of *Seattle* elides how controversial integrative busing was both at the time of that decision (1982) and when *Parents Involved* was decided (*Parents Involved in Community Schools v. Seattle School District No. 1*, 2007). In so doing, the plurality opinion renders the racial injury in *Seattle* clear and uncomplicated (like its assessment of *Mulkey* and *Hunter*) and a relic of the past. The plurality, then, imposes the current sensus communis over the obvious harms of housing discrimination and state-imposed school segregation on those previous cases, eliding the controversies engendered by the specific remedies the states in those cases sought to undertake. This elision renders the voters' "aggravating" actions in each case patently discriminatory. It also sets the plurality's opinion and the *Schuette* controversy in a new era – one where housing discrimination and school segregation are past problems duly acknowledged and addressed by law. In turn, this move articulates the present as one where race-based injuries have largely been alleviated and where classification on the basis of race itself is the primary evil the legal system must guard against.

This past/present divide aids the plurality in distinguishing the Michigan voters' efforts to remove affirmative action from the purview of university boards with the Washington voters' efforts to remove integrative busing from the purview of school boards. The opinion suggests that to find for the plaintiffs would require accepting the proposition that "all individuals of the same race think alike" (*Schuette v. BAMN*, 2014, p. 308) and would encourage "the creation of incentives for those who support or oppose certain policies to cast the debate in terms of racial advantage or disadvantage" (p. 309). The implication is that affirmative action, unlike fair housing or the integrative busing of yore, is an issue with neutral racial implications about which reasonable people disagree. What this implication denies is the possibility of any underlying race-based injury. While discriminatory housing practices and racially segregated schools are cast as clear race-based injuries that can be aggravated by voter action, the history of discrimination in higher education and the persistence of racial inequities in higher education admissions and attainment are, for the *Schuette* plurality, beside the point.

In rendering Seattle's integrative busing plan less a controversial measure to achieve racial balance in schools and more a necessary antidote to insidious, state-sponsored segregation, the *Schuette* plurality could represent controversy over affirmative action as something of a different kind, something untethered to racial injury and prejudice. If affirmative action is nothing more than a policy preference (about which many reasonable people disagree and to which we cannot assign race-based purpose, benefit, or preference), the voters' action is merely democratic decision-making in action.

Though the *Schuette* plurality declares at the outset that the case "is not about the constitutionality, or the merits, of race-conscious admissions policies in higher education" (*Schuette v. BAMN*, 2014, p. 300), its decision, and particularly its treatment of *Seattle*, suggests the opposite – that the outcome of the case was contingent on the Court's negative assessment of affirmative action itself. The plurality closes by declaring: "What is at stake here is not whether injury will be inflicted but whether government can be instructed not to follow a course that entails, first, the definition of racial categories and, second, the grant of favored status to persons in some racial categories and not others" (p. 300). This description draws into question the plurality's insistence that its assessment of affirmative action is not contingent on the outcome of the case. While the *Seattle* Court understood that integrative busing was controversial, that didn't keep it from acknowledging the underlying purpose of integrative busing, the injury it was designed to address, and the complex process voters had used to remove busing from school boards' purview. The difference between *Seattle* and *Schuette*, then, might be attributed not to the controversy around the respective policies but to the Justices' own opinions about those policies (as informed by those public controversies). In other words, the difference may be that the plurality of the Justices on the *Schuette* Court were interested in tipping the sensus communis toward a colorblind field of vision while the majority of the Justices on the *Seattle* Court still inhabited a sensus communis where it was common sense that the white majority might work to preserve its privilege, even absent overt racial animus.

At the time of *Washington v. Seattle School District No. 1* (1982), court-ordered busing was still relatively common and the Supreme Court continuously upheld the practice even in the face of public outcry. While public opinion was divided, the Court itself may have understood busing as a valuable tool in combatting segregation (especially when other methods like neighborhood integration were abandoned by the federal government). On the other hand, at the time of *Schuette v. BAMN* (2014), the Court had already begun to erode the constitutional basis for affirmative action, which may explain why the *Schuette* plurality could only envision the practice of affirmative action itself as inflicting racial injury (rather than the other way around). That the plurality understood the drawing of racial classifications as racial injury may also explain the plurality's tortured reading of *Seattle*. By explaining the *Seattle* Court's decision only in terms of de jure segregation and the Court's historic intervention in that presumed bygone practice, the *Schuette* plurality could draw a stark line between the era when race-based remedies were necessary and the present, where they are suspect and harmful. In this way, the plurality tries to fit history into its own sensus communis around Equal Protection – an understanding that we are past the era where racial classifications can combat prejudice because underlying state-backed prejudice has been confronted and vanquished.

The Court's assessment of affirmative action is perhaps more widely accepted than it sometimes appears. While Steve Sanders claims that "anybody who can read a poll knows that affirmative action is supported by an overwhelming number of blacks" (Sanders, 2016, p. 1448), in truth it is somewhat difficult to determine where the plurality's description lies within the (as yet) unsettled sensus communis. In 2014, the year *Schuette* was decided, Pew researchers asked respondents this question: "In general, do you think affirmative action programs designed to increase the number of black and minority students on college campuses are a good thing or a bad thing?" In the poll, 84 percent of Black respondents declared them a good thing, while 80 percent of Hispanic respondents and 55 percent of white respondents did (Drake, 2014). That polling would suggest that affirmative action was even more popular among Black Americans at the time of *Schuette* than desegregative busing was at the time of *Seattle*, where a poll found 60 percent of Black respondents in favor of desegregative busing (Steadman, 1981). But the wording of polling questions concerning approval for affirmative action has significant impact on outcomes. A 2021 Gallup poll asked respondents: "Do you generally favor or oppose affirmative action programs for racial minorities?" In that poll, 79 percent of Hispanic adults responded in favor, 69 percent of Black adults responded in favor, and 57 percent of white adults responded in favor (these are not tremendously different results than the 2014 poll) (Saad, 2021). However, in a 2022 Pew poll, when asked if race or ethnicity should be a factor in college admissions decisions, 39 percent of Black adults responded yes, while 37 percent of Asian adults, 31 percent of Hispanic adults, and 21 percent of white adults did (Gómez, 2022). These results suggest that when polling questions move from the level of abstraction to more specifically referencing the mechanics of affirmative action, support plummets. So, while polling data contemporaneous to *Schuette* suggests broad minority support for affirmative action, the wording of that polling question should give us pause. Perhaps, then, the *Schuette* plurality was right – Michigan voters' removal of affirmative action from university boards' otherwise complete discretion over admissions policies is not a violation of Equal Protection but a mere manifestation of democracy in action. And yet, the Court's precedent suggests that the analysis shouldn't rest on the popularity of a given practice but upon the racial injury effected when, through voter action, a practice designed to address racial injury is rendered more difficult to enact than any similar non-race-based practice.

Certainly, as I've suggested, we can (and should) attribute the outcome in the *Schuette* case both to the shifting composition of the Court and to the rise of what some critics have termed the Court's colorblind approach to the Equal Protection claims, where it tends to view any racial classification, whether designed to address historical and present inequities or to exacerbate inequities, as suspect (Roberts, 2014). However, some have criticized the precedent upon which the *Schuette* plurality relied for its failure to provide clear guidance as to the application of Equal Protection. Sanders argues that a "significant weakness" of the cases preceding *Schuette* "is the court's relative delicacy and indirection about the racial dynamics behind the challenged measures in those cases" (Sanders, 2016, p. 1438). He goes on: "The *Hunter* and *Seattle* opinions can be criticized for the Court's unwillingness to be more forthcoming and candid about the racial prejudice it perceived behind the restructurings" (p. 1438). Similarly, David Bernstein argues the court could have named the "substantial racist component" behind the voters' actions in *Mulkey* and *Hunter* but did not (Bernstein, 2013, p. 264).

Like the *Schuette* plurality opinion itself, these criticisms seem to abstract *Mulkey*, *Hunter*, and *Seattle* from their historical contexts. Suggesting that those earlier Courts should have predicted the colorblind approach that would come to dominate the Court's evaluation of Equal Protection claims, Sanders and Bernstein seem to want those earlier Courts to have anticipated the turns in both language and values that would develop around Equal Protection law. Bernstein charges that

> the *Mulkey* and *Hunter* Courts could have simply ruled that the referenda in question had discriminatory intent and discriminatory effects. From approximately 1948 to 1972, however, and to some extent through 1982, the Supreme Court openly allied with the civil rights movement but tried to do so without either overtly accusing anti-civil rights forces of racism or massively disrupting the federal–state-balance. (Bernstein, 2013, p. 278)

It's not clear that either decision Bernstein references fails to establish discriminatory intent and effects. In *Mulkey*, when the Court says that the amendment "was intended to authorize, and does authorize, racial discrimination in the housing market" and that this renders "the right to discriminate" one of the "basic policies of the State," the Court is clearly indicating the intended and actual effect of the amendment (*Reitman v. Mulkey*, 1967, p. 381). Bernstein's criticism seems more leveled at the Court's failure to assign the term "racist" to the amendment and the voters than its analysis of a clear violation of Equal Protection. Bernstein may have perceived that the Court handled the matter "delicately" less because the Court failed to outline the nature of the violation and more because the amendment looks egregious to us now (and didn't to many at the time of its passage). Similarly, the *Hunter* Court is clear that the Akron voters had singled out fair housing in an effort to place "special burdens on racial minorities within the governmental process" (*Hunter v. Erickson*, 1969, p. 391), explicitly holding that the amendment "discriminate[d] against minorities" (p. 393). Bernstein is correct that the Court failed to label the Akron voters themselves racist, electing to label the amendment itself discriminatory. But whether that's a "weakness" the Court should have avoided, as Sanders claims and Bernstein suggests, is less clear.

Bernstein and Sanders are right that in all three opinions – *Mulkey*, *Hunter*, and *Seattle* – the Court avoids labeling the voters' actions racist or even racially motivated. The Court's reticence to assign the label racist to each individual voter, especially in the case of *Seattle*, makes sense given that such a sweeping generalization would have been unsupported by evidence (though, undoubtedly, a significant portion of those opposed to busing were opposed to desegregation). After all, in *Seattle*, polling reflected that 30 percent of Black adults opposed desegregative busing, an opinion the Court may have known was shared by prominent civil rights activists including preeminent civil rights lawyer and scholar Derrick Bell (Cobb, 2021). Further, it's notable that at the time of *Mulkey* and *Hunter*, Southern politicians had been articulating the position that one could be a segregationist without being a racist. George Wallace proclaimed in 1964: "A racist is one who despises someone because of his color, and an Alabama segregationist is one who conscientiously believes that it is in the best interest of Negro and white to have a separate education and social order" (Bernard, 2022). While almost nobody would entertain the proposition now, at the time of *Mulkey*, the Warren Court had spent more than a decade combatting that very idea – that segregation and separation on the basis of race could be distinguished from the maintenance of white supremacy and the perpetuation of inequality – by chronicling the effects of segregation. The Court understood its role in confronting and altering the sensus communis around "separate but equal." So, while Bernstein is correct in indicating that the Court was navigating common opinion and controversy of the time, his suggestion that it could have just labeled the actions in question in *Mulkey* and *Hunter* racist seems ahistorical, as that label wouldn't have had the same relevance as it does in current judicial and cultural reasoning (because the meaning of the term was contested in different ways than it is today) and wouldn't have aided in resolving the underlying legal question (because the opinions already establish the creation of a suspect racial classification and discriminatory effect of that classification).

8.6 CONCLUSION

Reading these opinions through Vico's sensus communis reminds us that the *Mulkey*, *Hunter*, and *Seattle* Courts were accustomed to the particular sorts of evils the majority could undertake in the name of democratic action and in the service of preserving the racial status quo. *Schuette*, its precedent, and the criticisms of those precedents draw into stark relief how the *Schuette* plurality had to engage the settled sensus communis over the historical importance of Equal Protection, while continuing to revise its present meaning, all as a result of confronting a new necessity – the question of whether a state's voters can discriminate in their treatment of state universities' authority with respect to affirmative action. To achieve this result, the *Schuette* plurality worked to insulate the racial injuries of the past from any relationship to the present. In suggesting that *Seattle* concerned de jure segregation (something *Parents Involved* strenuously argued against), the opinion renders *Seattle* part of the kind of legally backed discrimination and segregation that we have moved past and beyond. In the *Schuette* plurality opinion, de jure segregation is classed with overt housing discrimination, and those issues are located in the Court's and our past. This move enables the plurality to articulate our present and future as one where it is possible for all to live as individuals untainted by stereotypes, where "the only way to stop discriminating on the basis of race is to stop discriminating on the basis of race" (*Parents Involved in Community Schools v. Seattle School District No. 1*, 2007, p. 748).

It's easy enough to assess precedent for its failure to be completely responsive to our current controversies. I would imagine that it's far more difficult to formulate precedent with an eye toward what future controversies might arise and the language in which those controversies will be unavoidably embedded. Certainly, we should continue to discuss how precedent does or doesn't respond to our current situation, but we should do so with an appreciation for the sensus communis out of which that precedent emerged and with an appreciation for how our discussions themselves either do or don't account for our history. Thus, our common law system and its reliance on precedent provides an opportunity to continually revisit our history and to struggle over what it was and what we value.

REFERENCES

Bayer, T. I. (2008). Vico's principle of sensus communis and forensic eloquence. *Chicago-Kent Law Review*, 83(3), 1131–1155.

Bernard, D. (2022). How a failed assassination attempt pushed George Wallace to reconsider his segregationist views. *Smithsonian Magazine*. www.smithsonianmag.com

Bernstein, D. E. (2013–2014). "Reverse Carolene Products," the end of the Second Reconstruction, and other thoughts on *Schuette v. Coalition to Defend Affirmative Action*. *Cato Supreme Court Review*, 261–284.

Brown v. Board of Education of Topeka, 347 U.S. 483 (1954).

Cobb, J. (2021). The man behind Critical Race Theory. *The New Yorker*. www.newyorker .com/magazine

Constable, M. (2014). *Our word is our bond: How legal speech acts*. Stanford Law Books.

Drake, B. (2014). *Public strongly backs affirmative action programs on campus*. www .pewresearch.org/fact-tank/2014/04/22/public-strongly-backs-affirmative-action-programs-on-campus/ [https://perma.cc/EZ58-UZ9A]

Epps-Robertson, C. (2016). The race to erase *Brown v. Board of Education*: The Virginia Way and the rhetoric of Massive Resistance. *Rhetoric Review*, 35(2), 108–120.

Gómez, V. (2022). As courts weigh affirmative action, grades and test scores seen as top factors in college admissions. *Pew Research Center*. www.pewresearch.org/short-reads/2022/04/26/u-s-public-continues-to-view-grades-test-scores-as-top-factors-in-college-admissions/ [https://perma.cc/W8EM-69ZY]

Hasian Jr., M., Condit, C. M., & Lucaites, J. L. (1996). The rhetorical boundaries of "the law": A consideration of the rhetorical culture of legal practice and the case of the "separate but equal" doctrine. *Quarterly Journal of Speech*, 82(4), 323–342.

Hunter v. Erickson, 393 U.S. 385 (1969).

King, Jr., M. L. (1963). Letter from Birmingham jail. *The Atlantic Monthly*, 212(2), 78–88.

Martin, J., & Glueck, K. (2019, July 4). Joe Biden and Kamala Harris bring their debate-stage fight to Iowa. *The New York Times*. www.nytimes.com

Parents Involved in Community Schools v. Seattle School District No. 1, 551 U.S. 701 (2007).

Paz, I. G. (2019, June 27). Kamala Harris and Joe Biden clash on race and busing. *The New York Times*. www.nytimes.com

Plessy v. Ferguson, 163 U.S. 537 (1896).

Reitman v. Mulkey, 387 U.S. 369 (1967).

Roberts, D. E. (2014). *Loving v. Virginia* as a civil rights decision. *New York Law School Law Review*, 59(1), 175–209.

Saad, L. (2021). Americans' confidence in racial fairness waning. *Gallup*. https://news.gallup.com/poll/352832/americans-confidence-racial-fairness-waning.aspx [https://perma.cc/H9DH-D6XN]

Sanders, S. (2016). Race, restructurings, and equal protection doctrine through the lens of *Schuette v. BAMN*. *Brooklyn Law Review*, 81(4), 1393–1462.

Schaeffer, J. D. (1990). *Sensus communis: Vico, rhetoric, and the limits of relativism*. Duke University Press.

(2001). Thomas More and the master tropes: The deep structure of a dialogue concerning heresies and Giambattista Vico. *Moreana*, 38(147/148), 5–24.

(2004). Commonplaces: Sensus communis. In W. Jost & W. Olmsted (Eds.), *A companion to rhetoric and rhetorical criticism* (pp. 278–293). Blackwell.

(2019). *Giambattista Vico on natural law: Religion, rhetoric and sensus communis*. Routledge.

Schuette v. Coalition to Defend Affirmative Action, Integration and Immigrant Rights and Fight for Equality by Any Means Necessary (BAMN), 572 U.S. 291 (2014).

Simone, N. (1964). Mississippi Goddamn. Mercury Records.

Steadman, J. (1981). *Busing for school desegregation: The debate on selected issues*. Congressional Research Service.

Students for Fair Admissions v. President and Fellows of Harvard College, 600 U.S. 181 (2023).

The National Advisory Commission on Civil Disorders. (2016). *The Kerner report* (2016 ed.). Princeton University Press. (Original work published 1968.)

United States Department of Justice. (2021, October 22). Justice department announces new initiative to combat redlining [Press release]. www.justice.gov/opa/pr/justice-department-announces-new-initiative-combat-redlining [https://perma.cc/YVB8-ASWW]

United States Government Accountability Office. (2022). Student population has significantly diversified, but many schools remain divided along racial, ethnic, and economic lines. United States Government Accountability Office. www.gao.gov/assets/gao-22-104737.pdf [https://perma.cc/T8F9-BAFL]

Vico, G. (2018). *On the study methods of our time* (E. Gianturco & D. P. Verene, Trans.). Cornell University Press. (Original work published 1709.)

(2020). *The new science* (J. Taylor & R. C. Miner, Trans.). Yale University Press. (Original work published 1744.)

Washington v. Davis, 426 U.S. 229 (1976).

Washington v. Seattle School District No. 1, 458 U.S. 457 (1982).

9

(Vernacular) Rhetorics for Women's Rights

Rasha Diab

9.1 INTRODUCTION

Misunderstood, decontextualized, or assum absent, the rhetorical discourses on women's rights in the Arab(ic)-Muslim world call for attention. To start, I revisit a moment when countering misrepresentations of and assumptions about Arab/ Muslim women's rights discourse becomes conspicuous and an exigence to write this chapter. At a conference in 2019, I was asked about the Arab Charter on Women's Rights (ACWR) launched by the advisory Federal National Council of the United Arab Emirates, or *al-Majlis al-Waṭanī al-Ittiḥādī* (Arab Parliament, 2021). After naming the charter as a "surprising and unprecedented feat," my interlocutor rapidly added, "how odd it is that this [Charter] moved forward?!" What's communicated is that it is odd that the charter materialized, given the assumed nature and state of *sharīʿa* law in the Middle East.

Such a reading matches English media representations that identify the moment as a striking "one-and-done" moment of exceptional work in a narrative of continual progress sponsored by and modeled after the West. At the time, the charter was celebrated; images and press releases circulated, often linking the feat mainly and sometimes only to Western instruments of rights.[1]

Citing international precedents especially when addressing international audiences is common practice. Unfortunately, this practice might be misread as a statement of absence of local and religious precedent, especially when such

[1] For example, Salama (2019) celebrates the moment and notes that "The Arab Charter for Women's Rights is the first legislation enacted by the Arab Parliament on women and the provisions of the International Covenant on Civil and Political Rights, the International Covenant on Economic, Social and Cultural Rights, and the principles of the 1979 Convention on the Elimination of All Forms of Discrimination against Women, as well as the Beijing Platform for Action of 1995, Security Council Resolution 1325 on Women, Peace and Security and subsequent resolutions." The article then states that the charter's core commitments are "in keeping with the guidance of Islamic Sharia, other divine religions, human values, and the international legitimacy of human rights."

information is buried in media representations. Also not commonly known is that the charter was years in the making, resulted from years of the Arab Parliament's multinational work, responded to feminist critiques of the invisibility of women in the Arab Charter on Human Rights (ACHR) (Arab League, 2004a, 2004b), and was preceded by centuries-old official and vernacular discourses on women's rights. Many don't know this history, and the ACWR doesn't disclose its rich history. Unsurprisingly then, my interlocuter reiterated, "Isn't this a huge legislative feat?!"

Since the conference encounter, addressing (mis)conceptions of Arabic-Islamic legal discourse and the long history of official and vernacular rhetorics on women's rights continues to be pressing. A simple Google/Google Scholar search for the ACWR takes us neither to the text of the charter in English or Arabic, nor to feminists advocating for rights, nor to a fifteen-centuries-old history of rights and women's rights in Islām. The search, however, repeatedly leads to the Arab League's ACHR. Drafted in 1994 and revised and adopted in 2004, the ACHR is an important precedent and context for the ACWR.

The rhetoricity of the conference encounter and the Google search are conspicuous. Settling a search for women's rights with the ACHR erases decades-long, complex debates about the far-reaching consequences of excluding/including women's rights in long-awaited regional instruments like ACHR. Centering *just* ACHR and ACWR is a selective remembering and misrepresentation of women's rights' long and contentious history. I argue that the misrepresentation, selective forgetting/remembering, and decontextualized reading of official and vernacular discourses of women's rights are telling and consequential, demanding scholarly attention.

9.2 SELECTIVE MEMORY AND (ASSUMED) CONTRADICTION OF TERMS

Though related to the limited visibility of Arabic-Islamic rhetorics in general (e.g., Diab, 2023), there is much more to this invisibility. Negative perceptions of women and women's rights in the Arab/Muslim world hinder a nuanced assessment of legal instruments like ACWR and their precedential history. This is especially the case if we explore women's rights only through the stereotypical and colonial prism of concerns about women who need to be saved because they can only be assumed "passive victims of religious patriarchy," as Howe (2020, p. 1) puts it. Attempts to interrogate this orientalist frame typically trigger variants of the following question: "When we take a look at the history of Arabic-Islamic legal-political rhetoric, aren't women 'passive victims'?" These negative perceptions center a history of impediments that women face in the Middle East and North Africa region (e.g., limited or not enforced laws promoting women's rights, backlash constraining and questioning women's rights). Unfortunately, these impediments and perceptions are often assumed to be fait accompli and are selectively made more visible. In the mix, an undeniably rich discourse of rights, including women's rights, remains invisible. It even seems hard to trace. This discourse comprises a legal–ethical rhetoric of rights (e.g., Diab, 2018) and vernacular rhetorics of women's rights with conspicuous religious roots. Selective remembering is perilous.

Furthering invisibility, such selective memory may result in an absence of guarantees to women's rights and accountability measures for the violation of their rights. Empowering advocacy for women's rights (discourses) hinges on knowledge of and access to the legislative record, cultural and historical precedents, and role models. What if such knowledge remains invisible and inaccessible? Why are the ACWR's present and past contexts invisible or ignored? *What* and *how* can we know differently about official and/or vernacular women's rights discourses in the Arab(ic)-Islamic traditions? Bringing attention to official and vernacular rhetorics of women's rights and the Arab(ic)-Islamic legal-rhetorical tradition might surprise some or seem like a contradiction in terms to others; however, they often intersect and can help us answer these questions.

I demonstrate that we can *know differently* Arab(ic)-Islamic women's rights discourses by undertaking a more nuanced study of multifaceted regional contexts, historical roots, formative texts, enthymemes, and *topoi* that underwrite this rights advocacy. Additionally, we can attend to ACWR and ACHR's immediate present and formative past, including official and vernacular rhetorics of rights.

Scholars study vernacular rights discourses to highlight how articulations and "demands for rights ... are inseparable from their particular cultures, histories and political contexts" (Dunford & Madhok, 2015, p. 605). Scholars also distinguish between thin and thick discourses of rights. In his work on the "Moral Vernacular of Human Rights," Hauser defines the thin moral vernacular of human rights discourse as a "form [of discourse] in which human rights are transformed from a discrete set of moral principles to a discourse, or human rights talk. It manifests human rights as open to interpretation and subject to continual revision. Human rights talk does not seek convergence on values but agreement on consequences for which there is accountability" (Hauser, 2008, p. 443), whereas the thick discourse is "the language used by victims of human rights abuses" (p. 442). I'll draw on this definition frequently in the rest of the chapter.

In what follows, therefore, I shed light on persistent, even if rocky, regional Arab (ic)-Islamic tradition of women's rights; a rich vernacular of women's rights; and, more important, a long history of doctrinally driven legal-ethical teachings and rhetoric advocating against the violation of women's rights and operationalizing accountability for such rights. More specifically, in what follows I *first* briefly chart the discourse of rights and women's rights in Islām. I situate this rights discourse within a vision for a moral order, which is operationalized using an ethical-legal code. I demonstrate how this code is prescriptive, proscriptive, and constitutive (Section 9.3.1). *Second*, I use the condensed argument "*ūṣīkum bil-nisā' khaīran*" (I advise you to observe women's rights) to show the recognition of women as rights holders and the commensurate obligation to observe their rights (Section 9.3.2). *Third*, I identify misconceptions of women's rights (Section 9.3.3). I end the chapter by shedding light briefly on illustrative moments of persistent advocacy for women's rights which manifest a rich blend of official and vernacular rhetorics (Section 9.4). All are invisible precedents of the 2019 ACWR.

9.3 RIGHTS DISCOURSE AND WOMEN'S RIGHTS IN ISLĀM

Arab(ic)-Islamic discourse on women's rights can be neither separated from a multifaceted discourse on rights nor abstracted from a multitude of socio-cultural and political forces that undermine them. These include social and cultural biases and organizing stereotypes within/outside the Arab-Muslim world, and it is a complicated history: A discourse on women's rights in Islām exists; a patriarchally justified/justifiable framework questioning, if not undermining, these rights exists; misconceptions of women's rights in Islām and Arab/Muslim communities also exist. Needless to say, tracing the history of women's rights discourse results in a story irreducible to polemical soundbites.

9.3.1 *Beyond Soundbites: Negative/Positive Rights and the Moral Order*

Going back to the seventh century, I trace roots for a legal-ethical discourse on rights and women's rights. Though not without setbacks and inconsistent enforceability, this discourse on rights lives and circulates – sometimes inconspicuously – and warrants attention. Reasons for the inconspicuous presence of articulations of rights might be attributed to assumptions that rights are *only* articulated positively or are indexed in modern-day terms as rights.

As a scholar of peace-making rhetorical practices and legal-political instruments in the Middle Ages and beyond, I center my work on articulations of rights. Clearly, articulations of rights take different forms. Some are articulated positively; some are articulated negatively. Scholars distinguish between positive and negative rights. The former addresses the right *to* things including life or a resource (e.g., medical or legal aid), whereas the latter addresses the right "*not* to be interfered with in forbidden ways" (e.g., Fried, 1978, p. 110; emphasis added). We assume positive rights to be the norm. However, in contexts of gross violations, negative rights ascertain protections from abuses or infringements on others' rights; negative rights imply duties to others (i.e., abstaining from harm). Therefore, they are undismissable forms of legal-ethical intervention. Like the right *to*, the right *not to* is a key topos of legal rhetoric that migrates beyond legal spheres. Regardless of how they are articulated, rights are inseparable from a discourse on justice and visions of a moral order. I turn now to shed light on an enduring history of rights and justice discourses that comprise positive and negative rights, underscore a vision of a moral order, and call for and authorize accountability to these rights.

Drawing on previous research (e.g., Diab, 2016; Fried, 1978; Khadduri, 1946), I situate positive/negative rights, including the ACWR, in the context of multifaceted, Arab(ic)-Islamic iterations of rights/obligations. This discourse spells out *acts* that lead to and deviate from what is just. These iterations conspicuously

- identify and counter aggression (*baghī*), injustice (*ẓulm*), or evil (*shar*);
- identify and affirm rights (*ḥuqūq*), what's right (*ḥaq*), and people as rights-holders, regardless of their identifications and social, political, or legal standing;[2]
- advise against injustice and advocate for realizing justice, or *'adl* and *qist* (i.e., actionable, just measures); and
- support/invite work to clarify what these teachings and legislation mean *now* about women's rights.

In these iterations, what seems most obvious is a discourse on conduct, or good/bad or permissible/impermissible actions. This discourse can be understood as a legal-ethical code mapped onto a spectrum of positive/negative actions; on this spectrum, actions are (1) mandatory (*farḍ*); (2) recommended (*mandūb* or *mustaḥabb*); (3) permissible (*mubāḥ*); (4) reprehensible (*makrūh*); or (5) impermissible (*ḥarām*). The fulcrum of this discourse on conduct is justice, which is operationalized in contemporary parlance in terms of rights/duties and good/wrong conduct. All the spectrum's actions are inseparable from an interlocking legal–political–ethical–religious discourse. This discourse centers (in)justice and has conspicuous features: It is prescriptive, proscriptive, constitutive, and telos driven. Each feature is briefly addressed below.

The legal-ethical code is prescriptive and proscriptive, and it seeks to establish a moral order (e.g., Smith, 2003). The moral order is *positively defined* and encourages positive conduct pursuing what is right, fair, and just, or *'adl* and *ḥaq* (e.g., responding in kindness and not in kind to resolve conflict; The Qur'an, 2008, 41:34). It is also *negatively defined* and discourages harmful conduct that is neither fair nor just (e.g., advising *against baghī*, *ẓulm*, and *shar*, including conceit, which is inconsistent with equality and indicative of supremacy logics; The Qur'an, 2008, 17:37). Proscription and prescription are premised on divine commands, which separate what's fair from unfair, just from unjust.

The legal-ethical code manifests as constitutive rhetoric (Charland, 1987); it constitutes a moral order and its members. The legal-ethical code is simplified and made actionable using the aforementioned conduct spectrum. Significantly,

[2] In Islām, there are two broad categories of rights, namely rights of God (*ḥuqūq Allāh* like *ṣalāh*, or prayer) and rights of people (*ḥuqūq al-'ibād* like *zakāh*, or alms). This list of themes (1) addresses the rights of people (e.g., right to life and fair trial), (2) identifies practices that manifest inequities and manipulative practices (e.g., usury), (3) names the legal standard (i.e., Qur'ān and *Ḥadīth*) and witnesses to this legislation/legal agreements. For more on taxonomies of *ḥuqūq*, see Diab (2016).

positive/negative conduct is linked to subjectivity. As noted earlier, the legal-ethical code is addressed in terms of actions to undertake/abstain from, and these choices and acts interpellate or call forth a Muslim subjectivity. Calling forth a Muslim is a long, multifaceted process: "[I]nterpellation hinges on socialization" (Charland, quoted in Diab, 2016, p. 105). "One aspect of this socialization is naming ... their ... group membership ... [Another is to] invite actions that maintain membership" (Diab, 2016, p. 105). Actions that sustain the moral order and Muslim subjectivity map onto the aforementioned spectrum's positive end and include mandatory (*farḍ*) or recommended actions (*fī ʻl mandūb* or *mustaḥabb*), whereas those that undermine the moral order and Muslim subjectivity map onto the spectrum's negative end and include condemned, reprehensible (*makrūh*), or impermissible (*ḥarām*) acts. Each act determines proximity/distance from Islām and Muslim subjectivity, which is read here as the path of peace and abstention from violence and harm. This legal-ethical code is the context within which discourses of rights emerge and are sustained. So, where do we see traces of this code conspicuously articulated?

To answer this question, I point to the two main sources of legislation in Islām, namely al-Qur'ān, and *ḥadīth* and *sunnah*, or the sayings, actions, and "lived example" of Prophet Muḥammad (e.g., Lowry, 2010; Quraishi, 2008). These two sources are interpreted and explained by "jurists – the legal scholars within Muslim societies – [who] developed a science (or art if you want to call it that) of interpreting those texts to come up with specific legal conclusions" (Quraishi, 2008, p. 164). In the Holy Qur'ān, the first source of law, both sources of legislation are named and linked to one another and to the *telos* of establishing and sustaining a just moral order.

Within this teleological frame, moral discord is explained as diverting from divine commands and as caused by and unleashed when one chooses might and inequity to reign over people and communities. In contrast, moral order is described as a structure with numerous building blocks to be deliberately chosen and invested in. Its building blocks are iterated in terms of (commands related to) rights and (im/perfect) duties. These rights and duties form a relational web. On one hand, rights and duties unite people and bind them to a legal-ethical code of conduct. The strengthening of this bond, in turn, guards against a permissive culture where the violation of people's rights is normalized. On the other hand, these rights and duties underscore obligations to God (*huqūq Allāh* and *sharʻu Allāh*). In the Islamic tradition, rights and duties are complex yet simple, separate and clearly interdependent, definitive and commodious. Abiding by God's law or way (*sharʻu Allāh*) realizes this *telos* (*maqāṣid*). Because of its centrality and conspicuousness, (non-)Muslim scholars underline this *telos*. For example, Sam Souryal explains that Islamic legislation is an ethical code of conduct, or "a nomos based on divine law and a spiritual commitment to social decency" (Souryal, 1987, p. 431). This legal-ethical code seeks to create and sustain a moral order, as noted earlier.

The connection between the two aforementioned sources of legislation and conduct is well defined. As Quraishi explains, "*shari'a* as 'God's Law,' capital 'L,' capital 'G' [. . . is] the ideal of how people should be in the world" (Quraishi, 2008, p. 164). Similarly, the centrality and constitutive dimension of the legal-ethical code is evident in short-hand constitutive teachings from *ḥadīth*: "A Muslim is the one who people are spared of [the excesses or abuses of] their tongues and hands, or al-muslim man salima al-nās min lisānih wa yadih" (Al-Nawawī, 2001, pp. 511–513). This ḥadīth explains that the path to belief and redemption hinges on following God's law or way (*shar'u Allāh*) and the Prophet's teachings, which in turn set people on the right path as described in the legal canon (e.g., Fakhry, 1991). Denying/observing (*kufr/ṭā'ah*) God and the Prophet's legal-ethical code makes Muslims positioned close to/far from the moral order. Accordingly, actions respond to what is right and just, and iterations of sanctioned and condemned actions further affirm the legal-ethical code that is prescriptive, proscriptive, and constitutive. So, where do we see traces of this legal-ethical code in terms of and to affirm women's rights?

9.3.2 "Ūṣīkum bil-Nisā' Khaīran" *and Prophet Muḥammad's "Farewell Speech"*

I trace early Arabic-Islamic legal rhetoric of women's rights to the "Farewell Speech" (*khuṭbat al-wadā'*), which was delivered at Mount 'Arafāt on 9 Dhū al-Ḥijjah and during pilgrimage in 10 AH (i.e., 6 March 632). I had long heard the statement "*ūṣikum bil-nisā' khaīran*," or "I [Prophet Muḥammad] advise you to treat women well or fairly," without realizing that this is a quotation from Prophet Muḥammad's *khuṭbat al-wadā'*, or "Farewell Speech" (Bassiouni, 2006, pp. 32–33). *Khuṭbat al-wadā'* is one of ten prominent Islamic instruments included in Bassiouni's *International Instruments on Human Rights* (2006, pp. 23–44). "*Ūsīkum bil-nisā' khairan*" is a condensed teaching that reiterates repeated messages in the Holy Qur'ān about equity and fairness to women, and to everyone. In general, teachings from al-Qur'ān and *ḥadīth* about doing *khaīr* circulate enthymematically in vernacular discourse to counter *baghī*, *zulm*, and *shar* (i.e., aggression, injustice, and evil), as well as misused legal precepts, which circulate enthymematically, too. (For more on enthymemes and legal rhetoric, see Tanner, Chapter 5 in this volume.) This circulation is seamless and often invisible.

Excerpts from *khuṭbat al-wadā'* circulate on different occasions, including Friday *Khuṭbah*, or Friday oration (a weekly oration delivered to guide Muslim congregants). Whether excerpted or read in full, *Khuṭbat al-Wadā'* is to this day widely recognized as encoding human rights topoi, including women's rights topoi; some of these human rights topoi are identified below because they are a crucial part of the immediate context of "*ūṣīkum bilnisā' khaīran*." Because "*ūṣīkum bil-nisā' khaīran*" typically circulates alone without an explicit reference to the speech, I briefly shed light on the speech, and then underscore the relation between this legal-political guidance to al-Qur'ān and Prophetic tradition (*sunnah*). Situating the "Farewell Speech" within an epideictic rhetoric on equality and reciprocal positive/negative rights and duties, I shed light on early Arabic-Islamic legal discourses on women's rights condensed in this Prophetic teaching, suggest reasons for the invisibility of this discourse, and then use the concept of vernacular rhetoric of human rights (e.g., Hauser, 2008; von Arnauld & Theilen, 2020) to draw attention to more recent iterations of women's rights.

Prophet Muḥammad gives the speech about three months before his death, and the speech reiterates principal Islamic teachings, including those on women's rights. Prophet Muḥammad's "Farewell Speech" addresses in/justice topoi. Farooq (2018) identifies twelve themes. The *sanctity of the moment* is emphasized: time (9 Dhū al-Ḥijjah), place (Mecca), occasion and ritual of pilgrimage, or *ḥajj*; transition from *jāhilīyah* (often translated as the age of ignorance) to Islām. The speech also reiterates key issues like pardon (i.e., "abolition of all prior claims to blood revenge"); abolition of usury; repudiation of racism; gender matters related to equity and rights; Qur'ān and Prophet Muḥammad's teachings as a legacy (for legal and ethical conduct); compliance with divine law and adherence to principles of Islām; and other teachings concerning rights, *ṣalāh* and *zakāh*, and debts. The speech identifies congregants (and secondary addressees) as witnesses (Farooq, 2018, pp. 325–330).

A bidimensional throughline unifies all topics: (a) advocacy against wrongful acts that cause harm and (b) advocacy for the negative right of the self and others to be free from manipulation or harm. For example, impermissible conduct is evident in references to supremacy, usury, aggression targeting other people's money (*amūālukum*), *a'rāḍukum* (honor or reputation), and lives (*anfusakum*). Based on these im/permissible actions, we can discern positive/negative rights. To name two examples, Prophet Muḥammad refers to women's right to equality and to the right to one's inheritance, which includes women's right to inheritance (addressed later). Relatedly, obligations, including obligations to self and others, are evident in the reference to abstaining from denying/disbelieving God ("*falā targa'na ba'dī ilá al-kufr*") and by extension God's laws. Across these themes, it's clear that Prophet Muḥammad underscores im/permissible conduct, positive/negative rights, and obligations; the three work together to establish and sustain a moral order and constitute the Muslim. It's within this context that women's rights are affirmed in the speech (Bassiouni, 2006, pp. 32–33).

In the speech, women's rights are mentioned in relation to reciprocity of rights. The section on women's rights begins by underscoring that "they have rights, which you [Muslim men and Muslims in general] are obligated to realize (*linisā'kum 'alikum ḥaqa*), and you [Muslim men] have rights, which they [Muslim men and Muslims in general] are obligated to realize" (Bassiouni, 2006, pp. 32–33).

What strikes me most is the accessible enthymematic force of the condensed teaching in "*ūṣīkum bil-nisā' khaīran*." An enthymeme is a truncated syllogism, which is often defined as a three-pronged argument by deduction. When one (or two) of the prongs is assumed, we are left with a shorthand deductive argument. The suasive potential of an enthymeme hinges on "the joint efforts of speaker and audience" (Bitzer, 1959, p. 408). In this case, the audience is a nascent community that is bound by a religion and its legal-ethical code. The truncated argument "*ūṣīkum bil-nisā' khaīran*" can be expanded as follows: Women have rights; their rights are diminished or undermined; therefore, I [Prophet Muḥammad] counsel you to treat women fairly and do good by them.

The enthymeme mirrors and condenses Islamic teachings about the pursuit of *khaīr*, or good, and the obligation to counter *baghī* and *ẓulm* (injustice) and *shar* (evil). The teachings condensed in "*ūṣīkum bil-nisā' khaīran*" are central to and recur in the two main sources of legal-ethical prescriptive/proscriptive and constitutive discourse in Islām, which are al-Qur'ān and *ḥadīth*, as noted earlier. Women's rights are so important that Prophet Muḥammad affirms them in his "Farewell Speech" and later in his last oration on the day he died. He reiterates, "*ūṣīkum bil-nisā' khaīran.*" I now turn to Qur'ānic verses that underwrite and provide divine legislation that "*ūṣīkum bil-nisā' khaīran*" condenses.

Numerous verses in al-Qur'ān reference women as created from one and the same self, and therefore equal to men in rights and responsibilities (and concomitantly rewards and punishment). These rights and responsibilities cover all dimensions of life, including religious, social, financial, inheritance, and ethical rights and responsibilities (e.g., The Qur'ān, 2008, 33:5, 7:189, 4:1, 4:124, 9:71, 3:195, 16:97, 2:286); these iterations of rights/responsibilities counter pervasive cultural misrepresentations of women (e.g., as intellectually or morally inferior) at the time. Among many verses that highlight a general principle guiding women's rights is the first verse of *Surat al-Nisā'* (Women; The Qur'ān, 2008, 4:1) and verse 228 of *al-Baqarah* (Cow; The Qur'ān, 2008, 2:228): "[W]omen have rights similar to those of men according to what is equitable."[3]

Numerous verses in al-Qur'ān underscore women's rights and duties. More importantly, articulations of im/permissible conduct and corresponding positive/negative rights/obligations are linked using connective tissue. Al-Qur'ān constantly emphasizes reverence and recognition of the sanctity of life. (This idea is affirmed in numerous verses in the Holy Qur'ān [e.g., *al-Mā'idah*, verse 32] and is addressed later.) Another, which is in line with the sanctity of life and a counter to objectification and dismissal, is identifying *all* people (e.g., women and people of other confessions, *ahl al-dhimah*) as rights holders and rights claimants. The sanctity of life and the representation of disenfranchised groups as rights holders are conspicuously iterated in al-Qur'ān. (This is an issue addressed in the following section.)

[3] Verse 228 of Surat al-Baqarah focuses on divorced women, and in this context the verse underscores women's marital and reproductive rights and duties (support and accountability measures during and after marriage, her rights and obligations during pregnancy).

Unsurprisingly, these ethical and rights topoi are ever-present and circulate in vernacular discourse. They are invoked to structure and amplify arguments, including those for women's rights; they are also partially quoted and weaponized to undermine women's rights, social authority, or standing. It is within this distant and enduring context that we need to question the invisibility of women's rights. Why are women's rights as articulated in al-Qur'ān and ḥadīth invisible? Why is recent advocacy for women's rights represented as an unprecedented victory while un(der)recognizing the recurrent backlashes against women's rights *in* and *outside* the Arab(ic)-Muslim world?

9.3.3 *Misconceptions of Women and Their Rights in the Arabic-Islamic Traditions*

Misconceptions block a more nuanced understanding of Arabic-Islamic women's rights discourse. Earlier in the chapter, I pointed to selective memory. In the following paragraphs, I deepen earlier reflections on selective remembering and highlight three interrelated phenomena that block the recognition and exploration of official and vernacular rhetorics of women's rights. These are conflating terms, historical forgetting, and decontextualizing rights from their socio-cultural and historical contexts.

From an analytical perspective, the conversation about women's rights in the Arabic-Islamic traditions abounds with conflations of terms and concepts. As a starter, Islām and Muslims are conflated. A parallel and related conflation results from fusing an edict embedded in and actualizing an Islamic worldview with enduring socio-cultural misogynistic legacies. Needless to say, misogyny as ideology and practice has a momentum and a quotidian, gripping force. The religious edicts of Islām seek to halt this momentum and loosen its grip. For a long time, scholars have been writing about these parallel conflations (e.g., Esposito, 1975; Syed, 2008). Just to illustrate, Khalida Tanvir Syed explains that, among many misconceptions, "perhaps the most controversial, is that Islam oppresses women. In reality, Islam offers women the right to make their own choices in the areas of education, business, and property, to name a few" (Syed, 2008, p. 245).[4] Where does this misconception come from then? It's partially due to the conflation of Islām and Muslims and misunderstanding of the history of interpretation of al-Qur'ān. Scholars illustrate how this conflation manifests again and again.

The conflation between Islām and Muslims is explicitly addressed by Esposito (1975): Islām brought about many legal reforms that actualized women's negative and positive rights (e.g., the rights to life, to inheritance, and to [withhold] consent

[4] Syed counters three misconceptions: that "Muslims are terrorists because they believe in Jihad," that "Muslims prohibit scientific knowledge and only aim to seek religious knowledge," and that "Islam oppresses women" (Syed, 2008, p. 245).

to marriage). As Esposito explains, "the implementation of Qur'ānic reforms markedly improved her position in the family and society in the classical period. However, subsequent historical events as well as assimilated cultural influences [impacting Muslims] at times seriously compromised her rights" (Esposito, 1975, p. 113).

Esposito clarifies that many biases are "assimilated cultural influences" that are antithetical to the teachings of Islām. Because they are assimilated, they are *not* recognized as projected cultural influences. The slippage from Islām to Muslim clouds debates and obscures the Islamic legal-ethical code. To clarify the role of these "cultural influences," scholars shed light on women's social, cultural, and legal status and (violation of women's) rights *before* Islām and contrast them with Islām's rights discourse since its stance is ignored in the mix. A brief introduction to highlight key points about these cultural influences is warranted.

As Syed (2008, p. 254) puts it, "Pre-Islamic practices have been very threatening for women." Women in pre-Islamic Arabia were situated culturally, financially, and economically in a subservient position in a power matrix which, to a large extent, is premised on controlling their bodies. Within this power matrix, women's bodies become the locus of articulations of control, power *over*, an impending threat. Collective gender anxieties (Adamson, 2007) about and responses to this perceived threat are seen in practices of female infanticide. Predictably, within this matrix, their killing is justified. Two verses of *Surat al-Naḥl* (The Bee; The Qur'an, 2008, 16:57–58) explicitly critique perceptions of and subsequent actions against women, especially those against the female child. The verses also provide a socio-psychological profile that makes this normalized violence perceptible.

> When news is brought to one of them of [the birth of] a female [child], his face darkens, and he is filled with inward grief! With shame does he hide himself from his people because of the bad news he has had! Shall he retain her [on sufferance and contempt], or bury her in the dust? Ah! What an evil [choice] they decide on! (Syed, 2008, pp. 253–254)

Even at birth, the rights of the female child are denied and her standing as a rights holder is rejected. Writing about these two verses, Syed explains that the "Qur'an also condemned the unwelcoming attitude of some parents upon the birth of a baby girl" (Syed, 2008, p. 253). This attitude justifies the violent practice of female infanticide and numerous other harmful practices; these include disregard of right to wealth, inheritance, or income; disregard of the right to choose a spouse; and disregard of true consent to marriage. All harm women and society at large. All of these practices were countered by Qur'ānic legislation.

Al-Qur'ān criticizes such practices in several verses. In *al-Takwīr* (The Qur'an, 2008, 81:8–9), al-Qur'ān condemns female infanticide, uses irony to make the unjustifiable harm against the child irrefutable, and offers us the analogy of a "trial scene." Al-Qur'ān exclaims, "And when the female (infant) buried alive is questioned – For what sin she was killed." The irony is coupled with role-reversal. Al-Maghāmsy (2019) explains that the killed female child is present(ed) on the day of reckoning so that she becomes *the interlocutor*; this is the reversal of the power dynamic that crushed her life and voice out of existence. So the child, who was the *object* of the aggressor's wrath, is an agentive subject. The child is presented as a rights holder and claimant bringing a grievance to a legal authority (i.e., God and the Prophet). Fully present(ed) here, her question(ing) centers the pursuit of justice, holding perpetrators accountable, and doing right by her. And by extension, doing right by all other children (and females), whose right to life is affirmed (Al-Maghāmsy, 2019).

In the context of verses 1–28 of *al-Takwīr*, verses 8–9 (quoted above) about female infanticide lead to accountability for human life and the rights of people; both are affirmed in this "trial scene." Enthymematically presented, we see mainly the conclusion of the syllogism in verse 14, which stipulates that "a soul will (then [on the day of reckoning]) know what it has brought (with it)." In the context of the "trial scene," or day of reckoning, the verse points to the presenting of evidence of injustice and the punishment incurred. Since al-Qur'ān represents God's law and commands, verses addressing im/permissible acts read as legislation clauses that spell out the consequences of im/permissible actions.

What corroborates this reading is that verse 14 is amplified by later verses, namely 18, 19, 20, 21, 27, and 28, which identify and confer about this guidance as divine law by asserting: "Verily this is the word of a most honourable Messenger, Endued with power, with rank before the Lord of the Throne, With authority there, (and) faithful to his trust ... (With profit) to whoever among you wills to go straight, or whoever wills among you to take a right course of action." In short, at the beginning of *Surat al-Takwīr* (verses 8–9) the killed child is present(ed) as a rights holder and plaintiff, and their categorical rights to life and justice are affirmed. A few verses later (verses 18–28), the terms of accountability (e.g., judgment event(s) and processes, record of deeds/evidence against aggressors, law and law enforcer against harm done) are named, and female infanticide is denounced.

Terms of accountability are asserted repeatedly in al-Qur'ān. One of the most crucial legal assertions of accountability to the right to life is in *Surat al-Mā'idah* (The Qur'an, 2008, 5:32), which addresses cases of murder. It comprises the stasis of quality and underscores the weight of the offense as an ultimate violence. To amplify the stasis of quality, the significance of work done to protect and/or sustain life and wellbeing is also underscored using parallel structure: "if any one slew a person – unless it be for murder or for spreading mischief in the land – it would be as if he slew the whole people: and *if any one saved a life, it would be as if he saved the life of the whole people*" (The Qur'an, 2008, 5:32, emphasis added). The right to life is complemented with a multitude of other legal assertions.[5]

[5] For more, see Islamic law, "Ḥadd." "In law, [*ḥadd* is] ... the technical term for the punishments of certain acts which have been forbidden or sanctioned by punishments in the Qur'ān

Zooming in on overt references to women's rights, we find that evidence in al-Qur'ān abounds. A broad Qur'ānic legal-ethical rights mandate is discernible in verse 228 of *al-Baqarah*: "[W]omen shall have rights similar to the rights against them according to what is equitable." This general rights mandate is matched with specific assertions of women's rights. To illustrate, among their financial rights, women have the right to their dowries and the right to inherit in their varied roles as spouses, daughters, sisters, and/or mothers in *Surat al-Nisā'*, or Women (The Qur'an, 2008, 4:10–11); specifying women's roles impresses on readers an image of women as partners and rights holders and not as objects (of desire) or extensions of others. In verses 10–11, women's right to inherit and the percentage of inheritance in numerous cases across the aforementioned roles are detailed. (Women's political rights will be touched on in the following section.) Financial rights are vital because they counter "assimilated cultural influences" (Esposito, 1975, p. 113). Before Islām, women often were denied financial rights. Patriarchal control, which is a manifestation of "assimilated cultural influences," deemed women as objects, and as objects they are owned and don't own. Terms of accountability work proactively when they center rights holders and underscore others' duties to rights holders. Terms of accountability also reactively respond to rights violation. Verses 12–13 underscore that inheritance rights as outlined are God's *hudūd* (singular *ḥadd*; The Qur'an, 2008, 4:12–13); those who observe God's laws are rewarded, and those who violate them are punished (de Vaux et al., 2012). Tracing terms of accountability helps us see the discourse of rights, which can be made invisible by unfair practices.

Unfortunately, sometimes readers of al-Qur'ān don't know this history or miss the point of the discourse on female infanticide and women's rights. Esposito (1975) highlights this as a methodological problem caused by unnuanced attention to context and urges scholars to detangle Qur'ānic legal reforms from (1) backlash against these reforms and (2) a history of "assimilated cultural influences." To reiterate, Esposito's critique seeks to clarify the conflation of Islām and Muslims, the context of Qur'ānic reforms, and the reforms themselves. His work clarifies how and why these important distinctions are often un(der)studied or just ignored for a simpler account premised on binaries.

Misconceptions have other causes. Misconceptions of women's rights in the Arabic-Islamic traditions are also partly due to the far-reaching consequences of the epistemic arm of colonial waves. Explaining this, Howe, in her "Introduction" to *The Routledge Handbook of Islam and Gender* (2020), underlines the contributions of decolonial studies of Islām and gender. Decolonial studies foreground the far-reaching consequences of orientalist misrepresentations orchestrated by the epistemic arm of colonial waves. Scholars trace orientalist misrepresentations to eighteenth- and nineteenth-century European colonial and mercantile expeditions and

and have thereby become crimes against religion ... [The type and] intensity [depend] on the severity of the crime" (de Vaux et al., 2012, n.p.).

then invasions of the Near and Far East. Howe (2020, p. 9) explicates that "Muslim female bodies have long been sources of *desire and disgust*." As a cultural and religious foil, "The female Muslim body became a ground through *which colonial actors constructed their versions of Islam as backward and uncivilized … European, Christian, societies were celebrated as the high point of civilization*" (p. 9; emphasis added). This profile of the Muslim woman and Islām doesn't align with a nuanced assessment of the discourse on rights or the discourse on women's rights in Islām.

Similarly, Khalida Tanvir Syed clarifies that misconceptions of "Muslim women as being ignorant and submissive" and Islām as repressive and backward are amplified by internal political forces: These "[m]isconceptions … are also created by ostensibly Islamic leaders who do not practice Islam. They may believe theoretically and gain the advantage of appearing to be knowledgeable or pious in the Islamic world, but their practices are contradictory to the teachings of the Qur'an and Hadith" (Syed, 2008, p. 247). Together, the aforementioned local, regional, and global imperial forces impact our conceptions of women's rights and assumed nonexistence of official and vernacular rhetorics of women's rights. The resulting misconceptions and binaries (e.g., civilized versus uncivilized) have emotional dimensions, and they feed into a desirable "progressive" narrative and epistemic agendas.

Notably, assumptions about and attachments to comfortable/comforting narratives of a linear, progressive march of human rights discourse make us forget about relapses and regressive politics. Recognized as political turns and not necessarily *the* norm, relapses and regressive politics alert us to the danger of forgetting the nonlinear march of history, humans, and rights discourses. Feminist scholars like Leila Ahmed (1992), Asma Barlas (2002), and Fatima Mernissi (1991) alert us to these narratives as forms of denial of the complexity of history and the persistence of patriarchy. Summarizing this point, Howe (2020, p. 11) explains "that while the early Muslim community enacted more egalitarian gender norms, patriarchal practices came to be hegemonic in the decades following the death of the Prophet Muhammad."

To illustrate, in *Unreading Patriarchal Interpretations of the Qur'ān*, Asma Barlas demonstrates how patriarchy is read into the Qur'ān. Explaining that "the Qur'an was revealed in/to an existing patriarchy and has been interpreted by adherents of patriarchies ever since," she underscores that "Muslim women have a stake in [explicating the methods and consequences of and, therefore,] challenging patriarchal exegesis" (Barlas, 2002, p. xi), which is beyond the scope of this chapter. Yet it warrants brief mention. Zooming in on the method of interpretation, Barlas continues to explain that early Muslim exegetes and Qur'ān commentators relied on a "linear-atomistic" method for interpretation (Mir quoted in Barlas, 2002, p. 8). This "linear-atomistic" method takes as its unit of exegesis a verse and, therefore, separates verses and reads them only linearly. "As a result, the Qur'ān is not read as a text possessing both 'thematic and structural *nazm* [coherence]'" (Mir quoted in Barlas, 2002, p. 8). Instead, "recognizing the Qur'ān's textual and thematic holism, and thus the hermeneutic connections between seemingly disparate themes, is absolutely integral to recovering its antipatriarchal epistemology" (p. 8). So, Barlas identifies guiding principles (e.g., unity of divine ontology and divine discourse and justness) to show that injustice to women is inconsistent with divine ontology and divine discourse:

> The principle of God's Unity (*Tawhīd*) has the most far-reaching implications for how we understand God and God's Speech. ... In its simplest form, *Tawhīd* symbolizes the idea of God's Indivisibility, hence also the indivisibility of God's Sovereignty. ... To the extent that theories of male rule over women and children amount to asserting sovereignty over both and also misrepresent males as intermediaries between women and God, they do come into conflict with the essential tenets of the doctrine of *Tawhīd* and must be rejected as theologically unsound. (Barlas, 2002, pp. 13–14)

Reading al-Qur'ān intra-textually, holistically, and contextually, we are better positioned to read how patriarchy is projected and used to justify injustice against women. (I tried to embrace these principles in the section on female infanticide and women's financial rights.) Reading al-Qur'ān intra-textually, holistically, and contextually, we are better positioned to address misconceptions, including misconception of cycles of rights discourse and how topoi of rights inform and circulate beyond official legal discourse. Part of this cycle is rights violation, articulation of grievance, denial of grievance, rights recognition, recognition of rights holders, actualizing rights and affirming rights holders, backlash and relapse, and repeats of the cycle, which will become obvious in the last section.

Centering narratives of Islām as patriarchal is a manifestation of historical forgetting, decontextualization, and conflation of Islām's legal rhetoric and Muslims' uptake of it. The historical record underscores *how* and *when* patriarchal, "linear-atomistic" hermeneutic practices came to be hegemonic after Prophet Muḥammad's death, as Barlas (2002) and Ahmed (1992) explain. Denying the historicity of patriarchy and the possibilities of legislation for a vernacular of rights rhetoric, patriarchy persists. In the next section, I expand my exploration beyond medieval historical and legislative roots of women's rights in Islām and their invisibility to address more recent roots in the Arab Renaissance. Beyond the Arab Renaissance, advocacy and legislation for women's rights continues, as I illustrate below.

9.4 ILLUSTRATIVE MOMENTS: THE ARAB RENAISSANCE AND CONTINUOUS ADVOCACY AND LEGISLATION

I fast forward from the seventh century to *al-Nahḍah*, or the Arab Renaissance or Awakening, to shed light on illustrative moments for women's rights. I begin with an illustrative moment that precedes the ACWR by a century and has had an enduring impact. Before the issuance of the ACWR, generations of women and men like Bint al-Shāṭi' ('Ā'ishah 'Abd al-Raḥmān's pen name; 1991) and Qāsim Amīn (2010a,

2010b) have advocated for women's rights. They implicitly and explicitly invoke earlier discourse on rights, including Qur'ān and ḥadīth, and the work on the ground by scholars and activists continues outside and within legislative and legal circles.

Al-Nahḍah refers to a historical period and a dynamic process. Historians describe this period as both a "cataclysmic, colonial event" marked by Napoléon Bonaparte's (1769–1821) invasion of Egypt and Syria and a massive regional, national, and intellectual awakening (El-Ariss, 2018, p. xxv). The military's resounding defeat was momentous, for it made clear that Egypt – and indeed the whole region – had become a proxy battlefield for British and French mercantile and political rivalry. Their subsequent colonization of Arab nations made conspicuous the undeniable cultural and technological gaps between Egypt and the colonizing powers. The interplay or collision of the military, economic, political, and cultural forces mandated introspection. In response, calls for cultural transformation, sifting through and reviving the Arab past, and embracing modernizing projects ensued and reverberated across the Arab world.

One of the most conspicuous shifts was a powerful discourse on the rights of women, who were now recognized as crucial partners of both national liberation and transformation, yet not recognized as political and legal actors with rights in these roles. In this context of transformation and reflection, presses and magazines thrived and literary salons proliferated (Diab, in press). These venues offered the space for envisioning, deliberating, and advocating for varied transformations. Key among these transformations was women's right to have rights, including marital and epistemic rights (i.e., the rights to know and interpret). To show the impact of this moment, I very briefly shed light on Bāḥithat al-Bādīyah's work. Joining leading feminists at the time, she identified ten articles in support of women's rights. The articles can be considered an early articulation of and precedent for numerous documents and legislative bills that eventually led, 100 years later, to the twenty-eight articles of the ACWR.

9.4.1 *Bāḥithat al-Bādīyah*

Bāḥithat al-Bādīyah is the pen name of Malak Ḥifnī Nāṣif (1886–1918), a noteworthy figure of al-Nahḍah. She was a well-known writer, first certified woman educator, social reformer, and advocate for women's rights. She tirelessly joined al-Nahḍah feminists and advocated for women's rights. Her testimonial and essayistic writing and speeches, published in *Nisā'iyāt* (Nāṣif, 2012), represent astute social critique, brim with justice and rights topoi, and exemplify a vernacular rhetoric of women's rights.

Breaking silence around social taboos, Bāḥithat al-Bādīyah spoke to and wrote about the right to have rights and the right to advocate for these rights. In this vernacular discourse, she named socio-cultural discourses that undermine women's potential and rights. She also underscored socio-cultural and educational changes needed to enhance women's potential and right to autonomy and equality. As a rights holder, she embodied and gave voice to women's suffering. As she testified, she was amplifying women's grievance articulations, and she explained how and why women's suffering is caused by restricted access to education, decision-making, and marital rights (e.g., choosing a spouse), let alone unquestioned cultural practices like polygamy, which she experienced herself. Leveraging the stance of a rights holder who could voice grievances, explain their root causes, and envision potential changes, Bāḥithat al-Bādīyah (and other al-Nahḍah feminists) constructed a vernacular rhetoric of gender equality.

Her advocacy for the right to learn is a case in point. As an educator, she had keen awareness of and interest in women's epistemic rights. She wrote about women's rights to education, (decolonizing) women's right to determine their fate and make decisions regarding education and work, and their rights to affirm their identity and cultural rights. For example, in one of her essays collected under the heading "Arā'" (View Points) (Nāṣif, 2012, pp. 13–77), she aligned herself with other advocates of girls' and women's education (e.g., 'Āishah al-Tīmūrīyah) and critiqued the current educational model, which sometimes undermined women's identity and cultural rights (Zīyādah, 2012, pp. 41–67). These concerns were amplified by Egypt's colonial context.

Under British rule, a meaningful discourse on liberation and rights entailed an investment in questioning the terms of liberation. Often modeled after Western norms and values, terms of liberation became her concern, and Bāḥithat al-Bādīyah attended to cultural and religious difference and centered the needs of the Egyptian woman. The question of the veil accrues ontological and epistemological meanings and becomes a way to address complex issues: Who sets the terms for the rights to know, represent, and testify to the self's needs and rights? This discourse predates and resonates with third-wave feminist rights discourse.

Among her works, her speech to the Nation's Party Club (Nāṣif, 2012, pp. 77–92) stands out. The content and location of her speech to the Nation's Party Club (Nādī Ḥizb al-Umah) are noteworthy. The Nation's Party Club was a dynamic political and cultural space sponsored by and directly affiliated with Ḥizb al-Umah (established in 1907 by Maḥmmūd Pasha Sulīmān as a political, liberal party that sponsored both a club and a paper). Bāḥithat al-Bādīyah spoke at the club and published in the party's paper, *al-Jarīdah*. Bāḥithat al-Bādīyah's speech was relatively long, addressed different issues, and drew on topoi that can be traced to Prophet Muḥammad's *Khuṭbat al-Wadā'* and al-Qur'ān (e.g., critique of injustice and critique for justice, or *'adl*, and fairness, or *inṣāf'*). She clearly echoed other al-Nahḍah feminists (e.g., Hudá Sha 'rāwī) who also advocated for equality, or *musāwāh*, and partnership. Two of the most important issues addressed are misconceptions of women and their roles, and misconceptions of men and their rights and responsibilities. She affirmed women's standing as rights holders.

This speech is often remembered because, while underlining women's lack of opportunities, Bāḥithat al-Bādīyah said that had she had the opportunity to be with Christopher Columbus, she, too, would have discovered America (Zīyādah, 2012, p. 81). However, this frequently quoted statement deflects attention from the most crucial moment in the speech. Bāḥithat al-Bādīyah's speech to the Nation's Party Club (*Nādī Ḥizb al-Umah*) is of special significance as a manifestation of a vernacular of rights discourse.

Characterized by being unofficial, citizen-driven, and bottom-up discourse that copies the genre and tone of bills, this vernacular centers topoi of justice, rights, and accountability. The speech comprises ten articles that testify to Bāḥithat al-Bādīyah's keen awareness of the importance of legislation to counter violence against women. Not only are these articles an early articulation of and precedent for the twenty-eight articles of the ACWR issued a century later. They also cannot be read outside of the context of Islamic legislation for women's rights and the discourse on the moral order enthymematically condensed in the Prophetic mandate, "*ūṣīkum bil-nisā' khaīran*," left un(der)realized.

At the end of her speech (Nāṣif, 2012, p. 92), Bāḥithat al-Bādīyah advocated for legal change, enumerated ten articles representing the needs of her time, and called for legislative changes. She introduced the articles as "practical steps to move forward" and declared that "had I [Malak Ḥifnī Nāṣif] had legislative power, this would be [her] bill." (Her "bill' was eventually read at the party.) In today's parlance, she enumerated negative and positive rights and modeled a bill addressing women's rights. The ten articles are additionally significant because they prefigure many legal articles that followed, including ones underlined by the ACWR. Together, the ten articles amplify two main clusters of rights.

The first cluster (Articles 1–6) centers women's rights to education. The second cluster (Articles 7–8) centers women's sovereignty, consent as manifest in women's marital rights, rights to choose educational and work careers, and right to move.[6] The articles are intrinsically important, and their significance is enhanced, as they are explicitly stated after a long speech that unmistakably (a) underscores how these rights are not antithetical to Islamic practice and history, and (b) explains the negative consequences of undermining these rights in the microsphere of individual and family and the macrosphere of society and nation. These points resonated with her audience. At the time, her audience struggled with the assumed tension

[6] The ninth article affirms the need for centering national interest, especially in relation to what I understand as cultural imposition, and the tenth article declares that "fellow brothers are to realize this project!" (Nāṣif, 2012, p. 92). This is similar to contractual terminal formulas, or discursive moves at the end of legal instruments (e.g., listing enforcers or witnesses, naming signatories). Sonia Dabbous reads Article 10 as a sign of Bāḥithat al-Bādīyah's conservatism and clarifies that "[a]s demonstrated by her ten-point programme of reform, Nassef did not envisage women's participation in politics. Indeed, her tenth point was that it was men's duty to carry out the programme" (Dabbous, 2004, p. 43). I read the tenth article as a call to action and a trace of those contractual terminal formulas.

between women's rights and Islām, which was perceived as threatened by imported ideologies. Her audience, too, comprised people aligned with and affiliated to Ḥizb al-Umah, so it's reasonable to assume that they shared the investment in national liberation and women's participation in it.

I think of Bāḥithat al-Bādīyah as a foremother. Her advocacy for women's rights carries the marks of the early 1900s. Because advocacy for women's rights is intimately connected to its historical, cultural, political, and national/regional need for liberation, advocacy during *al-Nahḍah* means that advocacy for women's rights is connected to national interest. Equally important, foremothers model and inspire. Indeed, some dimensions of Bāḥithat al-Bādīyah's advocacy for women's rights are (un)surprisingly current. These current aspects include, for example, her reference to the relation between access to domains of action, imagined/foreclosed possibilities, and actual participation in such domains (often condensed in phrases like "the glass ceiling" and "stained-glass ceiling") (e.g., Sullins, 2000). Both temporally situated and current, the discourse on women's rights we see in Bāḥithat al-Bādīyah's work cannot be seen outside of the buzzing spheres of political rhetoric at the time and shouldn't be severed from later vernaculars of rights that eventually led to legislation. I now turn to shed light on vernacular rhetoric about women's civil rights and Personal Status Law (El-Alamai, 1994).

9.4.2 *Women's Rights Rhetoric Amplified and Continued*

Bāḥithat al-Bādīyah died very young because of the influenza pandemic of 1918–19, but her work endured. Her contemporaries continued the work. Just to illustrate, as partners in political activism, women participated in the 1919 Revolution against British occupation and its impact on the political and economic spheres. United, Egyptian people asked for national independence. Yet women, especially women's rights advocates, were surprised by their exclusion from the commission of thirty people who pored over drafting the new constitution of 1923. Among the most notable features of this constitution, however, was absence. The 1923 constitution absented women and didn't recognize women's voting rights. This exclusion resulted in Hudá Sha'rāwī, a well-known Egyptian feminist and nationalist, establishing the Egyptian Feminist Union (*al-itiḥād al-nisā'ī al-maṣrī*) in 1923.[7] This was yet another crucial moment for the vernacular of women's rights. The Egyptian Feminist Union established two papers, *l'Egyptienne* and *al-Miṣrīyyah*. The Egyptian Feminist Union's main goal was to advocate for women's political participation, not just in terms of voting rights but also in terms of participating in

7 Hudá Sha'rāwī was the founder and president of the Arab Feminist Union in 1945, a transnational, and pan-Arabism, feminist union whose role cannot be underestimated. For more, see Arafa (1973).

legislative efforts and legislative bodies (i.e., the right to hold public office) and equity in/at work (Arafa, 1973).

Generations of feminists followed, and with each the vernacular of women's rights rhetoric evolved, persisted, and eventually intersected with and led to legislation. In the 1950s, there were other key advocacy moments and direct-action rhetoric. Before and after the 1952 Revolution, Durrīyah Shafīq advocated for women's political representation and participation. In front of the Egyptian Parliament, she led a demonstration of 1,500 women who asked for their right to political participation and for reforms to civil law; a bill for women to participate in elections to the parliament and to vote in these elections moved forward but didn't pass.

I fast-forward again and point to another key advocacy moment and direct-action rhetoric. In response to women's exclusion from another constitution-drafting commission, women organized a hunger strike, which the group ended when they won the promise of political rights. The 1956 Constitution and the laws that followed included articles for political participation and voting rights (Law 73/1956). A year later, eight women stood for elections; two won and became members of the National Parliament (*Majlis al-Ummah*). They were Rāwīyah 'Aṭīyah (1926–1997) and Amīnah Shukrī (1912–1964). The process and advocacy continued. Within a decade, the number increased from two to eight (1964). Within another decade, a quota system (for women representatives) was used to increase the number of women members of parliament to thirty-five in 1979. The work persisted because the quota system was repudiated and reinstated several times. The backlash was real, and legal reforms and legal advocacy rhetorics were cyclical (Elsadda & Hassan, 2018, p. 141).

A similar connection is evident between the vernacular of rights and "Personal Status Law (PSL)[, which] regulates marriage, divorce, child custody, and inheritance issues" (Singerman, 2005, p. 161) and was issued in 1920 and amended in 1929. The connection is, for example, evident in calls for two different reforms, which I address briefly. The first call for reform was energized by Ḥusn Shāh's writing and the literary dramatization of the urgent need for change in divorce laws. Ḥusn Shāh, a lawyer by training and a journalist, wrote a column titled "*Urīd Ḥala*" (I Want a Solution), in one of Egypt's most prestigious and widely read daily papers, *Akhbār al-Youm*. She was inspired by one of the column's true stories to write the film *Urīd Hala* (Marzūq, 1975) about three women. (In the film, Shāh centers and gives voice to the struggles of one woman, Durrīyah. Like many, for years Durrīyah tries to get a divorce but fails. Shāh successfully dramatizes women's struggle for divorce, presents reasons for women to have the right to initiate divorce, and holds the space for a societal awareness of and deliberation about the nature and scale of divorce problems.) A bill to reform the Personal Status Law garnered a lot of attention even from Egypt's First Lady, Jihān al-Sadāt, who lobbied publicly for the bill, which was named after her. The law passed (Law 44/1979). During the process, fifteen-century-old Islāmic legislation and precedent of the permissibility of this course of action became evident to many.[8] However, the Supreme Constitutional Court of Egypt found the law unconstitutional in 1985 based on a procedural matter. Despite this procedural matter, an almost identical law (Law No. 100 of 1985) was issued to replace Law 44/1979: "[W]ith one major exception which was the result of a compromise between religious circles and the feminist movement: A wife's right to a divorce from her husband in the event that he took a second (or subsequent) wife no longer would be automatic, but rather would depend on the discretion of the court" (El-Alami, 1994, p. 117).[9] Feminist legal advocacy continued. "Law No. 100 of 1985, which resulted in a significant improvement in the position of Egyptian women, has become the touchstone for future legal reform" (El-Alami, 1994, p. 117), including Law No. 1 of 2000 for a no-fault divorce, or khul'.

In 2022 and 2023, there were similar moments for societal concern, deliberation, and increased awareness of PSL. In 2022, debates about custody laws peaked: Egyptians watched and debated the series *Fātin Amal Ḥarbī,* written by Ibrahīm 'Eissá, which focused on women's struggles with custody and their potential loss of custody if they remarry. Similarly, in 2023, women's guardianship was on people's minds as they watched *Taḥt al-Uṣāiyah.* Debates trended on the suffering, social and legal strife of, and right to guardianship of a mother who battled against the children's grandfather's guardianship. (The grandfather was next in line and preceded the mother in claims for guardianship after a father died.) After watching the series, the hashtag "Guardianship is my right," advocating for women's right to guardianship, became viral and was complemented by numerous articles. For example, Ilhām Yūnis (2023), a columnist at *al-Ahrām* (a widely read Egyptian paper), connected the three works in her piece on "Taḥt al-Uṣāiyah and Urīd Ḥala." Calls for legal reform ensued; some members of the parliament are currently considering a bill to address this issue.

9.5 CODA

The advocacy continues. No single moment is most crucial or sufficient to disclose the deep roots and rich history of the vernacular and official women's rights discourse in the Arab(ic)-Muslim world. From the 1960s until now, the vernacular of rights has thrived and led to legislation, which is not without setbacks and inconsistent enforceability. It is worth noting that all the articles that were presented by Bāḥithat al-Bādīyah to the Nation's Party Club (*Nādī Ḥizb al-Umah*) became reality. Egyptian women do participate widely in religious activities (Article 1), have access to K-12 and higher education (Article 2), join nursing and medical schools, and more (Article 5). Women continue to advocate for anti-discrimination laws not

[8] For more on coalition politics to rewrite PSL, see Singerman, 2005.

[9] For Arabic/English text of Law 100/1985, see El-Alami, 1994, p. 117.

just by law enforcement personnel but in many aspects of private and public matters. Similarly, there is hope and a process for guardianship laws to be reformed to expand women's legal rights. It is in this context that I see the Arab Charter for Women's Rights, which was issued in 2019, as a moment worth celebrating only *in relation to* and *as a recognition of* a much longer, multidimensional, and ever-present advocacy for women's rights and a rich legal-ethical code for justice.

REFERENCES

Adamson, C. (2007). Gendered anxieties: Islam, women's rights, and moral hierarchy in Java. *Anthropological Quarterly*, 80(1), 5–37.

Ahmed, L. (1992). *Women and gender in Islam: Historical roots of a modern debate*. Yale University Press.

al-Maghāmsy, S. (2019). Ma ʻālim baīyānīyah fī aīyāt Qur'ānīyah [Rhetorical landmarks in Qur'ānic verses]. [Transcribed lectures]. *Qur'ānic Thought*. www.quranicthought.com/ar/books/%D9%85%D8%B9%D8%A7%D9%84%D9%85-%D8%A8%D9%8A%D8%A7%D9%86%D9%8A%D8%A9-%D9%81%D9%8A-%D8%A2%D9%8A%D8%A7%D8%AA-%D9%82%D8%B1%D8%A2%D9%86%D9%8A%D8%A9/ [https://perma.cc/89PV-QUE2]

Al-Nawawī, M. (2001). Book on impermissible acts. In Shu ʻaīb al-Arn'ūṭ (Ed.), *Rīyāḍ al-sāliḥīn [The meadows of the righteous] by Al-Nawawī, M*. Mu'assat Risālah.

Amīn, Q. (2010a). *Al-mar'ah al-jadīdah* [The new woman]. Hindawi.

(2010b). *Taḥrīr al-mar'ah* [The liberation of women]. Hindawi.

Arab League. (2004a). Al-*Wathīqah al-ʻArabīyah li ḥuqūq al-insān* [Arab Charter on Human Rights]. http://hrlibrary.umn.edu/arab/a003-2.html [https://perma.cc/N59A-RHTE]

(2004b). Arab Charter on Human Rights. https://digitallibrary.un.org/record/551368?ln = ar [https://perma.cc/AEL3-6TFX]

Arab Parliament. (2021). Al-wathīqah al-ʻarabīyah lilmar'āh [Arab Charter on Women's Rights]. http://ar-pr.org/AgreementsAnddocuments.aspx

Arafa, B. (1973). *The social activities of the Egyptian Feminist Union*. Elias' Modern Press.

Barlas, A. (2002). *"Believing women" in Islam: Unreading patriarchal interpretations of the Qur'an*. University of Texas Press.

Bassiouni, C. (2006). Al-wathā'iq al-Islāmīyah [Islamic instruments (Arabic)]. In Bassiouni, C. (Ed.), *Al-wathā'iq al-dawlīyah al-maʻnīyah bi-Ḥuqūq al-insān* [International instruments on human rights] (Vol. 2) (pp. 23–44). Dār al-Shurūq.

Bint al-Shāṭi'. (1991). *Ṣuwar min ḥīyātihin* [Scenes from their lives]. Al-Haī'ah al-Miṣrīyah al-ʻĀmah lil-Kitāb.

Bitzer, L. (1959). Aristotle's enthymeme revisited. *Quarterly Journal of Speech*, 45(4), 399–408.

Charland, M. (1987). Constitutive rhetoric: The case of the Peuple Quebecois. *Quarterly Journal of Speech*, 73(2), 133–150.

Dabbous, S. (2004). "Till I became a minister": Women's rights and women's journalism in pre-1952 Egypt. In N. Sakr (Ed.), *Women and media in the Middle East: Power through self-expression* (pp. 39–52). I. B. Tauris.

de Vaux, C., Schacht, B. J., & Goichon, A. M. (2012). Ḥadd. In P. Bearman, T. Bianquis, C. E. Bosworth, E. van Donzel, & W. P. Heinrichs (Eds.), *Encyclopaedia of Islam new edition online (EI-2 English)*. Koninklijke Brill NV. http://dx.doi.org/10.1163/1573-3912_islam_SIM_2586

Diab, R. (2016). *Shades of sulh: The rhetorics of Arab-Islamic reconciliation*. University of Pittsburgh Press.

(2018). Legal-political rhetoric, human rights, and the Constitution of Medina. *Rhetorica: A Journal of the History of Rhetoric*, 36(3), 219–243.

(2023) Engaging with Arab(ic)-Islamic religious rhetoric. In M. Depalma, P. Lynch, & J. Ringer (Eds.), *Rhetoric and religion in the twenty-first century: Pluralism in a postsecular age* (pp. 201–223). Southern Illinois University Press.

(In press.) Arabic rhetoric. In D. Gross, L. Mao, & S. Mailloux (Eds.), *Cambridge history of rhetoric: Rhetoric after 1900*. Cambridge University Press.

Dunford, R. F., & Madhok, S. (2015). Vernacular rights cultures and the "right to have rights." *Citizenship Studies*, 19(6–7), 605–619.

El-Alami, D. S. (1994). Law No. 100 of 1985 amending certain provisions of Egypt's Personal Status Laws. *Islamic Law and Society*, 1(1), 116–130.

El-Ariss, T. (2018). Introduction. In T. El-Ariss (Ed.), *The Arab renaissance: A bilingual anthology of the Nahda* (pp. xv–xxviii). Modern Language Association of America.

Elsadda, H., & Hassan, M. (2018). *Binā' wa niḍāl* [Founding and striving]. Women and Memory Forum.

Esposito, J. L. (1975). Women's rights in Islam. *Islamic Studies*, 14(2), 99–114.

Fakhry, M. (1991). *Ethical theories in Islam*. E. J. Brill.

Farooq, M. O. (2018). The farewell sermon of Prophet Muhammad: An analytical review. *Islam and Civilisational Renewal*, 9(3), 322–342.

Fried, C. (1978). *Right and wrong*. Harvard University Press.

Hauser, G. A. (2008). The moral vernacular of human rights discourse. *Philosophy & Rhetoric*, 41(4), 440–466.

Howe, J. (2020). Introduction. In J. Howe (Ed.), *The Routledge handbook of Islam and gender* (pp. 1–12). Routledge.

Khadduri, M. (1946). Human rights in Islam. *Annals of the American Academy of Political and Social Science*, 243(1), 77–81.

Lowry, J. E. (2010). The Prophet as lawgiver and legal authority. In J. E. Brockopp (Ed.), *The Cambridge companion to Muhammad* (pp. 83–102). Cambridge University Press.

Marzūq, S. (Director). (1975). *Urīd Ḥala* [I want a solution]. Salah Zulfikar Films.

Mernissi, F. (1991). *Women and Islam: An historical and theological inquiry*. Blackwell.

Nāṣif, M. Ḥ. (2012). *Nisā'iyāt* [Women's matters or essays on women's rights]. Hindawi.

Quraishi, A. (2008). Who says *shari'a* demands the stoning of women: A description of Islamic law and constitutionalism. *Berkeley Journal of Middle Eastern and Islamic Law*, 1(1), 163–178.

The Qur'an (A. Y. Ali, Trans.). (2008). Tahrike Tarsile Qur'an.

Salama, S. (2019, October). Arab charter on women's rights launched in Abu Dhabi. *Gulf News*. https://gulfnews.com/uae/arab-charter-on-womens-rights-launched-in-abu-dhabi-1.66992137 [https://perma.cc/8M36-DQAD]

Singerman, D. (2005). Rewriting divorce in Egypt: Reclaiming Islam, legal activism, and coalition politics. In R. W. Hefner (Ed.), *Remaking Muslim politics: Pluralism, contestation, democratization* (pp. 161–188). Princeton University Press.

Smith, C. (2003). Human culture(s) as moral order(s). In C. Smith (Ed.), *Moral, believing animals: Human personhood and culture* (pp. 7–44). Oxford University Press.

Souryal, S. S. (1987). The religionization of a society: The continuing application of Shariah law in Saudi Arabia. *Journal for the Scientific Study of Religion*, 26(4), 429–449.

Sullins, P. (2000). The stained glass ceiling: Career attainment for women clergy. *Sociology of Religion*, 61(3), 243–266.

Syed, K. T. (2008). Misconceptions about human rights and women's rights in Islam. *Interchange*, 39(2), 245–257.

von Arnauld, A., & Theilen, J. T. (2020). Rhetoric of rights: A topical perspective on the functions of claiming a "human right to . . ." In A. von Arnauld, K. von der Decken, & M. Susi (Eds.), *The Cambridge handbook of new human rights: Recognition, novelty, rhetoric* (pp. 34–50). Cambridge University Press.

Yūnis, I. (2023, April). *Taḥt al-uṣāiyah and Urīd ḥala* [Under guardianship law and I want a solution]. *Al-Ahram.*https://gate.ahram.org.eg/daily/News/896665.aspx .

Zīyādah, M. (2012). *Bāḥithat al-Bādīyah* [Seeker of the dessert]. Hindawi.

10

<Police Power> to Stop-and-Frisk

A Pattern for Persuasion

Lindsay Head

On a warm evening in late August 2008, Leroy Downs arrived home from work to an encounter like others he had experienced many times – a humiliating and dangerous encounter, which stripped him of his liberty and constitutional rights to be let alone and equally protected under the law. Standing there, in front of his own home, Downs spoke to a friend on his cellphone. Holding the mouthpiece of a headset connected to the phone by a cord, Downs watched as a black Crown Victoria drove by, stopped, reversed, and then double-parked directly in front of Downs and his home. Some people might hurry inside or prepare to call the police in this situation, but Downs, being all too familiar with this sort of thing, recognized that this *was* the police.

Officers Scott Giacona and James Mahoney, white men in plainclothes, aggressively approached Downs, saying it appeared he was smoking marijuana and forcing him to "get the fuck against" his own fence.[1] Downs explained that he was holding the mouthpiece connected to his phone, he was not smoking marijuana, and he is, in fact, a drug counselor. For unknown reasons, this response did not satisfy Giacona and Mahoney, who patted down the outside of Downs's clothes, reached into and emptied his pockets, and searched through his wallet. Downs neither consented to this search, nor was he asked for permission. Having found nothing with which to charge Downs, Giacona and Mahoney started toward their vehicle. Aware of his purported rights, Downs asked for the officers' badge numbers, a request which was "laughed off" with one officer saying Downs was fortunate not get locked up and the other saying, "I'm just doing my fucking job."

In this situation, only two people broke the law, and neither of them was punished. In fact, Officer Mahoney has since been promoted. Downs, the only innocent party, was, however, disciplined from the very moment Officers Giacona and Mahoney saw him standing in front of his home that evening. Indeed, Downs had been disciplined in this way, in his words, "many times" before. His neighbor

[1] The quotes and facts described throughout my introduction derive from *Floyd v. City of New York* (2013).

witnessed part of this demeaning encounter. The New York Police Department (NYPD) gave him the run-around when he tried to file a complaint. And when the officers were finally called to account for their actions – in *Floyd v. City of New York* (2013; hereafter *David Floyd*) – they feigned no recollection, an artifice which United States District Court Judge Shira Scheindlin did not find credible.[2]

The *David Floyd* case is a bright spot in New York's sullied history of stop-and-frisk. In this landmark case, twelve Black and Hispanic individuals, including Leroy Downs, succeeded in a class action lawsuit against the city, alleging that the NYPD's use of its stop-and-frisk policy violated their Fourth Amendment right to be free from unreasonable searches and seizures and their right to equal protection of the laws under the Fourteenth Amendment. Judge Scheindlin found that NYPD officials acted with deliberate indifference to unconstitutional stops, frisks, and searches, affirming that "suspicious blacks and Hispanics may not be treated differently by the police than equally suspicious whites" (*Floyd v. City of New York*, 2013, p. 667).

Sadly, the gross violations the *David Floyd* plaintiffs experienced are not uncommon, in New York and across the country, and this outcome might have been much less likely prior to 2013, when the case was decided. The cultural, political, and legal histories surrounding stop-and-frisk practices reveal discourses designed to privilege police power in the name of crime control and public safety and restrict liberty, particularly for Black and Hispanic Americans. The terms <police power>[3] and <liberty> can be understood as ideographs – links between rhetoric and ideology. These terms, alongside others, transform the legal landscape of stop-and-frisk across time. They emerge as evolving legal, political, and social terms within and beyond the opinion; and, indeed, a careful analysis of *David Floyd*'s contemporary rhetorical culture might have predicted the outcome.

This chapter first describes a method for that analysis: an ideographic analysis of <police power> and related ideographs in stop-and-frisk jurisprudence, specifically examining *David Floyd* as a textual archive of the times. First, I define and describe the ideograph and its intersection with legal texts, using Michael Calvin McGee's (1980) characterization of the ideograph as a link between rhetoric and ideology as my framework (Section 10.1). Following that framework, I identify some of the prevalent ideographs of stop-and-frisk, briefly tracing their use diachronically before turning to examine their synchronic use both within and outside *David Floyd* (Section 10.2). Finally, I highlight how Judge Scheindlin engages this vocabulary of ideographs and the law consequently changed in response to an evolving American rhetorical culture (Section 10.3). Ultimately, I argue that ideographic

[2] Because of legal citation conventions, this case is listed in the references as *Floyd v. City of New York*. The plaintiff's first name, David, is omitted. However, because of the more recent events surrounding the murder of *George* Floyd in Minneapolis, I have chosen to use David Floyd's full name when referring to his case in this chapter.

[3] Angle brackets (< >) conventionally indicate ideographs.

inquiry offers more than a useful tool for education and analysis or a method for predicting societal beliefs and behaviors. Ideographs are a *force* for persuasion.

10.1 IDEOGRAPHS AND RHETORICAL CULTURE

When we look at stop-and-frisk jurisprudence (or any text) ideographically, we consider the power of terms imbued with meaning through historical, social, and political use to influence related beliefs and behaviors. In "The 'Ideograph': A Link between Rhetoric and Ideology," Michael Calvin McGee wrote:

> The falsity of an ideology is specifically rhetorical, for the illusion of truth and falsity with regard to normative commitments is the product of persuasion. Since the clearest access to persuasion (and hence ideology) is through the discourse used to produce it, ... ideology in practice is a political language, preserved in rhetorical documents, with the capacity to dictate discussion and control public belief and behavior. Further, the political language which manifests ideology seems characterized by slogans, a vocabulary of "ideographs" easily mistaken for the technical terminology of political philosophy. (McGee, 1980, pp. 4–5)

That is, the language of ideology – or of the systems of ideas that influence behaviors and beliefs – is recorded textually and has the ability to influence what people think and how they act presently and in the future. This language of ideology, texts imbued with influence, is stamped with what McGee (1980, p. 5) described as "a vocabulary of 'ideographs.'" Consequently, the ability to view this embossed vocabulary imparts upon the spectator the ability to predict and describe ideology.

Ideographs are, in the plainest articulation, terms that conceptualize collective social commitments toward a practice or belief. They are not propositions because ideographs are "more pregnant than propositions ever could be," and they display an elasticity of meaning (McGee, 1980, pp. 6–7). They identify with and about an idea or ideal, but their interpretation is not fixed. We commonly recognize ideographs as slogans or key terms that defined a culture. McGee provided <property>, <religion>, <right to privacy>, <freedom of speech>, <rule of law>, and <liberty> as examples of ideographs, though there are many more (p. 7).

Within McGee's framework, ideographs are both "the building blocks of ideology" and "one-term sums of an orientation" because they form our beliefs and position us temporally and culturally (McGee, 1980, p. 7). Put another way, ideographs take on meaning and reflect societal beliefs in relation to both their historical use and contemporary context, particularly in the way they relate to other elastic terms within a rhetorical culture.

As "building blocks of ideology," ideographs reflect social commitments; "they exist in real discourse, ... They are not invented by observers; they come to be as part of the real lives of the people whose motives they articulate" (McGee, 1980, p. 7). McGee intended the ideograph as "purely descriptive of an essentially social condition. Unlike more general conceptions of 'Ultimate' or 'God' terms, attention is called to the social, rather than rational or ethical, functions of a particular vocabulary" (McGee, 1980, p. 8). In this way, ideographs define what it means to be part of a culture and how one should behave within that culture.

In this chapter, I examine a specific rhetorical culture – stop-and-frisk law – within a broader rhetorical culture – the American public – with attention to the social function of a vocabulary of ideographs in *David Floyd*. I'll borrow from Condit and Lucaites to explain the concept of rhetorical culture, which described "the range of linguistic usages available to … a group of potentially disparate individuals and subgroups who share a common interest in their collective life" (Condit & Lucaites, 1993, p. xii). We might describe a broad American rhetorical culture or a more discrete rhetorical culture, such as a group of civil rights advocates, a church congregation, or the legal profession. The law, like any other collective with shared interests and language uses, "exists as part of an evolving rhetorical culture" (Hasian et al., 1996, pp. 326). There we find "commonly used allusions, aphorisms, characterizations, ideographs, images, metaphors, myths, narratives, and … common argumentative forms," vocabularies that mark discursive and ideological boundaries within which members of the collective operate (Condit & Lucaites, 1993, p. xii).

Just as the law represents a discrete rhetorical culture, it often comprises a set of discrete ideographs – terms of art specific to legal practitioners. However, our social vocabulary can never be apart from our legal vocabulary because the law is a textile stitched primarily of social stories. To be sure, popular ideographs pop up within the discursive space of the law, but some change meaning after the courts continuously employ them within the constraints of that rhetorical culture. Ideographs specific to the law appear when courts and other legal practitioners use a term or phrase that turns in meaning, style, and manner over time and through repeated use. Some ideographs reach far back into the earliest foundations of the law. Others work their way in from broader or tangential rhetorical cultures. On some occasions, meanings neatly overlap; while on others, the distinctions are more palpable.

<Police power>, for example, is a term with elastic meaning – an ideograph – used both popularly and legally and reflective of a collective commitment to a practice (e.g., stop-and-frisk) and a belief or ideology (e.g., that this practice is necessary to deter criminal activity despite infringements upon personal liberty). The term's meaning is elastic because it depends upon when and where it is used. Today, in some segments of American rhetorical culture, <police power> takes on one elastic, often pejorative, meaning. In legal discourse environments – the rhetorical culture of law – it takes on a similarly elastic, though perhaps less pejorative, meaning. These connotations are subject to the evolutions of the rhetorical culture upon which the term is inscribed. The connotations are also reflective of the ideology of that rhetorical culture.

Ideographs are also "constantly sites of struggle, as those who successfully lay claim to [them] enjoy a significant persuasive advantage" (McCann, 2007, p. 385).

Examining the legal intersections of Black lives and <police power>, Carbado explained that we "would be right to wonder whether it is at all unusual for the Supreme Court to invent constitutional doctrine," although this, in fact, is common because "terms like 'due process' and 'equal protection' and 'liberty' require Courts to give them meaning" (Carbado, 2022, p. 113). The terms Carbado highlighted are ideographs, which have varied or elastic meanings in the law depending upon who is using them, when and how they are being used, and for what purpose. It might even be argued that these terms operate in tandem with the principle of *stare decisis* to give the law meaning *and* force, affording it the ability define and inform, but also to both act upon individuals and cause them to move or to act (Head, 2018). Ideographs have the potential to highlight social similarities or expose tensions in changing beliefs in evolving rhetorical cultures.

So, we see ideographs as the "building blocks of ideology" in rhetorical culture. People are "'conditioned,' … to a vocabulary of concepts that function as guides, warrants, reasons, or excuses for behavior and belief," rather than to belief or behavior itself (McGee, 1980, p. 6). We become inured to the ideology presented to us through ideographs. Thus, if the vocabulary available offers a reason for a belief or behavior, then we can predict how people will behave or what they will believe by examining the vocabularies they use. By viewing a rhetorical culture's textual archive (e.g., a judicial opinion) stamped with a vocabulary of ideographs, we can make such predictions and adjust our own language use accordingly.

The description of ideographs as "one-term sums of an orientation" offers an analytical framework for this sort of investigation: ideographic analysis as a means to predict and describe behaviors or beliefs. This analysis uncovers "interpenetrating systems or 'structures' of public motives" revealed in "'diachronic' and 'synchronic' patterns of political consciousness, which have the capacity both to control 'power' and to influence (if not determine) the shape and texture of each individual's 'reality'" (McGee, 1980, p. 5). In texts, the terms align with structures of social motives in order to persuade, influence, and control. The vocabularies evolve in meaning depending upon their positionality.

The patterns run diachronically reaching back into history and synchronically stretching out into rhetorical culture. McGee explained: "Chronological sequences are provided by analysis, and they properly reflect the concerns of theorists who try to describe what [the ideograph] *may* mean, potentially, by laying out what the term *has* meant" (McGee, 1980, p. 12). But when considering ideographs "as *forces*" to be used rhetorically in order to persuade others to action, we must view ideographs horizontally in conflict with other ideographs where meaning arises out of synchronic confrontations (p. 12). Ideographs are "connected to all others as brain cells are linked by synapses, synchronically in one context at one specific moment" (p. 16). Where the synchronic conflict happens, there you will find the "force and currency" of an ideograph and other terms in its cluster or "vocabulary" (p. 14). The complete ideological description, according to McGee, "will consist of (1) the isolations of a society's ideographs, (2) the exposure and analysis of the diachronic structure of every ideograph, and (3) characterization of synchronic relationships among all the ideographs in a particular context" (p. 16).

When specifically analyzing legal discourse, we identify ideographs in precedent cases, the Constitution, and statutory law. As McGee noted, "Formally, the body of nonstatutory 'law' is little more than a literature recording ideographic uses in the 'common law' and 'case law'" (McGee, 1980, p. 11). Notably, significant diachronic vocabularies lie in "'popular' history" whether we are analyzing legal discourse or not (p. 11). Popular history includes the sort of texts we might find in popular culture: songs, films, plays, and novels, for example. The diachronic analysis would also equally include political history and public discourse. "The significance of ideographs is in their concrete history as usages, not in their alleged idea-content," so a variety of sources should be considered (McGee, 1980, pp. 9–10). For these reasons, I chose to examine news and popular media sources, presidential speeches, and historical and critical commentary in my cursory diachronic analysis of <police power> below.

Indeed, McGee's methodology has proven quite useful to critics invested in cultural communication, argumentation, and rhetoric broadly. Since McGee first published his article in 1980, a vast literature of ideographic analysis has been produced by scholars identifying ideographs in the media (McDaniel, 2013), public address (Potter, 2014), legislation (Cuomo, 2020), legal opinions (Sinsheimer, 2005) (as I discuss here), related legal discourse (Langford, 2015), and public health policies (Allgayer & Kanemoto, 2021) – just to name a few. In keeping with McGee's description, the ideograph necessarily crosses a variety of contexts. Moreover, the persuasive impact of visual ideographs (Jones, 2009) represents yet another descendant of McGee's work. In fact, so much scholarship exists on ideographs that many simple examples that come to mind have already been subjected to rich scrutiny.

Some scholars employing McGee's ideographic method explore single terms diachronically, tracing their historical roots and uses. Others focus on a synchronic methodology, identifying how the term is presently situated or situated within a particular text to persuasive effect at a specific moment in time. McGee (1980, p. 14) explained that understanding and describing both the diachronic and synchronic patterns creates a theoretically accurate account of an ideology. So, this chapter proceeds first as a demonstration of that method, discussing some (certainly not all) diachronic patterns of <police power>, before narrowing in on the surrounding rhetorical culture and language use synchronous with *Floyd v. City of New York*.

In the process, I identify what we call a "vocabulary of ideographs" surrounding <police power> because ideographs do not exist in isolation; they exist in relation to other ideographs. If we charted all the ideographs used to justify a position, "they would form groups or clusters of words radiating" from original uses (McGee, 1980, p. 13). Some of the terms I highlight in the vocabulary of <police power> include

<liberty>, <high crime area>, <furtive movements>, and especially as it relates to *David Floyd*, <justice>.

With that said, my purpose is not solely demonstrative, nor is it to provide an exhaustive mapping of <police power>. Ideographs are *forces*, with rhetorical potential, bound up in their synchronic clusters (or vocabularies) – they offer more than mere description and analysis. Ideographs are influential, causing us to move and to act in response to the energy and ideas that they convey. I aim to show how McGee's historical text can intersect with a contemporary text (e.g., a legal opinion) in a way that is valuable not only for descriptions and revelations about a term's *prior* use and impact, but also for persuading and predicting *present* and *future* audiences – a valuable instrument in the practice of law or for any rhetorical purpose.

10.2 THE IDEOGRAPHIC PATTERNS OF <POLICE POWER>

Contemporary scholars look back on the last fifty years or so as a period when "the Supreme Court has interpreted the Fourth Amendment to allocate enormous power to the police: to surveil, to racially profile, to stop-and-frisk, and to kill" (Carbado, 2022, p. 11). While it is impossible to discuss a detailed history of <police power> to stop-and-frisk in every detail here, an ideographic analysis of *David Floyd* would be incomplete without examining the term's meaning and evolution – as well as its relationship to other related terms or vocabularies – diachronically.

In response to British soldiers searching their homes without restraint via general warrants and writs of assistance, the American colonists sought to include the Fourth Amendment in the United States Constitution to curb <police power>. Ratified in 1791, the Amendment provides:

> The rights of the people to be secure in their persons, houses, papers, and effects, against unreasonable searches and seizures, shall not be violated, and no warrants shall issue, but upon probable cause, supported by oath or affirmation, and particularly describing the place to be searched, and the persons or things to be seized.

The Amendment connotes personal <liberty> and a <right to privacy>. But let us not forget that personal <liberty> was denied to Black Americans until 1865 with the ratification of the Thirteenth Amendment. The law is riddled with disconcerting examples of a long history of racial disparity in its application, which is unmistakably apparent in stop-and-frisk practices – arising long after the Fourth Amendment's ratification – empowered by arguments for the necessity of <police power>.

What is stop-and-frisk? Generally, when officers suspect a crime has been or is about to be committed, stops are initiated. In *Florida v. Bostick* (1991, p. 437), the Supreme Court established the test for determining a stop as "whether a reasonable person would feel free to decline the officers' requests or otherwise terminate the encounter." That encounter advances to a frisk when suspicion is strengthened through the initial contact. Reasonable suspicion that criminal activity is afoot is enough to justify the stop. Reasonable suspicion that "the person stopped is armed and dangerous" is enough to justify the frisk (*Floyd v. City of New York*, 2013, p. 566).

"*Terry* stops," as they have come to be called, fluctuate in meaning over time. The foundational case is *Terry v. Ohio* (1968, p. 1), in which "rapidly unfolding and often dangerous situations on city streets" purported to necessitate expanded <police power>. The officer in *Terry* observed two unfamiliar men who appeared to be casing a store for a "stick-up." The officer approached the men, asked their names, spun one man around, and patted his clothing; the officer found a revolver. While the Court stated that personal security could not be violated, it saw tension between the rights of individuals and the role of police: "reflective of the tensions involved are the practical and constitutional arguments pressed with great vigor on both sides of the public debate over the *power of police* to 'stop and frisk' – as it is sometimes euphemistically termed – suspicious persons" (*Terry v. Ohio*, 1968, p. 9). Here, the Court homes in on the ideograph as a site of struggle. The Court places weight on the fact that the officer had a great deal of experience and the defendants were clearly suspicious persons. Sadly, the subjectivity of suspicion preordained that stop-and-frisk would open the door to state-sanctioned discrimination by the NYPD because the standard "promotes background social biases to normative status" (Gray, 2017, p. 280).

At the same time the Court was deciding *Terry*, it was also deciding *Sibron v. New York*, a case directly challenging the constitutionality of New York's stop-and-frisk statute, under which an officer could stop a person "whom he reasonably suspects is committing, has committed or is about to commit a felony [or other specified offense]" (*Sibron v. New York*, 1968, p. 43). There was no concern with the officer's safety specified in this statute, and the Court in *Sibron* sidestepped the question by noting that the officer suspected that the defendant was armed, so further inquiry into whether the statute permitted unconstitutional conduct was unnecessary.

New York defined <police power> further in *People v. De Bour*, determining that officers may approach individuals unengaged in "suspected criminal activity" and ask for information if "the encounter [does] not subject [them] to a loss of dignity, for where the police degrade and humiliate their behavior is to be condemned" (*People v. De Bour*, 1976, p. 210). The permissiveness in *De Bour* was clearly accepted; the prohibitions took a bit longer to sink in – after all, one person's interpretation of degradation might look different from another's. The Court noted that expanding <police power> in this way is supported by the fact that police play a multifaceted role in society, which includes acts of public service (*People v. De Bour*, 1976, p. 218). Essentially, police officers cannot do their jobs without these expanded powers. As we will later see in *David Floyd*, this emphasis on "suspected criminal activity" opens courts up to a new elastic term: <furtive movements>.

De Bour exposed even more complexity in the vocabulary of <police power>. For example, when does this "encounter" become a full-blown stop? *INS v. Delgado* attempted to clear things up by suggesting that <ordinary citizens> should know that they can "simply refuse to answer" or "disregard a police request" (*INS v. Delgado*, 1984, p. 218). Many in our contemporary culture would view this characterization of the <ordinary citizen> as severely misguided, which further illustrates the evolution of language use in our society. Then, however, concepts like "deterrence" and the balancing of "social costs" were woven throughout judicial history in apparent response to political and cultural cries for crime control and a brewing war on drugs.

The 1980s gave us "yuppies," MTV, and the first female Supreme Court Justice, Sandra Day O'Connor. The decade also gave us a revolution in the ideological predilections of Americans and the Supreme Court, now centering on a jurisprudence of crime control and engaged in a war on drugs. Embracing a "new conservatism" in response to the counterculture revolution of the 1960s and 1970s, the "Moral Majority" blamed permissiveness and welfarism of the 1960s for the deterioration of the country (Weiss, 2011 p. 90). Most legal and political critics blamed the Warren Court in significant part, arguing it was "too soft on crime" and its decisions were injurious to society because they limited the scope of <police power> (Merriman, 2011, p. 66). These critics lamented the substantial social cost of allowing criminals to go free, and they countered with a rhetoric of deterrence.

Two *Atlantic Monthly* articles in particular highlight the country's concerns at the time. The first, "Broken Windows: The Police and Neighborhood Safety," by Kelling and Wilson, appeared in March 1982. Kelling and Wilson (1982, p. 38) argued the "importance of maintaining, intact, communities without broken windows." Basically, the police have two major functions – fighting crime and maintaining order – and the latter stems from the belief that "if a window in a building is broken and is left unrepaired, all the rest of the windows will soon be broken" (Kelling & Wilson, 1983, p. 30).

This "Broken Windows" policy was not their own (the policy predates stop-and-frisk and tees up the practice nicely), but Kelling and Wilson (1982, pp. 32–35) used it to suggest that a vivid police presence, and deterrence practices more broadly, can impact and, ultimately, curb criminal activity. They argued that "serious street crime flourishes in areas in which disorderly behavior goes unchecked," so society "must return to our long-abandoned view that the police ought to protect communities as well as individuals" (pp. 33, 28). If police keep obstreperous people in check, it will prevent an increase in harmful or serious criminal activity. The emphasis on communities rather than individuals reflects a prioritizing of social costs over individual privacy protections running through interpretations of <police power> that eventually reach *David Floyd*.

The second influential *Atlantic Monthly* piece, "Thinking about Crime," more directly examines the question of deterrence. Wilson acknowledged the potential for deterrence efforts to have less of an impact than sociologists expect, but he nevertheless argues that "justice requires that we use [both deterrence and job-creation] because penalizing wrong conduct and rewarding good conduct are right polices in themselves" (Wilson, 1983, p. 88). For Wilson (1983, p. 72), the <police power> debate comes down to weighing "the costs and benefits of crime" because that supports an ideal policy. What's more, he noted that "experiments in deterrence have involved changes in police behavior rather than changes in the behavior of judges and prosecutors," and the consequence of changing police behavior seems "to indicate that the more focused and aggressive the police effort, the greater the chance it will make a difference" (Wilson, 1983, p. 79). As we have begun to see, similar language saturates the diachronic structures of <police power> in stop-and-frisk practices.

Of course, this conversation expanded far beyond the *Atlantic Monthly* at the time. These articles are only meant as representations of the rhetorical culture. Supporting the expansion or extension of <police power>, attention to crime control (and a resulting drug enforcement prerogative) can be seen in the other aspects of popular rhetorical culture as well. *Paste Magazine* describes the decade as "the coming of age period for TV crime dramas" (Jackson, 2014). Shows like *Magnum P.I.*, *Knight Rider*, *Miami Vice*, and *Hill Street Blues* topped the charts in the early 1980s, and even other popular shows seemingly unrelated to crime – such as *Cheers*, *The Facts of Life*, *Diff'rent Strokes*, and *Family Ties* – began systematically tackling the related issue of drug abuse, bringing these concerns to the forefront of the nation's cultural consciousness (Jackson, 2014). Concerns over rising crime rates and drug use pervaded American culture, and not without reason. The country was reeling in response to the fact that crime rates had increased sharply since the late 1960s, but "between 1980 and 1993 most FBI Index crimes declined and violent crime stabilized, while incarceration (especially Black) skyrocketed" (Weiss, 2011 n. 8).

This is perhaps because, as Erin Leigh Frymire (Chapter 11 in this volume) argues, in response to a perceived "alarming rise in the crime rate," President Reagan and his administration "shift[ed] the focus of representative legislation and criminal prosecution away from crimes of the powerful … to crimes of the powerless" (Weiss, 2011, p. 90). During his presidency, Reagan instructed the FBI "to resume aggressive domestic spying … [u]nder the rubric of fighting 'terrorism,'" marking that term part of the diachronic vocabulary of our ideograph (Greenberg, 2011, p. 43). Reagan initiated a responsive agenda that moved public policy sharply rightward, "diminishing legal rights, enhancing the authority of police and prosecutors, and creating an enormous penal state targeting young black and Latino offenders," and the administration created a firm foundation for mixing national security with criminal justice, further extending <police power> (Weiss, 2011, p. 89). But it was Reagan's War on Drugs that served as the "principal rationale for expanding state repressive apparatuses" like stop-and-frisk practices, declaring it a "national security objective" and calling for "greater militarization of crime control domestically" (Weiss, 2011, p. 89).

Rhetors often cite these <national security> concerns, or other similar ideographs, to sway the public toward a preoccupation with crime control. In *The Mark of Criminality*, McCann (2017, p. 6) suggested that these concerns stemmed from "discourses [that] almost always appealed to racialized fears associated with criminality," and this "shift in political rhetoric came in direct response to the growing strength and militancy of the civil rights movement." McCann (2017, p. 6) further explained, "As large social movements began to make major gains in the public square ... many prominent political figures began crafting messages that framed law and order as a matter of great national concern, arguing that crime control must be a federal priority to calm the tumult of the period." Reagan's political rhetoric certainly hit this mark and served to significantly bolster <police power>.

On October 2, 1982, Reagan pronounced on the radio, "We've taken down the surrender flag and run up the battle flag ... and we're going to win the war on drugs" (Reagan, 1982a). He outlined the impending confrontation twelve days later from the White House Rose Garden, saying "those of you engaged in law enforcement have struggled long and hard in what must often have seemed like a losing war against the menace of crime" (Reagan, 1982b). In that Rose Garden address, he called crime an "American epidemic," empowered the police, and noted that "[n]ine out of ten Americans believe that the courts in their home areas aren't tough enough on criminals, and cold statistics do demonstrate ... the failure of our criminal justice system to adequately pursue, prosecute, and punish criminals" (Reagan, 1982b).

Incidentally, Regan's ideographic identifications in this address are persuasive. If your audience thinks "a certain kind of conduct is admirable, then [you] might persuade the audience by using ideas and images [or ideographs] that identify ... with that kind of conduct" (Burke, 1950, p. 55). Pursuing, prosecuting, and punishing dangerous criminals is, of course, commendable. By citing a majority of Americans and referencing their homes, he further identifies with them, and by mentioning a war and an epidemic, Reagan established the division necessary for the ideographic identifications to influence changes in his audiences' beliefs about <police power>.[4]

New York City continued its fight against crime well into the 1990s. Police began to delineate certain factors or considerations for stop-and-frisk encounters. They learned the vocabulary, and it informed their actions. It even populated their official forms. One such term is <high crime area>, which carries with it varied denotations and connotations depending on where you are in the history of stop-and-frisk. Being in a <high crime area> is one factor that informed the Court's decision in *Whren v. United States* (1996) that a traffic violation (failing to use a turn signal and delaying to proceed at a stop sign) could justify a stop even where the officers conceded that they would not have made the stop outside suspicions of more "serious criminal activity" characteristic of the area in which the stop took place.

[4] See K. Burke's (1950) theory of identification and division. Moreover, division has long been considered a necessary part of discourse; the *Rhetorica Ad Herennium* ([Cicero], 1954, 1. 3) indicated it is "[b]y means of the *division* we make clear what matters are agreed upon."

However, in *Illinois v. Wardlow* (2000), the Court distinguished the <high crime area> factor as insufficient alone to justify a stop; the Court attended to the individual and his purpose for fleeing, and in doing so Justice Stevens appeared to be identifying with changes in his own rhetorical culture's altering image of <police power>:

> Among some citizens, particularly minorities and those residing in high crime areas, there is also the possibility that the fleeing person is entirely innocent, but, with or without justification, believes that contact with the police can itself be dangerous, apart from any criminal activity associated with the officer's sudden presence. (*Illinois v. Wardlow*, 2000, p. 132)

Here, Stevens connected legal ideographs to beliefs presented in the wider popular and political culture.

Uses and interpretations of <police power> emerge out of these historical vocabularies. The related terms in the ideograph's vocabulary are many and complex; they offer a variety of perspectives on the meaning of <police power> and, ultimately, the application of stop-and-frisk law. Indeed, the historical vocabularies of <police power> are too rich and detailed to fully cover here. For our purposes, it is enough to demonstrate how the term has expanded and contracted since its roots in the Fourth Amendment and now shift our focus to the synchronic vocabularies of <police power> in *David Floyd*'s contemporary rhetorical culture. It is in this that we find the most immediate persuasive value – the *force* of the ideograph.

10.3 A VOCABULARY OF IDEOGRAPHS IN *DAVID FLOYD*

As early as 1999, the City of New York was put on notice that "stops and frisks were being conducted in a racially skewed manner," but until 2013, it seems that "[n]-othing was done in response" (*Floyd v. City of New York*, 2013, p. 560). What changed in 2013? *David Floyd* was decided within a rhetorical culture attentive to the potency and pervasiveness of <police power>. In 2013, we ushered in the "Year of the Selfie." It was a time of over-exposure and rapid increase in technological growth. American culture entered a new "age of surveillance," made even more apparent with the 2013 Snowden Leaks. Many scholars mark the country's true turn toward unrestrained governmental surveillance on September 11, 2001; and, indeed, many American citizens had come to expect unfettered government surveillance in the years after 9/11, when the federal government made very real strides in obtaining the legal right to "engage in covert and overt surveillance" of its citizens (Hawkes, 2007, p. 344). By 2013, many Americans had become so desensitized to surveillance that they largely gave up concern and freely posted intimate details about their lives on the internet. Of course, coming to expect, or worse to ignore, surveillance intrusions creates firmer vocabularies that slowly erode privacy rights and expand <police power>.

This is what it had come to on the streets of New York City: overt <police power> and eroding personal liberties. The need for this surveillance can be traced back to the *war on drugs* and the *war on terror*, to a *jurisprudence of crime control* and its connection to <national security>. Overt surveillance expanded in more ways than just technologically. There was a rapid rise in stops-and-frisks in the first decade of the twenty-first century. In New York in particular, the police conducted over 4.4 million *Terry* stops between January 2004 and June 2012. Only 6 percent of those stops resulted in an arrest, and in only 10 percent of cases was the individual who was stopped white (*Floyd v. City of New York*, 2013, p. 559). In the decade or so before *David Floyd*, the NYPD significantly pressured officers to increase stop activity, the number jumping from approximately 97,000 in 2002 to approximately 686,000 in 2011 (*Floyd v. City of New York*, 2013, p. 590).

By 2013, police officers, once depicted as *crime fighters* in popular rhetorical culture, had increasingly exposed a tendency toward violence against Black and impoverished Americans. While much police work is service rather than fighting crime – offering assistance, negotiation, and peacekeeping – the image of "blue on Black" violence began to regularly appear in the synchronic structures of society, in the news and on the streets. So, rhetorical culture shifted further, resulting in changing narratives, vocabularies, and ideologies about <police power> and how stop-and-frisk practices were actually applied. People like Leroy Downs stood up to the existing structures and persisted toward changing them. The culture was ripe for a correction, and tensions were mounting.

<Justice> topped the list of social and political ideographs at the time, particularly in terms of *racial justice*. Recently, political science professor Juliet Hooker spoke on National Public Radio reflecting that in "the past 10 years, some of the moments where you see that the most amount of democratic energy and activity has been in movements for racial justice" (Baldwin, 2022). And she goes on, "These are the moments where you see ordinary citizens engaged in politics, trying to change policy, trying to address past wrongs." The collective social narrative concerning <police power> had certainly evolved.

This was the rhetorical culture of *David Floyd* – a strong specific example of which would be the Black Lives Matter (BLM) movement. BLM is committed to fighting racism, anti-Black violence, and police brutality. The vocabularies of BLM served to diminish societal beliefs about the necessity for broad <police power>. Most of that discourse appeared in the public sphere (though, as we will see, it made its way to the legal sphere in *David Floyd*). The BLM movement began in 2013 with the hashtag #BlackLivesMatter on social media after George Zimmerman was acquitted in the shooting death of Trayvon Martin, which occurred in February of 2012 (HUSL, 2023). The rhetorical culture pushed back hard against Florida's Stand Your Ground Law. Attorney Ben Crump described the public's swift reaction:

> More than 3.5 million people signed a Change.org petition. Basketball superstar LeBron James and the entire Miami Heat team tweeted a picture of themselves wearing Trayvon-style hoodies printed with the words: "We are all Trayvon," which was retweeted more than 5 million times. Thousands of young people occupied New York's Times Square for the Million Hoodie Rally. In a White House speech President Obama said, "This could have been my son." Trayvon Martin's story was the number-one news story in the world in 2012. (Crump, 2019, pp. 57–58)

It would be difficult to overestimate the importance of BLM and the Trayvon Martin case in the synchronic vocabularies of *David Floyd*. As we will see, Trayvon's name is embossed on the pages of the opinion itself, as are the words of President Obama's now famous speech.

President Obama spoke from the White House Press Room on July 19, 2013, concerning Trayvon's case. *David Floyd* was decided less than a month later on August 12. The Obama presidency (2009–2017) surrounds Trayvon's (and *David Floyd*'s) rhetorical culture; the President had been sworn in for his second term earlier that year. In his speech, he describes "a woman clutching her purse nervously" when a Black man joins her on the elevator, remarking, "That happens often" (National Archives, 2013). This and other experiences inform how the Black community views Trayvon's case, he says, and that "community is also knowledgeable that there is a history of racial disparities in the application of our criminal laws" (National Archives, 2013). This community and the hearers of these words create and operate within the social, synchronic vocabularies of *David Floyd*. The sordid history that led to this moment, and the contemporary cries for change in interpreting <police power> reverberating within it – all are imprinted on the pages of *David Floyd*.

* * *

> New Yorkers are rightly proud of their city and seek to make it as safe as the largest city in America can be. New Yorkers also treasure their liberty. Countless individuals have come to New York in pursuit of that liberty. The goals of liberty and safety may be in tension, but they can coexist – indeed the Constitution mandates it. (*Floyd v. City of New York*, 2013, p. 556)

These four sentences introduce Judge Scheindlin's opinion in *David Floyd*, which held the city liable for Fourth Amendment and Fourteenth Amendment violations arising out of the police department's widespread discrimination practices in the use of stop-and-frisk. In just these four sentences, an ideographic analysis reveals both diachronic and synchronic structures connected to American rhetorical culture, creating a persuasive vocabulary used to evolve <police power> to stop-and-frisk in response to evolutions in the culture that surrounds it.

The ideograph <liberty> is ever evolving in response to its meaning in contrast to other terms, such as <safety>. These terms necessarily connect to specific identifications with New York residents: “New Yorkers” coming to the “city in pursuit of liberty” mandated under the Constitution, “New Yorkers” wishing to “coexist” in “the largest city in America,” where “New Yorkers” are said to “treasure their liberty.” Sheindlin highlights New York's history as a safe haven of <liberty>, long protected by the Constitution, and she connects with a vibrant contemporary rhetorical culture of New Yorkers who are proud of their city and their freedoms under that Constitution. Of course, those are just the first four sentences.

The remainder of the introduction distances the opinion from the historical emphasis on “fighting crime,” mentioning the term just once throughout the entire case (*Floyd v. City of New York*, 2013, p. 557). And, in a subsequent paragraph, Scheindlin distances her opinion from the remnants of *Whren* and <high crime areas>, writing “[t]here is no basis for assuming that an innocent population share the same characteristics as the criminal suspect population in the same area” (p. 560). Scheindlin's initial privileging of <liberty> and distancing from vocabularies previously used to expand <police power> signals a shift in legal and cultural discourse surrounding stop-and-frisk jurisprudence. The remainder of the opinion does not disappoint that expectation.

Admittedly, the opinion becomes more persuasive with citation to legal precedent, which we have already seen to be riddled with ideographs. This is necessary to the practice of law. Others interrogating legal texts through an ideographic analysis similarly recognize that “when a significant change in the rhetorical culture occurs, the legal system ... must adhere to old vocabularies that inadequately encompass new situations” (Hasian et al., 1996, pp. 326). For example, identifying with the historical goals of <police power> centered on deterrence, Scheindlin acknowledges that “police will deploy their resources to high crime areas,” and that there are “benefits [to] communities where the need for policing is greatest” (*Floyd v. City of New York*, 2013, pp. 562–563). The legal precedent in *David Floyd* traces through the early vocabularies of <police power> and stop-and-frisk jurisprudence described previously. Beginning with the Fourth Amendment and working quickly through *Terry*, Scheindlin employs *Bostick*, *Warlow*, and *De Bour* to define stop-and-frisk law under the Fourth Amendment – just as we did before.

However, the notable synchronic interpretations of key terms in *David Floyd* significantly outnumber interpretations emphasizing their historical meanings. This is evident throughout Scheindlin's introduction, such as when discussing the “constitutionality of police behavior,” referencing the Supreme Court's concern for “community resentment” and “personal security,” espousing that “no one should live in fear,” and when acknowledging the need for improvements in fostering a community that is less “distrustful of the police” (*Floyd v. City of New York*, 2013, pp. 556–557). This language indicates to the contemporary reader a clear connection with the surrounding rhetorical culture – where BLM has begun to take shape, after Trayvon's killer was set free, and there is a strong sentiment among many in the

Black community that their children are not safe on the streets, not in spite of but because of <police power>.

While we read *David Floyd*, Scheindlin's antipathy for the stop-and-frisk practices of the NYPD becomes clear as she questions historical vocabularies that once supported expanding interpretations of <police power>. At times, she even seems incredulous. For example, when she remarks:

> One NYPD official has even suggested that it is permissible to stop racially defined groups just to instill fear in them that they are subject to being stopped at any time for any reason – in the hope that this fear will deter them from carrying guns in the streets. The goal of deterring crime is laudable, but this method of doing so is unconstitutional. (*Floyd v. City of New York*, 2013, p. 540)

At the time she is writing, the surrounding rhetorical culture is erupting with a similar incredulity that the law can be so devoid of racial <justice>. Scheindlin gives voice to these beliefs, and, by questioning deterrence practices that American rhetorical culture once praised, she creates a more persuasive demand for change.

The remainder of the case highlights many terms ("a vocabulary of ideographs"), including <liberty>, <high crime area>, and <furtive movements>. Stop-and-frisk opponents often home in on these terms in their critiques, noting the "ready vocabulary of rote platitudes that courts routinely accept as sufficient to show reasonable suspicion" (Gray, 2017, p. 279). These are the terms officers learned to incorporate into their vocabularies to bolster their authority to stop-and-frisk.

Some terms were even provided in a checklist on official forms, for example NYPD's Unified Form 250, which includes "furtive movements," "high crime area," "appropriate attire," and a "suspicious bulge" (Gray, 2017, p. 279). Officers need only check the correct term to justify their behavior. In *David Floyd*, Scheindlin posits that the number of NYPD stops from 2004 to 2012 that lacked reasonable suspicion is likely higher than 200,000 based upon that fact that "'furtive movements,' 'high crime area,' and 'suspicious bulge' are vague and subjective terms" (*Floyd v. City of New York*, 2013, p. 559). These terms, with elastic meanings, sometimes inhibit the clear articulation and implementation of the law, even if they also provide the law room to grow.

The trouble with <furtive movements> is particularly illustrative. <Furtive movements> can purportedly indicate criminal activity is afoot. While exemplifying inadequacies in NYPD training, Scheindlin describes one officer's testimony that "furtive movement is a very broad concept" (*Floyd v. City of New York*, 2013, p. 561). The ideographic nature of <furtive movements> is itself described in this portion of the opinion, as Scheindlin seems to question the law's commitment to this language. Language once customary and supportive of expanding <police power> to stop-and-frisk is viewed within the context of an evolving rhetorical culture and has lost nearly all meaning. According to officers, the term can include:

> a person "changing direction," "walking in a certain way," "[a]cting a little suspicious," "making a movement that is not regular," being "very fidgety," "going in and out of his pocket," "going in and out of a location," "looking back and forth constantly," "looking over their shoulder," "adjusting their hip or their belt," ... "hanging out in front of [a] building, sitting on the benches or something like that" and then making a "quick movement," such as "bending down and quickly standing back up," "going inside the lobby ... and then quickly coming back out," or "all of a sudden becom[ing] very nervous, very aware." (*Floyd v. City of New York*, 2013, p. 561)

The unsettled meaning of the term perhaps explains why there is a disconnect in the NYPD's application of stop-and-frisk law and a need for evolution in the law; the vocabulary of <police power> seems to have expanded into obscurity. As Scheindlin bemoans, "it is no surprise that stops so rarely produce evidence of criminal activity" (*Floyd v. City of New York*, 2013, p. 561).

David Floyd further provides descriptions of <furtive movements> as vague, subjective, and potentially "affected by unconscious racial biases" (*Floyd v. City of New York*, 2013, p. 578). Similarly, the term "fits description" is found troubling because it can be used to describe a large part of the population, "such as black males between the ages of 18 and 24" (*Floyd v. City of New York*, 2013, p. 579). A <high crime area> is similarly problematic because it might include all of Queens or Staten Island, according to Scheindlin, who employs voices outside the legal community to help demonstrate unconscious biases, citing a research study in psychology, with "evidence that officers may be more likely to perceive a movement as indicative of criminality if the officer has been primed to look for signs that 'crime is afoot'" (*Floyd v. City of New York*, 2013, p. 581). Scheindlin's opinion systematically questions the vocabulary of <police power> to stop-and-frisk, highlighting inconsistencies between interpretations in American rhetorical culture and the law.

While discussing the notion that Black individuals are more suspicious looking somehow, Scheindlin makes more synchronic connections, quoting President Obama's personal experiences with stereotyping in his Trayvon Martin speech and Ekow Yankah's op-ed in the *New York Times* (*Floyd v. City of New York*, 2013, p. 587). The portion of Yankah's piece that Scheindlin chooses to include reads in part: "Mr. Martin's hoodie struck the deepest chord because we know that daring to wear jeans and a hooded sweatshirt too often means that the police or other citizens are judged to be reasonable in fearing you" (*Floyd v. City of New York*, 2013, p. 588). The image of "Mr. Martin's hoodie," which takes on its own ideographic nature, embosses a rich rhetorical identification within the opinion, and the pejorative use of "reasonable" demonstrates a clear shift in the term's typical connotation in legal discourse. Ultimately, this language transforms stop-and-frisk practices, reflecting a shift in the surrounding rhetorical culture's beliefs about <police power> and demonstrating the power of the ideograph at work.

The opinion closes with a final cultural reference: Charles Blow's article, "The Whole System Failed Trayvon Martin," from the *New York Times*. Blow writes: "The idea of universal suspicion without individual evidence ... is pervasive in policing policies ... regardless of the collateral damage done to the majority of innocents. It's like burning down a house to rid it of mice" (*Floyd v. City of New York*, 2013, p. 667). Employing this cultural language bolsters the opinion's persistent questioning and condemning of pervasive <police power>. The vocabulary of ideographs and related language use in *David Floyd* results in a transformation in how our legal system applies a lengthy and complex legal history surrounding stop-and-frisk practices. But the opinion reveals more than changes in the law; it reflects changes in the surrounding rhetorical culture. Turning the last page of the opinion feels something like walking on fresh-cut grass. The world is familiar and changed all the same. After cursorily mapping the ideographic structures, we are left with the sense that some ideographs – <police power>, <liberty>, <justice> – are forever changed with the inclusion of *David Floyd* in the textual archive of our rhetorical culture.

Yet, even with *David Floyd* now in rearview, some would argue that "stop and frisk programs leave citizens more vulnerable to police than to criminals" even today (Gray, 2017, p. 277). Undoubtedly, *David Floyd*'s vocabulary of ideographs responds to changes in the surrounding rhetorical culture. The introduction of stop-and-frisk practices and expanding <police power> once intimated increased protections and security for the public in efforts to curb crime and wage war on drugs. Years later, just as *David Floyd* came before the court, there had been profound shifts in American rhetorical culture, where people began to truly question the costs of these practices – costs related to terms with fluctuating meanings: ideographs, such as <liberty>, <privacy>, and <police power>.

The concerns of the rhetorical culture transformed as the evolving vocabulary of ideographs informed cultural beliefs and behaviors, and so the law's discursive identifications with that rhetorical culture adjusted to align. The plaintiffs in *David Floyd* did not oppose the constitutionality of the NYPD's stop-and-frisk law as a tool. Rather, they opposed inflexible interpretations of <police power> and the constitutionality of how the tool is used by the NYPD. Judge Scheindlin's opinion adjusts and aligns the law in this landmark stop-and-frisk case, but perhaps that is not enough, and the tool (stopping and frisking) itself is unreasonable.

10.4 CONCLUSION

In the end, the law, like any other discourse object, is constantly in a state of flux. Legal ideographs ebb and flow with meaning, just as their cultural counterparts do. In *David Floyd*, the pendulum of stop-and-frisk swings away from <police power> and toward personal <liberty>. Although the data may still be underreported (Center for Constitutional Rights, 2020), the NYPD recorded just 8,947 stops

(61 percent innocent, 10 percent white) in 2021 compared with 532,911 (89 percent innocent, 8 percent white) in 2013 (New York Civil Liberties Union, 2023). Despite a reverberation of racial <justice> running vibrantly through American rhetorical culture, "the hard truth is that under Fourth Amendment law, Black life is [still] undervalued" (Carbado, 2022, p. 20). Notwithstanding, the reduction in stops is significant. *David Floyd* offers hope, but discursive and cultural changes can nudge the pendulum stealthily backward. When people identify with repeated calls for <public safety> and <national security>, they begin to form warranted beliefs about <police power>; they are more easily persuaded to limit the scope of <liberty>, for example, in the name of <necessity> (Hasian, 2012). This is the delicate, powerful, and essential tension imbedded in the Fourth Amendment.

Ideographic analysis illuminates embedded tensions in any rhetorical situation. When we extend beyond that analysis and begin to deploy ideographs ourselves, we no longer merely *see*, we *do*; we generate productive tensions rather than simply highlight them. Ideographic analysis would be particularly useful in legal writing education and for the professional legal practitioner, whose purpose is to persuade by identifying long-standing precedent (a diachronic analysis) and arguing for change in a present circumstance.[5] Knowledge of contemporary social commitments to evolutions in legal discourse, coupled with a rich understanding of the history of their use, results in the most effective advocate.

Of course, advocacy extends well beyond the courthouse. Ideographs in the public sphere, in community writing, and, as we saw with BLM, on social media platforms are perhaps the most apparent in terms of changing social beliefs. Employing ideographs in these contexts could significantly change the landscape of American rhetorical culture. What's more, ideographic analysis provides similar benefits in the private sphere. A term (e.g., <family>) may take on an elastic meaning within a personal relationship. Describing the ideograph diachronically and synchronically would show whether extending or limiting the term's use is likely to create a collective commitment within that relationship.

McGee understood the ideograph's present importance. He saw that "even a complete [historical] description ... leaves little but an exhaustive lexicon understood etymologically and diachronically – and no ideally precise explanation of how ideographs function *presently*" (McGee, 1980, p. 12). After all, persuasion is kairotic – it is fit for a particular occasion, aimed at an opportune and decisive moment rather than for just any general context. While the most effective rhetor will not ignore the historical lexicon of ideographic uses, they must understand the present function of

[5] I am not the first to promote ideographic analysis in educational and professional capacities. Sinsheimer (2005) models an ideographic analysis that would develop a lawyer's critical thinking skills and develop legal writing skills.

ideographs to employ them persuasively. Here, we recognize ideographs as *forces*, because they move us to act, rather than as merely tools for analysis.

McGee's process provides a theoretical framework for describing and explaining material and symbolic environments, as well as their latent rhetorical tensions. He efficaciously crafted this framework, as evident in spans of ideographic analyses following the publication of his piece. Still, we can do more with ideographs than analyze and explain. Mapping ideographs provides a lens of awareness, but also an educational tool, a pattern for persuasion, and perhaps even an apparatus for change. The value of attending to evolutions in a vocabulary of ideographs expands beyond mere academic musings on the intersections of law and rhetoric across time (although that can be diverting). People identify with this vocabulary in such a way that it influences what they think and how they act. That's powerful in any situation. Yet, despite several decades of ideographic inquiry, many simply gloss over the ideograph's potency in favor of the <safety> of analysis. Perhaps it is time to recirculate the argument that ideographs are *forces* of social commitment, conflict, and control.

REFERENCES

Allgayer, S., & Kanemoto, E. (2021). The <three Cs> of Japan's pandemic response as an ideograph. *Frontiers in Communication*, 6, 1–10.

Baldwin, R. (2022, February 26). *Trayvon Martin's killing 10 years ago changed the tenor of democracy*. NPR.org.

Burke, K. (1950). *A rhetoric of motives*. University of California Press.

Carbado, D. W. (2022). *Unreasonable: Black lives, police power, and the Fourth Amendment*. New Press.

Center for Constitutional Rights. (2020, May 6). NYPD continues to underreport use of stop and frisk; severe racial disparities persist. https://ccrjustice.org/home/press-center/press-releases/nypd-continues-underreport-use-stop-and-frisk-severe-racial [https://perma.cc/PDR2-NX6V]

Cicero, M. T. (1954). *Ad C. Herennium de ratione dicendi (Rhetorica ad Herennium)*. Harvard University Press.

Condit, C. M., & Lucaites, J. L. (1993). *Crafting equality: America's Anglo-African world*. University of Chicago Press.

Crump, B. (2019). *Open season: Legal genocide of colored people*. Harper Collins.

Cuomo, A. (2020). Constituting an audience against California state senate bill 48. *QED: A Journal in GLBTQ Worldmaking*, 7(1), 90–96.

David Floyd (see *Floyd v. City of New York*).

Florida v. Bostick, 501 U.S. 429 (1991).

Floyd v. City of New York, 959 F. Supp. 2d 540 (2013).

Gray, D. (2017). *The Fourth Amendment in an age of surveillance*. Cambridge University Press.

Gizzi, M. C., & Curtis, R. C. (2016). *The Fourth Amendment in flux*. University Press of Kansas.

Greenberg, I. (2011). Reagan revives FBI spying. *The 1980s: A critical and transitional decade*. Lexington Books.

Hasian, M. (2012). *In the name of necessity*. University of Alabama Press.

Hasian, M., Condit, C. M., & Lucaites, J. L. (1996). The rhetorical boundaries of "the law": A consideration of the rhetorical culture of legal practice and the case of the "separate but equal" doctrine. *Quarterly Journal of Speech*, 82(1), 323–342.

Hawkes, L. (2007). The impact of invasive web technologies on digital research. In H. McKee & D. N. DeVoss (Eds.), *Digital writing research: Technologies, methodologies, and ethical issues*. Hampton Press.

Head, L. (2018). Standing near(by) things decided: The rhetorical and cultural identifications of law. *Legal Communication & Rhetoric: JALWD*, 15, 189–207.

HUSL Library at Howard University School of Law. (2023, January 6). A brief history of civil rights in the United States: The Black Lives Matter movement. https://library.law.howard.edu/civilrightshistory/BLM [https://perma.cc/6DR3-874H]

Illinois v. Wardlow, 528 U.S. 119 (2000).

INS v. Delgado, 466 U.S. 210 (1984).

Jackson, J. (2014). *The 80 best TV shows of the 1980s*. Paste Magazine.

Jones, K. (2009). The persuasive function of the visual ideograph. In S. Barnes (Ed.), *Visual impact: The power of persuasion*. Hampton Press.

Kelling, G. L., & Wilson, J. Q. (1982). Broken windows: The police and neighborhood safety. *The Atlantic Monthly*, 249(3), 29–38.

Langford, C. L. (2015). On making <person>s: Ideographs of legal <person> hood. *Argumentation & Advocacy*, 52(2), 125–140.

McCann, B. J. (2007). Therapeutic and material <victim>hood: Ideology and the struggle of meaning in the Illinois death penalty controversy. *Communication and Critical/Cultural Studies*, 4(4), 382–401.

(2017). *The mark of criminality: Rhetoric, race, and gangsta rap in the war-on-crime era*. University of Alabama Press.

McDaniel, A. (2013). Obama-man: The fanboy ideograph for "hope and change." *International Journal of Comic Art*, 15, 338–353.

McGee, M. C. (1980). The "ideograph": A link between rhetoric and ideology. *Quarterly Journal of Speech*, 66(1), 1–16.

Merriman, S. (2011). The "real" right turn. In K. R. Moffitt & D. A. Campbell (Eds.), *The 1980s: A critical and transitional decade*. Lexington Books.

National Archives and Records Administration. (2013, July 19). Remarks by the president on Trayvon Martin. National Archives and Records Administration. https://obamawhitehouse.archives.gov/the-press-office/2013/07/19/remarks-president-trayvon-martin [https://perma.cc/5JTF-UUKN]

New York Civil Liberties Union. (2023, July 26). Stop-and-frisk data. www.nyclu.org/en/stop-and-frisk-data [https://perma.cc/TP6K-JVV5]

People v. De Bour, 40 NY2d 210 (1976).

Potter, J. (2014). Brown-skinned outlaws: An ideographic analysis of "illegals." *Communication, Culture, and Critique*, 7(2), 228–245.

Reagan, R. (1982a, October 3). Radio talk, vows drive against drugs. *The New York Times*. Reprint.

(1982b). Remarks announcing federal initiatives against drug trafficking and organized crime. White House Rose Garden, Washington DC Address, October 14, 1982.

Sibron v. New York, 392 U.S. 40 (1968).

Sinsheimer, A. (2005). The ten commandments as secular historic artifact or sacred religious text: Using Modrovich v. Allegheny County to illustrate how words create reality. *University of Maryland Law Journal of Race, Religion, Gender & Class*, 5, 325–350.

Terry v. Ohio, 392 U.S. 1 (1968).
Weiss, R. P. (2011). Privatizing the leviathan state: A "Reaganomic" legacy. In K. R. Moffitt & D. A. Campbell (Eds.), *The 1980s: A critical and transitional decade*. Lexington Books.
Whren v. United States, 517 U.S. 806 (1996).
Wilson, J. Q. (1983). Thinking about crime: The debate over deterrence. *The Atlantic Monthly*, 252(3), 72–88.

PART V

Law's Power to Exclude Voices

11

Framing the War on Drugs

Judith Butler and Legal Rhetorical Analysis

Erin Leigh Frymire

11.1 INTRODUCTION

Legal rhetorical study draws our attention to the constitutive power of legislation and judicial decisions. These documents not only establish legal precedent but mold our social and cultural realities via rhetorical and material means. Judith Butler's work explores this interaction between the rhetorical and the material, the discursive and the bodily. Though Butler is most widely known for their theories on gender (which certainly have important legal applications), I focus on Butler's later work on state power. In this work, Butler provides a theoretical framework for understanding law's constitutive power and its role in human lives. This framework can reveal how law constitutes social norms and how those in power deploy the law to protect those norms.

In this chapter, I use Butler's concepts of *frames of war* and *precarious life* to analyze the 1986 Anti-Drug Abuse Act (ADAA), which infamously mandated the same minimum sentence for the possession of 100 times as much powder cocaine as crack cocaine. The two forms of the drug are pharmacologically equivalent and yet, with this 100:1 ratio, they were (and still are) treated very differently by federal law. This difference is not chemical but social and rhetorical, as the two forms are associated with distinct socioeconomic and racial groups: powder cocaine with wealthy, white drug users and crack cocaine with poor, black drug users. Using Butler's theories to examine the ADAA and the contemporary political discourse on the War on Drugs, we can see how this law reinforced racist structures in the United States and how it gained public support.

After a brief introduction to Butler's body of work, particularly as it pertains to law, I turn to an overview of the ADAA, its features, and the legislative changes since it was passed in 1986. I then use Butler's frames of war and precarious life to demonstrate how these concepts shed light on the rhetorical strategies used by the state, as well as how they are useful in legal criticism more broadly. These concepts highlight not only the rhetorical strategies used within the ADAA and the political discourse surrounding it but also illuminate how the ADAA is itself a rhetorical strategy for reproducing norms and maintaining a racist status quo. This case demonstrates how Butler's work provides tools for legal criticism that can help us to understand law's social and cultural power, as well as its revolutionary potential to challenge the entrenched norms of racism and division.

11.2 BUTLER'S THEORETICAL FRAMEWORK

It is important first to elucidate central concepts in Butler's work: the formation of the subject and the function of cultural norms. For Butler, there is no a priori subject. Charlotte Chadderton, who examines how Butler's theories can be applied in the study of racism and education, explains that Butler sees the individual as "subjectivated, or rendered a subject, through norms and discourses. Identity is a normative ideal rather than a descriptive feature or experience" (Chadderton, 2018, p. 48). These "norms and discourses" come from the cultural, social, political – and legal – contexts surrounding the individual. As each person encounters these norms, they respond to them, and it is in this response that subjecthood forms.

Within their discussion of gender and identity formation, Butler explains how we act out gender and other aspects of identity as though acting out a play:

> The act that one does, the act that one performs, is, in a sense, an act that has been going on before one arrived on the scene. Hence, gender is an act which has been rehearsed, much as a script survives the particular actors who make use of it, but which requires individual actors in order to be actualized and reproduced as reality once again. (Butler, 1990, p. 272)

Thus, the "scripts" or norms of our cultural context constrain our performances and use us to maintain their power. It is by our acting out a "script" that the script lives on. Butler (2011, p. xxi) explains that "Performativity is thus not a singular 'act,' for it is always a reiteration of a norm or set of norms, and to the extent that it acquires an act-like status in the present, it conceals or dissimulates the conventions of which it is a repetition." Performativity, then, not only reifies the cultural codes in which we live, but also obscures these codes behind a façade of individual action or choice. The play we are performing may seem and feel original, because we are unconscious of the codes to which we are responding.

As in the construction of gender as a performative act, in which individuals enact (or reject) the cultural codes prescribed to them, Butler sees the formation of all aspects of self or subject in the same way. They explain that "in the first instance, a subject only becomes discrete through excluding other possible subject formations, a host of 'not-me's'" (Butler, 2008, p. 141). The subject is then formed by defining itself in contrast to others – choosing which "scripts" to perform and which to reject. By creating and performing these identifications and disidentifications, subjects define themselves, their gender, their race, and so on. In this process, "subject-positions are produced in and through a logic of repudiation and abjection, the specificity of identity is purchased through the loss and degradation of connection" (Butler, 2011, p. 114). The creation of identity is thus performed by the continued navigation of possible scripts.

Law is a uniquely powerful source of such scripts and norms. Unlike with most texts we encounter, legal interpretation, in Robert Cover's (1986, p. 1601) famous words, "takes place in a field of pain and death." It is this power of law over human lives that most concerns Butler. In Elena Loizidou's interpretation of Butler's views on law, she writes: "*[W]hen* the law and norms become one, or at least are presented as one ... then the possibility for survival as humans becomes delimited. A very small space for resistance remains" (Loizidou, 2007, p. 125). It is here in the human experience that Butler engages with the law. They write: "I am not interested in the rule of law per se, however, but rather in the place of law in the articulation of an international conception of rights and obligations that limit and condition claims of state sovereignty" (Butler, 2004, p. 98). This exploration of legal and state power and its limitation (or lack thereof) comprises much of Butler's work in recent decades.

Butler's work illuminates the broader function of discourse in determining the public's reaction to and interpretation of violence enacted by the state. In *Frames of War: When Is Life Grievable?*, Butler (2008) decries the suspension of habeas corpus and the many humanitarian abuses at Guantanamo Bay and other detention sites. Here, Butler helps us better understand how attitudes about war and the people involved are shaped rhetorically by the state. *Frames of War* focuses on the counter-terrorism policies of the United States post-9/11 and provides insight into how the idea of war functions rhetorically to gain public support. Generally, Butler uses *frames* to describe the social, cultural, and political norms that color our perspectives. It is the frame of war that leads us to interpret an act of violence in a state-sanctioned military action differently from how we might interpret or define the same act in another context – say two soldiers shooting at one another in battle versus two civilians shooting at one another in a personal conflict. We understand these two actions in different ways, use different terms to describe them, and apply different moral codes to evaluate them. The former, one might call battle, an act of patriotic duty; the latter, one might call murder, an act of evil criminality. Butler argues that "the frame works both to preclude certain kinds of questions, certain kinds of historical inquiries, and to function as a moral justification for retaliation" (Butler, 2008, p. 4). In essence, imposing the frame of war alters the moral and ethical rules by which we judge an event, policy, or action.

In a related work, *Precarious Life: The Powers of Mourning and Violence*, Butler (2004) focuses on the mechanism by which social hierarchies and divisions are established and maintained. One such mechanism, crucial to the frame of war, is the theory of precarious life. Butler (2008, p. 15) defines precariousness as the awareness of the fragility and value of life: "Precisely because a living being may die, it is necessary to care for that being so that it may live. Only under conditions in which the loss would matter does the value of the life appear." All humans die, yet not all human lives are viewed as precarious or protected from that precarity. Lives that the cultural, social, and legal structures seek to protect from precarity are those considered grievable. Butler explains that the "apprehension of grievability precedes and makes possible the apprehension of precarious life. Grievability precedes and makes possible the apprehension of the living being as living, exposed to non-life from the start" (Butler, 2008, p. 15). So, a life is only truly considered a life if its death would be grieved. The mosquito you reflexively squash when it bites you is not considered (by most people) a grievable life. Yes, we recognize that it was alive and is now dead, but that death is not grieved – it may even be celebrated, as the mosquito's life may be a threat to the human. However, cultures do not equate grievability with humanity. Cultural scripts, including and especially those in the law, enshrine the grievability of some human lives while denying the grievability of others, deeming them threats to the grievable population.

The lines separating the precarious lives from those not valued are created by establishing boundaries of disidentification. One draws these lines by choosing to recognize certain people or groups and by disavowing others. Butler (2011, p. 114) explains that the "repeated repudiation by which the subject installs its boundary . . . is not a buried identification that is left behind in a forgotten past, but an identification that must be leveled and buried again and again, the compulsive repudiation by which the subject incessantly sustains his/her boundary." If we apply this view of individual subjecthood to our national identity, we can see how identifications and disidentifications have been continuously performed. This need for "repeated repudiation" has driven the various American institutions that have upheld the norms of race and racism (slavery, segregation, mass incarceration) and "sustained" traditional "boundaries." Thus, Butler can help us understand how, despite social and legal progress, the racist disidentifications central to many of our cultural norms persist. Each time one form of dehumanization and segregation loses its legal status, another rises to take its place and maintain the boundaries of precarious, grievable life.

It is this reestablishment of boundaries that we see rhetorically enacted in the ADAA. This law did not solve our drug problem, but it did reestablish black Americans as an ungrievable population. In the dehumanizing political discourse surrounding the War on Drugs and in the mass incarceration of poor black and minority Americans, the ADAA is a new performance of a familiar script. The ADAA may be considered a failure in curbing drug use and related crime, but it was a rhetorical success in shoring up racial boundaries in the late twentieth century. After the gains of the 1960s, the ADAA redrew lines that had begun to blur, creating a revised system of division and disidentification. Butler can help us better understand this reestablishment of the racist norms expressed in (and imposed by) the ADAA as a performative, rhetorical act of federal law that defines national identity.

11.3 THE ADAA

Butler's concern for legal matters is ultimately a concern for the human beings on which the law operates. In Loizidou's (2007, p. 89) reading, Butler "is asking foremost about its [law's] place in relation to the question of life. Can it, in other words, promote and sustain a mode of life that is livable and viable?" As a powerful expression of cultural norms, law plays a role in the formation of us as individual subjects and of our national identity. In this way, the law – and the norms it expresses – can indeed help us create "a mode of life that is livable" for everyone, or one that continues to be "livable and viable" only for select groups. The 1986 ADAA is a clear example of legislation that has made life "livable and viable" for only some segments of the population. Legislation that was supposed to target high-level offenders instead became one of the engines driving mass incarceration.

For most of the twentieth century, prison rates were largely stable, at about 110 prisoners per every 100,000 people. However, from 1975 to 2005, incarceration rates in the United States more than quadrupled (Raphael & Stoll, 2009a, p. 3). Such a drastic increase in imprisonment would seem to indicate a significant increase in crime, yet the opposite is true. Crime rates were actually much higher in the early twentieth century than in later decades. Increased rates of incarceration were tied not to crime but to policy. Indeed, in "all but one crime category, the policy variables accounted for nearly 90 percent of the increase in incarceration rates" (Weiman & Weiss, 2009, p. 74). The policy changes that resulted in this drastic increase in incarceration included harsher drug laws and severe restrictions on judicial discretion. These tougher policies did coincide with other shifts, such as "changes in illicit drug markets, the deinstitutionalization of the mentally ill, [and] the declining labor-market opportunities for low-skilled men" (Raphael & Stoll, 2009b, p. 28). However, though they are significant, "the collective influence of these factors is minor relative to the impact of changes in sentencing and corrections policy choices" (p. 28).

The transformation of drug laws began in New York in the 1970s with the imposition of the Rockefeller laws, which ushered in similar measures across the country. Though the War on Drugs has been supported by both sides of the aisle, the 1981–1989 Reagan administration prioritized stricter federal drug laws, resulting in "mandatory prison sentences of five years for drug possession of shockingly small amounts (for example, 5 grams of crack cocaine)" (Clear, 2007, p. 51). Drug possession and small-scale distribution had previously been relatively minor crimes. For example, the sale of one ounce of cocaine or heroin used to be a class C felony offense. During the 1980s, these crimes were upgraded to a class A-1 drug felony, which is on the same level as "homicide, first-degree kidnapping, and arson" (Weiman & Weiss, 2009, p. 86). Therefore, individuals convicted of previously minor drug offenses began to be sentenced to lengthy prison terms, and drug crimes were implicitly likened to violent offenses such as murder and arson.

The ADAA is the legal centerpiece of the War on Drugs at the federal level. Its infamously harsh and uneven mandatory minimums continue to reverberate today. Prior to the late 1980s, the maximum sentence for any drug possession charge was one year (Alexander, 2012, p. 54). In fact, the Comprehensive Drug Abuse Prevention and Control Act of 1970 repealed mandatory minimums for most drug crimes (United States Sentencing Commission [USSC], 2011, p. 22), but this was reversed by a series of state and federal legislative changes following the Rockefeller laws. The ADAA reached new extremes that greatly expanded the carceral state by increasing the number of prisoners as well as the length of their sentences via mandatory minimums. Just prior to the ADAA, in 1984, Congress passed the Sentencing Reform Act. It eliminated parole in the federal system and established the United States Sentencing Commission (USSC), which is tasked with developing sentencing guidelines to counter bias in judicial discretion (Osler & Bennett, 2014, p. 121). The ADAA was partially the result of the USSC's work. The intent of implementing mandatory minimums was to erase judicial bias and sentencing discrepancies (p. 121). However, rather than avoid bias, the ADAA mandated it. A salient feature of this law is the extreme disparity; there is a 100:1 ratio of powder to crack cocaine in the amounts that trigger the same mandatory prison sentence. This disparity falls conspicuously along racial lines; most of those convicted of crack cocaine crimes were (and are) black. Black crack offenders made up 91.4 percent of all crack offenders in 1992 and 87.4 percent in 2000 (USSC, 2002, p. 62).

The harsh punishments in the ADAA were increased in the subsequent Anti-Drug Abuse Act of 1988, which created a five-year mandatory minimum for simple possession of crack (Osler & Bennett, 2014, p. 134). In addition to further expanding the quantity and length of prison sentences, the 1988 Act is also significant for establishing crack as the *only* substance for which simple possession triggers a mandatory sentence. These minimum sentences in the ADAA were legally mandatory until 2005. In the landmark case *United States v. Booker*, the Supreme Court altered the guidelines from mandatory to advisory. Legislative action, however, did not come until the Fair Sentencing Act of 2010, which changed the powder-to-crack ratio to 18:1 and got rid of minimum sentences for simple possession of crack – though it also created twelve new enhancements (Osler & Bennett, 2014, p. 158). Since 1994, there has also been a safety valve that can result in a lesser sentence if a first-time offender meets a list of criteria, but for the most part, the ADAA mandatory minimums decide the defendant's fate, not the judge. This is especially true for crack defendants, who "are less likely to receive the benefit of the safety valve than any other drug type" (Bennett, 2014, p. 882).

The problems in the ADAA have not gone unnoticed. The law that was supposed to target high-level traffickers has instead imprisoned everyday crack users. In 2002, the USSC reported that 79 percent of federal crack cocaine offenders had not performed the trafficking functions "described in the legislative history of the 1986 Act" (USSC, 2002, p. vii). Furthermore, the racial divide has been widely criticized.

In its 1995 report, the USSC recommended that Congress reconsider the 100:1 ratio, and in its reports to Congress in 1997, 2002, and 2007, it explicitly called for a revised 1:1 powder-to-crack ratio. While the USSC declared in 1997 that "there is no evidence of racial bias" and in 2002 that "this assertion [of racist motives] cannot be scientifically evaluated," the racial bias in the mechanized law is all too apparent if one considers the demographics associated with the two forms of cocaine. The reasoning for the distinction between crack and powder cocaine was the perception (or misperception) about the drugs and the contexts in which they circulated. In their 1997 report to Congress, the USSC explained that "crack cocaine is more often associated with systemic crime – crime related to its marketing and distribution – particularly the type of violent street crime so often connected with gangs, guns, serious injury, and death" (USSC, 1997, p. 4). These "associations," however, have proven to be incorrect when examined. In 2000 (during which the 100:1 ratio was still mandatory), only a quarter of federal crack offenders had any weapon and just 2.3 percent actually fired a weapon (USSC, 2002, p. vii).

In their discussion of the ADAA, legal scholar Mark Osler and retired federal judge Mark W. Bennett explain that at the center of these sentencing policies is "the myth that most of the Guidelines, including the drug guidelines, are based on empirical historical data, alleged special expertise of the Sentencing Commission, and the Sentencing Commission's exercise of its characteristic institutional role – when in fact they are not" (Osler & Bennett, 2014, p. 156). Racist attitudes permeate the construction and reviews of the ADAA, as well as its implementation. On top of the imbalanced regulations, black defendants "were indicted and convicted at much higher rates than whites ... and they were more likely to receive longer sentences" (Weiman & Weiss, 2009, p. 84). Even traffickers are sentenced differently: Street-level crack dealers receive sentences 300 times more severe than higher-level powder importers (Bennett, 2014, p. 894). As the USSC wrote in its 2002 report to Congress, the "overwhelming majority of offenders subject to the heightened crack cocaine penalties are black, about 85 percent in 2000" (USSC, 2002, p. viii). The years following the ADAA saw an immense spike in the incarceration of black men that continues today – all enabled by a simple, seemingly innocuous list of weights.

11.4 FRAMES OF WAR

The 1986 ADAA was a key weapon in the War on Drugs. This concept of a "war" on drugs and the use of explicitly militaristic discourse in discussions of drug policy may now seem so normal to us as to go unnoticed, but this ubiquity makes it all the more worthy of our consideration. Butler's discussion of the frame of war is therefore especially relevant to our analysis of the ADAA, as it became the cornerstone of the federal *War* on Drugs. The very term *War* tells us how to understand the issue – which frame to use. Other possible frames – such as "drug-related crimes" or "public health crisis" – would create a very different set of norms through which to interpret and evaluate the phenomenon itself as well at the state's reaction.

In the case of the ADAA, President Reagan and other officials have used the frame of war to gain public support for their efforts to maintain normative disidentifications. However, this frame is not merely a convenient metaphor to inspire public support. The frame of war not only sells the ADAA, it ideologically produces the ADAA and other legal manifestations of racial division. In other words, the strategic frame of war functions not only in the campaign to gain support for the legislation – it functions also in the mindset that created the ADAA and laws like it. These laws are themselves rhetorical tools for communicating ideologically and materially with the American people. The ideological motivation becomes clearer when we consider that the War on Drugs – presented as a response to a crisis – actually predates (and, some argue, created) that crisis. The notion of a "War on Drugs" began during the Nixon administration but hit its stride during Reagan's presidency. Curiously, as Michelle Alexander explains, the timeline demonstrates that "President Ronald Reagan officially announced the current drug war in 1982, before crack became an issue in the media or a crisis in poor black neighborhoods … The Reagan administration hired staff to publicize the emergence of crack cocaine in 1985 as part of a strategic effort to build public and legislative support for the war" (Alexander, 2012, p. 5). The crack epidemic began in poor, urban neighborhoods *after* the announcement of the War on Drugs, which emphasizes the War itself as a strategic rhetorical move rather than a practical response.

We see Reagan deploying the frame of war in speeches given around the passing of the ADAA. On September 14, 1986, six weeks before the signing, President Reagan and Nancy Reagan addressed the nation from the White House. The speech proclaims the dire need for a "crusade against drugs." Reagan declares that the "American people want their government to get tough and to go on the offensive. And that's exactly what we intend, with more ferocity than ever before" (Reagan, 1986, para. 4). Here we see the militaristic diction expanding beyond the title of the war to describe going "on the offensive" with "ferocity." Even moments that suggest another possible frame are quickly pulled back into war. Reagan says, "Today there's a new epidemic: smokable cocaine, otherwise known as crack" (para. 6). Here, "epidemic" seems to gesture toward a public health frame, but he immediately returns to the military language by following with "It is an explosively destructive and often lethal substance which is crushing its users. It is an uncontrolled fire" (para. 6). The likening of crack to explosives here positions the drug itself as a weapon of war. If crack is a "crushing," "lethal" weapon that has been deployed on American soil, a War on Drugs is the only possible recourse.

The frame of war is reinforced by the comparison of the War on Drugs to other conflicts in US history. In the 1986 address delivered with Nancy, Reagan explicitly links the War on Drugs to World War II and the Civil War. In calling for support, he says, "My generation will remember how America swung into action when we were attacked in World War II. . . . Well, now we're in another war for our freedom, and it's time for all of us to pull together again" (Reagan, 1986, para. 20). Later on, he comments that he's just down the hall from the Lincoln Bedroom, which Lincoln used as his office during the Civil War. He muses, "Memory fills that room, and more than anything that memory drives us to see vividly what President Lincoln sought to save" (para. 28). Here, crack is figured not as an "epidemic" but as an enemy force. Crack is Nazi Germany or civil war, and we all must band together to support the state's efforts toward victory.

If crack is an "explosive" deployed by the enemy, the ADAA is the defensive wall thrown up against it. The frame of war manifested quite literally in earlier versions of the bills that became the ADAA. The first version that passed in the House included "a death penalty provision, which would have applied to major drug dealers who committed murder" and "required deploying the military to stop drug smuggling at the borders" (Greenhouse, 1986, p. 1). These controversial elements were eliminated to secure Senate approval. Yet, even though these measures are not in the ADAA, we can see here how war is far more than convenient metaphor. The War on Drugs is imagined as an actual war, calling for military deployment and the killing of its enemies. Though these measures did not become part of the law, the majority of the House of Representatives supported them. In this frame of war, drugs (crack in particular) take on a level of danger that is beyond the risks to health and safety presented by any number of substances. In Butler's discussion of the suspension of rights for detainees in Guantanamo, they explain that "what counts as 'dangerous' is what is deemed dangerous by the state" (Butler, 2004, p. 76). This declaration of danger is what the state uses, in the case of the War on Terror, "for its own preemption and usurpation of the law" (p. 76). In the War on Drugs, the state is not suspending or transgressing the law, but using danger to create the law.

When seen through this frame of war, mandatory minimums are a necessary defensive strategy. Mandatory sentences have existed in the United States since its beginnings as a nation. However, they were formerly reserved for the most extreme crimes. The 1790 Crimes Act listed twenty-three such federal crimes, including "treason, murder, three offenses relating to piracy, forgery of a public security of the United States, and the rescue of a person convicted of a capital crime" (USSC, 2011, p. 7). Throughout their history, mandatory minimums have applied to crimes related to the conflicts of that period. During the Civil War, for example, mandatory minimums against Confederate allies were enacted – and it is worth noting that the minimum penalty for colluding with Confederates was only six months in prison, far shorter than minimum penalties for possessing 5 grams of crack under the ADAA (USSC, 2011, p. 13). Perhaps more important to observe is the implication of adding drug crimes to a list that formerly consisted of treasonous offenses; even low-level drug offenders are put on par with traitors and spies. The mandatory minimums solidify the War on Drugs as a true war.

The discursive efforts in the law and the speeches backing it were successful in gaining public support for the War on Drugs. Crime became a key concern for voters. As political scientist Marie Gottschalk notes, in polls during the mid-1990s, the public listed crime as a high concern, despite the fact that actual crime rates had dropped significantly (Gottschalk, 2006, p. 27). Politically popular "tough on crime" policies led politicians from both parties to support these measures, regardless of actual crime rates. This disconnect between crime rates and incarceration rates resulted in public misperception of the reality of crime that dramatically impacted policy: More prisoners implied more crime and justified harsher laws – leading to more prisoners.

Some scholars argue that such misperceptions were intentionally constructed, and some evidence suggests that the Nixon administration, whose second campaign heralded the "tough on crime" refrain that continues today (Clear, 2007, p. 50), intentionally used drug legislation to target minority communities. In a 2016 article for CNN, Tom LoBianco writes about a twenty-two-year-old interview with previously unreleased quotations from John Erlichman. Erlichman, who worked on domestic policy for the Nixon administration, stated: "We knew we couldn't make it illegal to be either against the war or black, but by getting the public to associate the hippies with marijuana and blacks with heroin. And then criminalizing both heavily, we could disrupt those communities" (LoBianco, 2016, para. 3). Though some contest this account, it is significant to see an insider so blatantly describe the use of drug policy as a means of social control.

The War on Drugs, foremost among so-called tough on crime efforts, was successful in maintaining this social control – provoking fear of crack users, as well as acceptance of the state's policies and practices. Even around the time the ADAA was on the floor, news coverage largely focused on the debate over the inclusion of death penalty measures and the political maneuvering to get the bill through the Senate. *New York Times* headlines covering the ADAA in the fall of 1986 state: "Issue of Financing the Key Obstacle for Antidrug Plan" (Roberts, 1986, p. A1) and "Congress Approves Anti-Drug Bill As Senate Bars a Death Provision" (Greenhouse, 1986, p. 1). The glaring disparity between two forms of the same substance was not spotlighted, nor were there accusations of racism. This lack of attention is perhaps a testament to the strength of the frame of war. As Gottschalk (2006, p. 19) explains, "the carceral state has been a largely invisible feature of American political development, not a contested site of American politics." I argue that it has not been a "contested site" because the frame of war has persuaded many to see incarcerated persons as the enemy. As cited above, Butler's frame of war "works both to preclude certain kinds of questions, certain kinds of historical inquiries, and to function as a moral justification for retaliation" (Butler, 2004, p. 4). We accept, and even welcome, things in the context of war that would be unimaginable in any other frame. The wartime rhetoric persuaded the American public to accept and support the ADAA and similar measures as necessary in combat. Butler's frame of war elucidates both the strategies used to garner support for the ADAA and how the ADAA is itself a rhetorical strategy seeking to persuade the American public how we ought to view drugs – and drug users.

11.5 PRECARIOUS LIFE

Using the frame of war has an important consequence that is crucial in understanding the ADAA and its rhetorical function. If the War on Drugs is indeed a war, then there must be an enemy. And that enemy is the drug user – especially the crack user. Alexander (2012, p. 105) explains that "although explicitly racial political appeals remained rare," in public discourse "the calls for 'war' at a time when the media was saturated with images of black drug crime left little doubt about who the enemy was in the War on Drugs and exactly what he looked like." The fear of drugs became an easy proxy for embedded cultural fears of racial minorities and black Americans in particular.

Here, Butler's concepts of grievability and precarious life can illuminate the state's rhetorical strategies. The question Butler poses is this: Which human lives are precarious? For not all are considered grievable according to cultural norms. To return to the frame of war, enemies in wartime are not grievable life. The fallen enemies are viewed not as precarious, grievable life but as a threat to such life. Thus, the frame of war divides "populations into those who are grievable and those who are not" (Butler, 2008, p. 38).

To kill an enemy while maintaining legal and moral authority, the state must transform the enemy into "ungrievable life." The War on Drugs, therefore, insists that drug users (especially black crack users) are ungrievable. This frame then reinforces the racist hierarchy. The black crack user is not merely an evil or enemy subject; they are not a human subject at all. The ADAA and the discourse of the War on Drugs draw clear boundaries between grievable and ungrievable lives to uphold the racist status quo that had been threatened by the progress of the mid-twentieth century.

These questions of who "matters" ring familiar to those of us in the age of the Black Lives Matter movement. In a *New York Times* blog with George Yancy, Butler speaks directly to this issue:

> If black lives do not matter, then they are not really regarded as lives, since a life is supposed to matter. So what we see is that some lives matter more than others, that some lives matter so much that they need to be protected at all costs, and that other lives matter less, or not at all. And when that becomes the situation, then the lives that do not matter so much, or do not matter at all, can be killed or lost, can be exposed to conditions of destitution, and there is no concern, or even worse, that is regarded as the way it is supposed to be. (Yancy & Butler, 2015, para. 2)

The last line here can help us understand the way in which racist policies tap into notions of grievable and ungrievable life. The ADAA can protect the majority (white) population from the enemy (black) crack user; therefore it is a moral and ethical tool according to our cultural norms and in the frame of war – it's "the way it is supposed to be."

The ADAA and the warlike discourse surrounding it draw clear lines between grievable and ungrievable life. In his remarks upon signing the ADAA into law, Reagan professes his concern and compassion for the drug user:

> We must be intolerant of drugs not because we want to punish drug users, but because we care about them and want to help them. This legislation is not intended as a means of filling our jails with drug users. What we must do as a society is identify those who use drugs, reach out to them, help them quit, and give them the support they need to live right. (Reagan, 1986, para. 2)

This statement of concern and assurance that the goal is to offer "help" and "support" rather than "filling our jails with drug users" is belied by the fact that the latter is precisely what the ADAA did. As a result of the ADAA and similar policy changes at the state level, the incarceration rate skyrocketed as prisons became overpopulated with nonviolent drug offenders. The number of people imprisoned for drug crimes in 2001 was ten times greater than it was in 1980 (Clear, 2007, p. 54). Put another way, in 1980, drug offenders made up 9 percent of all inmates; by 1988, they comprised 25.4 percent of the total prison population and 37 percent of new prisoners (Weiman & Weiss, 2009, p. 89). Even recently, in 2019, people incarcerated for drug offenses made up 46 percent of the total incarcerated population (both state and federal) (The Sentencing Project, 2021, p. 9) and at the time of writing, 45.2 percent of people in federal prisons were incarcerated for drug offenses (Federal Bureau of Prisons, 2022, Chart 1). Despite Reagan's assurances, the United States has indeed been "filling our jails with drug users" for decades.

Furthermore, Reagan's assurance of sympathy for the drug user is at odds with the vilification in the rest of his remarks. He states: "I ask each American to be strong in your intolerance of illegal drug use and firm in your commitment to a drug-free America. United, together, we can see to it that there's no sanctuary for the drug criminals who are pilfering human dignity and pandering despair" (Reagan, 1986, para. 5). The idea that drug criminals are "pilfering human dignity" implies that they are outside of this category of human – that they are a group apart. This image of criminals taking advantage of the "despair" of others implies that Reagan is directing his anger exclusively toward drug *dealers* – as the ADAA indeed promised to do. However, despite his claims that this new policy is aimed at high-level dealers, he makes no such distinction in stating, "Drug abuse is a repudiation of everything America is" (Reagan & Reagan, 1986, para. 23). Here, drug use itself – and by implication the drug user – is un-American. There is a "repudiation" here of the drug user (not only the dealer) as fundamentally *not* us, *not* American, and *not* a valued human person. Particularly in the late Cold War context during which these remarks were made, to be un-American was to be a wartime enemy – and a wartime enemy is not a grievable life.

Two years after the ADAA was passed, in a radio address on economic growth and the War on Drugs (perhaps a telling juxtaposition), Reagan uses even stronger dehumanizing language. Reagan (1988, para. 4) avows that "we will no longer tolerate those who sell drugs and those who buy drugs. All Americans of good will are determined to stamp out those parasites who survive and even prosper by feeding off the energy and vitality and humanity of others." Here, not only drug sellers but also users are "parasites" who are "feeding off" of "humanity." Quite explicitly, drug users are not human; furthermore, they are a danger to and enemy of humanity. In this way, drug users are crafted into what Butler (2008, p. 31) describes as "populations [that] are 'lose-able' ... cast as threats to human life as we know it rather than as living populations in need of protection." The ADAA itself may be less colorful in its language but is just as clear in establishing who this enemy, this "threat to human life," is. The drug user, yes, but the most dangerous enemy is specifically the crack user. The ADAA's most infamous provisions, the wildly disparate mandatory minimums for crack and powder cocaine, are stated thus:

> (1) (A) In the case of a violation of subsection (a) of this section involving – ...
>
> (ii) 5 kilograms or more of a mixture or substance containing a detectable amount of –
>
> (I) coca leaves, except coca leaves and extracts of coca leaves from which cocaine, ecgonine, and derivatives of ecgonine or their salts have been removed ...
>
> (iii) 50 grams or more of a mixture or substance described in clause (ii) which contains cocaine base ...
>
> such person shall be sentenced to a term of imprisonment which may not be less than 10 years or more than life. (ADAA, 1986, p. 2)

The subsequent section is identical, except for the amounts: 500 grams of cocaine or 5 grams of cocaine base results in a prison sentence not less than five years (p. 3). The ADAA states that "such person shall be sentenced to a term of imprisonment which may not be less than 10 years or more than life and if death or serious bodily injury results from the use of such substance shall be not less than 20 years or more than life" (p. 2). The enemy, or "such person," is defined primarily by the quantities and substances listed in the ADAA. Racial categories are, of course, absent from these descriptions. Yet we see how the drug user is framed as already violent, since the added penalty for "death or serious bodily injury" simply doubles the penalty attached to the substance alone. Imposing the severest penalties on crack users implies that they are the worst on the list, and the American public in 1986 and today knows who the implied crack user is.

These perceptions of crack as more dangerous and its trade more violent than its more expensive counterpart do not come from empirical data. Instead, they are directly indicative of racist attitudes toward the users of crack cocaine. Due to cost differences and relative availability, crack cocaine has been used more often by poor minorities, whereas powder cocaine has more often been used by wealthier whites (Alexander, 2012, p. 53). As this was the case prior to the ADAA, it is doubtful that Congress members could have been unaware of the demographic implications of their legislation. Therefore, the logical conclusion, as Clear (2007, p. 55) states, is that "the rules regarding drug-law enforcement were gerrymandered to show an even greater bias against poor minorities." This is one of the many patterns of bias within the legal system, which Yancy and Butler (2015, para. 24) argue "is engaged in reproducing whiteness when it decides that the black person can and will be punished more severely than the white person who commits the same infraction." A law that effectively allowed white drug offenders to have 100 times more of the same substance as black offenders to earn the same punishment draws a clear boundary between the lives that are precarious and grievable and those that are not.

As we consider the ADAA, we can see how it is this division, and not the purported efforts to target high-level players in the drug trade, that is its function. The ADAA does not allow consideration for one's role in the drug trade but is based entirely on weight. Osler and Bennett (2014, p. 164) describe these mandatory minimums as "a foolishness based on a lie, that lie being that the weight of narcotics at issue serves as a valid proxy for the relative culpability of a defendant." Foolishness indeed, if the goal is to dismantle the drug trade from the top. If, as Reagan says, the "legislation is not intended as a means of filling our jails with drug users," it was a colossal failure. However, if the goal is to maintain a white supremacist status quo, then the ADAA has been a rousing success. Black crack users are rhetorically constructed as the enemies in a War on that is excusing the state's policies. The ungrievable lives of "enemy" black drug users file into the prison system, maintaining the normative racial hierarchy that the ADAA reproduces.

11.6 REPRODUCING NORMS

Thus, the ADAA is another script that defines who is cast as an American citizen and who is left off the list. It is yet another rhetorical mechanism for delineating grievability along color lines. As Butler (2008, p. 24) explains, "Forms of racism instituted and active at the level of perception tend to produce iconic versions of populations who are eminently grievable, and others whose loss is no loss, and who remain ungrievable." Crowding the prison system with black drug users is "no loss" but instead necessary in the "war" to protect the grievable population. Sociologist Loïc Wacquant similarly argues that mass incarceration and other oppressive institutions are "instruments for the conjoint *extraction of labor* and *social ostracization* of an outcast group deemed unassimilable" (Wacquant, 2000, p. 379). The boom in imprisonment that began in the 1970s and hit its stride in the 1980s has overwhelmingly affected young black men from disadvantaged urban areas who have been targeted by the legal actions that created mass incarceration. Other racial minority groups and the urban poor more generally have also been impacted. Even with the subsequent changes to the ADAA, and the overall decrease in incarceration rates since they reached a peak in 2009, these disparities continue. The Bureau of Justice Statistics reports that 1,182,166 people were sentenced (in state or federal courts) to a prison term of more than one year in 2020. Of this group, 389,500 (30 percent) were black, 275,300 (23 percent) were Hispanic, and 358,900 (30 percent) were white (Carson, 2021, p. 10). We can better understand the significance of these ratios by comparing them to the United States as a whole. The 2020 US Census found that those identifying as black or African American (alone or in combination with other racial identities) make up 14.2 percent of the total population (Jones et al., 2021). Put another way, the imprisonment rates in the year 2020 were 223 per 100,000 white Americans and 1,234 per 100,000 black Americans (Carson, 2021, p. 14).

As Alexander (2012) and many other scholars have discussed, mass incarceration is yet another policy in a long line of efforts to maintain white supremacy in the United States. Slavery, segregation, and incarceration have all been efforts to deny the precarity of black American lives. Alexander concludes that "what has changed since the collapse of Jim Crow has less to do with the basic structure of our society than with the language we use to justify it. . . . Rather than rely on race, we use our criminal justice systems to label people of color 'criminals' and then engage in all the practices we supposedly left behind" (Alexander, 2012, p. 2). They are performances of the same script of racial hierarchy, seeking to define American identity by disidentifying from black Americans. In their explanation of frames of war, Butler (2008, p. 24) explains that all "frames are subject to an iterable structure – they can only circulate by virtue of their reproducibility, and that very reproducibility introduces a structural risk for the identity of the frame itself. The frame breaks with itself in order to reproduce itself, and its reproduction becomes the site where a politically consequential break is possible." Each norm that has been "broken" (slavery, segregation) has opened up a "politically consequential" moment, an opportunity to create new norms and frames. As Wacquant (2000, p. 384) observes, "by the end of the 1970s, then, as the racial and class backlash against the democratic advances won by the social movements of the preceding decade got into full swing, the prison abruptly returned to the forefront of American society and offered itself as the universal and simplex solution to all manners of social problems." Mass incarceration resulting from the War on Drugs, in that it targets primarily nonviolent offenders, functions not to preserve public safety, but to remove huge percentages of black and other minority populations from free society. This removal reinforces norms of precarious life and the racist boundaries between those lives that are grievable and those that are not. Therefore, mass incarceration of black and other minority Americans following the ADAA and similar legislation is itself rhetorical.

The incarceration and subsequent absence of those people from American families, neighborhoods, and towns or cities rhetorically shapes the nation and who comprises it.

11.7 CHALLENGING NORMS

Through the example of the ADAA and the surrounding discourse of the War on Drugs, we have seen how Butler's concepts of frames of war and precarious life enable us to interpret the law and its role in reproducing cultural norms and boundaries. The frame of war denies the precariousness of black lives as the state works to shape our views of one another. However, Butler (2008, p. 5) also argues that "what we are able to apprehend is surely facilitated by norms of recognition, but it would be a mistake to say that we are utterly limited by existing norms of recognition when we apprehend a life." We are deeply affected by the norms surrounding us, but we are not wholly determined by them. We can choose to challenge, adapt, or reject these norms. Indeed, this resistance is key to the formation of one's self and one's agency. The norms of racism supported by the ADAA seem insurmountable, because they have been so entrenched in our cultural, political, and social experiences. In their discussion of sex, Butler (2011, p. xix) explains that

> As a sedimented effect of a reiterative or ritual practice, sex acquires a naturalized effect, and, yet, it is also by virtue of this reiteration that gaps and fissures are opened up as the constitutive instabilities in such constructions, as that which escapes or exceeds the norm, as that which cannot be wholly defined or fixed by the repetitive labor of that norm.

Other identity categories and cultural concepts, like race, have become similarly "sedimented." What now appears to be solid stone is in fact the compressed layers of "ritual practice" performed over and over. Yet this sediment is not as stable as it may appear. As with the frame of war, these norms must be "reiterated" again and again, but these reiterations open "gaps and fissures" – opportunities for us to question these norms.

In this, I believe that Butler's work is not only useful in social and legal critique, but also in developing a productive, critical optimism. They tell us that "the problem is not merely how to include more people within existing norms, but to consider how existing norms allocate recognition differentially. What new norms are possible, and how are they wrought?" (Butler, 2008, p. 6). If norms – including those enforced by law – are ultimately shaped by our own performative acts, then these norms are rhetorically constructed. This recognition is always an empowering one, as anything we have created through discourse can thus be amended, altered, or overturned by discourse. Despite their criticism of law, Butler also sees law's discursive possibilities. Loizidou (2007, p. 125) explains that "law … becomes for Butler the only vehicle for resistance and, specifically through the practice of the trial, the only force for dissent." Though I don't see law as the only such vehicle, it is an undeniably powerful and far-reaching mechanism. Laws like the ADAA play a powerful role in shaping norms and performances as well as materially impacting our lives.

Just as Butler's ideas can help us interpret our legal history, they can also shed light on our current moment. In the last few years, restrictions on voting rights, which once seemed like a pre-Civil Rights artifact, have made a significant resurgence. Butler can aid us in seeing this resurgence as yet another performance of the script of white supremacy and to understand these moves as ultimately rhetorical rather than a response to a practical problem. According to researchers with the Brennan Center for Justice at NYU School of Law, nearly 400 restrictive voting bills were introduced in legislatures across the United States in 2021 and early 2022. In an extensive study, they found that, while the majority of these bills are Republican-sponsored, not every Republican-controlled state has seen the introduction of restrictive voting laws; instead, restrictive voting laws are "most prevalent in states where they [Republicans] have control *and where there are significant non-white populations*." Legislators who introduce such bills are "concentrated in the whitest parts of the most diverse states" (Morris, 2022, para. 32). In addition to this demographic analysis, the Brennan Center included data from the 2020 Cooperative Election Study, which found that these areas in which the restrictive voting bills were concentrated also had high racial resentment scores (Morris, 2022).

If we examine these recent legal trends through the lenses of precarious life and grievability, a familiar picture emerges. Much like the ADAA, these laws do not explicitly announce a racist agenda. Instead, they emphasize the need for measures to curb election fraud – despite the absence of evidence that such fraud is an actual problem. This absence calls into question the purpose of these bills and demonstrates how they are ultimately rhetorical tools rather than practical solutions. Instead of solving a fraud problem, these bills would disproportionally limit black and brown Americans' ability to vote. Measures such as requiring ID, limiting voting hours, and limiting or eliminating early and mail-in voting all have a greater effect on voters of color than on white voters (Brennan Center for Justice, 2022). Just as the ADAA has done, these bills make a clear argument of division and disidentification. They tell us whose voices should be included in our democracy and whose voices should be silenced yet again – whose lives are precarious and whose are ungrievable.

While the very existence of such bigoted legislation is disheartening, Butler enables us to understand legal and cultural norms as sedimented practices, rather than the bedrock they seem to be. The idea of unstable ground can be unsettling, but instability also signals possibility. If law can reinscribe the norms that create division and limit the scope of grievable life, it can also challenge those norms and reshape a broad and inclusive view of precarious life. Butler's work, then, can provide tools for analyzing our legal past and imagining our legal future.

REFERENCES

Alexander, M. (2012). *The new Jim Crow: Mass incarceration in the age of colorblindness*. The New Press.

Anti-Drug Abuse Act of 1986, Publ. L. No. 99-570, 100 Stat. 3207 (1986). www.govinfo.gov/content/pkg/STATUTE-100/pdf/STATUTE-100-Pg3207.pdf [https://perma.cc/FC62-LEEV]

Bennett, M. W. (2014). A slow motion lynching? The War on Drugs, mass incarceration, doing *Kimbrough* justice, and a response to two Third Circuit judges. *Rutgers Law Review*, 66(4), 873–919.

Brennan Center for Justice. (2022, January 10). The impact of voter suppression on communities of color. www.brennancenter.org/our-work/research-reports/impact-voter-suppression-communities-color [https://perma.cc/6VYM-69LR]

Butler, J. (1990). Performative acts and gender constitution: An essay in phenomenology and feminist theory. In S. E. Case (Ed.), *Performing feminisms: Feminist critical theory and theatre* (pp. 270–282). Johns Hopkins University Press.

(2004). *Precarious life: The powers of mourning and violence*. Verso.

(2008). *Frames of war: When is life grievable?* Verso.

(2011). *Bodies that matter: On the discursive limits of "sex."* Routledge Classics.

Carson, A. E., (Ed.). (2021, December). Prisoners in 2020: Statistical tables. Bureau of Justice Statistics. https://bjs.ojp.gov/content/pub/pdf/p20st.pdf [https://perma.cc/5FUD-GPFF]

Chadderton, C. (2018). *Judith Butler, race and education*. Palgrave Macmillan.

Clear, T. R. (2007). *Imprisoning communities: How mass incarceration makes disadvantaged neighborhoods worse*. Oxford University Press.

Cover, R. M. (1986). Violence and the word. *Yale Law Journal*, 95, 1601–1629.

Federal Bureau of Prisons. (2022, August 13). Offenses. www.bop.gov/about/statistics/statistics_inmate_offenses.jsp

Gottschalk, M. (2006). *The prison and the gallows: The politics of mass incarceration in America*. Cambridge University Press.

Greenhouse, L. (1986, October 18). Congress approves anti-drug bill as Senate bars a death provision. *The New York Times*, 1.

Jones, N., Marks, R., Ramirez, R., & Rios-Vargas, M. (2021, August 12). 2020 census illuminates racial and ethnic composition of the country. United States Census Bureau. www.census.gov/library/stories/2021/08/improved-race-ethnicity-measures-reveal-united-states-population-much-more-multiracial.html [https://perma.cc/JX5X-GNKX]

LoBianco, T. (2016, March 24). Report: Aide says Nixon's War on Drugs targeted blacks, hippies. CNN. www.cnn.com/2016/03/23/politics/john-ehrlichman-richard-nixon-drug-war-blacks-hippie [https://perma.cc/B8UF-93XG]

Loizidou, E. (2007). *Judith Butler: Ethics, law, politics*. Routledge-Cavendish.

Morris, K. (2022, August 3). *Patterns in the introduction and passage of restrictive voting bills are best explained by race*. Brennan Center for Justice. www.brennancenter.org/our-work/research-reports/patterns-introduction-and-passage-restrictive-voting-bills-are-best [https://perma.cc/44H7-5FDU]

Osler, M., & Bennett, M. W. (2014). A "Holocaust in slow motion?": America's mass incarceration and the role of discretion. *DePaul Journal for Social Justice*, 7(2), 116–178.

Raphael, S., & Stoll, M. A. (2009a). Introduction. In S. Raphael & M. A. Stoll (Eds.), *Do prisons make us safer? The benefits and costs of the prison boom* (pp. 1–24). Russell Sage Foundation.

(2009b). Why are so many Americans in prison? In S. Raphael & M. A. Stoll (Eds.), *Do prisons make us safer? The benefits and costs of the prison boom* (pp. 27–72). Russell Sage Foundation.

Reagan, R. (1986, October 27). Remarks on signing the Anti-Drug Abuse Act of 1986. Ronald Reagan Presidential Library & Museum. www.reaganlibrary.gov/archives/speech/remarks-signing-anti-drug-abuse-act-1986 [https://perma.cc/2NMX-5632]

(1988, October 8). Radio address to the nation on economic growth and the War on Drugs. Ronald Reagan Presidential Library & Museum. www.reaganlibrary.gov/archives/speech/radio-address-nation-economic-growth-and-war-drugs [https://perma.cc/459Z-5DFE]

Reagan, R., & Reagan, N. (1986, September 14). Address to the nation on the campaign against drug abuse. Ronald Reagan Presidential Library & Museum. www.reaganlibrary.gov/archives/speech/address-nation-campaign-against-drug-abuse [https://perma.cc/7CM7-EDH9]

Roberts, S. V. (1986, September 29). Issue of financing the key obstacle for antidrug plan. *The New York Times*, A1.

The Sentencing Project. (2021, May). Trends in U.S. Corrections.

United States Sentencing Commission. (1995, February). *Cocaine and federal sentencing policy*. www.ussc.gov/sites/default/files/pdf/news/congressional-testimony-and-reports/drug-topics/199502-rtc-cocaine-sentencing-policy/1995-Crack-Report_Full.pdf [https://perma.cc/Y4V2-VBW5]

(1997, April). *Cocaine and federal sentencing policy*. www.ussc.gov/sites/default/files/pdf/news/congressional-testimony-and-reports/drug-topics/19970429_RtC_Cocaine_Sentencing_Policy.pdf [https://perma.cc/B8T6-MPVF]

(2002, May). *Cocaine and federal sentencing policy*. www.ussc.gov/sites/default/files/pdf/news/congressional-testimony-and-reports/drug-topics/200205-rtc-cocaine-sentencing-policy/200205_Cocaine_and_Federal_Sentencing_Policy.pdf [https://perma.cc/G5LR-KRZU]

(2011). 2011 *Report to the Congress: Mandatory minimum penalties in the federal criminal justice system*. www.ussc.gov/research/congressional-reports/2011-report-congress-mandatory-minimum-penalties-federal-criminal-justice-system [https://perma.cc/DHA5-Y3VQ]

United States v. Booker, 543 U.S. 220 (2005).

Wacquant, L. (2000). The new "peculiar institution": On the prison as surrogate ghetto. *Theoretical Criminology*, 4(3), 377–389.

Weiman, D. F., & Weiss, C. (2009). The origins of mass incarceration in New York State: The Rockefeller drug laws and the local war on drugs. In S. Raphael & M. A. Stoll (Eds.), *Do prisons make us safer? The benefits and costs of the prison boom* (pp. 73–116). Russell Sage Foundation.

Yancy, G., & Butler, J. (2015, January 12). What's wrong with "All Lives Matter"? *The New York Times Opinionator*. https://archive.nytimes.com/opinionator.blogs.nytimes.com/2015/01/12/whats-wrong-with-all-lives-matter/ [https://perma.cc/NF9R-7Y7C]

12

Ensnared by Custom

Mary Astell and the American Bar Association on Female Autonomy

*Judy M. Cornett**

12.1 INTRODUCTION

Is it possible for women to thrive in a man's world? Do we even want women to thrive in a man's world? If we think that women should be able to thrive in a man's world, and if they aren't doing so, what should be done about it?

These are the questions addressed by two very different authors separated by almost four centuries. And although the two authors agree that women should be able to thrive in a man's world but aren't doing so, they use very different rhetorical strategies to reach very different conclusions about what should be done to remedy the problem. Ironically, the early feminist who wrote during the seventeenth century – when women could not vote, hold public office, or practice any of the learned professions – writes with greater confidence and authority than the twenty-first-century women who have risen to the top echelon of the legal profession. And the solution proposed by the early feminist relies on the empowerment of women, while the modern women lawyers appeal solely to the good graces of men to solve the problem of women's failure to thrive as large-firm lawyers.

Mary Astell, one of the earliest English feminists, examined the issue of women's intellectual and educational subordination in 1694 in *A Serious Proposal to the Ladies* (1970). She believed that women were not living up to their intellectual potential and were relegated to the realm of trivia and frivolity by the social norms of the period. In 2019, the American Bar Association (ABA) published a report entitled *Walking Out the Door: The Facts, Figures, and Future of Experienced Women Lawyers in Private Practice* (the ABA Report) (Liebenberg & Scharf, 2019). Focusing on America's 500 largest law firms,[1] the report found that women with

* The author is grateful to Austin Wall, UT Law Class of 2024, for outstanding research assistance.

[1] Elsewhere in the report, the number of firms surveyed is given as 350 (Liebenberg & Scharf, 2019, p. iii).

more than fifteen years' experience are leaving law firms in droves. Like Astell, the report attributed this failure to thrive to male-created cultural norms.

As Christine Mason Sutherland (2005) points out in *The Eloquence of Mary Astell*, one of Astell's signal accomplishments was her move from *sermo*, private conversational discourse, to *contentio*, the discourse of public debate. This move marked a significant moment in the history of feminist discourse, since women lacked the traditional platforms of public debate: politics, the church, and the academy. Astell's confidence in making the move from sermo to contentio resulted from a number of factors, including her own education, her successful dialogue with John Norris, and the Cartesian philosophy that liberated women's intellect from the perceived weaknesses of their bodies. Astell's transition from sermo to contentio can be seen in her sure-footed identification of her audience, her deft employment of metaphor and rhetorical questions, and her direct address to her critics. Unfortunately, these same characteristics are missing from the ABA Report. In addition to the report's challenges with ethos, it vacillates uneasily between sermo and contentio. By using Astell's rhetorical sophistication as a lens, we can view the rhetoric of the report more clearly, assessing its success or failure as a rhetorical document.

12.2 BACKGROUND: A SEVENTEENTH-CENTURY FEMINIST AND TWENTY-FIRST-CENTURY LAWYERS

Mary Astell (1666–1731) was a British philosopher, author, and early feminist whose influential[2] works challenged prevailing notions of a woman's intellectual ability while promoting her conservative Anglican values (Sutherland, 2005). Born in Newcastle upon Tyne, she moved to London in 1684, where she gained the patronage and companionship of several aristocratic women, including Lady Catherine Jones, Lady Mary Chudleigh, Lady Elizabeth Hastings, and Lady Ann Coventry (Perry, 1986, pp. 39–40, 68; Sowaal, 2023). Her first major work, and her most influential, *A Serious Proposal to the Ladies*, was published in 1694, with a second part published in 1697. In *A Serious Proposal*, Astell argues that women are the intellectual equals of men but have been debarred from exercising their intellects by social custom, which denied women an education equal to men's. This lack of education initiated a vicious circle, argues Astell: Because they are uneducated, they appear to be shallow and frivolous, lending support to the argument that they lacked the intellect necessary for a rigorous education. Because of the rhetorical sophistication of her works and her explicit attention to rhetoric, Astell has been recovered by contemporary scholars as an important rhetorical theorist.

[2] Astell's ideas in *A Serious Proposal to the Ladies* (1970) were so influential in their time that writers Daniel Defoe and George Berkeley are known to have plagiarized Astell's proposals and language (Sutherland, 2005, pp. 159–160).

To remedy this lack of education, Astell proposed the establishment of an "academical monastery," the equivalent of an all-female college, a plan which she elaborated in the second part of *A Serious Proposal*. These works went through several editions into the early eighteenth century and, together with her second major work, *Some Reflections upon Marriage* (1700), influenced later feminists such as Lady Mary Wortley Montagu (Perry, 1986, pp. 108–109). Astell was a devout Anglican, and her works reflect her conventionally Christian worldview, but she drew upon medieval spiritual concepts that extol the equality of the soul despite the inequality of the sexes and the Cartesian idea that a formal education is not necessary to engage in philosophy (Sutherland, 2005, pp. 11, 27–28). *A Serious Proposal* reflected a commitment to the conversational theory of rhetoric (Sutherland, 2005, p. 53), and among the subjects to be taught at the academy was rhetoric.

The American Bar Association is a voluntary association of attorneys founded in 1878 in Saratoga Springs, New York. Consistent with the composition of the legal profession at the time of its founding, the ABA was originally made up exclusively of white men. Only in 1950 did the ABA gain its first African American member. The first woman became an ABA member in 1918. Despite its deeply conservative roots, the ABA sponsors some progressive initiatives, such as the Special Committee on Legal Aid Work, founded in 1920. A half-century later, in 1974, the ABA supported legislation creating the federal Legal Services Corporation, designed to provide legal services to indigent clients in civil cases. According to the ABA, in 2022, there were 1,327,010 lawyers in the United States; of this number, 242,500, or approximately 18 percent, were members of the ABA (D. Lopez, personal communication, January 20, 2022)

Walking Out the Door: The Facts, Figures, and Future of Experienced Women Lawyers in Private Practice is the first report published as part of the Achieving Long-Term Careers for Women in Law initiative from the American Bar Association. This initiative is designed to study and understand the high attrition rate of female lawyers from large law firms. Former ABA president Hilarie Bass described this project as her greatest priority as president and commissioned this four-pronged research initiative to identify issues and provide solutions for firms (Liebenberg & Scharf, 2019, p. iii). The ABA used data collected by ALM Media regarding female attorneys' partnership status and longevity in the nation's 500 largest law firms as its metrics for success (p. iii). As of 2022, the ABA had published three reports (American Bar Association, n.d.-a). Following the first report, which discusses female representation and attrition broadly, the second report focuses on the experiences of women of color as represented by focus groups sponsored by the ABA. The third report reflects qualitative research, collecting the results of 12 focus groups and 12 individual interviews with 116 experienced female lawyers of all races practicing in a variety of settings in six large cities. The ABA made a concerted effort to market these reports on the internet with content branded with the tag

"#WhyWomenLeave" and videos expressing concern that women are "leaving the profession" (American Bar Association, n.d.-b).

The solution, according to the ABA Report, is for the predominantly male power structure at firms to, first, use gendered data collection to measure key factors relating to promotion and, then, overhaul the training and best practices of the firm to make them more conducive to retaining female attorneys (Liebenberg & Scharf, 2019). The ABA Report appeals to the existing hierarchy and provides recommendations for working within it to advocate for cultural change in the individual firms.

12.3 RHETORICAL SITUATION

12.3.1 *The Paradox of Ethos*

Both Mary Astell and the authors of the ABA Report[3] are engaged in a persuasive endeavor. They both describe a problem, diagnose the problem, and offer a solution to the problem. Astell wanted to persuade her audience that women are intellectually equal to men and that they should be afforded an equal education. She also wanted to persuade her readers that the best way of providing that education was through a female-only institution where women could separate themselves from the world and concentrate on reading and study. The ABA Report wants to persuade those with power in large American law firms that women are failing to become equity partners in those firms because of gender-based issues. The report also wants to persuade its readers to implement gender-conscious policies and practices in order to retain the women lawyers they hire.

Any author engaged in persuasion must rely on ethos, that is, "[t]he speaker or writer must be seen to have authority to speak upon this particular subject to this particular audience" (Sutherland, 2005, p. 4). The author's authority can derive from the power of the text itself – "intrinsic ethos" – or it can derive from the author's "already-established reputation" – "extrinsic ethos" (p. 4). The author's ethos engenders trust in their audience. A persuasive endeavor may founder if the author's ethos is insufficient to gain and maintain the reader's trust. Thus, it is imperative for an author to establish a stable ethos; a reader's uncertainty about the author's ethos raises doubts about the strength of the author's argument. Ironically, because Astell explicitly theorizes and deploys ethos in *A Serious Proposal*, it is the seventeenth-century feminist, not the twenty-first century authors of the ABA Report, who gains and keeps the reader's trust.

At first blush, it would seem that the ABA Report, backed by the authority of the nation's largest voluntary bar association and its immediate past president, Hilarie

[3] Because, as will be shown below, it is difficult to assign authorship of the ABA Report to individuals, the term "report" and "authors" will be used interchangeably when discussing the ABA Report.

Bass,[4] would have no trouble establishing and maintaining extrinsic ethos. However, the report displays anxiety about its authority. First, its title page credits two individual authors, Roberta D. Liebenberg and Stephanie A. Scharf. But the title page also bears the imprint of three organizations: ALM Intelligence Legal Compass,[5] ABA Presidential Initiative on Achieving Long-Term Careers for Women in Law,[6] and the American Bar Association. A disclaimer on the title page warns: "The views expressed herein represent the opinions of the authors. They have not been approved by the House of Delegates or the Board of Governors of the American Bar Association and, accordingly, should not be construed as representing the position of the Association or any of its entities."[7] Similarly, on the copyright page, the reader is warned: "The materials contained herein represent the opinions of the authors and should not be construed to be the views or opinions of the law firms or companies whom such persons are in partnership with, associated with, or employed by, nor of the American Bar Association or the Commission on Women in the Profession unless adopted pursuant to the bylaws of the Association." Interestingly, a Google search for "Walking out the Door" brings up the text of the report as the fourth result, with the caption, "Walking out the Door – American Bar Association,"[8] and the text is on the ABA's website (American Bar Association, n. d.-a). The report is copyrighted by the American Bar Association.

This authorship and ownership issue is damaging for building extrinsic ethos for the report. In an attempt to invoke the credibility of the national organizations and initiatives that support the work, the report undermines its own ethos by mentioning that those same organizations do not unquestionably endorse their research and conclusions. The intrinsic ethos that the authors stood to gain from their research and reporting is blunted by the disclaimer that the organization publishing the

4 Hilarie Bass is now the head of her own company, the Bass Institute for Diversity and Inclusion. According to its website, "The Bass Institute for Diversity & Inclusion was founded by Hilarie Bass, a leader in identifying why women leave companies before they reach senior management. An attorney and former American Bar Association president, Hilarie has more than 20 years in senior management, including six as co-president of 2,000-person law firm Greenberg Traurig and eight as head of the firm's 600-attorney litigation practice." https://bassinstitute.org/hilarie-bass.

5 According to the ABA website, "ALM Intelligence, a division of ALM Media LLC, supports legal, consulting, and benefits decision-makers seeking guidance on critical business challenges. Our [sic] proprietary market reports and analysis, rating guides, prospecting tools, surveys, and rankings, inform and empower business leaders to meet business challenges with confidence."

6 This program originated with Hilarie Bass, ABA President in 2017–18, and now operates under the aegis of the ABA Commission on Women in the Profession.

7 This disclaimer appears to be typical of those used by the ABA in connection with reports it coauthors with other organizations. See, e.g., American Bar Association Center for Human Rights. Center for Civil Liberties (2022); Blanck et al. (2020). However, reports authored solely by the ABA carry no such disclaimer. See, e.g., American Bar Association Commission on Immigration (2021).

8 Google search August 21, 2022.

report and the firms with which the individual authors are affiliated disclaim approval of its findings.

The report next attempts to bolster its ethos with fulsome framing documents. Three preliminary texts follow the title and copyright pages. First is "A Note from the Authors," featuring photos of Stephanie A. Scharf and Roberta D. Liebenberg, who were appointed by Bass as Co-Chairs of the Presidential Initiative on Achieving Long-Term Careers for Women in Law (Liebenberg & Scharf, 2019, pp. i–ii). Next up is a foreword from Hilarie Bass, who by the time of publication was the past president of the ABA. According to Bass, *Walking out the Door* is the first of four research reports to be published as a result of the presidential initiative (Liebenberg & Scharf, 2019, p. iii). However, only two additional reports have been published: *Left Out and Left Behind*, published in 2020, examining the "experiences women lawyers of color have in the profession," and *In Their Own Words*, published in 2021, subtitled "Experienced Women Lawyers Explain Why They Are Leaving Their Law Firms and the Profession" (American Bar Association, n.d.-a; Liebenberg & Scharf, 2019, p. 25).[9] Finally, a foreword from Patrick Fuller, Vice President of ALM Intelligence, notes that the report is the result of a "joint study" conducted by ALM and the ABA. Fuller explains his credentials: "I gave my first speech on diversity in 2002 for the Minority Corporate Counsel Association. … As the only son of a single mother, I witnessed first-hand the struggles that women faced in professional environments, from behavioral double-standards to the lack of advancement and recognition for achievements" (Liebenberg & Scharf, 2019, p. iv). As a male writing about the oppression of women, Fuller is at pains to bolster his ethos (and that of the report as a whole) by proving that he is an ally to women.

Like Astell, whose wealthy patrons supported her work, the ABA Report has its sponsors. The final page lists Platinum, Gold, and Silver Sponsors, along with Patrons. The Platinum Sponsors are the ABA Commission on Women, the Center for Women in Law, Teachers Insurance and Annuity Association of America, and Sheppard Mullin, described on its X.com (formerly Twitter) site as a "[f]ull-service AmLaw 50 firm with more than 1000 attorneys in 16 offices in the United States, Europe & Asia." Of the additional fifty-plus sponsors and patrons, all are large national law firms, with the exception of the ABA Section of Litigation, John Hancock Financial, the Ark Group, Charles River Associates, VISA, Wal-Mart Stores, Inc., Hilarie Bass, and Roberta (Bobbi) Liebenberg.

Clearly, these adjuncts to the text are intended to provide extrinsic ethos for the report: The two identified female authors do not stand alone; they are supported by a former ABA president, a prominent national research firm, a male ally, and a plethora of the very organizations the report critiques. But, paradoxically, the effect

9 The acknowledgments page at the end of the report lists a fourth project, "a representative survey of law school alumni," which "[has] been completed" and is in the course of publication. As of 2024, however, this fourth report has not appeared.

of all this hedging is to incite skepticism. The disclaimers, which try to distance the text from the very organizations that appear to sponsor it, create tension. Is the text so dangerous or controversial that these groups cannot appear to approve of it? Yet the nature of the sponsoring organizations – the most powerful lawyers' group in America, large corporations, and large multinational law firms – creates a halo of conservatism and convention around the text. Can a work supported by such groups say anything radical or revolutionary? The overall effect of these elaborate efforts to bolster the text's extrinsic ethos is to destabilize the text, to raise questions in the reader's mind at the outset, and to undermine the authors' extrinsic and intrinsic ethos.

In contrast to the energetic ethos-building of the report's authors, Astell does not see the need to bolster her authority in *A Serious Proposal*. The first edition was published anonymously by "A Lover of Her Sex," clearly indicating that the author is a woman. The work "burst upon London in 1694 and was read and talked of from Pall Mall to Grub Street" (Perry, 1986, p. 99). Despite the anonymous publication, Astell's authorship seems to have been an open secret, due perhaps to her network of aristocratic friends or the support of her publisher, well-known bookseller Rich Wilkin (Perry, 1986, pp. 68–69). Thus, while the author's anonymity would seem to defeat any extrinsic ethos, her readers' knowledge of her authorship would engender some extrinsic ethos. Of course, this knowledge was a two-edged sword: Respectable women of the period were relegated to the private sphere, meaning that only private genres, such as letters and diaries, were deemed appropriate. In seventeenth-century England, women were viewed as naturally deficient in intelligence, morality, and goodwill, the three elements of classical ethos (Sutherland, 2005, pp. 6–8). Once a woman entered the realm of commercial publication, her ethos was brought into question because she was engaged in an activity deemed inappropriate for women (Sutherland, 2005, p. 8). By publishing her theories publicly, Astell broke contemporary rules of decorum (Sutherland, 2005, p. 23). Perhaps recognizing that her authorship challenged contemporary norms, Astell attempts to identify her work as an acceptable genre: the letter. Without a dedication, foreword, or introduction, Astell begins her project with a straightforward salutation: "Ladies." She embarks upon her discourse with confidence, taking advantage of the intrinsic ethos of her work – its logic and clear style – to gain the trust of her readers.

While *A Serious Proposal* was widely admired, in the second part of the *Serious Proposal*, published three years later, in 1697, Astell supplements her reliance on intrinsic ethos with some extrinsic ethos building. In the period between 1694 and 1697, Astell published her second work, her correspondence with John Norris, a well-known philosopher, entitled *Letters Concerning the Love of God*. This work, published in 1695, came in for harsh criticism. Indeed, another well-known woman intellectual, Damaris Masham, John Locke's patron, published a pamphlet critical of Astell, *Discourse Concerning the Love of God* in 1696 (Perry, 1986, p. 87).

These intervening events may explain why the second part of *A Serious Proposal*, published anonymously, again by Wilkin, opens with a dedication to "Her Royal Highness, the Princess Ann of Denmark," signed only "Your Royal Highnesses Most Humble and most Obedient Servant." By 1697, this anonymity was certainly unnecessary, since Astell was openly credited as the author. Indeed, *A Serious Proposal* was so popular that it went through five editions by 1701 (Perry, 1986, p. 103). However, the first part of *A Serious Proposal* had been criticized for offering no practical scheme for bringing its vision of a Protestant nunnery to fruition. In the second part, Astell offers a program of education for the women who undertake to educate themselves, and she believes that Princess Ann can further this project:

> What was at first address'd to the Ladies in General, as seeming not considerable enough to appear in your Royal Highnesses Presence, not being ill receiv'd by them, and having got the Addition of a Second Part, now presumes on a more Particular Application to Her who is the Principal of them, and whose Countenance and Example may reduce to Practice, what it can only Advise and Wish. (Astell, 1970, p. 47)

Thus, it seems that the dedication to Princess Ann was not intended to bolster Astell's credibility as a form of extrinsic ethos so much as it served a more practical purpose: flattering a potential donor.

Following the dedication is a nine-page introduction, "containing a farther Perswasive to the Ladies to endeavor the Improvement of their Minds." Here Astell is more self-conscious, noting that she is taking a risk in publishing the second part, since she could more safely "content her self with the favourable reception which the good natur'd part of the World were pleased to afford to her first Essay" (Astell, 1970, p. 51). She declares that she is "very indifferent what the Critics say, if the Ladies receive any Advantage by her attempts to serve them," and asserts, "It were more to her Satisfaction to find her Project condemn'd as foolish and impertinent, than to find it receiv'd with some Approbation, and yet no body endeavoring to put it in Practice" (p. 51). The second part is neither a retraction, nor an explanation, nor an apology for the original. Instead, it is a further step along the path she marked out in the first part, which merely laid out her plan "in general," with "the particular method of effecting it left to the Discretion of those who shou'd Govern and Manage the Seminary" (p. 59). In the second part, she hopes "to lay down in this second part some more minute Directions" for achieving her vision (p. 59).

While the addition of a dedication and introduction could be interpreted as props to her credibility by invoking aristocratic authority and addressing criticism of the original, Astell, far from backing down from the original, sees these additions as aids to achievement of her original vision. Rather than simply restate her suggestion for a protestant monastery for female education, she includes philosophical theory that her stated audience of upper-class and middle-class literate women would have little experience with (Astell, 1970, pp. 65, 66). Astell increases her intrinsic ethos by demonstrating her ability to engage in rhetorical logos, propounding philosophy and educational theory at the same level as influential thinkers of her time (pp. 66, 80). The confidence she exhibited in the first part of *A Serious Proposal* seems undiminished in the second part, in which she broadens her audience to include not just other women but also other philosophers. Astell's refutation of her critics, including John Locke, signals a crucial step from the traditionally female and passive rhetorical style of sermo into the more confrontational and masculine contentio, which will be on display in her later works (Sutherland, 2005, p. 80).

12.3.2 *Argument: Who Caused the Problem and Who Should Solve It?*

12.3.2.1 Audience

Both Astell and the ABA Report address elite, conservative audiences. Astell expected her proposal to reach literate women, and literacy was far from universal among women in the seventeenth century. Certainly, her audience was limited to upper- and middle-class women. Similarly, the ABA Report is not directed to the general public, but to legal professionals. In fact, it is aimed at a particular set of lawyers – those in the 500 largest American firms. Even more particularly, it is aimed at the partners, especially the managing partners, of those law firms.

Thus, the two works have very different audiences: Astell addresses women, while the report addresses men. In fact, these differing audiences reflect the basic dichotomy that subsists throughout the two works. The most fundamental similarity between the two authors is their use of the dichotomy between men and women to describe the human experience. Omitted from this universe are nonbinary or gender-nonconforming individuals. However valid the dichotomy may have been in 1694, by 2019, when the ABA Report was published, the dichotomy certainly was not an accurate description of the universe of lawyers (National Association for Law Placement, 2010). Moreover, Astell theorizes her audience, while the ABA Report does not. Throughout *A Serious Proposal*, Astell is conscious of her audience. She addresses women using the second person. She describes them, analyzes them, and exhorts them. In contrast, the ABA Report does not directly address its audience, nor does it explicitly theorize those at whom the report is aimed.

Accepting the dichotomy between men and women, the two authors are surprisingly congruent in the assumptions they make about both groups. For Astell, men are in charge politically, socially, and personally. They have excluded women from positions of power within society. Even within the family, men (with the complicity of women) have created a culture that has unfitted women for serious thought or discourse. Indeed, they are not even fit to educate their own children. Astell takes a Christian view of women, seeing them as created by God and – radically for her time – equal to men in intellect. However, women have been acculturated to value only the most superficial things – dress, flirtation, accomplishments such as needlework. Women are enthralled to "Tyrant Custom."

Similarly, the ABA Report sees men as the source of power within large law firms. They are the ones who can make the changes advocated by the report. Emphasizing the number of managing partners who responded to their survey – only 28, a miniscule number given the number of law firms included in the survey (500) – the report speaks primarily to these few individuals. Although women make up a certain percentage of equity partners in large law firms, and may also serve as managing partners, the report does not explicitly recognize this fact. Congruent with its identification of its primary audience, the rhetoric of the report is male-centered. With the exception of a few passages, its discourse views women as victims of big firm culture and the sole caregivers within the family. Most importantly, however, the report depicts women as financial assets whose earning power can be exploited.

12.3.2.2 The Problem and Its Cause

Both Astell and the ABA Report maintain awareness of their respective audiences throughout their arguments, using rhetorical strategies, including figures of speech, that reflect their audiences' viewpoints. In diagnosing the reasons why women have not prospered in their respective cultures – seventeenth-century England and twenty-first century American large law firms – both authors assign the blame to men. In proposing a solution, however, the two authors diverge. Astell sees women as the agents of their own improvement, while the ABA Report believes that men hold the key to improving women's status. Consistent with her confidence in her own intellectual prowess, Astell moves eloquently from sermo to contentio in framing her argument. In contrast, the ABA lurches uncomfortably at times between sermo and contentio. At all times during her argument, Astell speaks to her audience as one of them, while the ABA Report mostly identifies with its male audience, but – perhaps reflecting the fact that its two named authors are female – at times takes a more adversarial stance.

Despite her assumption that men wield primary power within her society, Astell correctly assesses the needs of her audience by engaging in woman-centered discourse. Although her audience are women, Astell does not soft-pedal her views about her contemporaries. She begins her analysis by identifying the problem: the current state of Women, who are "cheap and contemptible" (Astell, 1970, p. 1). She deploys a variety of metaphors, many based upon natural phenomena, to describe her contemporaries. They are "useless and impertinent Animals" (p. 1). They are "Cyphers in the World, useless at the best, and in a little time a burden and nuisance to all about them" (p. 1). When women speak without education or understanding, "[p]rating like Parrots," their words are meaningless (p. 101). And in Astell's most famous simile, she asks her contemporaries, "How can you be content to be in the

World like Tulips in a Garden, to make a fine shew and be good for nothing; have all your Glories set in the Grave, or perhaps much sooner?" (p. 3).

Set against this pessimistic vision of women's current status is Astell's assessment of women's potential. Astell undertakes to "enquire what it is that . . . keeps you groveling here below, like Domitian catching Flies, when you should be busied in obtaining Empires" (Astell, 1970, p. 5). Thus, her argument begins in the sermo rhetorical style, using a conversational tone to instruct the reader that the current state of affairs for women is deleterious to women and the social order through its waste of God's natural gift of reason to women (Sutherland, 2005, pp. 53–54). Astell appeals to the readers through *pathos* in these descriptions, using pessimism and pity to motivate her reader to seek the solution that she intends for women of her standing. She also appeals to her audience by using the very style she advocates for the pupils in her academy: a "plain and explicit" style which persuades "by putting every thing in its proper place with due Order and Connexion" (Astell, 1970, p. 118).

If women are to obtain empires, they must first overcome the causes of their current debased state. Here, Astell employs a series of dichotomies to explain why women have not obtained empires and to describe what must happen for women to becomes empresses. The most important dichotomies are Body versus Mind, Vice versus Virtue, Ignorance versus Knowledge, and Custom versus Reason, but these align with subsidiary dichotomies of Appearance versus Reality, Affections versus Judgment, Chat versus Conversation, and Wit versus Wisdom, among others (Astell, 1970, pp. 1, 9, 10–11, 13, 15, 16, 73, 129). Although the overuse of dichotomies can feel simplistic and lack texture, Astell's copious use of more granular dichotomies largely avoids this danger. These dichotomies, in turn, align with Women as They Are and Women as They Might Be. Despite the scathing words Astell uses to describe her contemporaries, the overall effect of this constant dualism is optimistic: The present can be reformed; the future can be different from the past. Astell's use of metaphor and dichotomy signals her foray into contentio style of rhetoric that was typically reserved for men in her time (Sutherland, 2005, p. 65).

With respect to the cause of the problem, Astell has no doubt:

> [I]f our Nature is spoil'd, instead of being improv'd, at first; if from our infancy we are nursed up in Ignorance and Vanity; are taught to be Proud and Petulant, Delicate and Fantastick, Humorous and Inconstant, 'tis not strange that the ill effects of this Conduct appear in all the future Actions of our Lives. (Astell, 1970, p. 7)

Although Astell elsewhere identifies women as the primary caretakers of children (p. 129), she lays the blame for women's defective upbringing squarely at the door of men. It is clear to Astell that men are in charge. Metaphorically, men raise women as a crop or build women as a house:

> The Soil is rich and would if well cultivated produce a noble Harvest, if then the Unskilful Managers, not only permit, but incourage noxious Weeds, tho'

> we shall suffer by the Neglect, yet they ought not in justice to blame any but themselves, if they reap the Fruit of this their foolish Conduct. Women are from their very Infancy debar'd those Advantages, with the want of which they are afterwards reproached, and nursed up in those Vices which will hereafter be upbraided to them. So partial are Men as to expect Brick where they afford no Straw. (Astell, 1970, p. 6)

According to Astell, men cannot see any problem with keeping women in ignorance because they believe that women "were made for nothing else but to Admire and do them Service, and to make provision for the low concerns of an Animal Life" (p. 158).

Although she identifies men as the cause of women's current status, Astell broadens the circle of blame by personifying Custom as the ultimate force behind women's subordination. While men may have been "Unskilful Managers" who neglect women's education, Astell assigns a more active role to Custom: "Thus Ignorance and a narrow Education lay the Foundation of Vice, and Imitation and Custom rear it up" (Astell, 1970, p. 10). The nurturing role that should be played by virtuous women rearing virtuous children has been usurped by "Tyrant Custom," as she calls it (p. 11). The dichotomy between Custom and Reason explains what Astell means by "Custom." For her, it is received wisdom, the voice of authority, the socially accepted way of doing things (Broad, 2007, p. 168). Custom opposes Reason because it is collective rather than individual. Reason operates in the individual; placed within each individual soul by God, it empowers the individual to judge accurately between right and wrong. In contrast, Custom "reverses the proper relation between the understanding and the will" (Astell, 1970, p. 11). While the individual's understanding, operating on the basis of Reason, makes an accurate judgment about right and wrong, the will conforms to Custom, "becom[ing] a 'head-strong and Rebellious Subject'" (p. 84). Because, in Astell's view, the will develops before the understanding, humans are not initially governed by Reason but by "Education, Example, or Custom" (p. 63). Thus the need for a proper childhood education becomes paramount.

For Astell, Custom is what anthropologists today might call "culture"; it pervades society, dictating gender roles and valuing vice over virtue. It is a "merciless torrent that carries all before it" (Astell, 1970, p. 63). Of course, a culture is not created by one sex alone, and Astell clearly sees that women have contributed to the authority of Custom. However, she argues, they are not to blame for following its dictates. Although she urges her readers to "dare to break the enchanted Circle that custom has plac'd us in" (p. 3), she also realizes the cost to women of trying to swim upstream against the torrent: "For Custom has usurpt such an unaccountable Authority, that she [who] would endeavor to put a stop to its Arbitrary Sway and reduce it to Reason, is in a fair way to render herself the Butt for all the Fops in Town to shoot their impertinent Censures at" (p. 29).

Like Astell, the authors of the ABA Report identify the problem as the current status of women. Specifically, women are not becoming equity partners at large law firms in the numbers that would be expected based upon their representation in law schools. Although women now account for more than 50 percent of law school graduates, and although almost 45 percent of new associates at large law firms are women, only 20 percent of equity partners in large law firms are women (Liebenberg & Scharf, 2019, pp. iv, i). Data from the National Association for Law Placement show that the gender representation gap increases relative to seniority in law firms (p. 2). Thus, the ABA Report clarifies that the problem is not the failure to hire women into entry-level associate positions. Instead, the problem is the failure to promote women into the powerful, profit-sharing upper echelon of large law firms.

As for the cause of this disproportionate attrition of women, the ABA Report blames men, or, more generally, the workplace culture cultivated by the majority-male power structure in the firms. Of course, the few women who are equity partners contribute to the firm culture, but the report does not explicitly remind the reader of this fact. Consistent with its identification of its audience as men, the report conceptualizes firm leadership as male. However, to the extent that culture is the culprit, women are complicit in both the seventeenth-century culture described by Astell and the law firm workplace culture identified in the ABA Report. But Astell seems to be more aware of this complicity than are the authors of the report. Astell's reprimands to women show her awareness that the frivolity and triviality she abhors are partly created and maintained by women. On the other hand, the ABA Report does not exhibit any awareness that women contribute to the toxic culture in large law firms. Women are partners; they serve on compensation committees; they serve as managing partners. The conditions in large law firms that drive women away before they make partner are partly created and maintained by women who have achieved that status. Astell's clarity about her audience – literate, largely upper-class women – enables her to take better account of their role in maintaining the dominant culture. While Astell accurately recognizes that men operate the power structures in seventeenth-century Britain (government, judicial system, church, and most of the wealth), the ABA Report glosses over the fact that senior women lawyers are just as responsible as senior male lawyers for creating law firm culture.

Using survey results from 1,262 men and women lawyers with more than 15 years' experience in the nation's 500 largest law firms,[10] the ABA Report focuses on two categories of information: the everyday experiences that contribute to the success of both men and women, and, specifically, what causes women in particular to stay or leave their firms (Liebenberg & Scharf, 2019, pp. 3, 9). Ironically, the report highlights that when firm leadership genuinely believes that their practices infallibly create a meritocracy, they are less likely to be aware of the various biases that inhibit female attorneys from achieving partnership status (p. 4). This lack of awareness

[10] Women constituted 70 percent of respondents, while men constituted 30 percent of respondents (Liebenberg & Scharf, 2019, p. 3).

manifests itself in everyday practices that contribute to the dissatisfaction of women with the firm's status quo.

According to the survey results catalogued in the ABA Report, the cause of women's attrition from large firms is not one definite issue; rather, it is "a death by a thousand cuts," ranging from routine disrespect from all levels within the firm to overt violence in the forms of sexual misconduct and fear tactics (Liebenberg & Scharf, 2019, p. 4). Female attorneys are far more likely than their male counterparts to have negative workplace experiences, including being mistaken for a lower-level employee, being overlooked for advancement or salary increases, and missing out on desirable assignments (pp. 7–8). Additionally, the existing informal structure for compensation and recognition and the lack of female representation on compensation committees create a system that does not provide equitable treatment for female attorneys (p. 8).

Specifically, the survey presented women respondents with several reasons why they may choose to leave large private firms and asked women to report whether the reason was "a very or somewhat important reason for leaving." Fifty-eight percent of women said that caretaking commitments fell into this category and 50 and 51 percent said that the number of billable hours and the emphasis on marketing or originating business were important reasons for leaving (Liebenberg & Scharf, 2019, p. 16). In another study by the ABA related to female attrition, the focus groups reiterated the claims in *Walking Out the Door*, citing undercompensation and unreasonable time demands as their least liked aspects of practicing law in large private firms (Sterling & Chanow, 2021). In addition to caretaking demands, overwork, and undercompensation, the survey reported that 50 percent of women were sexually harassed at work and that 25 percent of women decided not to report their sexual harassment out of fear of retaliation (Liebenberg & Scharf, 2019, p. 8). The report describes these conditions of sexual misconduct as "pervasive" in large firms (p. 9).

Thus, while the underlying cause of women's failure to achieve and maintain equity partner status is big-firm culture, women's attrition also results from their own decisions to leave, to "walk out the door" – their refusal to continue to endure the conditions outlined in the report. Women lawyers are not interested in being the Stepford wives of the legal profession, being passed over for tangible and intangible forms of recognition and yet expected to continue in the industry that does not respect them and actually harasses them. Although the report at several point equates leaving Big Law with leaving the profession, it is likely that many, if not most, women who depart large law firms find more attractive practice environments elsewhere, recognizing that their efforts will be better compensated, or they will find more professional satisfaction, in government work or as in-house counsel (Liebenberg & Scharf, 2019, p. 2).

Both Astell and the ABA Report see women as the problem. For Astell, women are poorly educated, resulting in a shallow and frivolous life, devoid of the intellectual and spiritual rewards that would result if their minds were nurtured. But women are not the cause of their own intellectual failings. They are poorly educated, shallow, and frivolous because men have engineered the social structure to exclude them from the benefits of education. Tyrant Custom has imprisoned women. For the ABA, women have come a long way: They are educated, professionally equal to men, and capable of achieving the greatest heights in the legal profession (large-firm partnerships). But they are stymied by large-firm culture, a culture created by existing firm leadership, which is overwhelmingly male. Like the Custom of Astell's day, big-firm culture of twenty-first-century America creates an environment in which women cannot thrive. Treated with disrespect or active hostility, women lawyers exercise their power of choice by leaving large law firms behind.

12.3.3 *Argument: The Appeal and the Solution*

With the problem and its cause identified, both Astell and the ABA Report undertake to propose a solution. Here, perhaps, is their greatest challenge: They must ask their audiences to take action. While indicting those responsible for the problem, both authors must also appeal to the self-interest of their readers in order to motivate change. In meeting this challenge, Astell proves much more effective than the ABA Report. Her rhetoric skillfully appeals to her audience's self-interest while admitting the difficulty of implementing her proposed solution. In doing so, she moves appropriately from sermo to contentio. The ABA Report, on the other hand, remains embedded in male-dominated large-firm culture, even while trying to ameliorate it. Unlike Astell, who proposed a radical solution that women themselves should enact, the ABA Report proposes conservative steps that reflect the view of women as victims and as primary caretakers. In doing so, the report appeals primarily to the financial interests of law firm leadership, depicting women as assets to be exploited.

The difficulty of breaking free of the culture in which one is immersed motivates Astell to propose her "Academical Institution" for women (1970, p. 157). For Astell, the first advantage of "Retirement" is that "it helps us to [check]mate Custom and delivers us from its Tyranny, which is the most considerable thing we have to do, it being nothing else but the habituating our selves to Folly that can reconcile us to it" (p. 157). Separated from the social whirl, women will be able to achieve what Astell terms "the one great end of this Institution": "To expel that cloud of Ignorance which Custom has involv'd us in, to furnish our minds with a stock of solid and useful Knowledge, that the Souls of Women may no longer be the only unadorn'd and neglected things" (p. 17). Astell believes that women have the power to save themselves, to gain education and to put it to work once they return to the world. Her vision requires liberating women from the fetters of Custom by removing them to a safe haven where they can improve themselves through self-reflection. Although Astell envisions the women reading works of philosophy such as the works of

Descartes and Malebranche, she also prescribes self-knowledge, reflecting her belief in the power of women's minds (p. 20).

First, however, the process of gaining self-knowledge begins by stripping away the worldly trappings that distract women from their nobler quest. When the mind is constantly taken up with the sensations deriving from worldly trifles, it is impossible to focus the mind on itself.[11] Consistent with Astell's (1970) high-church Anglican loyalties, in the secular monastery women will regularly take communion, will hear preaching, and will observe all the holy days of the Church (Astell, 1970, p. 21). Their food and clothing will be "plain and decent," with no "superfluities" (p. 22). Their conversation will consist of "Friendly Admonitions," as opposed to the "Scoffing and offensive Railleries" of the world (p. 22). In the monastery, there will be "no impertinent Visits, no foolish Amours, no idle Amusements," and there will be very little time "spent in Dressing" (p. 25). Indeed, Astell's austere vision of her monastery also paints a vivid picture of its opposite, the social world, which is peopled by flighty but conniving women and arrogant, lustful men. Astell herself recognizes the self-perpetuating nature of that world. Women who feast on "Plays and Romances" see themselves reflected there, and this in turn confirms them in their "greatest Follies" (p. 19). Thus, in the Academical Institution, it is vital to eliminate these useless, and indeed vicious, works because "[a] rational mind *will* be employ'd, and it will never be satisfy'd in doing nothing, and if you neglect to furnish it with good materials, 'tis like to take up with such as come to hand" (pp. 19–20).

Unlike Astell's proposal of an entirely new institution with which to address the issue of women's education, the ABA's solution to the problem of female attrition in law firms is firmly grounded in existing Big Law structure. That structure is thoroughly capitalist, based on profits earned by equity partners by charging clients more than it costs the firm to pay associates and non-equity partners to staff the clients' cases. The pool of clients is generated by the lawyers' "rain-making" abilities, and it is primarily the firm's senior lawyers who attract wealthy clients. Thus, the report appeals primarily to its audience's self-interest in retaining senior female attorneys. Law firm managers are urged to "own the business case for diversity" (Liebenberg & Scharf, 2019, p. 19). Women's departure from Big Law constitutes, not a loss of intellectual energy or human potential, but rather a loss of clients – the lawyers' "books of business" – and a lost return on the firm's investment in those lawyers (p. 1). The report points out that "[l]aw firms devote substantial resources to hiring and training their lawyers, and the attrition of senior women lawyers causes substantial losses, both tangible and intangible" (p. 2). Even more bluntly, the internet marketing materials for the report include the following observations on the loss of female partners by Guy N. Halgren, chairman of the Executive Committee at Sheppard Mullin: "[I]f you're losing men or women during that time period, it's just very tough on your business . . . [I]t's not just that you're going to miss

[11] For a discussion of Astell's epistemology, see Goldie (2007).

out on business by not having folks around, but also that you've spent so much money getting them to that point" (American Bar Association, n.d.-b, 1:38, 1:38–2:07). Thus the ABA Report appeals to the self-interest of large firms by correlating attrition of female attorneys with financial loss and wasted investment:

> When senior women lawyers leave firms, the firm's relationship with those lawyers' clients suffer, there is a reduced range of legal talent to offer clients, a narrower base for firms and businesses to develop robust client relationships, a diminished ability to recruit and retain skilled women lawyers at all levels, and, ultimately, serious challenges to the firm's future growth and revenue. (Liebenberg & Scharf, 2019, p. 2)

The authors of the report expect firm management to be galvanized into action to change their culture and practices to ameliorate the issue of the gender gap because it affects the firms' ability to make a profit on their investment in hiring female attorneys.

Conversely, the ABA Report repeatedly notes that managers of large law firms often fail to properly recognize and compensate women for their success in rain-making, bringing new clients into the firm (Liebenberg & Scharf, 2019, p. 7). The report is not the first to recognize this disparity. The legal research firm Major, Lindsey & Africa has been tracking the gendered difference between compensation and client origination credit for years. From 2010 to 2018 male partners made between 32 and 53 percent more than female partners, and 48 percent of that difference is related to differences in origination credit (Lowe, 2018, p. 53). To address this issue, the report suggests that law firms develop a written policy for origination credit and a system to settle disputes of origination credit (Liebenberg & Scharf, 2019, p. 19). While mistrust of law firms' management echoes throughout the other solutions provided by the ABA Report, the suggested solution to this important problem is entrusted to the same managers who, according to the report, create the problem in the first place (p. 18).

Another of the primary causes of female attrition mentioned by women lawyers was the lack of time to fulfill their caretaking commitments (Liebenberg & Scharf, 2019, p. 12). The ABA Report recognizes that male attorneys in families that have children or elders requiring care do not carry the same burdens as female attorneys in similar family structures (p. 12). Firms often boast that female attorneys can still stay on the partner track while working part-time; however, even though nearly all large firms have this option, only 6–7 percent of attorneys make use of these policies (p. 13). The female attorneys realize that although this opportunity is afforded to them, actually using the part-time structure would likely ruin their timeline and goals of becoming partner (p. 13). The ABA Report notes with approval that some firms are implementing so-called concierge services to attract and keep female lawyers by hiring people to do the homemaking tasks that female attorneys typically would be forced to do on top of their work at the firm. Rather than encouraging men to do their fair share so that women don't have to work the "second shift," the ABA's suggested solution is to hire people to do those tasks, which reinforces the gender hierarchy by shielding men from their caretaking duties. This solution, reiterated in the section describing what firms should do to decrease attrition, negates a world-view where people have valuable and meaningful work outside of the firm in favor of facilitating the same high working hours that the report identified, just a few pages earlier, as a cause of female attrition (p. 11).

Most seriously, the ABA Report notes that 50 percent of women reported receiving "unwanted sexual conduct at work" and 16 percent of women "have lost work opportunities as a result of rebuffing sexual advances" (Liebenberg & Scharf, 2019, p. 8). Weirdly, in light of this revelation of the pervasiveness of conduct that, in some cases, could be criminal, the ABA Report recommends merely the implementation of "sensible and enforceable policies that incentivize women to report sexual harassment, protect them from retaliation, and punish those who engage in such conduct" (p. 9). This is the only use of the word "sensible" in the entire report. While insisting that "[l]aw firms must send a strong message that sexual harassment simply will not be tolerated," the policy that the ABA Report ultimately recommends as the remedy for sexual harassment at firms is to have more sexual harassment training (p. 19). The report fails to recommend firing lawyers who are guilty of sexual harassment, although such an example is provided in a footnote (p. 23 n.45).

This approach of identifying a serious and pervasive problem facing women in Big Law and then giving general advice in corporate-speak, touting strategy, targets, and metrics, is repeated throughout the solutions section of the report (Liebenberg & Scharf, 2019, p. 18). The logos of the report is sound, providing clear and specific evidence that points to a logical conclusion: The workplace culture and practices of large firms push women out before they are able to climb the hierarchy and become top billers for their firms. However, the lack of practical responses that firms or individuals can take harms the rhetorical strength of the authors' argument that firm behavior is both the cause of and the solution to this problem.

In sum, the attrition of female attorneys from large law firms is the result of toxic firm culture, but rather than advocate changing the culture to be more amenable to female lawyers, the ABA Report provides solutions that attempt to allow women to exist in the culture as it presently exists. Hiring concierge services, hosting more awareness campaigns, and adopting "sensible" policies on sexual harassment do not strike at the problem of female dissatisfaction with the current law firm culture. Consistent with the ABA's conservative history, and its donors' mainstream presence, the report seeks to solve the problem of female attrition by encouraging just enough change to quiet the complaints of female attorneys while maintaining the firms' basic capitalist structure. The report's tacit acceptance of this structure weakens the rhetorical logos that it crafted by using empirical evidence of the problem and its causes. The fate of women lawyers in large firms is in the hands of the same actors – primarily men – who have created and maintained the system that generates the problem. There is nothing radical to see here.

Similarly, despite the radical nature of Astell's proposal – creation of an entirely new institution for women's education – her assumptions and goals are deeply conservative, befitting a devout middle-class Anglican woman writing in the 1690s. What is the ultimate goal of Astell's proposal? She does not promote only one goal; instead, she elucidates a series of intermediate goals that will lead to what she sees as the ultimate good, expressed in a rhetorical question: "What End can Creatures have but their Creators Glory?" (Astell, 1970, p. 75). And along the way to this ultimate goal, women will achieve a number of concomitant goals that will benefit their families and society in general. Astell catalogues a number of ways in which the women's sojourn in the Academical Institution will benefit others. Aiming her argument toward men, she points out that a good education will make a woman a "better Wife" who will reclaim the brutish instincts of men and will make his life so "comfortable" that he will remain faithful (pp. 36, 38). Astell also argues that an educated woman will be a better mother by exerting a good influence on the impressionable child (pp. 38, 129). Surprisingly, perhaps, Astell urges her readers – primarily literate middle- to upper-class women – to nurse their children: "And if Mothers had due regard to their Posterity, how Great soever they are, they would not think themselves too Good to perform what Nature requires, nor through Pride and Delicacy remit the poor little one to the care of a Foster Parent" (p. 7). On the other hand, her position is consistent with her conservative Anglican values, which consign women to the private sphere. Astell disclaims any argument for a public role for women: "Women have no business with the Pulpit, the Bar or St. Stephens Chapel [i.e., Parliament]" (p. 123). However, Astell does envision a role for women as teachers. Disclosing her view of her audience, Astell notes that women educated in the seminary can "give the best Education to the Children of Persons of Quality, who shall be attended and instructed in lesser Matters by meaner Persons deputed to that Office" (p. 35).

But in Astell's view, the influence of educated women will extend beyond the family to a larger social circle. Women will not only educate children; they will educate one another. Although women have no place in the public pulpit, Astell insists that there can be no objection to women's educating one another, presenting a biblical example of a female teacher:

> I cannot imagine wherein the hurt lies, if … Women be enabled to inform and instruct those of their own Sex at least; the Holy Ghost having left it on record, that Priscilla as well as her Husband, catechiz'd the eloquent Apollos and the great Apostle found no fault with her. (Astell, 1970, p. 20)

Thus the education provided in the seminary will "fit us to propagate Religion when we return into the World" and to "make[] Proselytes to heaven" (pp. 33, 34). An educated woman can "improve her Sex in Knowledge and true Religion"; she can "revive the ancient Spirit of Piety in the World" (p. 14).

However, more important than the benefit that women will bestow on others is the benefit women themselves will accrue. One of Astell's most consequential positions is that women's "Soul," like men's, is created in the image of God (Astell, 1970, p. 78). Likewise, women, like men, are endowed with Reason and are equally capable of using it to develop their understanding (p. 18). Astell asserts that using the power of Reason to develop the understanding will enable women to choose right actions and to appreciate divine revelation, but Astell also conceives women's mental powers as being intrinsically valuable, not just instrumentally valuable (pp. 62, 98). She adopts, for women, the Cartesian model of man as a self-reflecting, self-knowing being. Astell explains to her readers that the retirement provided by the seminary will enable its residents to "know and reflect on our own minds" (p. 29). If women have done the difficult mental work necessary to clear their minds of prejudices, Astell assures her readers that Truth is easily accessible: "we have no more to do but to look attentively into our Minds" (p. 97). Education in the monastery will be valuable because it will enable her readers to "live up to the dignity of your Nature" (p. 4). Indeed, having chided her readers early on that they should be chasing empires instead of flies, Astell explains near the end of the Proposal what kind of dominions she hopes her readers will rule over. She hopes that by being "intimately acquainted with our own Hearts," women will become "Monarchs in our own Bosoms" (p. 159).

12.3.4 *Sermo and Contentio*

While Astell clearly moves from sermo to contentio – from her salutation to her audience as "Ladies," to her exposition of a full-fledged theory of rhetoric – the report mixes elements of sermo and contentio (Liebenberg & Scharf, 2019, p. 1; see Sutherland, 2005, chs. 9–10). The framing materials establish a familiar tone, complete with smiling photographs and use of the first person to address the reader, redolent of sermo (Liebenberg & Scharf, 2019, pp. i–v). Yet the report begins with reference to "facts" and "figures," invoking surveys and percentages and using distancing constructions such as "It is clear that" and "It is evident that" (p. 2). Instead of first-person pronouns, subjects of sentences become abstract nouns – for example, "implication," "problems," "satisfaction" (p. 7). This rhetoric of contentio comprises the majority of the twenty pages of the report. However, unlike Astell, who keeps her eye steadily on her female audience throughout the first part of the *Serious Proposal*, the authors of the report interrupt with first-person statements more suitable to sermo. In fact, these first-person statements, and the instability they inject into the discourse, reflect a bit of frustration with their audience. Although the report is clearly aimed at those in charge of Big Law firm culture, of the 1,292 respondents to their survey, only 28 were managing partners (p. 3). When the authors declare, "We also emphasize that there is no 'one size fits all' set of policies that suits all firms. We urge firms to tap into the creativity of their own lawyers"

(p. 13), they are pleading with the minority of their respondents, the ones whom they are depending on to make the changes necessary to improve women's positions in law firms.

This personal tone is more consistent with sermo than contentio, creating an uneasy slippage between the two discourses. Similarly, the contrast between Astell's and the report's style, especially their use of metaphor, shows the same slippage between sermo and contentio in the report. Astell's metaphors refer almost exclusively to nature – women are tulips in a garden, they are soil to be cultivated, they are straw to be used as bricks. In contrast, the report's metaphors are either competitive or mechanistic. According to the report, the goal of Big Law should be to "level the playing field" (Liebenberg & Scharf, 2019, p. ii). Currently, the report concludes, law firms are forcing women to "sidelin[e]" their careers by continuing to "move the goal posts" of equity partnership (pp. 1, 13). If equity partnership is a game to be won, it is also a vantage point to be achieved through utilizing "building blocks" and "climb [ing] up the ladder" (pp. 4, 7, 17). Thus, to Astell, the progress of women is a natural process; attention and conscious effort will yield fruit. True, women's minds have to be tended, and the people best able to do that are men, given the social arrangements of seventeenth-century Britain, but in Astell's Academical Retreat, women will be able to nurture themselves. In contrast, to the authors of the report, women in big law firms are competitors in a contest where those in charge of the game are men, who can move the goal posts and sideline women players at will. In the report, equity partnership is a prize to be won through competition or a position to be attained through the use of man-made (literally) tools such as building blocks and ladders. Metaphorically, big law firms must stop giving "lip service" to gender equality; instead, they must "give teeth" to the effort to promote women (pp. ii, 20).

But these metaphors, which support the contentio of the report, are belied by many of the emotion-laden adjectives deployed in the report, which are more appropriate to sermo and seem to deploy pathos in support of the report's argument. For example, women's lack of access to equity partnership is "undeniable and unfortunate" (Liebenberg & Scharf, 2019, p. 17). The gender differences revealed by the survey are "striking and alarming"; the results of the survey are "distressing" (pp. 8, 9). These overwrought adjectives might be appropriate in sermo – indeed, in his Foreword, Patrick Fuller of ALM calls the numbers "stunning" (p. iv) – but they create tension with the report's overall sense of contentio. Just after the survey results have been called striking, alarming, and distressing, the authors speak from a position of undoubted authority in diagnosing the shortcomings in Big Law and prescribing a solution:

> What is holding senior women lawyers back is not a lack of drive or commitment, a failure to promote themselves, or an unwillingness to work hard or to make substantial sacrifices. Simply put, women lawyers don't need to "lean in" any more than they have already done. What needs fixing is the structure and culture of law

firms, so firms can better address the needs of the many women they recruit and seek to retain. (Liebenberg & Scharf, 2019, p. 17)

In their passion, sincerity, and declaratory power, these sentences echo Astell. But they stand out in their context because of the uneasy mix of sermo and contentio that exists throughout the report. In fact, while the report uses emotional adjectives to label the results of the survey, its treatment of sexual harassment demonstrates this instability. The report reveals the truly shocking statistic that "one of every two women [respondents] said they had experienced sexual harassment" (p. 8). But in suggesting a solution to this sorry state of affairs, the authors use the most neutral of adjectives and even resort to bureaucratese: "[F]irm leadership and management [should] implement sensible and enforceable policies that incentivize women to report sexual harassment, protect them from retaliation, and punish those who engage in such conduct" (p. 9). It would seem that if there ever was a time for strong adjectives, the description of a solution to sexual harassment suffered by 50 percent of experienced women lawyers would be it.

Ultimately, the refusal of the ABA Report to suggest radical solutions and to maintain its rhetorical tone may result from its origin. The two named authors of the report, Roberta D. Liebenberg and Stephanie A. Scharf, were assigned the project conceived by former ABA President Hilarie Bass. They were provided a private sector partner, ALM Intelligence, to carry out the mandated survey. They were limited to examining the status of women in a specialized sector of the legal profession. Although the website hosting the ABA Report declares that "'Walking Out the Door' is making headlines with its shocking statistics and valuable recommendations" (American Bar Association, n.d.-a), it's easy to imagine the authors' belief that their report will merely take its place in a long succession of diversity, equity, and inclusion initiatives resulting in little change. As the authors declare in their introductory note, "We are way past the point where mere lip service to the goal of gender equality in the profession will suffice." Instead, they argue, the "market" for legal services is "increasingly demanding not only a professed commitment to diversity and inclusion, but actual proof of success in achieving that objective" (Liebenberg & Scharf, 2019, p. ii). Perhaps due to the conservative nature of the proposed solution, the women authors of the report occasionally lurch from sermo into contentio, revealing a certain level of frustration with attempting to motivate real change in large-firm culture.

In contrast, Astell chose her audience and her subject matter. Although she was constrained by the social mores of the time, her education and her network of friends and patrons gave her the confidence to advance her own views in her own voice. Her strong ethos, her explicit acknowledgement and direct address of her audience, and her plain, cogent style contrast with the insecure ethos, blindness to audience, and unstable style of the ABA Report.

12.4 CONCLUSION

Although Astell's *A Serious Proposal* and the ABA report *Walking Out the Door* have many similarities, ultimately they are very different. Both works divide the world into two genders, men and women. Both perceive a problem with women's status in the world – the social world, for Astell; the professional world, for the ABA Report. Both assign a gendered cause for the problem – Astell sees men as the culprit, although she acknowledges that men and women both create a culture that buttresses the problem; the ABA Report less perceptively blames (male) law-firm managers for creating a toxic work environment for women, while failing to explicitly recognize the role that women play in maintaining that environment.

Both works are deeply conservative. Astell writes from the perspective of a devout, middle-class Anglican. The ABA Report originates from the perspective of entrenched, well-established, moneyed law firms having traditional hierarchies of status and compensation. Both works are classist and elitist. Not only does Astell aim her proposal at literate, middle-class women, but she also asserts that human reasoning power is distributed on the basis of class. She asserts that some minds have a "larger Capacity" than others, and that "every one is placed in such a Station as they are fitted for" (Astell, 1970, pp. 90, 128). Because God has ordained every person's social class, each person's intellectual aspirations should align with their class; the "Plow-man" cannot be blamed for seeking less knowledge than the "Doctor" (p. 84).

Similarly, the thrust of the ABA Report is that equity partnership at a large law firm is the ultimate achievement for a woman lawyer. The report equates leaving large law firms with leaving the practice of law as a whole. The report seems blind to the fact that women who have spent the time and energy to go to law school, to get jobs at competitive firms, and to invest the time and energy to be successful at these firms might choose to work in a different legal setting. It is well documented that the onerous working conditions at large law firms have led women to disproportionately choose work in more hospitable settings such as in-house corporate counsel, government legal departments, or academia. Yet the ABA Report fails to acknowledge that these other roles might be as rewarding, or more rewarding, than equity partnership at Big Law. By walking out the door and voting with their feet, women lawyers might be sending a message to large law firms that exceeds a message about individual preferences.

Both works make conservative assumptions about their readers' worldviews. For Astell, the Christian religion is the commonly held orthodoxy; she expects her readers to understand and accept her assertions about the role of divinity in human life and the value of established religion in her culture. Therefore, Astell can pepper her work with rhetorical questions. Sharing a common cultural foundation with her readers, she can expect them to approve Astell's implicit or explicit answers. For example, when she asks the big question, "What did we come into the World for?," she does not expect her reader to argue with her answer: "to Prepare our selves and be Candidates for Eternal Happiness in a better [world]" (Astell, 1970, p. 67). Likewise, the ABA Report assumes that its readers share the large firms' capitalist worldview. Its readers are assumed to view law firms as businesses and women lawyers primarily as economic assets generating wealth for the members of the firms.

However, despite these many similarities between the two works, one overriding distinction separates the two. Astell empowers women to solve their own problem, to improve themselves and their lives. Even when she is scolding them, the women addressed by Astell always maintain their dignity. The ABA Report rejects a role for women lawyers in solving the problem of toxic big-firm culture, insisting that it is up to men to change the culture of Big Law. While this approach may seem salutary because it relieves oppressed women from responsibility and places blame on the true wrongdoers, in reality this approach patronizes women. When viewed through the lens of Astell's rhetorical practice, the myopia of the ABA Report becomes more understandable. Unlike Astell, who theorizes her audience, the ABA Report fails to acknowledge its audience. Although the report is designed to further the interests of women, its rhetoric moves them from the center of the discourse. The ABA Report exhibits a strong distrust of Big Law, blaming the problem of attrition on firms' work culture. In another report from this series, the ABA recognizes that the gender and diversity initiatives at most large firms do not effectively advocate for the needs of female lawyers of color (Peery et al., 2020, p. 24). However, in determining a solution for the problem, the ABA Report focuses only on solutions that are decided on by that same firm management. For example, the report urges law firms to redouble the efforts they have already undertaken: "The data lead us to conclude that firms need to look anew, from broader perspectives, at setting targets and implementing policies and practices that actually achieve meaningful progress and results" (Liebenberg & Scharf, 2019, p. 16). Yet the report's only specific suggestion is adoption of the so-called Mansfield Rule, an aspirational goal of 30 percent representation of women or ethnic minorities on firm committees (p. 19), which only 42 percent of experienced lawyers said was very or somewhat effective (p. 16). As envisioned by the ABA Report, large law firms thus play a double role of the oppressor and the savior whereby they are called on to rescue female attorneys from the very culture that the law firms have created.

Just as Mary Astell urged seventeenth-century women to "break the enchanted Circle that custom has plac'd us in" (Astell, 1970, p. 3), so large law firms should break out of the vicious circle of data, goals, targets, and policies. Unlike Astell, who argues for "a new vision of who and what women truly are and what they should see as their destiny" (Sutherland, 2005, p. 162), the ABA Report argues for maintaining the status quo. Ironically, now that women have become educated and have entered the public sphere, with few formal barriers to achieving the same professional goals as men, the ABA Report seeks to keep women in their place as traditional equity partners in traditional large law firms. But women lawyers who are walking out the door have an important message for Big Law that will be heard only if the focus shifts back to the women themselves. Their message cannot be heard if no one is listening.

REFERENCES

American Bar Association. (n.d.-a). *Achieving long-term careers for women in law – American Bar Association*. Commission on Women in the Profession. www.americanbar.org/groups/diversity/women/initiatives_awards/long-term-careers-for-women/

(n.d.-b). *#Whywomenleave* [Video]. Commission on Women in the Profession. www.americanbar.org/groups/diversity/women/initiatives_awards/long-term-careers-for-women/

American Bar Association Center for Human Rights. Center for Civil Liberties (2022). *Disappearing human rights defenders: Russia's human rights violations and international crimes in Ukraine*. American Bar Association.

American Bar Association Commission on Immigration. (2021). *Achieving America's immigration promise: ABA recommendations to advance justice, fairness and efficiency*. American Bar Association. www.americanbar.org/content/dam/aba/administrative/immigration/achieving_americas_immigration_promise.pdf

Astell, M. (1970). *A serious proposal to the ladies, for the advancement of their true and greatest interest*. Source Book Press. (Original work published 1694.)

Blanck, P., Hyseni, F., & Wise, F. A. (2020). Diversity and inclusion in the American legal profession: First phase findings from a national study of lawyers with disabilities and lawyers who identify as LGBTQ+. *University of the District of Columbia Law Review, 23*(1), 23–87.

Broad, J. (2007). Astell, Cartesian ethics and the critique of custom. In W. Kolbrener & M. Michelson (Eds.), *Mary Astell: Reason, gender and faith* (pp. 165–180). Ashgate.

Goldie, M. (2007). Mary Astell and John Locke. In W. Kolbrener & M. Michelson (Eds.), *Mary Astell: Reason, gender and faith* (pp. 65–85). Ashgate.

Liebenberg, R., & Scharf, S. (2019). *Walking out the door: The facts, figures, and future of experienced women lawyers in private practice*. American Bar Association. www.americanbar.org/groups/diversity/women/initiatives_awards/long-term-careers-for-women/walking-out-the-door/ [https://perma.cc/W393-EQV9]

Lowe, J. (2018). *2018 partner compensation survey*. Major, Lindsey & Africa.

National Association for Law Placement. (2010). *NALP bulletin: NALP research on non-binary law school graduates*. National Association for Legal Placement.

Peery, D., Brown, P., & Letts, E. (2020). *Left out and left behind*. American Bar Association.

Perry, R. (1986). *The celebrated Mary Astell: An early English feminist*. University of Chicago Press.

Sheppard Mullin [@SheppardMullin]. (n.d.) X (formerly Twitter) profile. Retrieved Spring 2024, from https://x.com/SheppardMullin

Sowaal, A. (Ed.). (2023). Mary Astell. *The Stanford encyclopedia of philosophy*. Stanford University. https://plato.stanford.edu/archives/sum2023/entries/astell/ [https://perma.cc/QAX8-W86L]

Sutherland, C. (2005). *The eloquence of Mary Astell*. University of Calgary Press.

Sterling, J., & Chanow, L. (2021). *In their own words*. American Bar Association. www.americanbar.org/groups/diversity/women/initiatives_awards/long-term-careers-for-women/in-their-own-words/

13

Dissoi Logoi, Rhetorical Listening, and Legal Education

Elizabeth C. Britt[*]

13.1 INTRODUCTION

Law schools should teach students not just to think like a lawyer but to listen like a sophist. The connection between these two rhetorical capacities was made clear by Anne-Marie Slaughter (2002), then a professor at Harvard Law School, when addressing students who had just completed their first year:

> You are now all well on your way to that magical state that is the end-product of your first year in law school: thinking like a lawyer. So what have we taught you? Thinking like a lawyer ... means that you can make arguments on any side of any question. Many of you resist that teaching, thinking that we are stripping you of your personal principles and convictions, transforming you into a hired gun. On the contrary, learning how to *make* arguments on different sides of a question is learning that there *are* arguments on both sides, and learning how to *hear* them.

Although not always recognized as such, these are ancient ideas and tensions. Teaching students to argue on either side of a question was common among sophists but decried by Plato for distracting speakers and listeners from truth and justice. Today, this practice is a given in legal pedagogy, embedded in the case method itself (Sullivan et al., 2007, p. 186). Less prominent in contemporary legal education is a focus on hearing. Yet for the ancient Greeks, listening was a rhetorical art (Johnstone, 2009).

This chapter explores the anonymous sophistic text *Dissoi Logoi* (written about 400 BCE) as a way of emphasizing the need to educate future lawyers not just to argue but to listen. Sophists were traveling intellectuals who in the fifth century BCE taught rhetoric, politics, and ethics in the newly emerging democracies of Greek city-states. Through their teachings, sophists equipped citizens (free, native-

[*] Thank you to the other contributors to this volume for their helpful feedback on earlier versions of this chapter.

born men) to participate in civic life, especially to speak in law courts, as there were no professional lawyers. Although the sophists were not a monolithic group, the overarching purpose of their pedagogy was "to demonstrate that the world could always be recreated linguistically, restated in other words, and thus understood otherwise" (Poulakos, 1994, p. 25). The world could always be "understood otherwise" because truth for the sophists was not certain and timeless but probable and contingent, something they learned through exposure to different cultures through travel.

The *Dissoi Logoi* illustrates the concept of "dissoi logoi" (or twofold arguments), an idea widely credited to the sophist Protagoras, but it also contains evidence of the sources of sophistic invention, namely listening to others. Like historian of rhetoric John Poulakos in his writing about the sophists, I seek less to arrive at fixed meanings of the *Dissoi Logoi* than to approach it as an "elusive" text that "can stimulate readers to rethink the constitution of their own lives" (Poulakos, 1994, p. 3). In particular, I connect the *Dissoi Logoi* to the contemporary notion of rhetorical listening – as theorized by Krista Ratcliffe (2005) – using appellate and North Carolina Supreme Court opinions in *State v. Norman* (1988 and 1989, respectively), a case about a woman convicted of voluntary manslaughter in the death of her abusive husband. *State v. Norman* is included in a number of criminal law casebooks, the compilations of opinions that dominate contemporary legal education. In the popular casebook analyzed in this chapter, editorial decisions thwart the efforts of readers to hear arguments on either side of this case. I use my analysis of this casebook to consider the possibilities for rhetorical listening in legal education more broadly. I argue that legal education should encourage students to listen rhetorically to the variety of materials they encounter – in casebooks and elsewhere – to hear not only the multiple voices present (and missing) from cases but also the voices framing them. My goal is to show how rhetorical listening can help law students and lawyers learn to avoid jumping to conclusions based on stereotypes, a prerequisite of cultural competence.

13.2 *DISSOI LOGOI* AND RHETORICAL LISTENING

Dissoi logoi is both a concept and the name of a text. The concept is thought to have originated with Protagoras, although we have no text on the subject from Protagoras himself. Instead, as rhetoric scholar Edward Schiappa notes, a number of ancient Greek writers credit Protagoras with the idea "that there are two *logoi* in opposition about every 'thing'" (Schiappa, 2003, p. 89). According to Schiappa, many translations reduce the idea "to the proposition that a debate is possible on any topic" (p. 90). These translations, he says, misinterpret Protagoras to be speaking narrowly about argumentative skills rather than more broadly about the relationship between language and reality, which he understood to concern the unity of opposites (p. 92). Protagoras's notion of *dissoi logoi*, he argues, is more accurately a claim that "there are two opposing ways (*logoi*) to describe, account for, or explain any given experience" (p. 92). As historian of rhetoric Susan Jarratt explains, Protagoras understood *dissoi logoi* as the foundation for seeing experience as the only source of knowledge (Jarratt, 1991, p. 50). Fellow rhetoric scholar Poulakos elaborates, explaining that "Protagoras' notion of *dissoi logoi* provides a worldview with rhetoric at its center ... [T]his worldview demands of the human subject a multiple awareness, an awareness at once cognizant of its own position and of those positions opposing it" (Poulakos, 1994, p. 58).

Legal scholar Francis J. Mootz sees in *dissoi logoi* the foundations of a rhetorical knowledge useful for law. The concept advances the idea that while knowledge is not absolute and eternal, neither is it completely relative. Instead, it "emerges in the creative refashioning of linguistically structured symbols of social cohesion by members of the public" (Mootz, 2006, p. 39). For law, the implications are "pragmatic, epistemic, and ethical," beginning with the idea that lawyering is comprised primarily of counseling clients and negotiating with other professionals (pp. 128–129). Legal scholar Eileen Scallen, who calls herself "a cheerful, unrepentant, out and proud, latter-day Sophist" (Scallen, 2006, p. 923), also values the sophists for their "contingent, but practical kind of truth," evidenced by the *Dissoi Logoi* (Scallen, 2003, p. 819). She considers their pragmatic approach to conflict particularly useful for teaching advocacy, procedure, and evidence.

The text known as *Dissoi Logoi*, which appears incomplete, has no title in the original but is so named because of its opening words: "Two-fold arguments [*dissoi logoi*] concerning the good and the bad are put forward in Greece by those who philosophize" (Sprague, 1968, p. 155). Many scholars estimate its date at 400 BCE, about a decade or two after the death of Protagoras. The text was found appended to the manuscripts of Sextus Empiricus, first published in 1570, and compiled with other pre-Socratic fragments into a critical edition (published in Greek and German by Hermann Diels) in 1903. It has only relatively recently been available in English. It was first translated into English by Rosamond Kent Sprague in 1968, and the first extended scholarly discussion of the text appeared in the introduction and notes to T. M. Robinson's English translation in 1979. As translated by Sprague, the text is about 5,400 words long.[1]

The first four sections of the *Dissoi Logoi* are arguments about pairs of terms (good/bad, seemly/disgraceful, just/unjust, and truth/falsehood). For each pair of terms, the author first argues that their meaning depends on context (e.g., "death is bad for those who die, but good for the undertakers and gravediggers") and then that their meaning is universal (e.g., "the good is one thing and the bad another, and ... as the name differs, so does the thing named"). The fifth section concerns whether all things are the same or different. The final four sections address the teachability of virtue, the assigning of public offices by lot, the qualities of a good speaker, and the

[1] An open access translation is also available. See Molinelli (2018).

training of memory. Although scholars disagree on whether the text has a unified theme, Robinson (1979, p. 79) argues that all the topics cohere under the theme of participation in public life.

Because of its association with sophistic ideas, most scholars see the text as a pedagogical artifact, a compilation of lecture notes created by a speaker or listener (Kerford, 1981). Although the writer was dismissed by Diels in 1903 as untalented because of inconsistencies in the arguments and argument structures, Robinson (1996) argues that the text demonstrates full awareness of contemporaneous philosophical discussion. For this reason, Robinson sees the *Dissoi Logoi* as a "genuine *teaching manual* for sophists" (p. 32) that compels those reading or listening to assess the arguments for themselves.

What can the *Dissoi Logoi* teach contemporary lawyers and legal educators? To be sure, the text illustrates how to argue on both sides of a question, linking contemporary legal education and practice with the rhetorical tradition. What classicist Michael Gagarin writes about the practice of *dissoi logoi* for the sophists – that it helped students "to explore new ways of thinking about ethical, legal, and political issues" (Gagarin, 2002, p. 22) – is equally applicable today. More significantly, though, it demonstrates the contingency and cultural specificity of knowledge and helps us recuperate the neglected rhetorical art of listening to recognize that knowledge, a capacity sorely needed by practicing attorneys.

Many scholars in rhetoric have focused on the multicultural perspective evidenced by the text, particularly in a passage on the "seemly and disgraceful." In this passage, the writer compares how pairs of cultures view the same practices, as in these two examples: "To the Spartans it is seemly that young girls should do athletics and go about with bare arms and no tunics, but to the Ionians this is disgraceful ... The Massagetes cut up their parents and eat them, and they think that to be buried in their children is the most beautiful grave imaginable, but in Greece, if anyone did such a thing, he would be driven out of the country and would die an ignominious death for having committed such disgraceful and terrible deeds" (Sprague, 1968, p. 158). For rhetoric scholars Patricia Bizzell and Bruce Herzberg, the passage reflects the pan-Hellenism of the sophists, the idea that communities could unite "on grounds of a common recognition that humanity could express itself in many ways and was not subject to an absolute standard that could mark some ways for annihilation" (Bizzell & Herzberg, 2001, p. 25).

Although speaking more broadly about sophistic rhetoric rather than the *Dissoi Logoi* text in particular, Mootz emphasizes the value of the sophists for thinking about our own multicultural challenges in a 1998 book review of *Beyond All Reason: The Radical Assault on Truth in American Law* by Daniel Farber and Suzanna Sherry. Farber and Sherry critique the relativism of radical multiculturalism in the legal academy and argue for the possibility of finding objective truth. Although the authors do not explicitly reference ancient philosophy, Mootz (1998, p. 637) sees their argument as a reenactment of Plato's attacks on the sophists, especially given their role as "professional provocateurs" in a society dealing with its own multicultural challenges. The radicals that Farber and Sherry critique (including critical race scholars, feminists, and queer theorists) are like the sophists, Mootz argues, in that they position rhetoric as a pragmatic alternative to philosophic discourse. Like Protagoras, these radicals do not embrace the idea that truth is chaotically and unpredictably relative but that it is created communally in discourse. Rather than "claiming that law is hopelessly irrational," then, Mootz (1998, p. 639) maintains "that law often requires a reasonable judgment as between two or more logically acceptable resolutions of a given issue," a lesson taught by the sophists through *dissoi logoi*.

The applicability of this multicultural perspective to our own moment seems clear. But how does one acquire it? The excerpt on "the seemly and the disgraceful" draws on cultural knowledge made available to the sophists through travel. In their search for students, the sophists were known for moving from city to city. Through encounters with potential students and others, they learned not only about various cultural practices but also the worldviews behind these practices. The sophists brought this knowledge along with them to each new city, using it to challenge the worldviews of students there. Like today's ethnographers, the sophists probably learned through observing and listening to others. Speaking methodologically, then, one strategy of invention (the practice of coming up with arguments) evidenced by the *Dissoi Logoi* is listening. Its arguments are grounded in cultural knowledge only available through this practice. As Poulakos (1994, p. 58) explains, "in order to understand an issue, one must be prepared to listen to at least two contrary sides; and in order to decide how to act, one must espouse one of the two sides or come up with a third."

Rhetorical theorist Krista Ratcliffe has recuperated listening as a practice rooted in the rhetorical tradition. Listening, she explains, was central to rhetorical training for 2,000 years but now runs a "poor, poor fourth" to reading, writing, and speaking, and is seen as "something that everyone does but no one needs study" (Ratcliffe, 2005, p. 18). By adding the term "rhetorical" to the word "listening," Ratcliffe emphasizes two things: First, listening, like other rhetorical practices, must be learned and can be taught. Second, listening, like other rhetorical practices, helps us decide how to conduct ourselves in relations with others. She defines rhetorical listening as a "stance of openness that a person may choose to assume in relation to any person, text, or culture" (p. 1). Rhetorical listening isn't something done just with the ears, although a person can take a rhetorical listening stance when encountering an aural text. Instead, it's an *attitude* that functions primarily to foster communication across difference. Ratcliffe defines four "moves" of rhetorical listening that can be modeled, taught, and practiced. The first, which I focus on in this chapter, is "promoting an understanding of self and other" (p. 26).

To explain this move, Ratcliffe (2005, p. 28) inverts "understanding" to "standing under" our own and others' discourses, or strands of thought that are at once individual, social, and cultural. When attempting to understand myself in this way, for example, I would identify the various discourses that I bring to encounters with other people or with texts. When attempting to understand others, I would listen not only for more legible discourses but also for "(un)conscious presences, absences, unknowns" (p. 29). In both cases, the idea is to let these discourses "wash over, through, and around us and then [let] them lie there to inform our politics and ethics" (p. 28). To see this move in action, consider this line from the section of the *Dissoi Logoi* on the seemly and disgraceful: "Egyptians do not think the same things seemly as other people do: in our country we regard it as seemly that the women should weave and work <in wool> but in theirs they think it seemly for the men to do so and for the women to do what the men do in ours" (Sprague, 1968, p. 158). As in other examples from the text, the listener has identified a strand of thought (here, what is seemly) in their own lives and in the lives of others. By identifying cultural assumptions about gender and work that often go unspoken, the listener is better prepared to engage ethically with others.

Similar moves to foster cross-cultural competence are receiving increasing attention in law schools, especially from faculty in clinical legal education. Most influential may be the five habits for cross-cultural lawyering developed by Susan Bryant and Jean Koh Peters (2005). The habits are designed to foster a nonjudgmental attitude and an ability to look "through the eyes and cultural lens" of another (Bryant et al., 2014, p. 350). "Attentive listening" is a component of the habits, aimed at helping students focus on the client's interpretation of a problem (Bryant, 2001, p. 73). For Bryant and Peters, this work is done in skills-training classes, when students are working with real clients or in hypothetical client scenarios. But is there a way to move this work earlier, into doctrinal classes that form the core of legal education? After all, as Elizabeth Mertz explains in her 2007 anthropological study of legal education, the first year is hugely influential in shaping how lawyers learn to think. In particular, the method of reading taught in the first year emphasizes "layers of textual authority as neutral sources for legal decision making" (Mertz, 2007, p. 5) rather than ideologically freighted selections of reality. Because casebooks dominate legal curricula, students learn this method of reading primarily in their encounters with this genre.

13.3 LISTENING RHETORICALLY TO *STATE V. NORMAN*

In the remainder of this chapter, I explore how students might gain cultural competence through learning to listen rhetorically to how a casebook presents the case of Judy Ann Laws Norman, a woman who had suffered decades of severe abuse and forced prostitution at the hands of John Thomas ("J.T.") Norman. After a particularly brutal two-day period, Judy had shot her husband as he napped. Indicted for first-degree murder, Judy Norman was convicted of voluntary manslaughter and sentenced to six years in prison. The trial judge had admitted evidence pertaining to self-defense but denied Norman's request to instruct the jury on that charge, instructing instead on first-degree murder, second-degree murder, and manslaughter. Judy Norman appealed based on that denial, and the North Carolina Court of Appeals found in her favor and remanded the case for a new trial (*State v. Norman*, 1988). The North Carolina Supreme Court disagreed, reinstating her conviction (*State v. Norman*, 1989). After serving two months and three days, Judy Norman was granted clemency by the governor and released (Ruffin, 1989).

At issue in the case was the definition of *imminence*: Only if Judy Norman reasonably believed she was in imminent danger at the time of J.T.'s death would she be entitled to an instruction on self-defense. In *dissoi logoi* terms, the Court of Appeals and North Carolina Supreme Court argued on both sides of this question: Did Judy Norman reasonably believe that J.T. Norman posed an imminent threat when she shot him? The Court of Appeals said yes. The North Carolina Supreme Court said no, despite recounting in their own opinion ample evidence of J.T.'s imminent threat to Judy, including testimony from expert witnesses and eyewitnesses to his abuse. The lone dissenter revisited this testimonial evidence, arguing forcefully that a reasonable juror would share Judy's belief that danger was imminent. All three opinions are included in Joshua Dressler and Stephen P. Garvey's popular casebook, *Criminal Law: Cases and Materials* (currently in its ninth edition, published in 2022), along with discussion questions and notes that frame them for the reader.[2]

Casebooks are the central genre of legal education, part of the case method developed at Harvard Law School in the late nineteenth century. Christopher Columbus Langdell, who is often credited as the originator of the case method and who created the first casebook, saw law as a science comprised of principles that could be extracted from appellate opinions (Stevens, 1983, p. 52). In the case method, professors focus on the language of these opinions in intense dialogue with students. To prepare students for these classroom discussions, faculty predominantly have students read opinions in casebooks, which usually compile them on a particular topic such as criminal law or contracts. For his own casebooks, Langdell chose cases based on how they contributed to the development of legal principles, while later authors chose cases that would help students understand legal process (Stevens, 1983, p. 56). The genre has evolved to include not only cases but also headnotes, discussion and study questions, and other materials designed to teach legal doctrine and procedure. Opinions themselves are often edited to narrow the reader's focus on the concepts central to the pedagogical purpose.

Although not necessarily obvious to their readers, opinions and casebooks demonstrate the sophistic principle that the world can be "recreated linguistically."

[2] According to one 2016 review of criminal law casebooks, Dressler and Garvey's sixth edition shared the biggest part of the market with just one other text (Ohlin, 2016, p. 1159).

In other words, the materials contained in them are not the actual world of conflict and resolution but representations of it embodied in language. These representations necessarily reflect and select certain realities while deflecting others.[3] The opinions themselves are not trial transcripts; they are instead "highly edited and abstracted versions of events" (Sullivan et al., 2007, p. 55). (And, of course, trial transcripts are themselves removed from the real events the proceedings adjudicate.) Once included in casebooks, as Mertz (2007, pp. 52–53) points out, opinions are "recontextualized"; they are removed from their original contexts (bound reporters and online services) and placed into a new context "formed by other case excerpts, notes on cases, occasional excerpts from articles or books, and the casebook author's commentary, typically bound together in a heavy book devoted to one area of law." Listening rhetorically to casebooks can give readers a window onto how events in the world are being recreated and how they could have been otherwise. Using Ratcliffe's first move, a reader can listen rhetorically to legal materials by "acknowledging the existence" of the various discourses as well as the "(un)conscious presences, absences, unknowns" (Ratcliffe, 2005, p. 29).

I offer the following focal points for using Ratcliffe's first move of rhetorical listening with Dressler and Garvey's treatment of *Norman*. First, we can pay attention to the multiplicity of voices within the text. We can listen to the Justices (including the dissenter), the trial court judge, and the casebook editors. We can listen to Judy Norman, to the police who testified, and to eyewitnesses who spoke about Judy's life and her husband's treatment of her. We can listen to the expert witness testimony and the psychotherapeutic discourses they represent. We can ask whose voices are missing. Second, we can pay attention to how we hear these voices. Which voices are included in some texts and not included in others? At what points are Norman's words taken literally from the transcript of the trial? From the accounts of police officers? From her family members? What is the effect of these mediations? In the casebook, how do discussion questions or headnotes direct the attention to some things rather than others? How do these questions frame what we see? What has been edited out of the opinions (as indicated by ellipses or asterisks)? In which chapter is the case placed? Under what heading? What other cases sit before and after? How do these placements prime us to understand the case in a particular way? Third, we can pay attention to how different voices select facts and explain the same facts or concepts. For example, how does each characterize J.T.'s act of sleeping? Which of Judy's acts are emphasized and which downplayed? How do the various legal experts explain "imminent" in relation to threat? How do they explain "reasonable" belief? Finally, we can pay attention to how discourses embodied within ourselves affect what we hear. What have I heard or seen about

[3] See Kenneth Burke's concept of terministic screens: "Even if any given terminology is a *reflection* of reality, by its very nature as a terminology it must be a *selection* of reality; and to this extent it must function also as a *deflection* of reality" (Burke, 1966, p. 45).

intimate partner violence? What explanations of intimate partner violence do I believe? How have my education and experiences taught me what to believe and value?

My analysis of Dressler and Garvey's casebook in the following pages shows that their editorial decisions thwart the ability of readers to ask many of these questions about the opinions in *Norman*. However, I also demonstrate that readers *can* ask them about the casebook itself. To establish the context within which Dressler and Garvey are writing, I first turn to how legal scholars have consistently misunderstood *Norman*, drawing upon the work of legal scholar Martha R. Mahoney.[4]

13.3.1 *Scholarly Misunderstanding and Misrepresentation of* State v. Norman

Norman is widely cited in law review articles on criminal law and intimate partner violence.[5] In a detailed analysis of this scholarship, Mahoney (2019, p. 677) argues that despite *Norman* being "one of the best-known cases in criminal law," scholars have almost uniformly misunderstood and misrepresented the case in regard to intimate partner violence. Through their work, these scholars have accepted and perpetuated stereotypes of intimate partner violence rather than listening to the variety of voices in the opinions, including those of Judy Norman herself and expert witnesses who testified at her trial. In particular, Mahoney (2019, p. 705) argues that scholars have misunderstood the use of expert witness testimony on the psychological effects of abuse, seeing this testimony as providing evidence that a victim's behavior cannot be understood as objectively reasonable. This misunderstanding stems from two quarters. First is confusion about the concept of "learned helplessness," a term of art used in psychologist Lenore Walker's theory of "battered woman syndrome." Scholars have often taken the term to mean that victims of abuse become completely passive and submissive, essentially "learning to be helpless" (Mahoney, 2019, p. 705). Walker (2000, p. 116) has written that she intended the concept, borrowed from psychologist Martin Seligman, to mean that victims lose "the ability to predict that what [they] do will make a particular outcome occur."[6] Second is that Walker's work (simplified and misunderstood as it is) has become entrenched in legal circles, even though current social scientific theories emphasize instead the coercive control of the abuser and the strategies that victims actively employ to mitigate abuse (Hamberger et al., 2017). As Mahoney (2019,

4 In addition to her scholarly analyses of *Norman*, Mahoney has also contributed a rewritten dissent to the case for *Feminist Judgments: Rewritten Criminal Law Opinions* (Mahoney, 2022).

5 In a Westlaw search in January 2023, I found nearly 300 citations in law reviews to *Norman* at either the appellate or NC Supreme Court level.

6 However, Walker's own writing has contributed to the confusion. In an earlier book, *The Battered Woman*, she writes: "Once we believe we cannot control what happens to us, it is difficult to believe we can ever influence it, even if later we experience a favorable outcome . . . Once the women are operating from a belief of helplessness, the perception becomes reality and they become passive, submissive, 'helpless'" (Walker, 1979, p. 47).

p. 671) argues, "battered woman syndrome" in its most simplistic form has become a generic and widely accepted shorthand for expert evidence about intimate partner violence in legal practice and scholarship, with pathologizing results. When a woman who kills her abuser is seen as suffering from an abnormal psychological condition that makes her passive and unable to accurately perceive reality, scholars immersed in this framework thus overlook evidence of her active responses to ongoing violence, the actual threat posed by the abuser, and the possibility that reasonable observers would share her sense of imminent danger.

Mahoney focuses primarily on how scholars have evaluated Judy Norman's perception of risk from her husband at the moment she killed him. If Norman had faced an imminent threat of death or great bodily harm, the judge should have instructed the jury on self-defense. Norman's perception of the *imminence* of the threat matters; her perception could be deemed to be either reasonable or unreasonable. Mahoney (2019, p. 711) found that many scholars evaluated Norman's perception through the lens of abnormal psychology because of the battered woman syndrome framework.

Yet, as Mahoney notes, the opinions themselves contain ample evidence that Norman's perceptions were reasonable. The majority opinion from the North Carolina Supreme Court, which reinstated her conviction, explains that under the imminence requirement, deadly force can be used only as a "last resort" (*State v. Norman*, 1989, p. 261). Judy Norman, they write, "had ample time and opportunity to resort to other means of preventing further abuse" (pp. 261–262). Yet their own narrative recounts the multiple ways that Judy Norman had exhausted these means: She had left numerous times in the past and had always been found and beaten by J.T. as a result; she called the police the day before the shooting, but the police advised her to file a complaint, told her that they couldn't arrest J.T. without a warrant, and left;[7] she attempted suicide after the police left that same day, and as the paramedics attended to her, J.T. cursed her and told them to let her die; and she sought help from a mental health center and a welfare benefits office the day of the shooting, only to have J.T. threaten to kill her (pp. 256–258).

Furthermore, although the majority declared that J.T. had done nothing "immediately prior to his falling asleep" (*State v. Norman*, 1989, p. 262) that would show an imminent deadly threat from him, they describe him earlier in the day "threatening to kill and to maim her, slapping her, kicking her, … throwing objects at her" (p. 257), and putting out a cigarette on her torso. Judy Norman's own testimony,

[7] Mahoney (2019, p. 670 n. 19) notes that the police were incorrect and that no complaint/warrant was required: "When the police told Judy they could not arrest J.T. unless she 'took out a warrant,' they were wrong – state law had changed years earlier to allow warrantless arrest for domestic violence."

included in their narrative, provides evidence of what she knew would happen when he awoke: "Asked why she killed her husband, the defendant replied: 'Because I was scared of him and I knowed when he woke up, it was going to be the same thing, and I was scared when he took me to the truck stop that night it was going to be worse than he had ever been'" (p. 257). As related earlier in the opinion, J.T. had for years forced her into prostitution at the truck stop, beating her if she resisted. She was expecting him to traffic her after he woke up, as he always did,[8] and the increased violence of the previous two days provided evidence that "it was going to be worse."

Mahoney pays considerable attention to the discrepancies in how the various opinions and subsequent commentaries characterize the time of day that J.T. was asleep. She argues that although the Court of Appeals accurately portrayed his sleep as a "nap" in the late afternoon, with the police arriving to find him dead at 7:30 pm, the North Carolina Supreme Court and scholars have characterized J.T. as asleep at night, with one scholar even portraying the event as a "midnight shooting" (Mahoney, 2019, p. 681). Mahoney argues that these errors "reveal stereotypes about impaired perception in battered women" and highlight the stubbornness of scholarly interpretation: "How else," she writes, "could 'afternoon' turn into 'midnight' without anyone noticing the change?" (p. 682).

The scholar who portrays Judy Norman's killing of her husband as a "midnight shooting" is Joshua Dressler (2006, p. 468 n. 27), who not only included *Norman* in his casebook with Garvey but has written several articles on women who have killed abusers. Dressler is outwardly sympathetic to Judy Norman; in an article in which he devotes extensive discussion to her case, he argues that he would defend her using an autonomy theory, writing that she "possesses a moral – if you will, natural – right of autonomy, a right that J.T. Norman violated on a daily basis by his physically injurious conduct, which right entitled Judy to kill him to protect her autonomy" (p. 466). Dressler embraces this theory because he claims that "there is simply no basis" to believe that J.T. Norman presented an imminent threat either in reality or in the mind of Judy Norman (pp. 463–464). Yet Justice Martin, who dissented from the North Carolina Supreme Court's decision, provides the basis that Dressler claims does not exist. Arguing that the doctrine of self-defense requires that imminence must "be grasped from the defendant's point of view," Justice Martin writes that testimony not only from Judy Norman but from other witnesses "could have led a juror to conclude that defendant reasonably perceived a threat to her life as 'imminent,' even while her husband slept" (*State v. Norman*, 1989, p. 271). To proclaim that "there is no basis" for arguments on one side of this question, as Dressler does, relies on stereotypes of intimate partner violence.

[8] The fact that he did traffic her every night comes from the transcript (Mahoney, 2019, p. 675 n. 1).

13.3.2 *Thwarting Rhetorical Listening through Editorial Decisions*

Stereotypes of any sort are harmful enough in scholarly articles. Unfortunately, Dressler and Garvey's (2022a) editorial choices in *Criminal Law: Cases and Materials* reinforce these stereotypes and hinder the reader's ability to listen rhetorically to the opinions so that they can come to a different understanding of Judy Norman's reasonableness. Readers can, however, listen rhetorically to the casebook itself by paying attention to what the editors cut from the opinions and how they framed them through headnotes, discussion questions, and placement.

Dressler and Garvey include excerpted versions of all three *Norman* opinions (the appellate opinion, as well as the majority and dissenting opinion from the North Carolina Supreme Court). Dressler and Garvey's edits make it difficult for students to assess Judy Norman's reasonableness for themselves. Although opinions included in casebooks must be shortened by necessity, casebook authors must be aware of how their choices affect readers. Importantly, Dressler and Garvey's choices direct students away from the actual question at issue between the appeals court and the North Carolina Supreme Court. Consider that the unedited opinion for the appeals court, which found in Judy Norman's favor, begins the legal analysis with a summary of self-defense law in North Carolina (*State v. Norman*, 1988, p. 390):

> In North Carolina a defendant is entitled to an instruction on perfect self-defense as justification for homicide where, viewed in the light most favorable to the defendant, there is evidence tending to show that at the time of the killing:
>
> (1) it appeared to defendant and he believed it to be necessary to kill the deceased in order to save himself from death or great bodily harm; and
> (2) defendant's belief was reasonable in that the circumstances as they appeared to him at the time were sufficient to create such a belief in the mind of a person of ordinary firmness; and
> (3) defendant was not the aggressor in bringing on the affray, i.e., he did not aggressively and willingly enter into the fight without legal excuse or provocation; and
> (4) defendant did not use excessive force, i.e., did not use more force than was necessary or reasonably appeared to him to be necessary under the circumstances to protect himself from death or great bodily harm.
>
> Under this standard, the reasonableness of defendant's belief in the necessity to kill decedent and non-aggression on defendant's part are two essential elements of the defense.

Dressler and Garvey omit this material, starting instead with a sentence that appears a page later: "The question * * * arising on the facts in this case is whether the victim's passiveness at the moment the [homicidal] act occurred precludes defendant from asserting * * * self-defense" (Dressler & Garvey, 2022a, p. 561). Coming at the beginning of their analysis, the court's summary of the relevant self-defense law prepares the reader of the opinion to understand Judy Norman's actions from her point of view. Omitting this summary, as Dressler and Garvey do, emphasizes instead J.T. Norman's passiveness. The edited version also replaces the word "unlawful" with "homicidal," a choice that seems unnecessary at best, given that the reader has just read an extensive description of the facts of J.T.'s death and so knows the nature of the act. At worst, it characterizes Judy Norman's act in the most culpable terms possible, conflicting with the court's ultimate decision to grant Judy Norman a new trial.

In another edit to the appellate opinion, Dressler and Garvey thwart readers from questioning different representations of J.T.'s act of sleeping. Although they retain the appellate opinion's statement that "in the late afternoon, Norman wanted to take a nap," Dressler and Garvey eliminate the time of day (7:30 pm) that the police had arrived at the Norman residence to find J.T. dead, reducing the possibility for students to question for themselves whether J.T. was asleep for the night.[9] In the unedited version, the time of day was especially prominent, coming in the first lines of the fact statement, while the description of J.T. deciding to take a nap comes three pages later. Notably, the teacher's manual also says that J.T. was "fast asleep" when Judy shot him (Dressler & Garvey, 2002b, p. 184), further influencing how instructors might frame the material for students. In the casebook, Dressler and Garvey also omit a crucial piece of the dissent. When explaining the evidence presented by the defense regarding whether Judy Norman believed she could escape J.T., the dissent had included the following testimony from a court-appointed forensic psychologist:

> Mrs. Norman didn't leave because she believed, fully believed that escape was totally impossible. There was no place to go. He, she had left before; he had come and gotten her. She had gone to the Department of Social Services. He had come and gotten her. The law, she believed the law could not protect her; no one could protect her, and *I must admit, looking over the records, that there was nothing done that would contradict that belief.* (*State v. Norman*, 1989, p. 269 [emphasis added])

Not only does this expert highlight what Judy had actively done to leave, he also declares that he found nothing that she had overlooked. By omitting this part of the dissent, Dressler and Garvey (2022a) prevent students from seeing that the trial court's own appointed expert had independently validated the reasonableness of her fear.

Dressler and Garvey's (2022a) choices in framing the case reinforce stereotypes about intimate partner violence. The case appears in Chapter 9 General Defenses to

9 Compare the original to the edited version, with asterisks representing omissions. Original: "At trial the State presented the testimony of a deputy sheriff of the Rutherford County Sheriff's Department who testified that on 12 June 1985, at approximately 7:30 p.m., he was dispatched to the Norman residence" (*State v. Norman*, 1989, p. 254). Edited: "At trial the State presented the testimony of a deputy sheriff * * * who testified that * * * he was dispatched to the Norman residence" (Dressler & Garvey, 2022a, p. 557).

Crimes, in a section on the "reasonable belief" requirement for self-defense. Dressler and Garvey's recontextualization of the case relative to others prepares students to see Judy Norman through the syndrome framework: The case is given its own section called "Battered Women, Battered Woman Syndrome and Beyond" that follows a section about the reasonable belief requirement "in general" and the "reasonable person." To be sure, all three opinions discuss Judy Norman's situation in terms of the syndrome testimony presented at trial. However, both the appellate opinion and the North Carolina Supreme Court dissent see no contradiction between this syndrome testimony and the possibility that Judy Norman acted reasonably. Placing *Norman* into its own section primes readers to see Judy Norman's behavior as outside the realm of reasonable.

Dressler and Garvey's headnote to *Norman* reinforces this perception. Headnotes in the chapter are inconsistent; most cases have no headnotes, a few briefly explain a legal concept the case is meant to demonstrate, one directs students to an interview with the controversial defendant,[10] and one (regarding a woman who killed her four children) contains just a short warning that it "is an emotionally difficult case to read" (Dressler & Garvey, 2022a, p. 678). The headnote for *Norman* jumps out in comparison. It features two items. First is a four-paragraph summary of the case of Francine Hughes, whose story was the basis of the book and TV film *The Burning Bed*. The summary describes the abuse that Hughes endured at the hands of her husband, as well as how she killed him by dousing him with gasoline while he was asleep and lighting the bed on fire. Hughes was acquitted after she pleaded "temporary insanity" (Dressler & Garvey, 2022a, p. 556). The second item in the headnote is a two-sentence summary of Lenore Walker's book *The Battered Woman*, which names "battered woman syndrome" but does not define, contextualize, or historicize it (p. 556). This introduction simultaneously sensationalizes both cases and prepares the law student reader to understand *Norman* as being primarily about abnormal psychology. In the notes following the opinions, the only explanation of battered woman syndrome is taken from a 2004 judicial opinion (*State v. Smullen*, 2004) that misrepresents learned helplessness as "when, after repeated abuse, women come to believe that they cannot control the situation and thus become passive and submissive" (as cited in Dressler and Garvey 2022a, p. 571). The opinion also claims that battered woman syndrome explains "why the defendant, having been previously subjected to abuse, simply did not leave the home or take some other action against her abuser" (as cited in Dressler and Garvey 2022a, p. 571), an assertion at odds with research available at the time explaining both substantial obstacles to leaving as well as how often victims do leave only to be pursued and punished, often killed.[11] This description certainly does not accord with the facts of *Norman*; even the North

[10] Bernard ("Bernie") Hugo Goetz, otherwise known as "the subway vigilante" (Dressler & Garvey, 2022a, p. 536).

[11] For example, see Barnett (2000).

Carolina Supreme Court majority opinion details how many actions Judy Norman took to keep herself safe, including leaving on multiple occasions only to be found, brought home, and beaten, and later attempting what legal scholar Marina Angel (2008, p. 70) calls the "ultimate exit, suicide."

Dressler and Garvey's discussion notes regarding imminence further shape the student's perception of the case, leaving no room for considering the possibility that Judy Norman *did* face an imminent threat, even though arguments on both sides of this question frame all of the opinions. At the North Carolina Supreme Court level, the question of imminence is *the* primary question, with the majority arguing that because J.T. was asleep when he was shot, "there was no action underway by decedent from which the jury could have found that the defendant had reasonable grounds to believe ... that a felonious assault was imminent" (*State v. Norman*, 1989, p. 262). In response, Justice Martin argues in his dissent that "'imminent' is a term the meaning of which must be grasped from the defendant's point of view," assuming that this belief "was reasonable in the mind of a person of ordinary firmness" (p. 271). He continues, writing that Judy Norman's "intense fear" of grievous bodily harm or death, supported not just by her own testimony but by that of witnesses, "could have led a juror to conclude that defendant reasonably perceived a threat to her life as 'imminent,' even while her husband slept" (p. 271). Although the appeals court does not use the term "imminent," they write that "a jury, in our view, could find that decedent's sleep was but a momentary hiatus in a continuous reign of terror by the decedent [and] that defendant merely took advantage of her first opportunity to protect herself" (*State v. Norman*, 1988, p. 392). Despite the centrality of the issue of imminent threat to all of the opinions, Dressler and Garvey treat the question as settled. Rather than asking students to think through whether Judy Norman faced an imminent threat, they ask whether the imminence requirement should be abandoned. This omission reinforces the idea that Judy Norman's perception can be understood only through the lens of abnormal psychology.

The teacher's manual for the casebook reinforces this idea. Providing Dressler as a model for how to teach the case, the manual describes him starting his own class discussions with the question of whether the trial jury should have been instructed on self-defense without testimony on battered woman syndrome. The answer he provides for other instructors is short and clear: "Not under traditional standards, in which 'imminent' means (as defined here) 'immediate danger, such as must be instantly met'" (Dressler & Garvey, 2022b, p. 183). In his own classes, he then asks students to consider whether Judy Norman would be entitled to this defense under the Model Penal Code (§3.04), which allows for the use of force when the defendant "believes that such force is immediately necessary." For Dressler, these discussions should make it "clear that Judy Norman is not entitled to a self-defense instruction" without testimony about battered woman syndrome (Dressler & Garvey, 2022b, pp. 182–183). Dressler then turns to whether this testimony would help Judy Norman's defense, directing instructors to a summary in the casebook itself of how courts currently treat expert testimony about battering. Although the trend in this testimony, according to Mahoney (2019, p. 572), is away from the pathologizing syndrome framework, the casebook inaccurately refers to this testimony as "BWS testimony" and "syndrome evidence." The casebook explains that although courts routinely admit this testimony in "confrontational homicides," they are divided about whether to admit them in "nonconfrontational" ones such as *Norman*. Labeling *Norman* a case of nonconfrontational homicide further reinforces the idea that Judy Norman's assessment of the threat from J.T. was unreasonable.

My critique of Dressler and Garvey's casebook has focused on the effects of their treatment of this case on readers' understanding of Judy Norman's reasonableness and, by extension, of intimate partner violence. After all, Judy Norman's reasonableness is at the heart of the question of imminence about which contrasting arguments are made in the opinions. Yet Dressler and Garvey treat the question of imminence as settled, perhaps because the North Carolina Supreme Court settled it *legally* in this case. Understanding the law in this way is integral to the case method. Once decided, a case becomes part of the body of law from which principles can be deduced. Given the casebook's focus on criminal law, the question of imminence in self-defense is a principle that Dressler and Garvey probably wanted to highlight. Seeing the question of imminence as legally settled by *Norman*, Dressler and Garvey might have imagined instructors using the North Carolina Supreme Court opinion to apply the principle of imminence to various hypothetical situations to determine, for example, whether imminence was definitely present, arguably present, or not present. Unfortunately, such a conversation would further reify the North Carolina Supreme Court's definition of imminence rather than helping readers see this definition as the result of contested viewpoints, of *dissoi logoi*.

13.4 IMPLICATIONS FOR INTIMATE PARTNER VIOLENCE AND BEYOND

Stereotypes of intimate partner violence likely informed the North Carolina Supreme Court's decision in *State v. Norman*. Although their opinion recounts facts that strongly support a conclusion that Judy Norman's behavior was reasonable, the majority reached the opposite conclusion by relying on stereotypes of victims of intimate partner violence as passive and damaged. Through their editorial choices, Dressler and Garvey reinforce these stereotypes. These stereotypes are potentially hugely influential on future practice, especially considering that the vast majority of law students are exposed to legal treatment of intimate partner violence only through this casebook. Most of the students who encounter *Norman* in their criminal law classes will never take a seminar devoted to intimate partner violence or have other opportunities to think about how this widespread social problem might affect their clients. And because intimate partner violence affects a victim's family life, employment, and financial affairs, lawyers in all areas of practice are likely to work with victims. At the very least, law students should not be misguided by outdated approaches that they are led to believe are current.

But the problem presented by casebooks goes beyond intimate partner violence. Although I have focused on the treatment of a single case in a single casebook, the casebook genre by definition recontextualizes its materials. All readers, students included, need to be aware of how this recontextualizing can frame their understanding. Readers can use rhetorical listening, especially its first move, to help recognize this framing. "Standing under" the discourses of a casebook means listening for both "(un)conscious presences, absences, unknowns" and legible discourses (Ratcliffe, 2005, p. 29). Becoming aware of asterisks (sometimes used in legal writing, as in Dressler and Garvey's casebook) or ellipses can draw attention to absences, even if the reader does not compare the edited version in the casebook to the original, as I have done here.

To hear legible discourses in a casebook, readers can listen for the categories that a case has been placed into. At the broadest level, we hear the area of law covered by the casebook. For example, reading *Norman* in a criminal law casebook forces us to understand it in a different context than if we had read it in one on intimate partner violence. The case is framed by different questions and surrounded by different cases and commentary. As readers, we can also hear the placement of the case *within* the casebook. Listening to how Dressler and Garvey place *Norman* in their casebook, for example, makes psychotherapeutic discourse even more prominent than it is in the opinions themselves. Readers might not initially know what to make of this discourse, but Ratcliffe advises also listening to the discourses embodied within ourselves, with the goal of understanding how these discourses influence how we perceive the discourses of others. What are my assumptions about intimate partner violence, and where did they come from? What psychotherapeutic explanations for intimate partner violence have I heard before, and what do I think of them? Letting these discourses "wash over, through, and around us and then letting them lie there to inform our politics and ethics" (Ratcliffe, 2005, p. 28), we can come to see how Judy Norman's actions have been further pathologized, as well as our own participation in (or resistance to) this pathologizing.

Readers of any casebook can listen for *dissoi logoi*. If the casebook presents only one opinion for a case, we can listen for how the opinion, as well as the headnotes and discussion notes, presents the central question and the answers to it. If the casebook contains dissents or lower court opinions that were reversed, we can ask ourselves the following: About what central question do the opinions disagree, and what arguments do they offer? Although the concept of *dissoi logoi* assumes a binary argumentative framework, we can also imagine other possible positions on the question by listening for "(un)conscious presences, absences, unknowns" (Ratcliffe, 2005, p. 29). For example, in *Norman* the opinions argue on both sides of the question of whether Judy Norman reasonably believed that J.T. Norman posed an imminent threat when she shot him. A third position on this question is that imminence should not be a universal requirement for self-defense. This position has been taken up by a number of feminist legal theorists who argue that the law of self-defense has been universalized from male experience, presuming the kinds of situations in which men typically use deadly force rather than those in which women do.[12]

13.5 CONCLUSION

The predominant lesson of the *Dissoi Logoi* – that rhetors should learn to argue on both sides of a question – is alive and well in contemporary legal education. This practice helps law students in an adversarial system develop the skills necessary to advocate successfully, such as identifying the strengths and weaknesses on each side and anticipating an opponent's argument. But, as this chapter argues, the *Dissoi Logoi* offers other lessons, most importantly an awareness of the subjectivity of our own perspectives. If law students can learn that any issue can be seen from (at least) two sides, they can begin to see that there is no neutral position from which to observe and arrive at the truth. This recognition does not mean that truth does not exist. Instead, law students can learn that truth is created communally through the clash of discourse. They can recognize that rhetoric isn't just a tool to be deployed but the means by which our world is created.

In this chapter, I have offered rhetorical listening as a way of hearing differing perspectives. As an attitude that one can take toward any discourse, rhetorical listening provides a foundation for challenging stereotypes and communicating across cultural divides. I have focused here on casebooks because they are the dominant genre in the first-year curriculum in American law schools. But law students need to learn to listen rhetorically to all of the materials they encounter throughout the curriculum to prevent jumping to conclusions, whether based on stereotypes, insufficient information, or the desire to solve problems quickly. Rhetorical listening, like other rhetorical skills, can be learned and taught. Law students need to learn not just to argue on both sides of a question but to listen for what they do not expect to hear.

REFERENCES

Angel, M. (2008). Why Judy Norman acted in reasonable self-defense: An abused woman and a sleeping man. *Buffalo Women's Law Journal*, *16*, 65–88.

Barnett, Ola W. (2000). Why battered women do not leave, part I: External inhibiting factors in society. *Trauma, Violence & Abuse*, *1*(4), 343–372.

[12] See, for example, Schneider (2000, pp. 112–147). Although Dressler and Garvey ask in a discussion question whether the imminency requirement should be abandoned, they do not include any feminist rationale for doing so.

Bizzell, P., & Herzberg, B. (Eds.). (2001). *The rhetorical tradition: Readings from classical times to the present* (2nd ed.). Bedford/St. Martin's Press.

Bryant, S. (2001). The five habits: Building cross-cultural competence in lawyers. *Clinical Law Review*, 8, 33–107.

Bryant, S., & Peters, J. K. (2005). Five habits for cross-cultural lawyering. In K. Barrett & W. H. George (Eds.), *Race, culture, psychology, and law* (pp. 47–62). Sage Publications.

Bryant, S., Milstein, E. S., & Shalleck, A. C. (2014). *Transforming the education of lawyers: The theory and practice of clinical pedagogy*. Carolina Academic Press.

Burke, K. (1966). *Language as symbolic action*. University of California Press.

Diels, H. (1903). *Die Fragmente der Vorsokratiker*. Weidmann.

Dressler, J. (2006). Battered women and sleeping abusers. *Ohio State Journal of Criminal Law*, 3, 457–471.

Dressler, J., & Garvey, S. P. (2022a). *Criminal law: Cases and materials* (9th ed.). West Academic Publishing.

(2022b). *Teacher's manual to Criminal law: Cases and materials* (9th ed.). West Academic Publishing.

Gagarin, M. (2002). *Antiphon the Athenian: Oratory, law, and justice in the age of the sophists*. University of Texas Press.

Hamberger, L. K., Larsen, S. E., & Lehrner, A. (2017). Coercive control in intimate partner violence. *Aggression and Violent Behavior*, 37, 1–11.

Jarratt, S. C. (1991). *Rereading the sophists: Classical rhetoric refigured*. Southern Illinois University Press.

Johnstone, C. L. (2009). *Listening to the logos: Speech and the coming of wisdom in ancient Greece*. University of South Carolina Press.

Kerford, G. B. (1981). *The sophistic movement*. Cambridge University Press.

Mahoney, M. (2019). Misunderstanding Judy Norman: Theory as cause and consequence. *Connecticut Law Review*, 51(3), 671–767.

(2022). Judgment: *State v. Norman*. In B. Capers, S. Deer, & C. R. Yung (Eds.), *Feminist judgments: Rewritten criminal law opinions* (pp. 230–252). Cambridge University Press.

Mertz, E. (2007). *The language of law school: Learning to "think like a lawyer."* Oxford University Press.

Molinelli, S. (2018). *Dissoi Logoi: A new commented edition* [Doctoral dissertation, Durham University]. Durham E-Theses Online: http://etheses.dur.ac.uk/12451 [https://perma.cc/6DHA-C988]

Mootz, F. J., III. (1998). Between truth and provocation: Reclaiming reason in American legal scholarship. *Yale Journal of Law & the Humanities*, 10(2), 605–646.

(2006). *Rhetorical knowledge in legal practice and critical legal theory*. University of Alabama Press.

Ohlin, J. D. (2016). The changing market for criminal law casebooks. *Michigan Law Review*, 114, 1155–1172.

Poulakos, J. (1994). *Sophistical rhetoric in classical Greece*. University of South Carolina Press.

Ratcliffe, K. (2005). *Rhetorical listening: Identification, gender, whiteness*. Southern Illinois University Press.

Robinson, T. M. (1979). *Contrasting arguments: An edition of the "Dissoi Logoi."* Arno Press.

(1996). The *Dissoi Logoi* and early Greek scepticism. In R. H. Popkin (Ed.), *Scepticism in the history of philosophy* (pp. 27–36). Springer Dordrecht.

Ruffin, J. (1989, July 8). Battered wife released from prison. *The News and Observer* [Raleigh], 1A.

Scallen, E. A. (2003). Evidence law as pragmatic legal rhetoric: Reconnecting legal scholarship, teaching and ethics. *Quinnipiac Law Review*, 21(4), 813–891.

(2006). Nobody likes a sophist until they need one. *Penn State Law Review*, 110(4), 923–931.
Schiappa, E. (2003). *Protagoras and logos: A study in Greek philosophy and rhetoric* (2nd ed.). University of South Carolina Press.
Schneider, E. M. (2000). *Battered women and feminist lawmaking*. Yale University Press.
Slaughter, A. (2002, May). On thinking like a lawyer. *Harvard Law Today*.
Sprague, R. K. (1968). Dissoi logoi or dialexeis. *Mind*, 77(306), 155–167.
State v. Norman, 89 N.C. App. 384 (1988).
State v. Norman, 324 N.C. 253 (1989).
State v. Smullen, 380 Md. 233 (2004).
Stevens, R. (1983). *Law school: Legal education in America from the 1850s to the 1980s*. University of North Carolina Press.
Sullivan, W. M., Colby, A., Wegner, J. W., Bond, L., & Shulman, L. S. (2007). *Educating lawyers: Preparation for the profession of law*. Jossey-Bass/Carnegie Foundation for the Advancement of Teaching.
Walker, L. E. (1979). *The battered woman*. Harper & Row Publishers.
(2000). *The battered woman syndrome* (2nd ed.). Springer.

PART VI

Looking Outward and Forward

14

An Unconventional Call for Proposals

Brian N. Larson and Elizabeth C. Britt

14.1 INTRODUCTION

We began this volume by describing it as a mosaic of theories and texts contributing tesserae – the small pebbles, stones, and glass that make up mosaics – to a larger picture of legal rhetoric. We are proud of the ways that this volume fills in a segment of this picture. First, the volume points to the richness of ancient texts. While much contemporary American legal thought relies on Aristotle, his work is often mischaracterized or simplified. The chapters by Mark Hannah and Jay Mootz on ethos (Chapter 2) and by Susan Tanner on the enthymeme (Chapter 5) challenge and complicate these received understandings. Other contributors illustrate the continued relevance of other figures of Greece and Rome – Brian Larson's chapter on Cicero (Chapter 4), Vasileios Adamidis and Laura Webb's chapter on the Attic orators (Chapter 3), and Beth Britt's chapter on a text by an anonymous sophist (Chapter 13) – while Rasha Diab rereads early Arab-Islamic discourses on women's rights (Chapter 9).

Second, the volume demonstrates the importance of closely attending to rhetorical theory as it developed in the West during the Enlightenment, a crucial period not only for the disciplines of both rhetoric and law but also for their relationship. Jennifer Andrus' chapter on John Locke (Chapter 6), and Laura Collins' chapter on Giambattista Vico (Chapter 8), illustrate opposite ideologies about language that largely represent how law and rhetoric became estranged. Judy Cornett's chapter shows us that the work of Mary Astell, an Enlightenment thinker ignored as a rhetorical theorist until relatively recently, can still teach us how to deploy ethos when addressing social problems (Chapter 12). And third, the volume demonstrates the need for engaging the rhetorical theory of the recent past and present. Kelly Carr's chapter engages with the classical notion of topoi, updated through the lens of Chaïm Perelman and Lucie Olbrechts-Tyteca (Chapter 7). Chapters by Lindsay

Head and Erin Frymire offer analyses based on the more fully contemporary theories of Michael Calvin McGee (Chapter 10) and Judith Butler (Chapter 11), respectively.

Nonetheless, as our introduction acknowledges, this collection "provides an imperfect and incomplete description of the scholarly matrix in which this volume intervenes." With the exception of Rasha Diab's chapter, the volume is limited in scope first by a focus on American law and second by a focus on rhetorical thinking from European and American traditions. Even within these traditions, this collection cannot pretend to be comprehensive.

We would like to see future work similar to this volume that engages a broader range of rhetorical traditions and applies them to a broader range of contemporary legal texts (or rhetorical performances). We would also like to see contributions whose authors reflect more of the diversity of the fields of law and rhetoric visible in the American academy and in the world. We think this desire is consistent with the invitation of Berenguer and colleagues (2023) to focus attention on a different portion of the law-and-rhetoric mosaic, including "Indigenous, African Diasporic, Asian Diasporic, and Latine" rhetorics, but in no way seeking to limit contributions only to those traditions. What's more, we believe that such efforts would benefit from extending what we mean by *rhetoric* to cover other discursive arts, including argumentation theory, dialectic, logic, and their analogs in other traditions.

In this afterword, we describe the process that led us to make invitations to scholars who could aid us in such an extension, and we make an unconventional call for proposals to scholars interested in extending this work – interested in filling in more of the tesserae in the mosaic of rhetoric and law.

14.2 GETTING HERE

The intellectual roots of this volume go back thousands of years, but its publication history begins in 2017 with Brian Larson's formation of a reading group among scholars of legal communication that explored ancient Western rhetorical traditions and considered their utility for understanding contemporary American law. Some of the authors of this volume (e.g., Francis Mootz and Laura Webb) were participants in that group. By 2019, some group members felt they wished to produce scholarship from the reading group. The first result was the 2019 symposium at University of Nevada, Las Vegas, William S. Boyd School of Law titled *Classical Rhetoric as a Lens for Contemporary Legal Praxis*. Participants in the symposium included members of the reading group but also a number of new faces. Some participants, such as Linda Berger, Michael Cedrone, Kirsten Dauphinais, Kirsten Davis, Lori Johnson, Melissa Love Koenig, Sue Provenzano, Susie Salmon, Laura Webb, and Melissa Weresh, came from the longstanding "wedge" of legal scholars using rhetoric in their thinking and approaches, while others hailed from the rhetorical side of academia but sought to take account of the law, including Jeff Bennett, Beth Britt, Robert Gaines, Mark Hannah, Clarke Rountree, Joseph Sery, and Isaac West. A direct consequence of the symposium was volume 20, issue 3, of the *Nevada Law Journal*, which included articles by many of these folks.

Much slower to develop from the 2017 reading group were two other outgrowths: this volume and the Mootz and colleagues (2024) reader containing excerpts of primary texts from the ancient Western rhetorical tradition. Jay Mootz was a member of the reading group and felt that contemporary scholars and students needed greater exposure to the primary texts about which we were all talking. He took the lead, with Kirsten Davis, Brian Larson, and Kristen Tiscione supporting. That project was somewhat drawn out by the complexity of selecting texts, getting permissions for some of the translations, finding the right publisher, two rounds of peer review, and complications of copy-editing the excerpts with contributors' and editors' notes.

Meanwhile, Clarke Rountree introduced Larson to Robert Gaines, an internationally recognized expert in the history of rhetoric, who agreed to become co-editor of this volume. Larson and Gaines' great concern, though, was that things had changed profoundly between 2019, when this project was conceived, and 2020, when the world faced COVID-19 and the United States faced racial reckonings, initiated in part by the Black Lives Matter movement, in the aftermath of the murder of George Floyd.

Though Gaines and Larson had proposals from some contributors already, they asked Beth Britt to join the editorial team to help recruit a more diverse group of contributors and traditions. In time, other pressing responsibilities drew Gaines away from this project, though Britt and Larson are grateful for his early participation in its formation. At that point, Britt and Larson worked to extend the scope of the volume's contributions in three ways: First, we expanded our sense of what *rhetoric* might include so that we could draw upon scholars of argumentation theory, critical studies, philosophy, and other fields that focus on the constitutive nature of discourse; second, we actively recruited junior scholars and scholars from marginalized groups; and third, we extended our recruitment to include scholars specifically from Asia, the Middle East, and the Global South.

As for the first expansion, we viewed works of scholars *who might not see themselves as doing rhetoric* and recognized that they might have a great deal to say that would be of value to readers of this volume. For example, we believed that philosophers such as Danielle Allen (e.g., 2006) and Robin Dembroff (e.g., Kohler-Hausmann & Dembroff, 2022) might make valuable contributions. We reached out to them and others. For the second expansion, we looked at the excellent scholarship in law or rhetoric by people from underrepresented groups, such as, for example, Martin Camper (2018), Rasha Diab (2016; and appearing in this volume,

Chapter 9), Sarah Hakimzadeh (2023), Annie Hill (2020), Lolita Buckner Innis (2009), Teri McMurtry-Chubb (2019), Ersula Ore (2019), and Anjali Vats (2016, 2019, 2021). We also reached out to promising junior scholars such as Susan Tanner (also appearing in this volume, Chapter 5). Finally, we identified scholars in Brazil, Europe, and Asia writing at the intersection of law and discourse studies. In all, we personally invited more than thirty scholars to propose chapters for the volume. Most responded to our invitations, and most of them were at least conceptually interested in the project. But the great majority of them explained that they were already fully (or overly) committed.

In the end, this volume achieved strong representation from women and from junior scholars, as well as one essay focused on non-Western thought (Chapter 9). Given, however, that the resulting volume is not balanced to represent the diversity of scholars even in the field of rhetoric, let alone the diversity of the *world's* rhetorical traditions, laws, and people, our efforts might seem a failure. But we recount our endeavors to recruit a more diverse group not because we are unhappy with the contributors that we have; we are delighted with the work we have published here. Rather, we believe that editors of collections like this ought to explain their efforts to include even more diverse viewpoints, regardless of the outcomes.

We also anticipate that we missed good candidates, scholars writing at or near the intersection of rhetoric and law that we did not find in our searches. (If you are one of them, did not receive in invitation from us, and think you should have, please see the next section.) The remedy to that problem is to publish more such volumes that include tesserae representing more diverse viewpoints. Only then can we begin to sketch out and fill in (more portions of) the mosaic.

14.3 GETTING THERE: A CALL FOR PROPOSALS

It's not typical to include a call for proposals in an edited collection, but we wish to extend our hands here. We invite scholars using a diverse range of discourse (and rhetorical) traditions to address questions or issues in contemporary law (American law or the law of other lands) – to edit, coedit, author, or coauthor a new volume that begins to fill in another section of the mosaic. We are prepared to assist: as coeditors, as contributors, or just as supporting advisors. We are also pleased to work as "match-makers" of a kind: If you are a scholar of rhetoric and believe you have insufficient expertise in law to carry out your project, or a scholar of law and believe you have insufficient expertise in rhetoric, perhaps we can match you with a complementary scholar. (We have done this before.)

We think a year is probably enough time to leave this call open. And we plan to reach out to the scholars we have previously contacted and others to invite them to contribute to another volume. But if you are interested and don't hear from us, reach out to us (we are pretty easy to find online). Pitch your topic.

If you recognize that we are a couple of cisgender scholars of European heritage at the cusp of the Boomer generation, and you believe the *editors* of the next volume should be more diverse, reach out to us. Pitch your editorial role. We can open the circle, or even step out of the circle, to make room for new editors.

If you conclude that you want to do your own thing but want supportive words or proposal templates, and so on, from two experienced scholars, reach out to us. We can share drafts of communications, point you toward publishers who seemed interested in our proposal, and maybe help you find grants or other support for an Open Access subvention (something we think is important for this kind of work to reach the widest possible audience).

As we converse, we hope, with interested parties through 2025 and in early 2026, we should see the outline of a second volume come together in the second quarter of 2026 with contributions late in 2026 or in the first half of 2027. You might be able to put a volume together much more quickly. If we can help you do that, please reach out to us.

REFERENCES

Allen, D. (2006). *Talking to strangers: Anxieties of citizenship since* Brown v. Board of Education. University of Chicago Press.

Berenguer, E., Jewel, L., & McMurtry-Chubb, T. A. (2023). *Critical and comparative rhetoric: Unmasking privilege and power in law and legal advocacy to achieve truth, justice, and equity*. Policy Press.

Camper, M. (2018). *Arguing over texts: The rhetoric of interpretation*. Oxford University Press.

Diab, R. (2016). *Shades of ṣulḥ*. University of Pittsburgh Press.

Hakimzadeh, S. (2023). Reclaiming the commons: Law, rhetoric, and C. S. Peirce's pragmatic philosophy. *Law, Culture and the Humanities*, 19(3), 603–623. https://doi.org/10.1177/1743872120935934

Hill, A. (2020). Free Speech v. Free Blacks: Racist policing and calls to harm. *First Amendment Studies*, 54(2), 190–196. https://doi.org/10.1080/21689725.2020.1837655

Inniss, L. B. (2009). A critical legal rhetoric approach to *In Re African-American Slave Descendants Litigation*. *St. John's Journal of Legal Commentary*, 24(4), 649–696.

Kohler-Hausmann, I., & Dembroff, R. (2022). Supreme confusion about causality at the Supreme Court. *CUNY Law Review*, 25, 57–92.

McMurtry-Chubb, T. A. (2019). Still writing at the master's table: Decolonizing rhetoric in legal writing for a "woke" legal academy. *The Scholar: St. Mary's Law Review on Race and Social Justice*, 21(2), 255–291.

Mootz, F. J., III, Davis, K. A., Larson, B. N., & Tiscione, K. (Eds.). (2024). *Classical rhetoric & contemporary law: A critical reader*. University of Alabama Press.

Ore, E. J. (2019). Lynching: Violence, rhetoric, and American identity. University of Mississippi Press.

Vats, A. (2016). (Dis)owning Bikram: Decolonizing vernacular and dewesternizing restructuring in the yoga wars. *Communication and Critical/Cultural Studies*, 13(4), 325–345. https://doi.org/10.1080/14791420.2016.1151536

(2019). Prince of intellectual property: On creatorship, ownership, and Black capitalism in purple afterworlds (prince in/as blackness). *Howard Journal of Communications*, 30(2), 114–128. https://doi.org/10.1080/10646175.2018.1523760

(2021). Temporality in a time of *Tam*, or towards a racial chronopolitics of intellectual property law. *IDEA: The IP Law Review*, 61(3), 673–734.

Index

1919 Revolution. *See* Egypt
1952 Revolution. *See* Egypt
1956 Constitution. *See* Egypt

ABA. *See* American Bar Association
ABA Commission on Women. *See* American Bar Association
ABA Section of Litigation. *See* American Bar Association
ʿAbd al-Raḥmān, ʿĀʿishah, 195
abortion. *See* reproductive rights
ACHR. *See* Arab Charter on Human Rights
ACWR. *See* Arab Charter on Women's Rights
ADAA. *See* Anti-Drug Abuse Act of 1986
Adams, John Quincy, 76
Adeodato, João Maurício, 101
adversarial system, 58, 65, 290
Aeschines
  Against Ctesiphon, 58–60
affirmative action, 174, 176
African Diasporic rhetorical tradition, 4, 296
Against Aristocrates. *See* Demosthenes
Against Athenogenes. *See* Epicrates
Against Ctesiphon. *See* Aeschines
Against Leocrates. *See* Lycurgus
Against Timocrates. *See* Demosthenes
Ahmed, Leila, 194–195
Akhbār al-Youm (newspaper), 200
al-Ahrām (newspaper), 201
Alexander, Michelle, 236, 239, 243
Alito, Samuel, 97, 103–116, 153, 165
al-Jarīdah (newspaper), 197
All Writs Act of 1789, 151–152
ALM Media, 250, 252–253, 269
al-Majlis al-Waṭanī al-Ittiḥādī. *See* Federal National Council of the United Arab Emirates
al-Miṣrīyyah (newspaper), 199
al-Nahḍah. *See Nahḍah*
al-Qur'ān. *See* Qur'ān
al-Sadāt, Jihān, 200
ambiguity, 33, 74, 80, 82, 84, 86, 116
  strategic, 116
American Bar Association, 143, 248–272
  ABA Commission on Women, 253
  ABA Section of Litigation, 253
  Achieving Long-Term Careers for Women in Law initiative, 250, 252–253
amicus/-i curiae, brief, etc., 64, 107, 145, 149–150, 154
Amīn, Qāsim, 195
Anglican Church, 249–250, 263, 270
Anti-Drug Abuse Act of 1986, 229, 232
Anti-Drug Abuse Act of 1988, 234
apagoge, 50
Arab Charter on Human Rights, 182
Arab Charter on Women's Rights, 181–182
Arab League, 181
Arab Parliament. *See* Arab League
Arab Renaissance or Awakening. *See Nahḍah*
Arab(ic)-Muslim world, 181–202
Arabic-Islamic rhetoric, 181–202
arete, 18–19
argumentation schemes, 100
Aristotelian revival, 17th century, 124
Aristotle, 3, 6, 18–19, 24, 73, 102, 161, 295
  Prior Analytics, 97
  Rhetoric, 3, 43, 73, 97–100, 121–122, 145
  On the Soul, 124
Ark Group, 253

ars dictaminis, 75
ars notaria, 75
Asian Diasporic rhetorical tradition, 4, 296
assimilated cultural influences, 191, 193
assisted suicide, 52, 110
Astell, Mary
  A Serious Proposal to the Ladies, 248–272
  Letters Concerning the Love of God, 254
  Some Reflections Upon Marriage, 250
'Aṭīyah, Rāwīyah, 200
Athens
  ancestral constitution, 42
  democracy, 73
  forensic rhetoric, 42–66
  judges, 43
  legal procedure, 45, 50
Atlantic Monthly, 213
Attic orators, 42–66
Augustine of Hippo, 4
autonomy theory, 283

Bāḥithat al-Bādīyah (pen name). *See* Nāṣif, Malak Ḥifnī
Balkin, Jack, 33, 54
Barlas, Asma, 194–195
Barrett, Amy Coney, 150–153
Bass, Hilarie, 250, 252–253, 269
Battered Woman, The. *See* Walker, Lenore
battered woman syndrome, 281–283, 285–288
Baude, William, 141, 143
Bell, Derrick, 178
Bennett, Mark W., 235, 242
Berenguer, Elizabeth, 4, 46, 55, 296
Berger, Raoul, 18, 36
  Government by Judiciary, 22, 24
Bernstein, David, 177–178
Beyond All Reason: The Radical Assault on Truth in American Law. *See* Farber, Daniel; Sherry, Suzanna
Bible, 75
Biden, Joe, 170
big law firms and culture, 260–261, 263–267, 270
Bint al-Shāṭi' (pen name). *See* 'Abd al-Raḥmān, 'Ā'ishah
Bizzell, Patricia, 276
Black Lives Matter, 217, 219, 223, 239, 297
Blackmun, Harry A., 111, 115, 128
Blackstone, William, 90
BLM. *See* Black Lives Matter
Blow, Charles, 222
bon sens, 160
Bowers v. Hardwick, 61–63
Brandeis, Louis B., 54, 106
  The Right to Privacy, 106
Brennan Center for Justice, 245
broken windows policy, 213
Brown v. Board of Education of Topeka, 18, 23, 26, 28, 34, 64, 166, 171
Bruen. *See New York State Rifle & Pistol Association v. Bruen*
Brutus. *See* Cicero, Marcus Tullius
Bryant, Susan, 278
Buller, Francis, 125
Bureau of Justice Statistics, 243
Burke, Kenneth, 55–56
Bush, George W., 21, 143
busing, 170–176
Butler, Judith, 229–232, 237–245
  Frames of War, 231
  Precarious Life: The Powers of Mourning and Violence, 231

Camper, Martin, 75
canons of construction or interpretation. *See* interpretation
canons, rhetorical, 74
Carbado, Devin W., 209
carceral state, 234, 238
Cartesian thought, 160, 249–250, 267
case method (legal education), 288
casebooks, 274, 278–281, 284, 287, 289–290
Center for Women in Law, 253
Chadderton, Charlotte, 230
character. *See ethos*
characterology, 147
Charles River Associates, 253
Chettle v. Chettle, 125
Chudleigh, Mary, 249
Cicero, Marcus Tullius, 73, 76, 91
  Brutus, 73
  De Inventione, 72–75, 145
  De Oratore, 73
  Topica, 73
Civil War, United States, 236–237
Classical Rhetoric as a Lens for Contemporary Legal Praxis (UNLV symposium), 296
clear and present danger, 54
Clear, Todd R., 242
CNN, 238
cocaine, 229, 233–236, 241–242
colonialism, 182, 193, 196–197
colorblind jurisprudence, 176
Columbus, Christopher, 198
common sense. *See sensus communis*
communal indwelling, 21
compelling state interest, 106, 108, 173

Comprehensive Drug Abuse Prevention and Control Act of 1970, 234
Condit, Celeste M., 208
Confrontation Clause. *See* United States Constitution
confrontational homicides, 288
congressional redistricting, 141
Connecticut National Bank v. Germain, 86–87
constitutional interpretation. *See* interpretation
constitutive rhetoric, 105, 185
constraint principle, 31
construction zone, 32
contentio, 249, 256–257, 262, 267–269
context, 77
Convention on the Elimination of All Forms of Discrimination against Women, 181
Corax of Syracuse, 46
Coventry, Ann, 249
Cover, Robert, 231
COVID-19, 149, 297
crack cocaine. *See* cocaine
Crawford v. Washington, 119–120, 122, 126, 128, 131–136
Crimes Act of 1790, 237
criminal law, 218, 281
Criminal Law: Cases and Materials. *See* Dressler, Joshua; Garvey, Stephen P.
Critique of Practical Reason. *See* Kant, Emmanuel
Crump, Ben, 217
Ctesiphon, 58–60
cultural biases, 184
cultural competence, 274, 278
cultural memory, 54
culture. *See* legal culture; rhetorical culture

D.A. v. Texas Health Presbyterian, 72, 76, 78–81, 90–91
Dabbous, Sonia, 198
Damele, Giovanni, 101, 111
David Floyd. *See Floyd v. City of New York*
Davis v. Washington, 122, 133–136
Davis, Kirsten K., 4
De Inventione. *See* Cicero, Marcus Tullius
De Oratore. *See* Cicero, Marcus Tullius
deadly force, 282, 290
death penalty cases, 143
decolonial studies, 193
deduction, 4, 71, 84, 100, 116–117, 189
deference. *See* judicial deference
Demosthenes, 58–60
  Against Aristocrates, 51, 59
  Against Timocrates, 52
  On the Crown, 43, 60
  On the Dishonest Embassy, 60
Descartes, René, 160, 263
desegregation, school, 170–173, 176
determinacy, 70, 72, 82–87
determinist imaginary, 70–91
dicast, 43
Diels, Hermann, 275
Discourse Concerning the Love of God. *See* Masham, Damaris
disidentification, 232
dissenting opinions, 28, 63–64, 85, 109, 112–113, 141, 143, 148–151, 168, 279, 283–287
Dissoi Logoi, 73, 273–279, 288–290
District of Columbia v. Heller, 29, 34, 46, 48–50, 53
diversity, 253, 263, 269, 271
divorce, 201
Dobbs v. Jackson Women's Health Organization, 52, 56, 97–117
dokimasia rhetoron, 60
domestic violence, 32, *See also* intimate partner violence
Downs, Leroy, 205, 217
doxa, 161
Draco, 42, 52, 54, 60
Dressler, Joshua, 283
  Criminal Law: Cases and Materials, 279–281, 284–290
Due Process Clause. *See* United States Constitution

Egypt, 196
  1919 Revolution, 199
  1952 Revolution, 200
  1956 Constitution, 200
  Personal Status Law, 200
Egyptian Feminist Union, 199
Egyptian National Parliament, 200
'Eissá, Ibrahīm, 201
election cases, 143
Eloquence of Mary Astell, The. *See* Sutherland, Christine Mason
Elrod v. Burns, 152
emergency orders, 141
Employment Division v. Smith, 153
endeixis, 50
enthymeme, 97–117, 183, 187–188, 198
Epicrates
  Against Athenogenes, 53
epideictic rhetoric, 188
Equal Protection Clause. *See* United States Constitution
equity, 27, 74–75, 91, 145, 187–188, 200
  inequity, 166, 174, 176, 185
  racial, 168, 174
Erickson. *See Hunter v. Erickson*

Erlichman, John, 238
Esposito, John L., 190, 193
Essay Concerning Humane Understanding. *See* Locke, John
ethical surplus, 37
ethos, 17–38, 43, 54, 56, 58, 66, 119–137, 151, 249, 251–256, 269, 295
  as dwelling, 20
  extrinsic, 251–254
  as indwelling, 26, 30, 35, 37
  intrinsic, 251–255
eunoia, 18–19, 21
Euthycles, 51
executive privilege, 23
expert witness testimony, 279–281, 285
extrinsic context, 77
eyewitness, 125, 279

fair housing, 167–170
Fair Sentencing Act of 2010, 234
Farber, Daniel
  Beyond All Reason: The Radical Assault on Truth in American Law, 276
Farewell Speech. *See* Muḥammad
Farooq, Mohammad Omar, 188
Fātin Amal Ḥarbī (TV series), 201
Federal National Council of the United Arab Emirates, 181
Federal Rules of Evidence, 126
female infanticide, 191–193, 195
Feminist Judgments, 8, 281
firearms, 46, 50
fixation thesis, 31–33
Florida v. Bostick, 211, 219
Floyd v. City of New York, 205–207, 210, 216–222
Floyd, George, 206, 297
Forensic Oratory: A Manual for Advocates. *See* Robinson, William C.
formalism, legal, 7, 100
Fourteenth Amendment. *See* United States Constitution
Fourth Amendment. *See* United States Constitution
Framers. *See* United States Constitution
frames of war, 229, 231, 235–239, 243–244
Frames of War. *See* Butler, Judith
Free Exercise Clause. *See* United States Constitution
freedom of speech, 54
Fuller, Lon L., 70, 82
Fuller, Patrick, 253, 268
furtive movements (ideograph), 211, 220

Gagarin, Michael, 276
Gaines, Robert N., 297
Garner, Bryan A., 70–91, 97
  Reading Law: The Interpretation of Legal Texts, 72, 81–87, 89–91
Garver, Eugene, 18, 37
Garvey, Stephen P.
  Criminal Law: Cases and Materials, 279–281, 284–290
gender, 188, 191, 193, 197, 230–231, 251, 259–260, 264–265, 268–271, 278
gender-nonconforming persons, 256
Gilbert, Geoffrey, 125–126
Ginsburg, Ruth Bader, 63
glass ceiling, 199
Glucksberg. *See Washington v. Glucksberg*
goodwill. *See eunoia*
Gordon, Thomas F., 100
Gore, Al, 21
Gorgias, 73
Gorsuch, Neil, 35, 150, 153–154
Gottschalk, Marie, 238
Government by Judiciary. *See* Berger, Raoul
grammar canon, 84
Greece, ancient, 3, 6, 38, 53, 73, 156, 273–275, 295
Greek city states, 3
Greek lawgivers, 53
Greek legal system, 156
Greenberg Traurig, 252
grievability, 232, 242–243, 245
Guantanamo Bay, 231

habeas corpus, 231
ḥadīth, 186–187, 194
Halgren, Guy N., 263
Hamilton, Alexander, 25
Hammon v. Indiana, 122, 133–136
Hardwick, Michael, 62
Harlan, John Marshall, II, 168–169
Harris, Kamala, 170
Harvard University, 6, 71, 76, 273, 279
Hastings, Elizabeth, 249
Hauser, Gerard A., 183
headnotes, 286
hearsay, 119–137
Hearsay Rule, 126–128
Heidegger, Martin, 18–20
Heller. *See District of Columbia v. Heller*
Herzberg, Bruce, 276
high crime area (ideograph), 211, 215, 219–220
Ḥizb al-Umah, 197, 199
Hobbes, Thomas, 75
Holmes, Oliver Wendell, Jr., 71
homicides, 288
homosexuality. *See* same-sex attraction
Hooker, Juliet, 217

House Judiciary Committee, 144
Howe, Justine, 193–194
Huhn, Wilson, 43
Hunter v. Erickson, 165, 168–172, 177

identification, 55–57, 215–216, 230–232
identity formation, 230
ideograph, 205–224
ideology, 122–123, 130–131, 136–137, 190, 206–209
imaginary. *See* determinist imaginary
imminence or imminent danger or threat, 279, 282–283, 287–288, 290
indeterminacy, 70–91
Indigenous rhetorical tradition, 4, 296
indwelling, 21, 26, 30, 35
inequity. *See* equity
influenza pandemic of 1918–19, 199
INS v. Delgado, 212
International Covenant on Civil and Political Rights, 181
International Covenant on Economic, Social and Cultural Rights, 181
interpellation, 186
interpretation
  Biblical, 75
  canons, 38, 76, 79, 81–87
  constitutional, 17, 22, 28, 30
  extrinsic aids, 87
  interpretation–construction distinction, 35
  legal, 17, 43, 47, 64, 72, 89, 98, 231
  Qur'ānic, 190, 194
  statutory, 28, 38, 72, 76, 81, 117
interpretation–construction distinction. *See* interpretation
interpretive-direction canon, 86
intimate partner violence, 133, 280–283
intrinsic context, 77
invention (canon of rhetoric), 71–74, 142, 144–153, 155, 274, 277
IRAC model, 102

Jackson, Ketanji Brown, 57
Jarratt, Susan, 275
Jefferson, Thomas, 53
Jewel, Lucy, 4, 46, 55, 296
Jim Crow, 243
John Hancock Financial, 253
Johnson, Lyndon, 166
Jones, Catherine, 249
Jost, Walter, 20
judicial activism, 115
judicial deference, 18, 23, 25–26, 29–30, 36
judicial restraint, 89–91
judiciary, role of, 103
jurisprudence of rules, 28
justice (ideograph), 211, 217, 220, 222–223

Kagan, Elena, 17, 35, 37, 141
kairos, 223
Kant, Emmanuel
  Critique of Practical Reason, 76
Kapoor, Vetan, 154
Kavanaugh, Brett, 150, 153
Kelling, George L., 213
Kennedy, Anthony, 28, 38, 62–63, 165
Kennedy, George A., 3
Kerner Commission, 167
Kerner Report, 169
khuṭbat al-wadā'. *See* Muḥammad, *Farewell Speech*
King, Martin Luther, Jr., 167
  Letter from Birmingham Jail, 168
Koran. *See* Qur'ān

l'Egyptienne (newspaper), 199
Langdell, Christopher C., 71, 279
Larson, Brian N., 4, 6, 100
last-antecedent canon, 79, 85
Latine rhetorical tradition, 4, 296
law and literature movement, 7
law as constitutive activity, 105
lawgiver, 45
Lawrence v. Texas, 28, 38, 62, 65
learned helplessness, 281, 286
legal culture, 146–149
legal education, 273–274, 278, 288–290
legal interpretation. *See* interpretation
Legal Services Corporation, 250
legal-ethical rhetoric of rights, 183
legislative history, 77, 84, 86
Leocrates, 46, 48
Leptines, 59
Letter from Birmingham Jail. *See* King, Martin Luther, Jr.
letter vs. intent, 74–75
Letters Concerning the Love of God. *See* Astell, Mary
liberty (ideograph), 206–207, 211, 218, 222
Liebenberg, Roberta D., 252–253, 269
Lincoln, Abraham, 237
Lithwick, Dahlia, 103
living constitutionalism, 27, 33
Llewellyn, Karl, 37
LoBianco, Tom, 238
Locke, John, 75, 119, 122–126, 135, 254, 256
  Essay Concerning Humane Understanding, 121–122, 124–125
logographer, 45

logos, 17–18, 32, 36, 120–123, 125–126, 128–132, 136, 256, 265
Loizidou, Elena, 231, 233, 244
London, 249, 254
Loving v. Virginia, 64
Lucaites, John L., 208
Lycurgus
  Against Leocrates, 46, 48
Lysias, 51

Macagno, Fabrizio, 101, 111
Madison, James, 25, 53
Maḥmmūd Pasha Sulīmān, 197
Mahoney, Martha R., 281–283, 288
Majlis al-Ummah. *See* Egyptian National Parliament
Major, Lindsey & Africa, 264
Malebranche, Nicolas, 263
Mancusi v. Stubbs, 130
Manning, John, 30
Mansfield Rule, 271
marriage, 38, 64, 191, 200
Martin, Harry C., 283, 287
Martin, Trayvon, 217, 221
Masham, Damaris
  Discourse Concerning the Love of God, 254
mass incarceration, 232–233, 242
Mattox v. United States, 129–130
McFadden, Tervor N., 154
McGee, Michael Calvin, 207–211, 223
McMurtry-Chubb, Teri A., 4, 46, 55, 296
memory, cultural, 54
memory, traditional, 54
Mernissi, Fatima, 194
Merrill v. Milligan, 141
Mertz, Elizabeth, 278
metaphor, 160, 208, 236–237, 257–258, 268
Middle East, 181–182
Mississippi Goddamn. *See* Simone, Nina
Montagu, Mary Wortley, 250
Moore v. City of East Cleveland, 52
Mootz, Francis J., III, 4, 70, 275–276
moral discord, 186
Moral Majority, 213
moral order, 184–186, 188, 198
Moskal v. United States, 85
Mount ʻArafāt, 187
MTV, 213
Muḥammad, 186–189, 197
  Farewell Speech, 187–189, 197
Mulkey. *See Reitman v. Mulkey*
multiculturalism, 276
Muslim world. *See* Arab(ic)-Muslim world

Nādī Ḥizb al-Umah. *See* Nation's Party Club
Nahḍah, 195–199
Naples's legal system, 159
Napoléon, 196
narrative, 6, 29, 42–66, 105, 194–195, 217
narrowly tailored. *See* strict scrutiny
Nāṣif, Malak Ḥifnī, 196–199
Nation's Party Club, 197, 201
National Advisory Commission on Civil Disorders, 167
National Association for Law Placement, 260
National Public Radio, 217
Nazi Germany, 237
nearest-reasonable-referent canon, 80, 85
negative rights. *See* rights
negligence, 77
Nevada Law Journal, 297
New Deal, 72
New Science, The. *See* Vico, Giambattista
New York City, 215–219
New York Police Department, 206, 212, 217, 220–222
New York State Rifle & Pistol Association v. Bruen, 50
New York Times, 221
Newcastle upon Tyne, 249
Nixon, Richard M., 23, 236, 238
non-binary persons, 256
nonconfrontational homicides, 288
Norman, John Thomas ("J.T."), 278
Norman, Judy Ann Laws, 278
Norris, John, 254
North Africa, 182
North Carolina Supreme Court, 282
NYPD. *See* New York Police Department

O'Connor, Sandra Day, 213
Obama, Barack H., 143, 218, 221
Obergefell v. Hodges, 29, 38, 61, 64, 110
Ohio v. Roberts, 120, 128–131
On Invention. *See* Cicero, Marcus Tullius
On Rhetoric. *See* Aristotle
On the Crown. *See* Demosthenes
On the Dishonest Embassy. *See* Demosthenes
On the Soul. *See* Aristotle
ordinary meaning, 17, 27
orientalism, 182, 193
original meaning, 22, 24–27, 31–34, 52, 131
originalism, 17–38, 71, 108, 164
Osler, Mark, 235, 242

Parents Involved in Community Schools v. Seattle School District No. 1, 170, 173
pathos, 17–18, 57, 66, 99, 121, 129, 258, 268

patriarchy, 46, 55, 182, 184, 193–195
patrios politeia, 42
People v. De Bour, 212, 219
Perelman, Chaïm, 147
Personal Status Law. *See* Egypt
Peters, Jean Koh, 278
Phaedrus. *See* Plato
Philip of Macedon, 48, 58
phronesis, 19, *See* practical wisdom
pistis/-eis, 18
plain language, 78
Planned Parenthood v. Casey, 104, 109, 115
Plato, 6–7, 46, 56, 73, 273, 276
  Phaedrus, 56
Plessy v. Ferguson, 166
Polemarchus, 51
police power (ideograph), 206, 208, 210–224
Pollock, Frederick, 84
polygamy, 197
positive rights. *See* rights
postmodernism, 99
Poulakos, John, 274–275, 277
practical reason, 18–21, 23, 26–27, 30, 32, 34, 70, 72–73, 76, 81, 83, 87, 89
practical wisdom, 4, 18, 20
precarious life, 229, 231, 239–243, 245
Precarious Life: The Powers of Mourning and Violence. *See* Butler, Judith
precedent, 28, 45, 55–56, 103, 111, 115–116, 144–145, 147–156, 209
premises (argumentative), 97–98, 101
  implicit, omitted, or hidden, 98, 100–101, 103–105, 111
Priester, Benjamin, 30
Prior Analytics. *See* Aristotle
privacy rights. *See* rights
progressive advocacy, 46
progressive movements, 44
Prophetic tradition. *See sunnah*
Proposal 2 (Michigan constitutional amendment), 164
prostitution, 60, 278, 283
Protagoras, 274–275
PSL. *See* Egypt, Personal Status Law
psychologist, forensic, 285
psychology, abnormal, 286
psychotherapeutic discourse, 289
public arguments, 142, 146, 154
punctuation canon, 85

quasi-logical reasoning, 99, 103, 116
Quintilian, 6, 19
Qur'ān, 186, 189–195
Qur'ānic interpretation. *See* interpretation

racial biases, 221
racial status quo, 166, 172
racism, 232
racist hierarchy, 239
Ratcliffe, Krista, 274, 277, 280, 289
Reading Law: The Interpretation of Legal Texts. *See* Garner, Bryan A.; Scalia, Antonin
Reagan, Nancy, 236
Reagan, Ronald, 214–215, 233, 236, 240–242
reasonable suspicion, 211, 220
Rehnquist, William H., 52
Reitman v. Mulkey, 165–169, 172, 177
related-statutes canon, 80, 86
reproductive rights, 52, 56, 102 117
Rhetoric. *See* Aristotle
rhetoric, definition of, 6
rhetorical culture, 207–209, 214, 216–222
rhetorical listening, 274, 277–278, 280, 289–290
rhetorical traditions
  African Diasporic, 4, 296
  Arabic-Islamic, 181–202
  Asian Diasporic, 4, 296
  Indigenous, 4, 296
  Latine, 4, 296
  traditional texts, 5
  Western, 4–6, 44, 55, 66, 296
Rhodes, 46
Rich Wilkin, 254
right to privacy (ideograph), 207
Right to Privacy, The. *See* Brandeis, Louis B.; Warren, Samuel D.
rights
  in Arab(ic)-Islamic discourse, 185
  epistemic, 197
  fundamental, 49, 51, 62, 64, 106, 108, 110
  to learn, 197
  negative, 184, 188–190, 198
  positive, 184, 188–190, 198
  privacy, 105–110
  unenumerated, 108, 110, 112, 114
  vernacular discourses, 183, 187–188, 196, 199
  women's, 181–202
Roberts Court, 47
Roberts, John G., Jr., 47, 72, 143, 165
Robinson, Thomas M., 275
Robinson, William C.
  Forensic Oratory: A Manual for Advocates, 76
Rockefeller laws, 233
Roe v. Wade, 81, 103, 107, 109, 111, 115
Roman Catholic Diocese of Brooklyn NY v. Cuomo, 142, 150–154

Rome, ancient, 6, 295
  history, 160
  legal arguments, 145
  oratory, 160
Romer v. Evans, 28
Rountree, Clarke, 297

Salama, Samir, 181
same-sex attraction, 38, 61–64
same-sex marriage, 64
Sanders, Steve, 176–177
Saratoga Springs, New York, 250
Scalia, Antonin, 18, 36, 38, 50, 57, 63–64, 70–91, 97, 119, 126, 131–133, 151, 153
  Reading Law: The Interpretation of Legal Texts, 72, 81–87, 89–91
Scallen, Eileen, 275
Schaeffer, John, 159–161, 164
Scharf, Stephanie A., 252–253, 269
Scheindlin, Shira, 206, 218–222
Schiappa, Edward, 274
Schrag, Calvin, 20
Schuette v. BAMN, 158, 164–179
Schuette v. Coalition to Defend Affirmative Action, Integration and Immigrant Rights and Fight for Equality by Any Means Necessary. See Schuette v. BAMN
scripts, cultural, 230–232, 242, 245
Seattle. See Washington v. Seattle School District No. 1
Second Amendment. *See* United States Constitution
Security Council Resolution 1325 on Women, Peace and Security, 181
Segall, Eric, 30, 35
segregation, 232
segregation, de jure, 173
self-defense, 46, 49, 279, 282–287
Seligman, Martin, 281
sensus communis, 158–179
Sentencing Reform Act, 234
September 11, 2001, 216
series-qualifier canon, 80, 85
Serious Proposal to the Ladies, A. See Astell, Mary
sermo, 249, 256–257, 262, 267–269
Sextus Empiricus, 275
sexual abuse, 265
sexual harrassment, 265
shadow docket, 141
Shafīq, Durrīyah, 200
Shāh's, Ḥusn, 200
shared identity, 55
sharī'a law, 181, 187
Shaw, Kate, 57
Sheppard Mullin, 253
Sherry, Suzanna
  Beyond All Reason: The Radical Assault on Truth in American Law, 276
Shukrī, Amīnah, 200
Sibron v. New York, 212
Siegel, Neil S., 103
Simone, Nina
  Mississippi Goddamn, 168
Sinsheimer, Ann, 223
Sixth Amendment. *See* United States Constitution
Slaughter, Anne-Marie, 273
Snowden Leaks, 216
social biases, 184
social class, 270
social hierarchies, 231
sodomy, 61–63
Solon, 42, 52, 54, 59–60
Solum, Lawrence ("Larry"), 18, 31–36
sophists, 4, 6, 73, 273–277
Sotomayor, Sonia, 154
soundness (logical), 113–115
South Bay United Pentecostal Church v. Newsom, 149
Special Committee on Legal Aid Work, 250
speech, freedom of, 54
Sprague, Rosamond Kent, 275
stained-glass ceiling, 199
stand your ground legislation, 217
stare decisis. See precedent
stasis of quality, 192
State v. Norman, 274, 278–290
statutory construction. *See* interpretation
statutory interpretation. *See* interpretation
stereotypes, 179, 184, 274, 281, 283, 285, 288, 290
Stevens, John Paul, 29, 87, 216
stop-and-frisk policies, 205–224
Story, Joseph, 71
strategic ambiguity. *See* ambiguity
strict scrutiny, 106, 108, 112, 166, 173
Strict Scrutiny (podcast), 57
Students for Fair Admissions v. Harvard, 166
subjectivity, 7, 100, 121, 125, 128, 130, 134, 136, 186, 230, 290
suicide, assisted, 52, 110
sunnah, 186, 188
Supreme Constitutional Court of Egypt, 201
surplusage canon, 85
surveillance, 216
Sutherland, Christine Mason
  Eloquence of Mary Astell, The, 249
Syed, Khalida Tanvir, 190, 194
syllogism, 4, 97–117, 188, 192
Syria, 196

Taḥt al-Uṣāiyah (TV series), 201
Taylor, Charles, 71
Taylor, John Pitt, 125
Teachers Insurance and Annuity Association of America, 253
techne, 19
Terry stops. *See Terry v. Ohio*
Terry v. Ohio, 212, 219
testimonial statements, 131, 134
Texas Court of Appeals, 72, 78–81
Texas Health Presbyterian v. D.A., 72, 76, 87–89, 91
Texas Supreme Court, 87–89
textual integrity, 25, 29
textual interpretation. *See* interpretation
textualism, 71, 76–77, 90
Thirteenth Amendment. *See* United States Constitution
Thomas, Clarence, 150, 153
Thompson v. Travanion, 125
Timarchus, 60
Tiscione, Kristen K., 4, 6
Topica. *See* Cicero, Marcus Tullius
topos/-oi, 20, 43, 142, 144–147, 150, 152–154, 183–184, 187, 190, 195–197, 295
tradition, 5, 42–66, 89–91, 160
traditional memory, 54
Trump, Donald J., 36
tyrant custom, 257, 259

underdeterminacy, 70–91
unenumerated rights. *See* rights
ungrievability. *See* grievability
United States Census, 243
United States Constitution, 21–27, 30–37, 49, 54, 71, 76, 90, 98, 104, 127–128, 131, 147, 210
  Article III, 90
  Confrontation Clause, 119–120, 131–134
  Due Process Clause, 23, 52, 61, 104, 110–111
  Equal Protection Clause, 158, 165–168, 170, 173, 176, 206, 209
  First Amendment, 54, 149, 152
  Fourteenth Amendment, 22, 25, 51, 65, 104, 110, 112–113, 165–166, 206, 218
  Fourth Amendment, 206, 211, 218–219, 223
  Framers, 20, 22–26, 33, 37, 53, 57, 73, 112, 131
  Free Exercise Clause, 149, 152–153, 155
  Second Amendment, 29, 46, 49–50, 53–54
  Sixth Amendment, 119, 127, 131–132
  Thirteenth Amendment, 211
United States Sentencing Commission, 234–235
United States v. Booker, 234
United States v. Virginia, 63
University of Naples, 159
unreasonable searches and seizures. *See* United States Constitution, Fourth Amendment
Urīd Hala (film), 200
Urīd Ḥala (newspaper column), 200
ūṣīkum bil-nisā' khaīran, 183, 187–189, 198
USSC. *See* United States Sentencing Commission

validity (logical), 113–115
veil, 197
vernacular rhetorics, 182–184, 187–188, 196, 199
vernacular rights discourses, 183, 187–188, 196, 199
Vico, Giambattista, 158–164
  New Science, The, 161, 164
Virginia Military Institute, 63
Virginia, Commonwealth of, 64
VISA, 253
Vladeck, Stephen I., 143, 152–153, 155
Voting Rights Act, 141

Wacquant, Loïc, 242–243
Walker, Lenore, 281
  Battered Woman, The, 286
Walking Out the Door: The Facts, Figures, and Future of Experienced Women Lawyers in Private Practice, 248–272
Wallace, George, 178
Wal-Mart Stores, Inc., 253
Walton, Douglas, 100
war on drugs, 213–214, 217, 222, 229, 233, 235–242, 244
war on terror, 217, 237
Warren Court, 23, 72, 178, 213
Warren, Samuel D., II, 106
  Right to Privacy, The, 106
Washington v. Glucksberg, 49, 52, 110–112
Washington v. Seattle School District No. 1, 165, 170–174, 177
Western rhetorical tradition, 4–6, 44, 55, 66, 296
Wetlaufer, Gerald, 7
white supremacy, 46, 166, 172, 174, 178, 239, 242–243, 245
White, James Boyd, 7, 105, 155
Whitney v. California, 54
Whren v. United States, 215, 219, 238–239
will (testament), 74
willful and wanton negligence, 78

Williams, Patricia J., 7
Wilson, James Q., 213
women in the legal profession, 248–272
women of color, 109, 250
women's rights, 181–202
World War II, 236

Yale University, 76
Yankah, Ekow, 221
Yūnis, Ilhām, 201
yuppies, 213

Zimmerman, George, 217

For EU product safety concerns, contact us at Calle de José Abascal, 56–1°,
28003 Madrid, Spain or eugpsr@cambridge.org.

www.ingramcontent.com/pod-product-compliance
Lightning Source LLC
LaVergne TN
LVHW052036200926
848481LV00005B/1701